Public Service Management and Employment Relations in Europe

T0384258

'The dynamics of employment relations in the wake of the financial crisis have become an issue of major political and social concern, nowhere more than so than in the public sector. As this outstanding collection of essays from leading scholars in the field demonstrates, public service employment relations in Europe have been profoundly influenced by the crisis, but in divergent, distinctive and quite different ways. By comparing and contrasting the experience of European countries, this book lays out the challenges facing policy makers, public managers and employees as they seek to make sense of the new post-crisis environment. Highly recommended'.
—*Rhys Andrews, Cardiff University, UK*

Has there been a transformation of public service employment relations in Europe since the crisis? *Public Service Management and Employment Relations in Europe* examines public service employment relations after the economic crisis, including an analysis of more than thirty years of public service and workforce reform, and addresses the interplay between an emerging post-crisis public service sector and the consequences for the state, employers and trade unions in core public services.

Written by leading national experts, this book places the economic crisis in a longer time frame and examines how far trends in public sector employment relations were reinforced or reversed by the crisis. It provides an up-to-date analysis of the restructuring of public service employment relations in 12 major European countries, including an analysis of little-studied Central and Eastern European countries.

This book will be vital reading for researchers, academics and Ph.D. students in the fields of public management, public administration, employment relations and human resource management.

Stephen Bach is a Professor of Employment Relations at King's College London, UK.

Lorenzo Bordogna is a Professor of Economic Sociology at the University of Milan, Italy.

Routledge Critical Studies in Public Management

Edited by Stephen Osborne

For a full list of titles in this series, please visit www.routledge.com

The study and practice of public management has undergone profound changes across the world. Over the last quarter century, we have seen

- increasing criticism of public administration as the overarching framework for the provision of public services,
- the rise (and critical appraisal) of the 'New Public Management' as an emergent paradigm for the provision of public services,
- the transformation of the 'public sector' into the cross-sectoral provision of public services, and
- the growth of the governance of inter-organizational relationships as an essential element in the provision of public services

In reality, these trends have not so much replaced each other as elided or coexisted together—the public policy process has not gone away as a legitimate topic of study and intra-organizational management continues to be essential to the efficient provision of public services, while the governance of inter-organizational and inter-sectoral relationships is now essential to the effective provision of these services.

Further, while the study of public management has been enriched by contribution of a range of insights from the 'mainstream' management literature, it has also contributed to this literature in such areas as networks and inter-organizational collaboration, innovation and stakeholder theory.

This series is dedicated to presenting and critiquing this important body of theory and empirical study. It will publish books that both explore and evaluate the emergent and developing nature of public administration, management and governance (in theory and practice) and examine the relationship with and contribution to the overarching disciplines of management and organizational sociology.

Books in the series will be of interest to academics and researchers in this field, students undertaking advanced studies of it as part of their undergraduate or postgraduate degree and reflective policy makers and practitioners.

Public Service Management and Employment Relations in Europe

Emerging from the Crisis

Edited by Stephen Bach and
Lorenzo Bordogna

Routledge
Taylor & Francis Group

NEW YORK AND LONDON

First published 2016
by Routledge
711 Third Avenue, New York, NY 10017

and by Routledge
2 Park Square, Milton Park, Abingdon, Oxon OX14 4RN

First issued in paperback 2018

Routledge is an imprint of the Taylor & Francis Group, an informa business

Library of Congress Cataloging-in-Publication Data
Names: Bach, Stephen, 1963– editor. | Bordogna, Lorenzo, editor.
Title: Public service management and employment relations in
   Europe : emerging from the crisis / edited by Stephen Bach and
   Lorenzo Bordogna.
Description: New York : Routledge, 2016. | Series: Routledge
   critical studies in public management ; 26 | Includes
   bibliographical references and index.
Identifiers: LCCN 2016007390 | ISBN 9781138851467
   (hardback : alk. paper) | ISBN 9781315724096 (ebook)
Subjects: LCSH: Employee-management relations in government—
   European Union countries—Case studies. | Civil service—
   European Union countries—Case studies. | Public
   administration—European Union countries—Case studies. |
   Financial crises—European Union countries.
Classification: LCC HD8013.E854 P85 2016 | DDC 352.6094—dc23
LC record available at https://lccn.loc.gov/2016007390

ISBN 13: 978-1-138-34000-8 (pbk)
ISBN 13: 978-1-138-85146-7 (hbk)

Typeset in Sabon
by Apex CoVantage, LLC

Contents

vi *Contents*

Tables and Figures

Tables

Figures

Preface

This book is the result of a lengthy period of collaboration that has involved working with an established network of colleagues across Europe with a shared interest in comparative public service employment relations, as well as being experts on their own national experiences. We have benefitted immeasurably from the discussions we have had with our contributors over the recent years and thank them for their patience in responding to our numerous queries while editing this book. Many of the contributors to this volume have collaborated on several comparative European Union-funded projects that have centered on the changing character of employment relations in the public services. Between 2011–2013, the research project, *Strengthening social dialogue and the public services in the aftermath of the economic crisis: strengthening partnership in an era of austerity*, considered how employers, trade unions and public authorities were managing workforce changes in a period of widespread restructuring. Fieldwork in each country considered the contribution of employee consultation and involvement in maintaining high-quality public services and focused in particular on the experience of the local governments in selected European countries.

In this project, we were not only struck by the variation in experience between and within countries, but also noted the severe pressure on systems of collective employee voice, the disorientating effects on trade unions of the turn to austerity and the extent to which the state was prepared to recentralize employment relations and act unilaterally in a period of crisis. Public service employment relations was clearly in transition, but did these developments signal a shift away from decentralization and measures to bring public and private sector employment relations closer together? Our discussions also indicated that an evolving system of European Union governance with explicit rules on deficits and debts and pressure from financial markets was challenging the sheltered national character of public service employment relations. These findings informed special issues of journals in the *European Journal of Industrial Relations* in December 2013 (edited by Stephen Bach and Lorenzo Bordogna) and in *Transfer* in July 2014 (edited by Peter Leisink and Stephen Bach).

Public service employment relations was also in flux as a result of other challenges that extended beyond austerity measures. Between 2013–2015, the European Union funded our comparative research project on *New Challenges for Public Services Social Dialogue: Integrating Service User and Workforce Involvement*, which examined the role of service users in shaping employment relations, focusing on the experience of hospitals and schools. It was notable how, despite widely differing national patterns of public service employment relations, a more prominent role was emerging for service users in shaping public services, with important implications for employment relations. In addition to these projects, we were invited by the European Commission to contribute to the 2012 and 2014 *Industrial Relations in Europe Report*, which took stock of the state of public sector employment relations in Europe.

These projects raised important questions about to what extent we are witnessing a transformation of public service employment relations, and what form any such transformation is taking. There has long been a standing preoccupation with the transformation of private sector employment relations, but there has been a much more cautious and equivocal view about such trends in public services. Indeed, we have highlighted many of these ambiguities and contradictions in our own interpretation of developments, including in the precursor to this book, *Public Service Employment Relations in Europe: Transformation, Modernization or Inertia?* (Routledge, 1999), prepared with our colleagues Giuseppe Della Rocca and David Winchester.

This book therefore has its origins in a concern to examine public service employment relations as it emerges from the crisis and has been informed by three main considerations. Firstly, there has been much interest in the immediate consequences of the economic crisis for public service employment relations, but findings from our related research projects indicated the importance of an extended time horizon in understanding changes in public service employment relations. We therefore encouraged our contributors to place their findings in a longer historical time frame and to look beyond the immediate consequences of austerity agendas to illuminate the longer-term consequences of current developments.

A second consideration has been informed by the reluctance of much academic writing to move beyond narrow silos that are increasingly a prerequisite of publishing in many highly regarded journals. We encouraged our contributors to integrate insights from the fields of public management *and* employment relations. These areas of study are usually dealt with separately, with contributions concentrating on the reform of the organization and management of public services or the institutions and practices of workforce management, but rarely provide an integrated understanding of these increasingly connected fields.

Thirdly, the selection of countries was based on several criteria. We wanted to include a variety of countries whose economies had been differentially exposed to the economic crisis, enabling us to examine the consequences for public service employment relations of being directly or indirectly subject to the intervention of the European Commission and the Troika. Different levels of financial vulnerability was therefore a key selection criteria that enabled us to address explicitly variations in the extent and scope of change. We also wanted to reflect the changing geometry of the European Union to include the influx of new member states after 2004. We have included analyses of Central and Eastern European countries—Czechcia (the Czech Republic), Hungary and Slovakia—countries in which there is a limited but emerging tradition of analyzing public sector reform and employment relations.

There was an opportunity to present some of the advanced drafts of the papers and to discuss them at a special symposium organized as part of the ILERA (International Labor and Employment Relations Association) World Congress in Cape Town in September 2015. The congress plenary session also enabled us to gain feedback for some of the ideas that inform the first chapter of this book. Following this conference, we commenced the final writing and editing of this collection. We are especially grateful to Alexandra Stroleny of King's College London, who provided invaluable assistance in preparing the data and tables for this book. Finally, completing a book manuscript over the Christmas/New Year period is not ideal timing, and we are therefore very grateful for the patience and understanding of our wives, Caroline and Benedetta, who accepted our absence for lengthy periods of time as we prepared the final stages of this manuscript.

Stephen Bach and Lorenzo Bordogna
London and Milan
December 2015

About the Contributors

Stephen Bach is a Professor of Employment Relations and Head of School of Management and Business at King's College London. His research interests include comparative public service employment relations, the international migration of health professionals and work reorganization in the public sector. He has led several EU-funded research projects on the consequences of austerity and the role of service users in shaping employment practices. His research has been published in the *British Journal of Industrial Relations, Human Relations, Public Administration and Work* and *Employment and Society*. His recent books include: *The Modernisation of the Public Services and Employee Relations: Targeted Change* (2012, with Ian Kessler) and *Managing Human Resources* (2013, edited with Martin Edwards).

Lorenzo Bordogna is a Professor of Economic Sociology at the University of Milan, Italy. His research interests include labor market institutions and economic performance, public service employment relations in a comparative perspective, industrial conflict in advanced economies, EU economic integration and national industrial relations systems. He has been a member of the Executive Committee of the International Labor and Employment Relations Association and the president of the Italian Association of Industrial Relations. He has participated in several international research projects. His recent articles have been published in the *European Journal of Industrial Relations*, the *International Journal of Human Resource Management, Transfer, Comparative Labor Law & Policy Journal* and the *Indian Journal of Industrial Relations*.

Nana Wesley Hansen is an Assistant Professor at the Employment Relations Research Centre in the Department of Sociology, University of Copenhagen. She specializes in studies of social dialogue and collective bargaining in the public sector at the sector and workplace levels. Her key publications include Hansen, N. W. & M. Mailand (2014), 'Public service employment relations in an era of austerity: The case of Denmark', *European Journal of Industrial Relations*, 19:4.

Marta Kahancová is a senior researcher and managing director at the Central European Labour Studies Institute in Bratislava, Slovakia. Her research interests are in the sociology of organizations and work, and in particular, comparative industrial relations, atypical employment, work practices and social interaction in multinational firms, and work-related migration. She has participated in many international research projects and been published in various peer-reviewed journals in industrial relations, sociology and human resource management. She obtained her Ph.D. at the University of Amsterdam, the Netherlands, in 2007.

Berndt Keller is a Professor Emeritus of Employment Relations at the University of Konstanz, Germany. He is the author of numerous articles and several books on German and European employment relations, including *Einführung in die Arbeitspolitik* (7th ed., Oldenbourg, 2008), *Arbeitspolitik im öffentlichen Dienst* (Edition Sigma, 2010) and *Atypische Beschäftigung zwischen Prekarität und Normalität* (with H.Seifert, Edition Sigma 2013). His research has focused on various national as well as comparative public sector issues. He was co-editor of *Industrielle Beziehungen. The German Journal of Industrial Relations*, was president of the German Industrial Relations Association and was a member of the Executive Committee of the International Labour and Employment Relations Association.

Christos A. Ioannou, an economist (Ph.D.), is Deputy Greek Ombudsman in charge of social protection, health and welfare issues since 2013. He has served as a mediator and arbitrator in collective bargaining with the Organisation for Mediation and Arbitration in Greece since 1991. His research work has been in the areas of labor markets, human resources, collective bargaining and wage and employment policies. His latest published work refers to the comparative analysis of financialization's impact on collective bargaining (in Christian E. Weller (ed), 2015), and his current research focuses on paradigm changes in wage formation and on productive reforms in the Greek economy.

Peter Leisink is a Professor of Public Administration and Organizational Science in the Utrecht University School of Governance, the Netherlands. His research interests are in strategic HRM and service performance in public and non-profit organizations, changes in employment relations, public service motivation and life-stage related personnel policies. A sample of his research group's work can be found in Leisink *et al.* (2013) *Managing social issues: A public values perspective* (Edward Elgar Publishing). His research has been published in the *European Journal of Industrial Relations, Human Resource Management Journal*, the *International Journal of Human Resource Management*, and the *Review of Public Personnel Administration*.

Mikkel Mailand is the Head of Research and an Associate Professor at the Employment Relations Research Center in the Department of Sociology at the University of Copenhagen. His research interests cover public sector industrial relation, neo-corporatism, EU-level labor market regulation and non-standard employment. His key publications regarding public sector industrial relations include M. Mailand (2014), 'Austerity measures and municipalities—the case of Denmark', *Transfer*, 20:3.

Monika Martišková is a researcher at the Central European Labour Studies Institute in Bratislava, Slovakia, and a Ph.D. candidate at the Institute of Economic Studies at Charles University in Prague, the Czech Republic. Her research covers labor markets institutions and collective bargaining in Central and Eastern European countries. She regularly participates in various international research projects addressing precarious work, industrial relations, income inequalities, regional disparities and active labor market policies in Slovakia and Czechia.

Oscar Molina is a lecturer in the Department of Sociology and a researcher at the Centre d'Estudis QUIT/Institute for Labour Studies, Universitat Autònoma de Barcelona. He obtained his Ph.D. in social and political science at the European University Institute in Florence. His research interests include changes in collective bargaining systems in Italy and Spain since the early 1980s. His work has been published in a number of journals, including the *European Journal of Industrial Relations*.

Imre Szabó is a doctoral student at the Central European University in Budapest. His dissertation examines the shift of bargaining conflicts from the private to the public sector across the EU, focusing on recent protest events organized by nurses, doctors and teachers. He is also an expert on Hungarian industrial relations as well as on healthcare and education human resource developments. He has published in *Transfer: European Review of Labour and Research* and in the *European Journal of Industrial Relations* (together with Marta Kahancová).

Catherine Vincent is a senior researcher at IRES (Noisy-le-grand, France) and an associate professor at the Universities of Paris-Dauphine and Paris 13-Villetaneuse. She is a sociologist who specializes in industrial relations. Her current research interests focus on collective bargaining, employee workplace representation and social dialogue in the public sector. She has been involved in a broad range of European research projects. She recently co-authored *Minimum Wages, Collective Bargaining and Economic Development in Asia and Europe* (Palgrave Macmillan 2015) and *Wage bargaining under the New European Economic Governance* (ETUI 2015).

1 Emerging From the Crisis

The Transformation of Public Service Employment Relations?

Stephen Bach and Lorenzo Bordogna

Decades of public service reform have highlighted the extent of change in the organization and management of public services, but the consequences for public sector employment relations have been more ambiguous and less straightforward to categorize (Christensen and Lægreid 2011; Pollitt and Bouckaert 2011). As the economic and financial crisis took hold and austerity measures were adopted widely across the European Union (EU), it would be easy to assume that these uncertainties have been dispelled as far-reaching reforms of public service employment relations have been implemented in many EU countries.

This book has two main purposes. The first is to provide national studies of public sector employment relations in twelve EU Member States, both inside and outside the Eurozone. It is recognized that there are varied employment relations and administrative traditions within Europe, and this book covers the main countries that have been the focus of political economy, public management and comparative employment relations literature (Esping-Andersen 1990; Crouch 1993; Hall and Soskice 2001; Pollitt and Bouckaert 2011). We include countries with differing systems of public sector employment regulation and public management reform and consider how these differing reform legacies shaped each country's response to the crisis as well as how pre-crisis patterns were affected. The dominant tradition in the public management literature is to focus on organizational reform, largely to the neglect of workforce issues, while comparative employment relations has paid limited attention to analysis of public management reform. By contrast, we encouraged contributors to connect employment relations and public management scholarship to develop *integrated* accounts of public sector workforce reform.

A novel feature of this collection is a recognition of the importance of Central and Eastern European countries, and by extending our analysis to a number of these countries, we start to address their neglect within studies of public management and comparative employment relations (for an exception, see Vaughan-Whitehead 2013). To maintain depth without sacrificing breadth, we limited the book to twelve countries: Greece, Italy, Spain, France, Germany, the Netherlands, Denmark, Sweden, Britain, Slovakia, the Czech Republic and Hungary. Five of them do not belong to the Eurozone: Britain, Denmark, Sweden, the Czech Republic and Hungary, while Slovakia joined in 2009. In each case, public service employment relations are examined within the wider context of national administrative systems, with particular attention to public management reforms that have occurred in most countries since the 1980s.

The second purpose of each chapter is to provide an in-depth analysis of the longer-term consequences of the economic crisis that erupted in 2008 and of governments' responses in relation to public service working conditions and employment relations institutions and practices. The economic recession and ensuing sovereign debt crisis had immediate implications for the public sector (Bach and Pedersini 2013; Bordogna and Pedersini 2013; Vaughan-Whitehead 2013), and we develop these accounts of the crisis. Each chapter places these crisis effects in a longer historical time frame, assessing public management reforms from the 1980s, but also extending its analysis beyond the preoccupation with immediate austerity measures to consider the legacy of the crisis from the vantage point of 2015.

Accordingly, the structure of each chapter follows a common framework to facilitate comparative analysis and is organized around a set of core themes and issues. Each chapter identifies the main features of public sector employment regulation up to 2008, covering state, employer and trade union policies and highlights shifts in public sector employment relations during previous periods of public sector management reform. The volume provides both a detailed analysis of evolving systems of public sector employment relations that will be of value to policy makers and students of public management and comparative employment relations and contributes to scholarship on the effects of the crisis on public sector employment relations. In particular, it addresses whether the crisis, and governments' policies in response to it, have had a temporary effect on public sector working conditions and employment relations or more enduring structural consequences.

In this introductory chapter, the focus is mainly on the second theme, namely on the question of whether the crisis has brought about a major transformation in public service employment relations in Europe or even a paradigm shift compared with pre-crisis patterns. A similar issue has been raised with regard to the United States' experience. Katz (2013) questions whether the 2008 crisis brought about a 'fundamental transformation' in public sector labor relations similar to the radical change that occurred in the US private sector in the 1980s. In the private sector, this transformation was associated with a shift in bargaining power in management's favor due to increased international competition, the growth of a highly competitive domestic non-union sector, the economic recession of the early 1980s and deregulation processes in several key industries (Katz 2013: 1031–1032). The conclusion reached by this analysis in relation to the public sector is negative, although with various qualifications. Are similar conclusions warranted in terms of the European experience?

To address this question, the chapter is organized as follows. The next section will present in a stylized way the key features of the two main public service employment relations models that prevailed in European countries until the 1980s. The following section recalls two decades of public service reforms often inspired by the new public management approach (NPM) and argues that the double process of convergence that NPM promised to deliver—across countries, and between the public and private sector in each country—did not materialize. We turn then to our core question: did the crisis, and governments' response to it, bring about the fundamental transformation in public service employment relations that NPM-inspired reforms failed to deliver? As countries emerge from the crisis, is a paradigm shift clearly detectable? Or is the picture more nuanced, comprising both new and longstanding features, convergent and divergent trends, depending on country-specific legal and institutional traditions and related to the intensity of the crisis experienced by the different countries? To address these questions, we draw on Eurostat data primarily for the twelve countries that are the main focus of our analysis, but extended to a wider group of EU countries.

The Past: Two Models of Public Service Employment Relations and Their Distinctiveness

For about three decades after WWII, the public sector in Europe has comprised a key part of a system of social protection in which employers and trade unions cooperated with the state to coordinate and implement welfare policies, albeit with significant variations across countries, in particular between liberal-market and coordinated-market economies (Hall and Soskice 2001). The public sector, nurtured by Keynesian economic policies, became a very significant employer and comprised an integral component of the so-called full employment welfare state, mitigating risk from job loss and ill health and providing secure employment with high social standards (Hay and Wincott 2012; Gottschall *et al.* 2015). Central and Eastern European countries followed a different trajectory with a distinctive state socialist tradition, in which the autonomous role of the social partners was suppressed and welfare services were a low priority for the state. EU membership, however, exposed these countries to pressures to conform, bringing their administrative systems more into line with practice in other EU member states.

Within this context, public service employment relations were characterized by special rules and institutions, separate and distinct from those governing private sector employment relations. Two models tended to prevail (Beaumont 1992; Bach and Kessler 2007), with some variants within each of them. The first one is often labeled as the 'sovereign employer' model, to stress the unilateralism that characterizes it, representative of countries with a *Rechtsstaat* tradition, either of Napoleonic or Prussian origin, and with a Weberian ideal-type of bureaucracy (Kickert 2007; Peters 2010). In this model, a clearly identifiable professional cadre of employees entered government through rigorous recruitment and selection procedures and evaluated against universal criteria. These public servants were expected to serve impartially and to pursue the general interest of the nation, fulfilling these 'sovereign' functions on behalf of the state. It was considered almost inconceivable that these public servants could have their own distinctive interests separate from the general interest of the state and the importance of values of loyalty, trust and stability featured in the regulation of their employment relationship. On the one hand, public servants enjoyed special substantive and procedural prerogatives, often established by a public law statute subject, if disputes arose, to administrative courts and tribunals. They had a formalized and protected position with employment security and generous pension treatment, and career development was mostly linked to seniority, or to a mixture of seniority and performance (Kickert 2007; Bordogna and Pedersini 2013). On the other hand, they were denied collective bargaining rights; their terms and conditions of employment were unilaterally determined by the state through laws or administrative measures. The right to strike was in some cases subject to special restrictions or even denied altogether, while the right of association was usually constitutionally protected, with little or no distinction between public and private employees. France and Germany (with regards to *Beamte*) were the exemplary cases of this model, but it also characterized the experience of Austria, Belgium, Italy (until the 1980s), the Netherlands and other cases in continental Europe.

The second model is typical of the common law tradition of Britain, where no fundamental division exists between public and private sector employment legislation and separate administrative law and employment tribunals for civil servants do not exist (Winchester and Bach 1999). Despite the absence of a legal distinction, however, public services employment relations in Britain still differed significantly from patterns prevailing in the private sector. This difference was associated with the 'model employer' approach that highlighted the greater degree of job security, better benefits such as pensions and the generally more benign attitude towards trade unions than in the private sector, including well-established forms of joint regulation (Fredman and Morris 1989). Other countries in Northern Europe were closer to this tradition than to the sovereign employer model, including Denmark and Sweden from the mid-1960s (Ibsen *et al.* 2011; Sundström 2016).

Irrespective of the differences between them, especially in terms of unilateralism (sovereign employer) versus joint regulation (model employer), what these models had in common was a recognition of the distinctive character of the employment relations institutions and practices that differed from those prevailing in the private sector. Another common and related feature was (and is) a trade union density rate systematically higher than in the private sector (Visser 2011; Bordogna and Pedersini 2013).

The reasons for this peculiarity are well known. They are mostly due to the basic features of the public sector employer, as stressed by two partly different but converging traditions of analysis. One line of analysis (Katz *et al.* 2015: 248) highlights that 'the public sector is in some ways fundamentally different from the private sector. Government is not just an employer and a provider of services: it is a provider of public services and the public sector is affected more significantly than the private sector by political pressures and the demands of the public'. In particular, drawing on Alfred Marshall's work, this argument stresses how the four Marshallian conditions that influence workers' bargaining power operate differently in the two sectors (Katz *et al.* 2015: 246–248). Two of these conditions are on average more favorable to public than to private sector employees. In general, there is a lower substitutability of labor in the public sector (i.e. less scope to use alternative labor suppliers or other factors of production) because public services are usually delivered locally and, like all services, depend on the interaction between the provider and the client, making it more difficult to use alternative suppliers. There is also a lower price elasticity of demand for the final product because public services are often essential services (defense, education, health etc.), and end users are often sheltered from paying directly for public services. Consequently, the trade-off between wages and employment is less severe (Katz 2013: 1034). One condition—the importance of being unimportant, that is, a low ratio of labor cost to total production cost—is likely to be disadvantageous for public employees because of the labor-intensive nature of public services, while the last one is neutral. This implies that on the whole, irrespective of the legal regulation of the employment relationship and regardless of the prevailing employment relations model, the demand for labor in the public sector is relatively inelastic and insensitive to increases in wages. Therefore, although differences between specific public sector industries (education, health etc.) make generalization hazardous, public employees enjoy on average stronger bargaining power than private sector employees, which in turn would 'justify' a special regulation of employment relations in the public sector (Katz 2013: 1033–1036; Katz *et al.* 2015: ch. 10).

These considerations are consistent with another long-standing line of analysis, which similarly stresses the unique role of the state as employer and the particular context in which it operates (Ferner 1985; Beaumont 1992). Public sector organizations are mainly financed through public funds and are subject to a higher degree of public scrutiny, and their employers/ managers are sensitive to the political consequences of their actions and are answerable to a wider range of stakeholders than private sector organizations (Bach and Kessler 2007). Consequently, the public employer is a political institution embedded in a system of constraints and incentives that leads to a logic of action that is quite different from that prevailing in the private sector. A political dimension is an intrinsic feature of public service employment relations, and this political component cannot be removed despite many organizational and managerial reforms that claim to do just that (Bordogna 2008; OECD 2015: ch. 8).

The Challenges of Two Decades of NPM-Inspired Reforms

The distinctiveness of public service employment relations started to be challenged in the mid-1980s by the cycle of public service reforms, frequently associated with the agenda of new public management. This reform trajectory originated in the main Anglophone countries (the UK, the US, Australia and New Zealand) and was endorsed and popularized by the OECD and management consultants (OECD 1995; Bach and Della Rocca 2000). NPM recipes spread beyond these 'first movers', although with variations between countries, often related to their distinctive administrative tradition rather than the political complexion of the party in office (Hood 1995; Pollitt and Dan 2011a; 2011b; OECD 2015). It was part of a broader shift in many democratic, advanced political economies from a Keynesian to a monetarist macroeconomic regime that favored market-driven public services (Hay and Wincott 2012).

With slower economic growth in the aftermath of the oil shocks of the 1970s and a deepening process of internationalization, nation states were increasingly concerned with the sustainability of their public finances. Pierson (2001) referred to a state of 'permanent austerity' arising from governments' inability to generate sufficient revenue to accommodate rising demands for public services and fierce opposition to welfare cuts from the beneficiaries of these services. At the same time, pressure from corporations to maintain lean taxation regimes was reinforced by the increased scope for employers to relocate to more favorable taxation jurisdictions and by continuing pressure to enhance national competitiveness (Schafer and Streeck 2013). The size and cost of the public sector became a more prominent focus of government attention, and in EU countries this preoccupation was strengthened by the fiscal discipline and requirements of the Stability and Growth Pact. Although this period from the late 1980s onwards did not constitute a frontal attack on public services, the need to recalibrate public services and, more generally, the welfare state (Ferrera 2005), encouraged more concerted efforts to reform public management *and* associated systems of public sector employment regulation (Bach *et al.* 1999).

The traditional distinctiveness of public service employment relations, with separate institutions and practices from the private sector, was challenged, although to varying degrees and with different effects across countries (Bach and Bordogna 2011). Despite definitional ambiguities, there is agreement that in broad terms, NPM aimed to remove differences between the private and public sectors, importing business techniques and values as the only way to improve public service efficiency and effectiveness (Hood 1991, 1995; OECD 1995; Pollitt and Dan 2011a, 2011b). Essential components of its recipes were the adoption of market-oriented mechanisms of governance in conjunction with private sector management techniques using policies of privatization and marketization. Privatization indicated the necessity to shift ownership and employment practices towards patterns prevailing in the private sector. Marketization stressed the need to shift the internal governance of public service organizations from a Weberian bureaucratic model based on formal rules, hierarchical relations and process accountability towards a market-like model based on competition, contracts and accountability for results. NPM-inspired reforms aimed to modify profoundly the system of constraints and opportunities, of incentives and controls governing the entire functioning of the public services, with a view to promoting a paradigm shift in the organization and management of public administration (Hood 1991). Moreover, given the claim that NPM was universal in its application (Hood 1995: 95), the implication was that a process of global convergence could be expected. Any variations across countries in the application of NPM could only be understood in terms of 'leaders' and 'laggards', excluding the possibility that other reform trajectories could be pursued (Bach and Bordogna 2011: 2282).

Changing the traditional patterns of public service employment relations and HRM practices was an essential part of this program. With regard to the sovereign employer model, the focus was on the special employment status of public employees (not limited to civil servants) and on the substantive prerogatives attached to such a status. With regard to the model employer approach, there was a rejection of the presumption that the public sector should be a 'model employer', and policies targeted national systems of employment regulation and the role of trade unions in jointly regulating pay and conditions (Winchester and Bach 1999; Bordogna and Winchester 2001). In both cases, NPM advocated less emphasis on equity issues and national comparability standards and the replacement of automatic and collective mechanisms of pay increases and career promotion with more discretionary and individualized mechanisms (such as performance-related pay and variable bonuses). The promise was a fundamental transformation, with the expectation of a double process of convergence between different countries and between public and private sectors within each country (Bordogna 2008).

However, after more than two decades of NPM-inspired reforms, these expectations have not been fulfilled, even if change is apparent. The dominant message of many studies is that outcomes are mixed with significant variations across countries, in different segments of the public sector and in relation to different measures (Pollitt and Dan 2011a, 2011b; Alonso *et al.* 2015). A few common trends are apparent, for instance, regarding the weakening of the special prerogatives of civil and public servants, the reduced importance of seniority in career development and pay systems and, more generally, the hybridization of the career-based and position-based models, as documented by the chapters in this volume. However, it remains unconvincing to argue that there has been a radical convergence across countries or between public and private sectors in each country. Country-specific legal, institutional and administrative traditions have proven to be particularly strong in the public sector, resulting in national path dependencies that hindered marked processes of convergence between countries.

Furthermore, the unique role of the state as employer and the particular context in which the public employer operates have proven more resistant than anticipated by the NPM program, continuing to affect many features of public service employment relations and preventing full convergence with private sector employment relations (OECD 2010, 2012, 2015; Pollitt and Dan 2011b; ILO 2013; Katz *et al.* 2015).

In several cases, the adoption of private sector institutions and practices brought about unintended and even perverse effects. Instructive examples are the decentralization of collective bargaining over pay and conditions of employment, the replacement of automatic and 'collectivist' systems of pay increases and career promotion based on seniority with more discretionary and selective procedures, and forms of performance-related-pay (PRP) and individualization of employment conditions. When these types of measures have been imported from the private sector neglecting the peculiarities of the public employer and without the appropriate financial and institutional arrangements, the effects have often been quite distant, if not opposed, to those obtained in the private sector (Bordogna 2008). A much more cautious and questioning attitude towards NPM has emerged over the last decade (OECD 2010; OECD 2012). A particularly instructive example is that of PRP, once among the most advocated NPM measures promoted by the OECD. A 2015 study, however, including Denmark, the Netherlands and Sweden, amongst others, underlines the costs and the lack of evidence about its benefits (OECD 2015: 224–226). This does not mean that NPM is dead (de Vries 2010; Pollitt and Dan 2011a, 2011b) or that none of its components may be fruitfully imported into the public sector and public service employment relations. But it signals that even amongst influential proponents of NPM, there is greater acknowledgement of the *pros* and *cons* of its recipes, of their potential unintended and even perverse effects (OECD 2015).

It can be concluded, therefore, that the fundamental change, or paradigm shift, promised by the NPM approach in the organization and management of public administration, including public service employment relations, did not materialize. Instead of a universal and linear process of change towards a common destination, with a distinction only between leaders and laggards, alternative reform trajectories have been pursued that combine NPM elements with long-standing features of 'classic' public administration and other more novel aspects of reform (Christensen and Lægreid 2007, 2011; Ongaro 2009; Osborne 2010; Pollitt and Dan 2011a, 2011b). In summary, until the economic crisis and despite ongoing reforms, country-specific and institutionally embedded patterns of public sector employment regulation continued to differ from private sector employment relations (Bach and Bordogna 2011).

The Economic Crisis and Its Effects

The financial and economic crisis that erupted in 2008, with a new marked downturn in 2012–13, hit the public sector with particular strength. In many EU countries, the public sector has been a prime target of government austerity policies. Working conditions, employment levels, pay dynamics and pension benefits of public employees have all been widely affected, in some cases with implications also for the quality and quantity of services provided (Bach and Pedersini 2013; Bordogna and Pedersini 2013; Della Rocca 2013; Vaughan-Whitehead 2013; Leisink and Bach 2014). Did these changes also impact on traditional public service employment relations institutions and practices with lasting, structural consequences for the pre-crisis configuration, to some extent resembling the transformation that occurred in the 1980s in the US private sector (Kochan *et al.* 1986)?

The argument supporting a radical change in the US private sector since the early 1980s was based on the Marshallian conditions about the sources of bargaining power. In particular, the focus was on a shift of bargaining power in management's favor due to four main factors: increased international competition, growth of a highly competitive domestic non-union sector, severe economic recession and deregulation in a number of key industries. The effect of these factors was to pressure 'private sector unions into concessions and other related bargaining outcome and process changes' (Katz 2013: 1036). In contrast with the private sector experience, the influence of these contextual changes in the public sector seems 'much more modest' than in the private sector. The role of international sourcing and of multinational corporations is limited, while privatization processes, which make alternative providers more feasible and therefore weaken unions' bargaining power, have expanded only gradually since the early 1990s in the US experience, and their increase after the 2008 crisis has not been on the scale capable of leading to transformative change (Katz 2013: 1037). Regulatory changes in the public sector have been limited compared to the deep deregulation that took place in key private sector industries in the 1980s (e.g. airlines, telecommunications). Overall, the argument concludes, these differences in the two contexts explain why the fundamental transformation that occurred in the US private sector did not affect, and is not affecting, public sector labor relations.

Are these conclusions tenable in relation to the European experience and, in particular, in the countries covered in this collection? Utilizing the same Marshallian approach, an important difference is apparent in the European context (Bordogna 2015). Given the depth and length of the economic crisis and its transformation into a sovereign debt crisis, at least one of the Marshallian conditions, the importance of being unimportant, worsened markedly to the further detriment of public sector employees and trade unions. For many EU governments, not only those under a rescue program established by the Troika (European Commission, European Central Bank, International Monetary Fund), the need to reduce or keep under tight control public finances became an absolute imperative, and the easiest and quickest way to achieve this result was by intervening to limit the total public sector pay bill. Was this change significant enough to substantially alter in management's favor the overall balance of the four Marshallian factors and therefore to bring about a fundamental change in public service employment relations? If so, are uniform trends evident across European countries, or do cross-national variations still prevail?

Financial Vulnerability and Austerity Measures

The degree of financial vulnerability of each country is a crucial variable in explaining government responses to the crisis and, in turn, their effects on public service working conditions and employment relations institutions. The constraints on the fiscal policies of member states, especially but not only in the Eurozone, have tightened markedly during the crisis within the framework of the new EU economic governance, especially the provisions of the 2011 'Euro Plus Pact' and the 2012 'Fiscal Compact' (European Commission 2012, 2016).

Table 1.1 presents the evolution between 2007 and 2015 of the financial vulnerability of the countries included in this volume and selected other countries. Refining a procedure utilized by Lodge and Hood (2012) and also Bach and Bordogna (2013), financial vulnerability comprises the two basic criteria of the EU Stability and Growth Pact (budget deficit and accumulated gross debt), adjusted to include real GDP growth. Two features are evident: a dramatic worsening of financial vulnerability between 2007 and 2009 and again in 2012, as well as wide cross-national differences. In 2007, most countries and the EU27 as a whole were included in the bottom left corner of the table, with the lowest degree of vulnerability. By 2009, all countries moved markedly upward: four countries and the EU27 as a whole to the highest vulnerability box, four other countries just below and no country was located in the lowest box. Something similar occurred between 2011 and 2012. Greece, Italy, Spain and France, followed partly by the UK, feature among the most heavily hit countries, while Denmark, the Netherlands, Sweden, the Czech Republic, Slovakia and Germany are generally at the opposite end of the spectrum with the exception of 2009, when some of these countries' positions deteriorated. Ireland and Portugal are also present amongst the most vulnerable group in both 2009 and 2012, while the remaining Central and Eastern European (CEE) countries generally indicate a stronger position, with the exception of Slovenia in 2013.

The severity and duration of austerity policies reflect this ranking, although with some qualifications (Table 1.2). The countries under the program of financial assistance by the Troika (Greece and partly Spain in our sample, but Portugal and Ireland exhibit similar patterns) are the clearest examples of the link between financial vulnerability and austerity policies, with the largest pay-bill cuts and measures covering all the relevant areas— employment levels, wage dynamics, working time and pension systems. Italy and France also feature strongly, although the first austerity measures predated the crisis in Italy (2008) and were less severe and partly delayed in the case of France. Milder measures have generally been adopted by countries with lower financial vulnerability, like Germany, Denmark and Sweden, but this was not the case in the Netherlands, especially with regard to employment, and was only partly the case in the Czech Republic. These variations and qualifications confirm that national dynamics are not entirely and exclusively accounted for by the economic and financial conditions of a country. They depend also on the traditional role and regulation of the

Table 1.1 Degree of Financial Vulnerability 2007–2015 of Selected EU Member Countries

	2007	2008	2009	2010	2011	2012	2013	2014	2015*
High (8/9)	EL	EL	**EU27**; EL; IE; FR; IT; PT; UK	EL; ES; PT	EL; ES; PT	IE; EL; ES; IT; PT	CY; EL; ES; PT	CY	EL; FR; IT; PT
Medium/High (7)	IT; HU; PT	IE; IT; UK	DE; ES; HU; SK	**EU27**** FR; IE; IT; UK	IE; IT; UK	**EU28**; CY; NL; UK	IE; IT	IT; PT	
Medium (6)		FR; HU; PT	CY; CZ; NL	HU	**EU28**; CY; HU; NL	CZ; DK; HU; SK	**EU28**; FR; NL; UK	IE; EL; ES; FR	CY; ES; UK
Medium/Low (5)	FR	**EU27**** DK; DE; ES; SE	DK; SE	CY; CZ; DE; NL; SK	FR	DE; FR; SE; SK	CZ; DK; DE; HU	**EU28**; DE; NL; UK	**EU28**; DE; IE; NL
Low (3/4)	**EU27**** CY; CZ; DE; ES; IE; NL; SE; SK; UK	CY; CZ; NL; SK		DK; SE	CZ; DK; DE; SE; SK		SE; SK	CZ; DK; HU; LT; SE; SK	CZ; DK; HU; SE; SK

[1]Sum of: GDP growth (GDP at market prices, Change on previous period) + Public deficit (% GDP) + Public debt (% GDP)

GDP growth (GDP at market prices)
(1) LOW: over 2.5%
(2) Medium: 0.1–2.5%
(3) HIGH: (0 and below)

Public deficit (% GDP)
(3) High: above 6%
(2) Medium: 3–6%
(1) Low: below 3%

Public debt (% GDP)
(3) High: over 90%
(2) Medium: 60 to 90%
(1) Low: Below 60%

* GDP growth (year 2015) data consists of average of Quarter 1, Quarter 2 and Quarter 3, not seasonally adjusted, growth rates with respect to the same quarter of the previous year; Public deficit (not seasonally adjusted) and Public debt data (year 2015) consist of average of Quarter 1 and Quarter 2.

** based on Eurostat data accessed 2015

Table 1.2 Austerity Measures Affecting Public Sector Pay, Employment, Pensions and Working Time 2008–2014

	Wages	Employment	Pensions and working time	Implementation process
CZ	Pay cuts (2010–2013) for most public service occupational groups, commencing with a 10% nominal wage cut in 2010. The main exception was teachers; gradual compensation through wage growth since 2014	Employment reductions (2010–2012) concentrated in central government. Modest employment growth in other subsectors	Raising the retirement age, freezing or reducing the value of pensions, increases in worker contributions, financial penalty for early retirement	Imposed by government despite trade union protests and demonstrations
DE	Small but continuous rises of nominal wages between 2010–2014; reduction of annual bonus	Increase in employment, mainly via increased use of part-time and temporary contracts	Raising the retirement age	Collective bargaining for employees (but not for civil servants)
DK	Pay freeze (2011); limited increases in nominal wages (2012 and 2013); removal of seniority bonuses (2011)	Employment has remained relatively stable since 2008, but employment in local government has declined since 2010	Raising the retirement age, limiting early retirement	Negotiation within a fiscal framework in which the Ministry of Finance is dominant
EL	Pay cuts to bonus payments and allowances and subsequent abolition of 13th and 14th monthly salary. Total pay cut since 2010 could not exceed 25% Average pay reduction of 12% in the 'special wage regimes' (2012) covering specific occupations. Planned introduction of new civil service pay structure (2015/6)	Target of -20% (150,000) to be achieved by end of 2015. This process was managed by establishing the 'mobility' and 'availability' scheme. Employees placed in the availability scheme receive 75% of their wage. Replacement of 1 in 5 staff that retire from the public sector	Weekly working hours increased from 37.5 to 40 (2011). Raising the retirement age and one-off pension fund levy of 7% of workers' after tax pay.	Initial pay cuts imposed by government and subsequent measures formed part of funding agreements concluded with the Troika

FR	Pay scales frozen 2010–2014, but with individual safeguards as a result of the purchasing power guarantee	Aggregate employment levels have changed little since 2008, but while local government employment increased, state civil service employment declined. Replacement of 1 in 2 staff that leave the state civil service	Raising the retirement age; reform of final salary arrangements	Imposed by government legislation, although government reforms aim to strengthen social dialogue
ES	Average 5% pay cut in 2010 followed by wage freezes (2010–2013) Removal of Christmas bonus payment (2012); reductions in sick pay (2012)	Reductions in public sector employment with largest reductions in local government. Replacement rate of 1 in 10 for retiring civil servants until 2013	Raising the retirement age, limiting early retirement, changes to final salary calculations. Increase in working hours (35 to 37.5 hours per week)	A tradition of social pacts survived the early period of the crisis (2009), but gave way to government imposition, prompting protests, strikes
HU	Abolition of 13th month salary (2009), small wage supplement to compensate the low paid	Public sector employment has increased substantially mainly because of employment creation in public works programs.	Raising the retirement age	Imposed by government
IT	Pay freeze and bargaining freeze (for 2010–12, later prolonged to 2013–14/15), freeze on seniority increments for public employees (2010–2015) not covered by collective bargaining, but repealed in June 2015 following Constitutional Court ruling. Cuts in resources for decentralized collective agreements. Pay cuts of 5% and 10% on earnings over an upper limit, but repealed end of 2012 following Constitutional Court ruling	Staff turnover cut down initially (2009) to 10–20% of retired personnel, depending on sector and category; turnover cut prolonged in 2010, 2011, 2012, 2013, 2014, 2015, with small changes; permanent employees decreased by 5–6% between 2007 and 2014 2008–on: tight financial constraints on the renewal of flexible employment contracts; decrease of these employees by 32% between 2007 and 2014	Cut in personnel training activities. Stricter performance assessment systems. Cuts in financial transfers to local governments	Wage and bargaining freeze imposed by a center-right government in 2010, prolonged until 2015 by different governments; pension reform approved in December 2011 by a center-left + center-right coalition government (Monti)

(Continued)

Table 1.2 (Continued)

	Wages	Employment	Pensions and working time	Implementation process
NL	No wage agreement in central government (which includes primary education) after 2010; a wage freeze that was formalized by government in 2013. Successive agreements in local government and healthcare enabled wage increases of 1–2% per annum.	Public sector employment has decreased except in hospitals. Reductions have affected central and local government	Raising the retirement age, reductions in value of pensions	Wage freeze imposed by government for central government, collective bargaining maintained in other sectors
SE	Wage moderation in a context of individualization and decentralization	Overall employment growth; reductions in employment of staff on fixed-term contracts		Collective bargaining
SK	Wage freeze in central and local government (2011–2013). Wage increases for specific groups (teachers, nurses, doctors) after 2012 following trade union mobilization	Substantial growth in core public services	Raising the retirement age, change to indexation	Collectively agreed wage increases
UK	Pay freeze for fiscal years 2011/12 and 2012/13, except local government that started a year earlier in 2010; some protection for lowest paid, followed by an ongoing 1% pay cap on the public sector pay bill. Reductions in premium payments and redundancy pay	Employment reductions of 15% between 2010–2015. Larger proportion reductions in local government. Recruitment freezes	Raising the retirement age, increases in worker contributions, phasing out of final-salary pensions and an overall reduction in the value of pensions.	Government unilaterally sets civil service pay guidelines, remit for the pay review bodies and pay policy; collective bargaining continued in attenuated form to negotiate reform (e.g. pensions)

Source: Chapters in this collection supplemented by European Foundation for the Improvement of Living and Working Conditions reports.

public sector, as shown by the differences between Italy and France, as well as on government political and ideological orientation, as the case of the UK government's commitment to shrinking the state indicates, and some of the same dynamics are apparent (in a more moderate form) in the Netherlands.

Quantitative Effects: Employment Levels

The most visible effects of austerity policies relate to employment levels and pay dynamics, given that in most countries, the quickest way to reduce the total pay bill, repeatedly pursued since 2008 through various measures, has been to decrease the number of public employees and to cut or freeze their wages and salaries. Many countries have reformed the pension system as well (see Table 1.2). Leaving aside some country variations, the overall trend is that the standard retirement age for receipt of a pension has been raised and linked to life expectancy and the value of pensions has been reduced, in part by lowering the protection from inflation and shifting all employees from an earnings-related to a contributions-related system. With some exceptions, however, these reforms have usually affected all employees, private and public, although in several cases, this implied a larger reduction in benefits for public employees with long-term implications for public expenditure (European Commission 2016).

Bearing in mind that between 2007 and 2014, employment levels decreased in the public sector and in the entire economy, Table 1.3 is based on the EU statistical classification of economic activities (NACE) and includes information on all NACE activities for comparative purposes over the entire period (2007–2014) and in two sub-periods (2007–2009 and 2010–2014). Moreover, the table reports data of only one of the three subsectors that cover public employees in Eurostat statistics, that is, Public Administration, Defense and Compulsory Social Security, since the other two categories (Education; Human Health and Social Work Activities) also include private providers whose employees have a private sector employment contract. Some reference will be made, however, to these subsectors as well.

Between 2007 and 2014, employment levels in the Public Administration subsector have decreased in 16 out of the EU27 countries, in several cases by a two-digit percentage. Four groups are detectable (Table 1.4). Eleven countries have seen a decrease of employment levels both in Public Administration and in the entire economy, including Greece, Italy, the Netherlands and Denmark; in general, the decrease has been notably more marked in Public Administration than in the entire economy. In five other member states, a reduction in Public Administration employment levels has occurred despite a positive development in the economy as a whole, including the Czech Republic, France, Germany and the UK. Only a minority of countries, albeit a significant minority, has recorded an increase of Public Administration

Table 1.3 Employment Levels: Percentage of Change

	All activities			Public Administration, Defense, Compulsory Social Security		
	2014/07	2009/07	2014/10	2014/07	2009/07	2014/10
EU-27	−0.87	−0.66	0.73	−3.20	0.99	−3.27
EU-15	−0.79	−0.84	0.43	−5.23	0.21	−4.68
Euroarea-18	−2.20	−0.97	−0.67	−4.17	0.85	−4.81
Belgium	3.73	0.92	1.22	−11.98	−3.06	−6.84
Bulgaria	−8.34	0.03	−2.34	−6.53	−1.59	−1.28
Czech Rep.	1.06	0.25	1.82	−2.14	−1.56	−3.01
Denmark	−3.20	−1.18	0.30	−5.60	10.75	−4.82
Germany	4.96	1.27	2.93	−2.36	−3.24	−0.38
Estonia	−4.99	−9.69	10.00	15.94	−4.63	11.91
Ireland	−10.69	−8.48	1.68	−7.92	1.43	−7.83
Greece	−22.52	−0.18	−19.45	−19.72	−2.68	−15.90
Spain	−15.72	−7.16	−7.37	3.94	10.21	−9.04
France	3.09	0.34	2.51	−4.44	2.07	−4.94
Croatia	−9.69	1.34	−7.37	8.52	13.18	2.15
Italy	−2.69	−0.85	−1.10	−8.86	0.64	−8.94
Cyprus	−4.02	1.32	−8.22	−14.74	−8.01	−9.22
Latvia	−16.34	−14.08	3.98	−28.19	−13.60	−1.84
Lithuania	−9.13	−9.24	5.71	2.45	2.71	3.38
Luxembourg	21.04	7.05	11.23	23.21	10.27	8.24
Hungary	5.09	−3.95	9.87	40.63	6.84	25.19
Malta	16.73	2.64	11.56	9.63	2.96	8.03
Netherlands	−2.69	1.57	−1.60	−13.53	0.05	−9.52
Austria	4.82	1.49	2.39	0.07	−1.25	−0.11
Poland	4.07	4.12	2.51	13.43	8.90	5.36
Portugal	−11.64	−2.43	−8.14	−1.40	2.03	2.90
Romania	−7.91	−1.17	−1.14	−16.42	4.59	−12.18
Slovenia	−6.94	−0.46	−5.09	4.96	11.76	−3.71
Slovakia	0.23	0.36	1.97	31.96	11.63	11.70
Finland	−1.78	−1.38	−0.01	−9.50	−0.60	−9.27
Sweden	5.10	−0.91	5.49	18.37	2.93	13.34
UK	4.72	−0.69	5.21	−11.09	−3.85	−4.36
Norway	7.90	2.68	5.03	11.31	1.51	8.56

Source: Eurostat, LFS

Extracted on 16.11.15; last update: 28.10.15.

employment between 2007 and 2014, including Sweden, Hungary and Slovakia, in addition to several other CEE countries. It is notable that in some countries, such as Spain, public administration employment has continued to grow despite a negative trend in the entire economy.

In many cases, austerity policies were not adopted until 2009–2010, with visible effects only or mostly apparent in the second sub-period, but not all countries follow this pattern.

Table 1.4 Change in Employment Levels, 2007–2014

		Public Admin., Defense, Social Security	
		Increase	*Decrease*
All Activities	Increase	LU, HU, MT, AT, PL, SK, SE, NO	BE, CZ, DE, FR, UK
	Decrease	ES, EE, LT, SI	DK, EL, IT, NL, BG, IR, CY, LV, PT, RO, FI

The picture is rather different in the other two subsectors (education; human health and social work activities), where employment levels have generally increased with a few exceptions (Italy in the education subsector and Greece and the Netherlands in both the education and health subsectors). The latter two countries are the only ones in our group that have recorded a decrease in all three subsectors (-15.4% in Greece and -5.5% in the Netherlands), which is somewhat surprising with regard to the Netherlands, given its comparatively limited financial vulnerability. At the other end of the spectrum, the largest increase in the three subsectors as a whole has been recorded in two of the three CEE countries (Hungary and Slovakia more than 15%), followed by France, the UK and Germany (around 10–11%), followed by Spain, Sweden, Denmark and the Czech Republic (between 4 and 7%); Italy is below a 1% increase. The UK is an unusual case in which the 11% decrease in the public administration subsector, already underway in 2009 but subsequently accelerated, contrasts strongly with the increase by 20% and 16% in the education and health sectors respectively, reflecting their political priority and relative budgetary protection.

In many cases, the negative trend in the employment levels of public administration has been due also to a decrease in the number of temporary, and often young, employees, who have been particularly hit by the crisis (Table 1.5). The largest decrease, above or around 30%, has occurred in Italy, Greece, Spain and the UK, followed by the Netherlands (-21%), Germany (-16%) and Denmark (-10%). This contrasts with the exceptionally high increase in Slovakia and Hungary and the more moderate one of the Czech Republic, Sweden and France. In three countries—Italy, the Netherlands and the UK—the number of temporary employees in public administration has diminished despite an increase in the economy as a whole, while in Denmark and Germany, the decrease has been greater than in the entire economy. These trends are partly different in the other two public service categories, education and health, but Eurostat data do not allow one to distinguish between employees with a public or a private sector employment contract. However, in Greece and Spain,

Table 1.5 Temporary and Part-Time Employment, Percentage of Change 2007–2014

	Temporary Employment		Part-Time Employment	
	2014/07 All Activities	2014/07 PA, Defense, Social Security	2014/07 All Activities	2014/07 PA, Defense, Social Security
European Union 27	−4,23	−7,46	12,23	1,59
European Union 15	−7,31	−16,49	13,10	−0,73
Euro area 18	−8,80	−13,62	13,95	3,51
Belgium	4,12	−34,12	12,86	−16,26
Bulgaria	−3,47	−55,26	47,85	n/a
Czech Republic	17,08	12,05	28,67	0,00
Denmark	−8,92	−10,26	4,28	−13,76
Germany	−5,50	−15,52	11,31	13,01
Estonia	43,31	n/a	11,75	53,33
Ireland	−2,35	−28,57	17,47	−11,81
Greece	−18,43	−27,12	29,91	−66,67
Spain	−35,96	−28,31	15,69	19,89
France	8,91	2,14	12,72	−3,64
Croatia	23,28	88,52	−26,90	−15,38
Italy	2,35	−38,43	31,11	−11,98
Cyprus	41,46	−31,82	86,55	n/a
Latvia	−33,93	−50,00	−2,39	n/a
Lithuania	−31,18	n/a	−8,94	n/a
Luxembourg	42,19	83,33	28,61	60,00
Hungary	56,91	243,19	61,18	84,21
Malta	77,94	83,33	77,98	66,67
Netherlands	10,83	−21,25	4,74	−11,37
Austria	9,29	5,85	28,79	21,74
Poland	7,65	7,30	−12,13	27,14
Portugal	−9,22	−20,89	−6,02	−6,78
Romania	−11,45	n/a	−5,62	n/a
Slovenia	−19,04	−4,11	11,64	8,33
Slovakia	71,17	520,00	104,80	686,54
Finland	−5,83	−28,13	7,52	−17,57
Sweden	5,41	13,73	12,98	25,24
United Kingdom	12,75	−28,82	11,71	−10,18
Norway	−10,59	−22,95	1,91	−27,64

Source: Eurostat, LFS

Extracted on 16.11.15; last update 5.11.15

temporary workers decreased also in the education and health sectors, although to a lesser extent than in the public administration, defense and social security categories; in France, Hungary and Sweden, they increased, although to a notably lesser extent than public administration in Hungary and to a notably higher extent in France. The other countries present a varied picture. In Denmark, Germany, the Netherlands and the UK, temporary workers increased both in Education and Health sectors, while they decreased in public administration, defense and social security. In Italy, they significantly decreased in the education sector, also as effect of stabilization processes of public school teachers, and increased in the health sector; the same occurred in the Czech Republic and the opposite occurred in Slovakia.

More varied developments are detectable in part-time employment. While in the economy as a whole, it has increased in all our countries and in most EU27 countries, in the public administration subsector, it has decreased in half of our twelve countries (DK, EL, FR, IT, NL, UK), increased in five (DE, ES, HU, SK, SE) and remained unchanged in the Czech Republic. In five of our countries, the public administration subsector has recorded a decrease of both temporary and part-time employees (DK, EL, IT, NL, UK). In this case as well, partly different trends are observable in the education and health sectors, although part-time workers increased in both sectors in the majority of our countries (CZ, DE, ES, FR, IT, HU, SW, UK).

The reduction in employment levels, temporary workers included, often obtained through severe cuts in staff replacement ratios and outsourcing processes, has implied a further, relative aging of public sector employees, especially in the EU15 countries, with effects also on the quality of services provided (Bach and Pedersini 2013; Bordogna and Pedersini 2013; Vaughan-Whitehead 2013; Leisink and Bach 2014; Mori 2015). In many cases, it has also had an adverse gender impact on the public sector workforce (Rubery 2013).

Quantitative Effects: Pay Dynamics

The other main target of austerity policies, widely testified by the national chapters in this volume, has been the wage and salary dynamics of public employees (Table 1.2). While in the pre-crisis period, between 2001 and 2008–2009, approximately half of the 22 EU countries for which data are available recorded a faster growth of wages in the public than in the private sector, and in some cases much faster growth (mostly CEE countries, in a type of catching-up process: RO, BG, SK, HU, EE, CZ, LT, plus MT, IE and IT), the reverse is true after 2009. Between 2010 and 2013, in only four countries out of 27, including Slovakia and the Netherlands, wage growth in the public sector exceeded that of the private sector, with a wage gap that was particularly large in Portugal, Hungary, Spain, Italy and the UK, among others (Müller and Schulten 2015: 21–24; data refer to all the three public sector NACE categories). Four of our twelve countries have recorded at least three years between 2009 and 2013 with a negative or close to zero wage dynamic (EL, HU, IT, UK).

The total pay bill reflects variations of both wages and employment (Table 1.6). Between 2007 and 2014, the total compensation of general government employees has markedly decreased in four of our twelve countries (IT, EL, HU, UK), particularly in the latter three (-16.5% in Greece and -6.9% both in HU and UK). The number of countries affected by a negative trend or by a markedly slowing increase is higher after 2009–2010 and especially until 2013, when government policies reacted with more urgency to the 2009 and 2012 downturns. In three of our countries, however, the decrease was concentrated mostly or exclusively

Table 1.6 Compensation of Employees (payable), General Government: Percentage Change

	2014/2007	2009/07	2014/10
European Union 27	9.95	3.10	3.84
European Union 15	9.13	2.71	3.58
Euro area 18	12.24	8.48	2.31
Belgium	28.48	10.39	13.38
Bulgaria	48.29	27.51	17.61
Czech Republic	41.29	14.56	20.95
Denmark	21.02	13.10	3.04
Germany	21.96	7.40	10.36
Estonia	41.29	16.25	26.28
Ireland	-6.56	4.06	-3.60
Greece	-16.50	20.31	-23.18
Spain	6.97	16.86	-7.96
France	15.64	5.62	7.07
Croatia	1.97	11.53	-7.77
Italy	-0.31	4.47	-5.06
Cyprus	-0.98	17.51	-16.80
Latvia	0.38	-0.18	22.81
Lithuania	21.75	20.31	12.82
Luxembourg	63.67	13.76	35.01
Hungary	-6.92	-9.20	1.50
Malta	47.18	17.11	23.20
Netherlands	15.65	11.45	1.11
Austria	18.57	9.00	6.88
Poland	30.41	6.11	7.30
Portugal	-10.92	6.96	-16.72
Romania	-5.51	6.64	-4.71
Slovenia	16.87	20.83	-6.70
Slovakia	63.10	34.09	16.61
Finland	24.41	10.00	10.39
Sweden	24.12	-9.43	20.58
United Kingdom	-6.87	-18.78	6.60
Norway	48.66	7.59	20.17

Source: Eurostat, Government revenue, expenditure and main aggregates [gov_10a_main]

Extracted on 14.12.15; last update: 11.11.15.

Table 1.7 Change in Employment Levels and Total Pay Bill, 2007–2014

			Employment (Public Administration, Defence, Compulsory Social Security)	
			Increase	Decrease
Compensation of employees (general government)		Increase	ES, SK, SE, EE, MT, LT, LU, AT, PL, SI, NO	CZ, DK, DE, FR, NL, BE, BG, LV, FI
		Decrease	HU	EL, IT, UK, IR, CY, PT, RO

in the 2007–09 period (HU, SE and UK), which sharply contrasts with the experience of countries that in the 2007–2009 still recorded a notable growth of the total pay bill, such as Greece, Italy and Spain, prior to the decrease in the following years. Five countries (DK, DE, FR, CZ and SK) stand out for a positive dynamic in their total pay bill in the entire 2007–2014 period as well as in all the other sub-periods examined, although to a different extent and at a slower pace compared with pre-crisis trends. Particularly high is the increase in the two CEE countries, probably, as already noted, part of a catching-up process with the private sector.

Combining changes in employment levels and total pay bill between 2007 and 2014, four groups of countries are visible (Table 1.7). The linkage with the degree of financial vulnerability is testified by the group with negative trends in both variables. Greece, Italy and the UK, but also Ireland, Cyprus, Portugal and Romania, are all countries either under a Troika assistance program or with the highest degree of vulnerability in one or more years covered by the table. However, the relationship is not a linear one and other explanatory factors play a role, as shown by the opposite cases of Spain and the UK. The latter country only in one year, 2009, displays the highest degree of financial vulnerability, but its government has adopted severe policies that led to marked decreases of both employment levels and pay bill. At the opposite extreme, Spain has been for four years in a row (2010–2013) in the group of countries with the weakest financial position, but has recorded an increase both in the total pay bill and employment levels, along with Sweden, Norway and several CEE countries.

Effects on Employment Relations Institutions and Practices

In most countries, the crisis affected also public service employment relations institutions and practices, reshaping existing patterns. Three main interconnected trends can be highlighted, although with variations between countries: a revival of unilateralism, a recentralization of employment relations and a weakened regulatory capacity of trade unions. These trends are linked to an altered context in which the increased importance of international forces and supranational actors in influencing public service employment relations is evident. This trend represents the broadest and most significant legacy of the crisis: a shift away from an institutional context traditionally sheltered from external pressures, conceived as at the exclusive disposal of domestic actors—national governments and social partners (Bach and Bordogna 2013).

As the following chapters show, and as Table 1.2 summarizes, in many cases, austerity measures were unilaterally decided and adopted by governments without negotiation, or even consultation, with trade unions. In some cases, governments openly disregarded the opposition of trade unions and wider social movements, and these trends extended well beyond the countries receiving financial assistance from the Troika. Combining a wage freeze, restrictions on recruitment and pension reform, Italy is a clear example of these trends, in a country with well-established collective bargaining institutions introduced in the public sector by a major 1993 reform and where concertation practices and trade union veto powers have a long and strong tradition. Many other examples are provided by the national chapters, such as the UK or France, despite the model employer tradition in the first case and legislation in 2010 on the renewal of social dialogue in the public sector in France.

The revival of unilateralism was often due to governments' need to make urgent decisions on contentious issues under the pressures of financial markets, irrespective of pressure from the Troika or from EU authorities. Usually, a sense of urgency and crisis in terms of time and financial resources made it very challenging to open negotiations and reach agreement with the social partners. In some cases, similar restrictions have been applied in the institutional relationships between central government and lower levels of government or decentralized authorities, in particular regarding financial transfers.

In many countries, especially the old EU15, this trend contrasts markedly with the experience of previous decades when social partners played a significant role, through social pacts, income policy or similar institutional arrangements, in supporting governments' effort to meet the conditions for access to the Economic and Monetary Union or to approve important labor market and welfare reforms (Avdagic et al. 2011). But it contrasts, at least partly, also with the experience of those CEE countries where forms of tripartite concertation, admittedly weaker than in the EU15 tradition, were practiced during and after the accession to the European Union.

The second effect has been a process of recentralization of wage-setting systems linked to the spread of centrally defined horizontal measures uniformly applied to all services and all employees and frequently adopted under the pressure of an economic emergency. This process contrasts with previous, often NPM-inspired, trends towards the decentralization of negotiations and forms of individualization of pay and career systems that aimed to develop more flexible local responses to varied labor market and organizational conditions. In some cases, the downsizing or the demise of previous forms of decentralization and individualization of employment conditions predated the crisis. This reflected the acknowledgment, also on the part of previously enthusiastic advocates, of the risk of unexpected and perverse effects of some NPM-inspired reforms, mostly based on agency theory, like the decentralization of collective bargaining and systems of performance-related pay if not accompanied by adequate institutional arrangements (OECD 2012; OECD 2015).

The third effect concerns the diminished regulatory capacity of public sector trade unions, which in a sense is the other side of the coin of the revival of unilateralism. Although public sector unions, despite some reduction in membership, remain almost everywhere the stronghold of national trade union movements (Visser 2011, 2015; Bordogna and Pedersini 2013), the crisis has generally weakened their capacity to influence governments' and public employers' policies in the new context dominated by international forces and supranational actors. On the one hand, the shift in decision-making power to the EU level, accelerated by the new EU economic governance, substantially limits the scope for independent action of national government in relation to economic policies, and this, in turn, curtails trade union bargaining power. On the other hand, trade union bargaining power is undermined also by governments' imperative, under the intensified constraints exerted by the international financial markets, to keep tight control of public expenditure, of which the total pay bill of public employees is a key component. This affects one of the Marshallian conditions of trade union bargaining power, i.e. the 'importance of being unimportant', further disadvantaging public sector trade unions. Despite some variation at local and decentralized levels (Leisink and Bach 2014; Grimshaw *et al.* 2015), the overall result is both limits on trade union scope to influence decision-making processes at the EU level and weaker veto powers at the national level, compared with the sheltered environment of the past. Episodes of mobilization against austerity policies have occurred, especially but not only in the countries receiving financial assistance from the Troika, but often they were forms of spontaneous protest and mass demonstrations against political elites rather than strike action in a strict sense. In most cases, unions took a defensive position, occasionally able to delay or modify some aspects of austerity measures, but unable to stop or substantially change them.

Conclusions and Prospects

Returning to our initial questions—did the crisis, and governments' response to it, bring about the fundamental transformation in public service employment relations that two decades of NPM reforms failed to deliver? Is a paradigm shift visible, compared with pre-crisis patterns, as it occurred in the US private sector in the 1980s?—the answer is not straightforward, reflecting the continuing and uncertain consequences of the crisis (Streeck 2014).

On the one hand, government policies in response to the economic and sovereign debt crisis have not only adversely affected in many countries employment levels, working conditions, salary dynamics and pension benefits of public employees, but they have also strained public service employment relations institutions and practices beyond the usual variations linked to the vagaries of the business cycle (Bach and Bordogna 2013). The traditional sheltered character of public service employment relations has been markedly eroded by the crisis, and this is not a temporary effect. External forces, namely, international financial markets and supranational actors (EU Commission, European Central Bank, International Monetary Fund), have moved center stage, tightly constraining governments' responses to the crisis, although with variations depending on the relative financial vulnerability of each country. The end of the crisis will ease these constraints, but the novelty of the new context compared with the pre-crisis environment will not disappear. In addition, the crisis has proved a catalyst for ongoing changes in employment relations and working practices. The quantitative reduction in employment in many countries and tight budgets put pressure on employers to change the way work is organized and employees rewarded. Governments are also using these external constraints to challenge more forcibly the remaining benefits (e.g. pension rights) attached to public sector employment. The main effect of this changed context is to weaken union bargaining power in relation to national governments—which could suggest that a fundamental transformation has occurred or is under way, to some extent resembling what occurred in the US private sector in the 1980s (Bordogna 2015).

On the other hand, the chapters in this volume seem to testify that, while important and at times dramatic changes have occurred in some countries, especially those under the assistance of the Troika, but partly also in Italy and the UK, a 'fundamental transformation' is not a universal trend. The experiences of Germany, Denmark, Sweden, the Netherlands, the CEE countries and to some extent France indicate more continuities with pre-crisis institutional arrangements. In particular, although in the new context the balance of power has generally shifted in favor of national governments and public employers, as in the private sector (Baccaro and Howell 2011; Streeck 2014; Marginson 2015), this has not eroded the distinctive character of public service employment relations linked to the unique role of the state as employer. Paradoxically, the economic crisis has strengthened its role because crisis conditions provide more scope for the state to act unilaterally and downgrade or abandon consultation with the social partners, as national governments appeal to the national interest and intervene to restore national competitiveness by maintaining tight control of public expenditure.

In conclusion, a markedly altered context has emerged in which the public sector is no longer sheltered from internationalization, enabling shifts in bargaining power and reforms that favor employers. These trends are likely to remain an enduring legacy of the crisis. Nonetheless, there are wide variations across the European Union linked to country-specific institutional and legal traditions and related to the financial vulnerability of each country. But while emphasizing these variations in response to the crisis, our study also points to the distinctiveness of public service employment relations that has proved resistant to change despite two decades of NPM inspired reforms. The return to unilateralism and forms of recentralization of employment relations indicate that the unique role of the state as an employer remains as relevant to understanding contemporary public sector employment as in the pre-crisis period.

References

Avdagic, S., Rhodes, M. and Visser, J. (eds) (2011) *Social Pacts in Europe: Emergence, Evolution, and Institutionalisation.* Oxford: Oxford University Press.

Alonso, J. M., Clifton, J. and Diaz-Fuentes, D. (2015) 'Did New Public Management Matter? An Empirical Analysis of the Outsourcing and Decentralization Effects on Public Sector Size', *Public Management Review*, 17(5): 643–660.

Baccaro, L. and Howell, C. (2011) 'A Common Neoliberal Trajectory: The Transformation of Industrial Relations in Advanced Capitalism', *Politics and Society*, 39(4): 521–563.

Bach, S. and Bordogna, L. (2011) 'Varieties of New Public Management or Alternative Models? The Reform of Public Service Employment Relations in Industrialized Democracies', *International Journal of Human Resource Management*, 22(11): 2281–2294.

Bach, S. and Bordogna, L. (2013) 'Reframing Public Service Employment Relations: The Impact of Economic Crisis and the New EU Economic Governance', *European Journal of Industrial Relations*, 19(4): 279–294.

Bach, S., Bordogna, L., Della Rocca, G. and Winchester, D. (1999) *Public Service Employment Relations in Western Europe: Transformation, Modernisation or Inertia?* London: Routledge.

Bach, S. and Della Rocca, G. (2000) 'The Management Strategies of Public Service Employers in Europe', *Industrial Relations Journal*, 31(2): 82–97.

Bach, S. and Kessler, I. (2007) 'Human Resource Management and the New Public Management', in Boxall, P., Purcell, J. and Wright, P. (eds.) *The Oxford Handbook of Human Resource Management*, Oxford: Oxford University Press, 469–488.

Bach, S. and Pedersini, R. (2013) 'The Consequences of the Crisis for Public Sector Industrial Relations', in European Commission (ed.) *Industrial Relations in Europe 2012*, Luxembourg: Publications Office of the European Union, 129–161.

Beaumont, P. (1992) *Public Sector Industrial Relations*, London: Routledge.

Bordogna, L. (2008) 'Moral Hazard, Transaction Costs and the Reform of Public Service Employment Relations', *European Journal of Industrial Relations*, 14(4): 381–400.

Bordogna, L. (2015) *Reforming Public Service Employment Relations: Past, Present and Future Prospects*, Keynote Address to Track on Employment Relations in the Public Sector, 17th ILERA World Congress, Capetown, 7–11 September.

Bordogna, L. and Pedersini, R. (2013) 'Public Sector Industrial Relations in Transition', in European Commission (ed.) *Industrial Relations in Europe 2012*, Luxembourg: Publications Office of the European Union, 93–127.

Bordogna, L. and Winchester, D. (2001) 'Collective Bargaining in Western Europe', in Dell'Aringa, C., Della Rocca, G. and Keller, B. (eds.) *Strategic Choices in Reforming Public Service Employment*, New York: Palgrave, 48–70.

Christensen, T. and Lægreid, P. (2011) 'Introduction', in Christensen, T. and Lægreid, P. (eds.) *The Ashgate Research Companion to New Public Management*, Farnham: Ashgate, 1–13.

Christensen, T., Lie, A. and Lægreid, P. (eds.) (2007) *Transcending New Public Management: The Transformation of Public Sector Reforms*, Aldershot: Ashgate.

Crouch, C. (1993) *Industrial Relations and European State Traditions*, Oxford: Oxford University Press.

Della Rocca, G. (2013) 'Employment Relations in the Public Services', in Arrowsmith, J. and Pulignano, V. (eds.) *The Transformation of Employment Relations in Europe: Institutions and Outcomes in the Age of Globalization*, London: Routledge, 51–68.

de Vries, J. (2010) 'Is New Public Management Really Dead?' *OECD Journal on Budgeting*, 1: 1–5.

Esping-Andersen, G. (1990) *The Three Worlds of Welfare Capitalism*, Cambridge: Polity Press.

European Commission (2012) *Treaty on Stability, Coordination and Governance in the Economic and Monetary Union*, Brussels. http://www.consilium.europa.eu/european-council/pdf/Treaty-on-Stability-Coordination-and-Governance-TSCG

European Commission (2016) *Fiscal Sustainability Report 2015*, Brussels: Directorate General for Economic and Financial Affairs.

Ferner, A. (1985) 'Political Constraints and Management Strategies: The Case of Working Practices in British Rail', *British Journal of Industrial Relations*, 23(1): 47–70.

Ferrera, M. (ed.) (2005) *Welfare State Reform in Southern Europe: Fighting Poverty and Social Exclusion in Italy Spain, Portugal and Greece*, London: Routledge.

Fredman, S. and Morris, G. (1989) *The State as Employer: Labour Law in the Public Services*, London: Mansell.

Gottschall, K., Kittel, B., Briken, K., Heuer, J. O., Hils, S., Streb, S. and Tepe, M. (2015) *Public Sector Employment Regimes: Transformations of the State as an Employer*, London-New York: Palgrave McMillan.

Grimshaw, D., Rubery, J., Anxo, D., Bacahe-Beauvallet, M., Neumann, L. and Weinkopf, C. (2016) 'Outsourcing of Public Services in Europe and Segmentation Effects: The Influence of Labour Market Actors', *European Journal of Industrial Relations*, 21(4): 295–313.

Hall, P. and Soskice, D. (eds.) (2001) *Varieties of Capitalism: The Institutional Foundations of Comparative Advantage*, New York: Oxford University Press.

Hay, C. and Wincott, D. (2012) *The Political Economy of European Welfare Capitalism*, Basingstoke: Palgrave Macmillan.

Hood, C. (1991) 'A Public Management for All Seasons?', *Public Administration*, 69(1): 3–19.

Hood, C. (1995) 'The "New Public Management" in the 1980s: Variations on a Theme', *Accounting, Organizations and Society*, 20(2/3): 93–109.

Ibsen, C., Larsen, T. and Madsen, J. (2011) 'Challenging Scandinavian Employment Relations: The Effects of New Public Management Reforms', *International Journal of HRM*, 22(1): 2295–2231.

ILO (2013) *Collective Bargaining in the Public Service: A Way Forward*, General Survey Concerning Labour Relations and Collective Bargaining in the Public Service, International Labour Conference, 102nd Session, Geneva.

Katz, H. (2013) 'Is U.S. Public Sector Labor Relations in the Midst of a Transformation?', *Industrial and Labor Relations Review*, 66(5): 1031–1046.

Katz, H., Kochan, T. A. and Colvin, A. (2015) *Labor Relations in a Globalizing World*, Ithaca, NY: Cornell University Press.

Kickert, W. (2007) 'Public Management Reform in Countries with a Napoleonic State Model: France, Italy and Spain', in Pollitt, C., van Thiel, S. and Homburg, V. (eds.) *New Public Management in Europe: Adaptation and Alternatives*, London: Palgrave, 26–51.

Kochan, T., Katz, H. and McKersie, R. (1986) *The Transformation of American Industrial Relations*, New York: Basic Books.

Leisink, P. and Bach, S. (2014) 'Economic Crisis and Municipal Public Service Employment: Comparing Developments in Seven European Countries', *Transfer—European Journal of Labour and Research*, 20(3): 327–342.

Lodge, M. and Hood, C. (2012) 'Into an Age of Multiple Austerities? Public Management and Public Service Bargains across OECD Countries', *Governance*, 25(1): 79–101.

Marginson, P. (2015) 'Coordinated Bargaining in Europe: From Incremental Corrosion to Frontal Assault?' *European Journal of Industrial Relations*, 21(2): 97–114.

Mori, A. (2015) 'Outsourcing Public Services: Local Government in Italy, England and Denmark', in Drahokoupil, J. (ed.) *The Outsourcing Challenge: Organizing Workers Across Fragmented Production Networks*, Brussels: ETUI, 137–155.

Müller, T. and Schulten, T. (2015) *The Public-Private Sector Pay Debate in Europe*, Brussels: ETUI, Working Paper 8.

OECD (1995) *Governance in Transition: Public Management Reforms in OECD Countries*, Paris: OECD.

OECD (2010) *Value for Money in Government: Public Administration After 'New Public Management'*, Paris: OECD.

OECD (2012) *Public Sector Compensation in Times of Austerity*, Paris: OECD.

OECD (2015) *Building on Basics, Value for Money in Government*, Paris: OECD.

Ongaro, E. (2009) *Public Management Reform and Modernisation: Trajectories of Administrative Change in Italy, France, Greece, Portugal and Spain*, Cheltenham: Edward Elgar.

Osborne, S. (ed.) (2010) *The New Public Governance: Emerging Perspectives on the Theory and Practice of Public Governance*, London: Routledge/Taylor and Francis.

Peters, B. G. (2010) *The Politics of Bureaucracy: an Introduction to Comparative Public Administration*. 7th ed., London: Routledge.

Pierson, P. (2001) 'Coping with Permanent Austerity: Welfare State Restructuring in Affluent Democracies', in Pierson, P. (ed.) *The New Politics of the Welfare State*, Oxford: Oxford University Press, 416–456.

Pollitt, C. and Bouckaert, G. (2011) *Public Management Reform: A Comparative Analysis. NPM Governance and the Neo-Weberian State*, Oxford: Oxford University Press.

Pollitt, C. and Dan, S. (2011a) 'The Impact of New Public Management in Europe: A Meta-Analysis', European Commission-European Research Area, Seventh Framework Programme: COCOPS Working Paper No. 3, 1–39.

Pollitt, C. and Dan, S. (2011b) 'The Impact of New Public Management (NPM) Reforms in Europe', European Commission: COCOPS European Policy Brief, December, 1–8.

Rubery, J. (2013) 'Public Sector Adjustment and the Threat to Gender Equality', in Vaughan-Whitehead (ed.) *Public Sector Shock: The Impact of Policy Retrenchment in Europe*, Cheltenham: Edward Elgar, 22–43.

Schafer, A. and Streeck, W. (2013) 'Introduction: Politics in the Age of Austerity', in Schafer and Streeck (eds.) *Politics in the Age of Austerity*, Cambridge: Polity, 1–25.

Streeck, W. (2014) *Buying Time: The Delayed Crisis of Democratic Capitalism*, London: Verso.

Sundström, G. (2016) 'Administrative Reform', in Pierre, J. (ed.) *The Oxford Handbook of Swedish Politics*, Oxford: Oxford University Press, 316–331.

Vaughan-Whitehead, D. (ed.) (2013) *Public Sector Shock: The Impact of Policy Retrenchment in Europe*, Cheltenham: Edward Elgar.

Visser, J. (2011) 'Variations and Trends in European Industrial Relations in the 21th Century First Decade', in European Commission (ed.) *Industrial Relations in Europe 2010*, Luxembourg: Office for the Official Publications of the European Communities, 17–53.

Visser, J. (2015) *ICTWSS: Database on Institutional Characteristics of Trade Unions, Wage Setting, State Intervention and Social Pacts in 34 Countries Between 1960 and 2012, Version 5*. http://www.uva-aias.net/208.

Winchester, D. and Bach, S. (1999) 'Britain: The Transformation of Public Service Employment Relations', in Bach, S., Bordogna, L., Della Rocca, G. and Winchester, D. (eds.) *Public Service Employment Relations in Western Europe: Transformation, Modernisation or Inertia?* London: Routledge, 22–55.

2 Greece: Public Service Employment Relations

Adjustments and Reforms

Christos A. Ioannou

Introduction: A Persistent Failure of Reforms

Public sector reform is an old and recurring issue in Greece. Since the 1950s, after the end of World War II and the Greek Civil War (1944–1949), public sector reform has been a permanent government priority. Public sector reform formed a part of reconstruction plans from the 1950s onwards of all governments (Danopoulos and Danopoulos 2009). Governments are not famous for efficiency (Olson 1973: 355), but after a variety of political dynasties (notably the Karamanlis and Papandreou families), the Greek government became infamous for the triple public sector bailout in 2010, in 2012 and in 2015. In the Third Hellenic Republic, since 1974 after the fall of the 1967–74 military regime and the end of autocratic regimes, public sector expansion and change has been continuous. Expansion and reform have been incorporated in more than 4,400 pieces of legislation adopted by the Parliament (not to mention tens of thousands of Presidential Decrees), 1,000 of which have been adopted since 2010 when the EC-ECB-IMF adjustment programs for Greece started (EC 2010, 2012).

The Greek case of public sector financial management failure found a prominent place in the literature (CGMA 2012: 9) as one that can trigger an economic failure. For years, the budget exceeded its deficit target, leading to rapid public debt accumulation. The 2009 budget had a deficit target of 3.7% of the GDP, but the final deficit (as confirmed in July 2010) was 15.3%. This led, in April 2010, the government to request bilateral financial assistance from Euro area Member States and a standby arrangement from the IMF. In November 2011–February 2012, a second request was made for a new, broader program. In July 2015, a third request was made for another European Stability Mechanism program.

Greece has been a unitary state (of Napoleonic origin) that in the 1980s and the 1990s, under PASOK socialist governments, moved towards some decentralization, but with a dominant position of the central government. Since 2010, the risk of public sector default on its sovereign debt added urgency to the need to reform the very fragmented structure of the Greek public sector, which in 2009 had four layers of administration. First, there were 15–20 ministries (it is customary after parliamentary elections or government reshuffles to merge, split or rename ministries, without any significant structural change). Each ministry, at the beginning of the crisis, had on average roughly five secretariats or single administrative sectors, each of which had general directorates, with subsidiary directorates and departments. There were on average 302 departments per ministry plus 137 decentralized structures at the regional level (OECD 2011b: 56). Second, there were 13 regional administrations, established as part of the PASOK regional decentralization reform in two stages; in 1986 (Law 1622) when established, but they remained under the central government control, and in 1998 (Law 2647), when they became subject to regional elections. Third, from 1986 there were 54 prefectures, initially appointed by the government and constituted as a second-tier local self-government with elections from 1994 onwards. Fourth, until 2010–2011, there were 1,037 municipalities and communes (established in 1997–1998) as part of an earlier phase of merger activity (Law 2539/1997). Another reform in 2010 (Law 3852) led to further mergers into 325 municipalities and communes. There were also extensive health (146 public hospitals, 250 (regional) health centers and more than 400 health service points of variable size, provided by the Social Insurance Funds, mainly the IKA), education networks (nearly 16,000 primary and secondary schools), fragmented social security funds (successive mergers reduced them from 170 in 2002 to 16 in 2013 and brought under the control of the Ministry of Labour and Social Security) and a wide range of more than 8,000 public sector entities and enterprises (of which 6,000 were related to first-tier local government institutions under the 2010 reform (Law 3852) that were supposed to merge into less than 2,000).

Since 2010, major reforms have been proposed in relation to employment relations, pay determination and the role of management and unions (see overview in Table 2.5). Since then, debate and conflict have been dominated by short-termism and the extent to which public sector workforce demands and political promises can restore the pre-crisis status quo in terms of public expenditure, public management and public employment relations. At the same time, citizens face important challenges, unprotected from the public services as a provider of individual and collective security and services. Unemployment is over 25% (and only 1/10 receive unemployment benefits) and 25% of the population is uninsured, without social security coverage and access to public health services. These are two areas indicative of the fact that state services have been simply 'coping' and where societal and local communitarian activism has developed in the crisis years. It is not only that, because of the crisis, the 'public service bargain' (Hood and Lodge 2006) has been broken; it had been poorly constructed before the crisis. As indicated in successive Eurobarometer findings (European Commission 2013c, 2014b), public trust in government, politicians, public services, public servants and public sector trade unions, which before the crisis had been comparatively low amongst EU member states, reached a new low. Until a new 'public service bargain' is reached, third parties—society and citizens—suffer the repercussions and bear the costs. In addition, the Greek public sector seems indisposed to address structural reforms and mid-term and long-term challenges lie ahead, including public debt, population aging, environmental risks and the massive influxs of unregulated migration.

The Centrality of Public Sector Employment Before and After the Crisis

'How large is public employment in Greece?' has been an open question for many years (OECD 2011: 71–72). The 'OECD Government at a glance 2013' concluded that 'with less than 8 % of the labour force employed by the government, Greece has one of the smallest government work-forces among OECD countries' (OECD 2013a), based on 2008 data, when another 12.8% of the labor force was classified as employed in public sector corporations. This brings Greece well above the OECD average (Ioannou 2013). This misleading OECD statement was subsequently corrected and public sector employment as a percentage of total employment was cal-culated in 2009 as 24.9% and 23.5% in 2013, above the OECD average (2009: 21.1%, 2013: 21.3%) (OECD 2015b: Figure 3.1). Since 1974, the number of permanent civil servants has been continuously increasing from nearly 130,000 in 1974 to nearly 693,000 in 2009; the ratio of permanent civil servants to the population increased five times from 1.26 in 1974 to 6.2 in 2009. It doubled from 1.26 in 1974 to 2.51 in 1991 and doubled again to 5.33 in 2006. It started falling gradually from 2010, but in 2014, it is just below its 2006 value (Table 2.1).

The number of permanent civil servants and the relevant ratios, however, does not provide the full picture of public sector jobs in Greece, which has proved difficult to measure accurately. Numerous official government pub-lications report public sector jobs only partially, i.e. referring to permanent civil servants and omitting other types of contracts (for example, Ministry of Interior 2008: 13). This is not simply a case of statistical or technical errors; it is mainly related to the tradition and legacy of patronage hiring (Ioannou 1996, 2013). Despite the 1994 legal provision that all public sec-tor recruitment is undertaken by the Public Sector Hiring Authority (ASEP), many loopholes and exceptions exist. The bulk of public sector recruitment between 1994–2009 occurred through the use of private employment fixed-term contracts without any formal, standardized and centralized selection procedure. These contracts were at a later stage (directly linked to the elec-toral cycles) transformed into permanent public law contracts. This repre-sented continuity with the situation before 1994. Even in the 1960s and the 1970s, public sector recruitment was supposed to be regulated by the High Council of the Civil Service, but most public sector recruitment was made

Table 2.1 Permanent Civil Servants and Population in Greece 1974–2014

Year	1974	1981	1987	1991	2001	2006	2009	2011	2013	2014
Population	8986153	9757874	10015863	10319672	10968542	11143780	11183516	11082566	10926807	10993000
Permanent Civil Servants	112896	121789	196556	259159	450259	594658	692907	646657	599207	576856
Permanent Civil Servants to Population ratio (1/100)	1,26	1,25	1,96	2,51	4,11	5,33	6,20	5,83	5,48	5,25

Sources: Population Censuses 1971, 1981, 1991, 2001, 2011, ELSTAT and 2006, 2009, 2013, 2014 Eurostat.
Civil servants 1974–2006 Various administrative sources, 2009–2014 Ministry of Administrative Reform and E-Governance (MAREG).

through ad hoc 'exceptional' procedures (Papagaryfallou 1973: 56–57). Despite the 1994 legislation, this pattern of 'exceptional' recruitment continued with recruitment to temporary or fixed-term contracts subsequently transformed into permanent contracts. This process, labeled as 'titularization', was quite common in Southern Europe (Sotiropoulos 2004: 411).

This is why during the EC-ECB-IMF adjustment programs in 2010–2014, the Greek government had to comply with the condition to provide a full and updated picture of public employment with detailed monthly data on ordinary staff (full-time public sector employees) and other staff (contractual employees, political appointees etc.), which since 2013 has been published, on a monthly basis, on the ministry's (Ministry of Administrative Reform and E-Governance, or MAREG) website. By mid-2011, the government had to record all central government employees into a census database and then bring all employees into the Single Payment Authority to complete the monitoring framework for government employment and the wage bill. That was not an easy task. The registration was planned to be fully implemented by end of April 2014, but it was never fully completed because of opposition and lack of cooperation by local government authorities, managers, employees and trade unions.

The Adjustment of Public Sector Employment After the Crisis

Public sector employment has been increasing and remains central to the Greek economy and society. Greek Labour Force Survey data indicate that the share of public sector jobs in Greece has been rising since the early 1990s and remains high in the periods before and after the crisis. In 1994, it accounted for 13.7% of total employment and for 25.7% of dependent (salary and wage earners) employment. Two decades later, after the crisis, in 2014q1, public sector employment accounted for 22.9% of total employment and 36.1% of dependent (salary and wage earner) employment (Table 2.2).

The census database provides a detailed picture of public employment in 2009–2013. In absolute numbers, the total public sector employment was reduced between the end of 2009 and 2013 from 942,625 to 675,330 employees. A proportion of the job cuts were amongst permanent contract employees that retired, but the majority of job cuts were employed on fixed-term contracts that were not renewed. As a proportion of total employment, public sector employment was reduced from 20. 9% to 19.4% between 2009–2013 (Table 2.2). The abolition of all recruitment exceptions in December 2009 was an initial break with the tradition of political clientelism in public sector recruitment (Ioannou 2013: 299), but the extent of growth before this period is unknown. It was this buffer of private fixed-term and temporary contracts that accounts for the main public sector employment adjustment since 2010. It is noteworthy that the share of permanent jobs in central government and local government in total employment increased from 15.4% to

Table 2.2 Public Sector Employment in Greece 2009–2014

	31.12.09	31.12.10	31.12.11	31.12.12	31.12.13	31.12.14
Population	11.183.516	11.123.392	11.082.566	10.991.400	10.926.807	10.993.000
Total Employment	4.508.600	4.278.500	3.886.900	3.597.000	3.479.900	3.535.300
Salary and Wage Earners in Employment	2.910.400	2.746.400	2.459.700	2.274.800	2.203.900	2.255.100
Public Sector Employment	942.625	866.658	772.460	735.561	675.530	
Public Sector Percent of Employment	20,9	20,3	19,9	20,4	19,4	
Public Sector Percent of Waged Employment	32,4	31,6	31,4	32,3	30,7	
General Government	865.153	796.947	715.686	682.289	635.338	
General Government Percent of Employment	19,2	18,6	18,4	19,0	18,3	
Permanent Staff (public law status)	692.907	667.374	646.657	629.114	599.207	576.856
Permanent Staff as Percent of Employment	15,4	15,6	16,6	17,5	17,2	16,3
Permanent Staff as Percent of Waged Employment	23,8	24,3	26,3	27,7	27,2	25,6
Total Temporary Staff (private law contract)	150.478	107.805	56.434	48.782	14.097	
Temporary Staff as Percent Employment	3,3	2,5	1,5	1,4	0,4	
Temporary Staff as Percent of Waged Employment	5,2	3,9	2,3	2,1	0,6	
Public Sector Utilities (Chapter B)	56.295	56.295	52.138	41.189	34.714	
As Percent of Employment	1,2	1,3	1,3	1,1	1,0	
As Percent Waged Employment	1,9	2,0	2,1	1,8	1,6	

Source: Population : 2011 Census, 2009, 2010–2014 Eurostat Total Employment and Salary & Wage Earners in Employment : Greek Labour Force Survey, relevant years Public Sector Employment: 2009–2014 Census Database Ministry of Administrative Reform and E-Governance (MAREG).

17.2 % between 2009–2013, while the share of private-law fixed-term and temporary jobs reduced from 3.3% to 0.4% (Table 2.2).

This has been the outcome of the EC-ECB-IMF programs and governments' commitment to deliver the decrease in general government employment by 150,000, with the deadline set for the end of 2015. The reduction in ordinary staff with permanent public law status was already evident by the end of 2013; it was based on a rigorous application of a 1:5 attrition rule (only 1 employee hired for every 5 retirements), with an additional boost from civil servants' retirement (civil servants retirement required fewer years at work and offered more generous pensions compared to private sector employees). It is not the first time that such an attrition rule was imposed in the Greek public sector. In the early 1990s, an EU loan to assist Greece in a balance of payments crisis included the governmental commitment to EcoFin to reduce public sector employment by 10% in the period 1992–94 (Ioannou 1996: 7). In the late 1990s, Greece's efforts to qualify for the European Monetary Union translated into quantitative restrictions on public employment policy. Recruitment was tightened, and the replacement of retiring personnel was limited to 1:3 or 1:5, although these measures did not apply to the public sector as a whole (i.e. both the administration and the public sector institutions and utilities) and were implemented unevenly, and in some cases gradually abandoned (OECD 2011: 71).

In sectoral terms, at the end of 2013, the main segments of public sector employment (mainly of permanent status) were: the Ministry of Education, Lifelong Learning and Religious Affairs as the biggest employer of permanent contracts with 29.6% of public sector permanent contracts (mainly public education—primary and secondary schools), the Ministry of National Defence accounts for 14.7% of public sector permanent contracts, the Ministry of Health and Social Solidarity (for public health services) with 14.4%, the Ministry of Citizen Protection (police officers etc) account for 10.5%, while local government accounts for 14.2%. A second category of smaller public sector employers, ranging between 2,5 and 3%, includes the Ministry of Labour and Social Security, the Ministry of Finance and the Ministry of Justice.

This distribution relates to the fact that in Greece, all levels of public administration provide public services and the largest sectors (education, national defense and health) are centralized. Since the mid-1980s, parallel to the decentralization reforms, local government employment has risen faster than general government employment (Table 2.3); from 9.3% of permanent contracts in 1987 to 12.8% in 2006, and then its share remained above 14%. The 1987 data suggests that 50% of local government employees were on private law contracts. The high share of fixed-term contracts (28. 9%) is indicative of what followed; local government converted most private sector fixed-term contracts into permanent contracts (Table 2.3). However, the fiscal decentralization in Greece has been the lowest in the EU-28 (Halásková 2015: 53).

Table 2.3 Local Government Public Employment in Greece 1987–2014

	1987		2006		2012		2013		2014	
	Employees	%	Employees	%	Employees	%	Employees	%	Employees	%
Local Government total	36484	8,1								
Permanent contracts	18207	9,3	75918	12,8	94386	15,0	84541	14,1	81810	14,2
Private contracts open-ended	11576	5,0	7611							
Private contracts fixed term	6701	28,9	n/a							
Regional Government total	n/a									
Permanent contracts	n/a		9678	1,5	6786	1,1	6454	1,0	6811	1,1
Number of Local Government institutions										
Municipalities	457	100	910		325		325		325	
Communes	5318	100	127		-		-		-	
Regions	13	100	13		13		13		13	
Total Public Sector	452046	100								
Permanent contracts	196556	100	594658		629114		599207		576856	
Private contracts open-ended	232343	100	n/a							
Private contracts fixed term	23147	100	n/a							

Source: 1987, 2006 Census of public sector employment, 2012–2014 MAREG

Public Sector Wage Leadership and Wage Premia Without Formal Collective Bargaining Rights

The Importance of Informal Collective Bargaining

Pay determination in the Greek public sector for civil servants under permanent, public law contracts has never been subject to formal collective bargaining regulation because of constitutional restrictions. This has been the pattern since the end of the Greek Civil War (1944–1949). This pattern did not change even after the 1974 political change and the move to the post-authoritarian period of parliamentary democracy, i.e. the Third Hellenic Republic. Pay determination has been excluded from the jurisdiction of collective bargaining rights for civil servants, even after these rights were recognized in 1999 (Law 2738), following the transposition of the ILO conventions 151 and 154; their bargaining rights have been restricted to subjects such as education and training, health and safety issues above and beyond the mandatory legislation, job mobility and transfers, trade union rights and the interpretation of collective agreements.

In spite of the 1999 reform, civil servant pay has been determined unilaterally by the government in the context of its annual budgetary policy. There has been more continuity than change. Since 1974 and especially after 1984, when the civil servants' national confederation ADEDY was reconstituted, the pattern emerged that the official announcement of the public sector wage policy led to the mobilization of civil servants unions and of their confederation ADEDY for informal collective bargaining at the level of each ministry. Since the mid-1980s, these gatherings organized by ADEDY 'condemned austerity' and the 'restrictive wage policy of the government'. This became an established ritual every December, when the annual budget was debated in Parliament. But officially, ADEDY, their secondary/sector-level federations and their primary/workplace-level unions did not have the formal right to bargain over pay. Bargaining procedures had been informal, normally taking place with the Finance Minister or his deputy, or at the ministerial level in each ministry (Ioannou 1996). The 1999 reform that introduced formal collective bargaining procedures for public law civil servants excluded matters of terms and conditions of employment of public law employees such as pay, pensions, creation of posts, qualifications and appointments due to constitutional constraints. This restriction was accommodated by introducing non-binding collective agreements in the form of joint conclusions (article 13.1 of Law 2738/1999). These were subject to further governmental review rather than being binding collective agreements. The 1999 reform therefore aimed to formalize and regulate previous practices of informal collective bargaining for civil servants.

Before the 1999 reform, these informal bargaining procedures did not lead to formal collective agreements. If unions were successful, they obtained a Ministerial Decision relating to the disputed issue, mainly pay, which in this context acquired certain peculiar characteristics. A pattern was established that aimed to leave untouched the legislated basic salary and allowed some flexibility for bonuses and allowances in the pay package. The Ministry of Finance opted for these additional pay raises to take the form of benefits and bonuses to avoid including these increases in pensions; pensions had to follow the legislated pay increase for basic public sector salaries. Although there were attempts by the Ministry of Finance to centrally manage this pay drift, informal bargaining, legal and judicial procedures ended up in permanent 'leapfrogging'; individual employees or trade unions succeeded in obtaining favorable court decisions on the grounds of comparability and equal treatment. In this widely used informal collective bargaining, the bargaining power of groups of civil servants varied. For instance, the Ministry of Finance employees were more influential because of their control over tax collection. Not surprisingly, they have been in the pay (and bonuses) leadership in the Greek public sector, and civil servants from other Ministries 'fought' to secure a secondment or job transfer to Ministry of Finance positions.

Despite the 1999 reform, not much of this procedure was formalized or changed. The 1999 reform provided for two types of collective agreements: a) the General (national) covering all civil servants across the board (excluding diplomatic employees, National Health System doctors and the employees of Parliament) and b) the Special (decentralized) covering groups of employees by ministry, organization, sector or job specialty. But after the adoption of the reform, there has never been a general collective agreement for civil servants, although there were initiatives, attempts and formal applications by the ADEDY Confederation in the first three years (2000–2002). In the same period, there were a number of formal initiatives for special collective agreements (2000: 25, 2001: 30, 2002: 39) that were mainly unsuccessful and led to few signed collective agreements (2000: 3, 2001: 4, 2002: 10) and non-binding/joint conclusion/collective agreements (2000: 3, 2001: 15, 2002: 14), the latter dealing mainly with pay-related issues (Drosou 2003). The implementation of the new system of collective bargaining for civil servants vanished, back to its previous informality, amidst waves of discontent in 2003 and a renewed wave of strikes mainly in the public sector, in the context of which ADEDY withdrew from formal collective bargaining. The strikes followed the announcement of the failed social dialogue reforms and the 'social package' of the then-PASOK socialist government (Ioannou 2010: 96–98).

The Sisyphean Reforms for a Service-Wide Unified Pay System

Since 1984, there have been successive governmental attempts to introduce a service-wide unified pay system for the public administration. But the informal and decentralized collective bargaining led to its continuous 'destruction' and turned the implementation of a simplified and unified remuneration system towards a pay grid into a Sisyphean task (Ioannou 2013). Until the 2009–2010 crisis, the pay structure in the Greek public sector remained balkanized and microcorporatist. The long list of additional pay bonuses, which were the outcome of successful informal collective bargaining, included off-budget ministry-specific bonuses that were financed by ministries' specific off-budget special accounts, usually financed by a percentage of revenues or expenditure of each ministry's activities e.g., drawing on the tax receipts of the Ministry of Finance or a share of the revenues of the museums for the employees of the Ministry of Culture etc. Bringing these off-budget pay accounts into the government budget controlled by the Parliament has been pending for many years and caused numerous strikes. It became feasible only after 2010 under the emergency conditionalities of the EC-ECB-IMF adjustment programs. It is also noteworthy that these expenditure and income items were not incorporated in the official statistics for public sector pay expenditure. Despite this systematic underreporting, every year since 1995, the wage bill has overrun the amounts budgeted (Manesiotis and Reischauer 2001: 108).

The labyrinth of Greek public sector pay determination as it developed until 2009 incorporated also pay formation for public sector employees under private law contracts. Some 150,000 public sector employees that, at the end of 2009, were employed under private law fixed-term or temporary contracts had the right to have their pay determined through collective bargaining. Their collective bargaining activity resulted in, on average, 50 collective agreements per year at the ministerial, occupation or organization/institution level (OMED 2010). Their main objective was to follow (and occasionally to leapfrog) the pay of the relevant (and comparable) civil servants.

In 2010, under the pressure of the EC-ECB-IMF program, the government started controlling and cutting the public sector wage bill (see Table 2.5), which constituted a key segment of the public sector financial management failure. These efforts to bring the general government deficit under control led, on the one hand, to a freeze in any formal and informal collective bargaining in the public sector, and in turn to successive incremental cutbacks and systemic attempts to bring every public sector pay item under the control of the Single Payment Authority. On the other hand, these efforts led to the implementation of a long overdue 'unified remuneration system', which took effect from January 2012 for civil servants in the central and local governments and became the model for the remaining private law contracts in public sector organizations and utilities. The new 'unified remuneration system', which has been, as the previous ones, based on seniority, provided for a) basic wage, b) qualifications allowance (educational level), c) functions allowance (level of responsibility and special areas of work) and d) component based on results or performance (which has been frozen for the period of the adjustment program); it was never fully implemented (Ioannou 2013). Amendments and exceptions allowed some 66,000 employees (mainly in the Ministries of Finance, Justice, Development and in local government, i.e., an important share, between 1/5 and 1/6 of the total number of civil servants supposed to be covered) to preserve their pay above the legislated limits in the form of 'personal pay differences' to avoid adjusting to the 'unified remuneration system'. Other groups of civil servants, i.e. judges, military personnel, university teachers, public health doctors, diplomats etc. had been exempted from the provisions of the new 'unified remuneration system' and enjoyed their own special wage grids.

The full implementation and the comprehensive application of the wage grid reform across the public sector, the rationalization of the public sector wage structure in a fiscally neutral way, including decompressing the wage distribution in both directions in connection with the skill, performance and responsibility of staff, was supposed to be legislated by November 2014 and made effective from January 1, 2015 (IMF 2014: 80–81). It was never brought to Parliament and political developments resulted in new elections. A new coalition government led by the left-wing SYRIZA took office in January 2015 and again (after snap elections) in September 2015. The pending reform for a service-wide unified wage grid, effective January 1, 2016, became a key commitment of the third bailout MoU (EC 2015: 30).

The Public Sector Pay Wage Premium Left Untouched

Despite all the freezes, the cutbacks and the changes in the wage setting procedures (see Table 2.5), the public sector remains the wage leader with a wage premia compared to the private sector. Many studies summarized in Ioannou (2013) suggest that there was a pre-crisis public wage premium, when adjusted for individual characteristics. According to Christopoulou and Monastiriotis (2013), in 2009, it was at the order of 11%. Christopoulou and Monastiriotis (2014) report that in 2009–2013, public premia for monthly regular wages never fell during the crisis; rather, they initially increased and subsequently returned back to their original level. While the private sector recorded a substantial adjustment, in the public sector, despite significant wage cuts, the public wage premia has become smaller, but survived the crisis. Giannitsis and Zografakis (2015: 49) report similar findings on the continuing inequality between private and public sector pay: 'the evolution of wages and pensions during the crisis highlights, on the one hand, the policy discrimination towards employees in the private versus the public sector and, on the other, the introduction or maintenance of incentives for a mass exodus of workforce to retirement. Behind this policy was an effort to cushion the public sector from the most adverse effects of the crisis, even if this implied that the private sector would be called on to bear the brunt of the adjustment'.

This pattern of public sector wage leadership has been dominant since the end of the Civil War in 1949. The pattern has been that, instead of public sector wage increases being linked to those in the private sector or in the export-oriented sector of the economy, the public sector acted as a wage leader. Any further wage drift was accommodated by new tax measures or upward adjustment of public sector deficits and debt. At the same time, especially during the EC membership period since 1981, and indeed, during the EMU membership since 2002 (Ioannou 2010), private sector pay and especially pay in the (diminishing) export-oriented sector of the Greek economy were subject to market pressures and restrictions of the open economy, resulting thus into a systematic labor market and growth model distortion.

In Search of Public Employers to Deliver Public Goods and Services

What Is Public in the Greek Public Sector?

The public sector is supposed to provide public goods and services, such as education, health, social security, justice, environmental protection etc. by taxing citizens and providing these services. However, well before the 2009–2010 Greek crisis, the provision of public goods and services has been dysfunctional. Measuring efficiency in education (student performance and spending per student at primary and secondary education) placed Greece at the bottom of OECD countries, second only to Mexico (OECD 2007: 264–265). The Greek NHS, which was legislated in the early 1980s by the then-new PASOK government, was never fully implemented and has been riddled with inequalities and occupational fragmentation, falling far short of satisfactory outcomes. In the years before the crisis, it developed as a costly technological model and not as a health system based on primary care and public health and has been subject to extensive criticism (Kyriopoulos *et al.* 2011; Stamati and Baeten 2014: 12–13).

Public education and public health in Greece are prominent cases of individual service provision where public sector mismanagement on the one hand and interest groups on the other have transposed the provision of these public goods and services as sources of additional private income, allowing further private rent seeking by public sector employees. In education, this occurs via shadow education services such as private tutoring services (Ioannou 2013: 305). Teenagers have a double school life; from 8 a.m. to 2 p.m. attending their standard secondary education classes and in the afternoon attending private tutoring for school courses that are part of their university entry exams (plus for foreign languages at all education levels). After being re-elected in September 2015, the coalition government decided to impose a 23% VAT on private education services (aimed at taxing wealthy segments of society with children in private schools), but realized this created a major political and societal problem because most households pay for private tuition in a well-established parallel private education sector. In health, this has been made possible by means of undeclared private payments to public sector doctors to get access to and avoid queuing for public health services. Consequently, Greek citizens pay twice for these public goods and services. First to the state, through taxes and social security contributions, that in

Greece account for an above-OECD-average 'tax wedge' and the highest for an average married worker with two children (OECD 2015a). Second, they pay in private for either additional shadow or parallel education services to their children or for proper access to the NHS. The provision of most other individual and collective public goods and services has also been dysfunctional. In the provision of justice and social security payments, there are long backlogs, and tax collection is also ineffective, with widespread non-compliance (European Commission 2013b).

Recent Attempts to Establish an Efficient Public Employer

Making the Greek public administration more efficient and effective to serve its citizens has been a long-standing issue, but either reforms were annulled, (e.g. hiring through the Public Sector Hiring Authority, implementation of a service-wide wage grid) or were unsuccessful (Spanou 2008). Basic personnel management and public administration procedures (e.g. job descriptions, performance management systems, rational pay and grading structures) were either nonexistent or dysfunctional (Argyriades 2013: 82). Civil service politicization has never been publicly admitted but was very widespread in terms of high-level appointments (Spanou and Sotiropoulos 2011: 729). The public administration was administered by large numbers of deputy ministers and political appointees as general (or special) secretaries in ministries, and performance standards and evaluation was absent.

After the 2009–2010 crisis, it was recognized that comprehensive reform of the Greek public sector in terms of tax policy, financial management, fighting corruption and the provision of public services constituted an essential step to increase efficiency and productivity and to ensure the sustainability of public expenditure and the wage bill. This led to plans for reorganization of ministries and entities based on the OECD analytical review of central administration intended to improve performance (OECD 2011). It proposed: the reallocation and streamlining of staffing, transparent recruitment procedures, competence evaluation for managers and staff, broader use of public procurement and better financial management, introduction of e-government and reduction of scope for corruption. A two-year administrative reform action plan for 2014–2015, also encompassing a comprehensive human resources strategy, has been adopted through the newly established Government Council of Reform. The plan dealt with mobility and deployment, performance management, disciplinary cases, training, selection of top management, roles and assessment of management and HR managers' network. Legislation to improve the existing evaluation system was to be adopted in April 2014, and a comprehensive reform of the system was to be introduced from 2015. A new system for the recruitment of managers was to be legislated in order to bring a complete renewal of management staff by June 2015. More careful assessment of new entrants was planned by stronger probation arrangements.

New staffing plans for line ministries (excluding the Ministries of Foreign Affairs, Public Order and Citizens' Protection and National Defence) were approved by the Government Council of Reform to cover 577,106 employees, (95% of the permanent workforce). Local governments, regions and decentralized administrations' staffing plans were to follow by December 2014. Presidential Decrees and other legal instruments to implement the new organizational structures for the line ministries were submitted to the State Council and were adopted in summer 2014 (EC 2014: 39). HR services were brought under common and horizontal standards to develop a coordinated and efficient HR network within and across different ministries, to improve efficiency and facilitate the evaluation and development of senior management competences and other staff. The plan was a) to introduce a new, competence-based, legal framework for the recruitment of top management in May 2014 (Law 4275/2014) with all senior appointments filled on this basis with heads of units appointed by June 2015 and b) to introduce, as of January 2015, a permanent system of individual evaluation, including performance-based incentives, with 2014 performance evaluated by March 2015. As a transitional measure, the previous system of individual evaluations was revised during 2014, with a ceiling placed on the proportion of employees that could be assigned a top grade and a floor to limit low grades. This became a major source of conflict with ADEDY, its federations and unions. ADEDY called for a permanent strike and for employees to boycott the implementation of the transitional appraisal system. Although the strike was declared illegal and abusive by a court decision in autumn 2014, the transitional evaluation scheme was not implemented during 2014. In spring 2014, the EC-ECB-IMF reported that 'on public administration reform, progress is mixed as Greece is struggling to introduce performance-based management and address the taboo against mandatory dismissals' (IMF 2014: 1). In summer 2015, the pending and identical administrative reform became a key commitment of the third bailout MoU (EC 2015: 29–31) signed by the new coalition government.

'Availability' and 'Mobility': The Mother of all Battles for Public Jobs Protection

In 2011–2013, the adjustment program aimed primarily to record all public sector employees into the census database and to pay wages through the Single Payment Authority. That was a prerequisite for expenditure and staff planning. In 2013, attrition reached its limits (see Table 2.2). To further reduce public sector jobs, the schemes of 'availability' and of 'mobility' were introduced. Employees placed in the 'availability' scheme had their wages reduced by 25% and were to be assessed, within a centrally defined evaluation framework, before reallocation to new positions or exit. The 'mobility' scheme was to operate as a permanent mechanism for voluntary and mandatory transfers for better allocation of personnel within public administration. The overall goal was to establish an internal job market and to implement mandatory rotation within the public sector to facilitate continuous renewal of skills (EC 2014a: 39). The internal job market was to replace the extensive practice of long secondments, while time-limited secondments were only to be allowed in very specific cases. The tools for the functioning of the internal job market included setting up a database for the management of personnel, committees for personnel selection, a database for the management of open positions and other matters such as termination packages. The internal job market was to start operating via the new 'mobility' scheme, clearly distinguished from the 'availability' scheme (which addressed both mobility and exit). The plan was that a minimum of 6,000 employees would be involved in the new mobility scheme in 2014 with further expansion in 2015, but was left in abeyance because of European Parliament elections in May 2014 and uncertainty surrounding subsequent parliamentary elections, which ended in January 2015 with a coalition government led by SYRIZA.

To set the impact of the 'availability' and 'exit' schemes in context, it is noteworthy that at the end of 2013, 12,799 employees were included in the 'availability' scheme. The cumulative target of 25,000 employees for 2013–2014 was only achieved symbolically by placing in the scheme 7,659 employees—doctors from the National Health Service Organization, who were in parallel practicing physicians in private activity, and 6,967 reallocations that were planned or implemented without prior placement in the 'availability' scheme (3,395 teachers from the Ministry of Education and 3,572 employees from the tax administration of the Ministry of Finance, both under mandatory transfer). Another 3,000 local government employees were to be placed in the 'availability' scheme under the competency of Ministry of Interior, but both the reluctance of the ministry and the mobilization of the federation of local government employees (POE-OTA) left these plans on paper.

The program target for personnel exits for 2013–2014 from public sector jobs was for 15,000 employees. This comprised dismissing people unlawfully appointed, those subject to disciplinary procedures and those who had been in the 'availability' scheme without being moved to another position. The government revised the legislation on the 'availability' scheme to reduce the time spent in the scheme from 12 months to 8 months to achieve its 'exit' targets. By mid-2014, actual exits comprised 6,651 employees. They were mainly one-offs from narrow groups: 2,662 employees from the closure of the public broadcasting company, 1,235 employees from disciplinary and incompetency cases, 1,657 employees from temporary injunctions, doctors in the public healthcare system who chose to exit rather than accept full-time public sector jobs and school guards. These exits were not based on performance; constitutional restrictions against mandatory, performance-based dismissals remained an impediment. The SYRIZA coalition promised to reinstate these employees.

In 2013, 'mobility' schemes were legislated for in primary and secondary public education (Law 4172/2013), but the Ministry of Education, while employing more than 177,000 employees, had difficulties in transferring 450 teachers from secondary education to the administration and 950 teachers from secondary to primary education. The plan was that a further 850 teachers be transferred to the administration and 3,600 to primary education, but this met successive mobilizations and strikes.

The 'availability' and 'mobility' schemes have caused widespread confusion and conflict across the public sector. The government program simultaneously included quantitative targets for both exits and 'mobility'. An employee agreeing to 'mobility' questioned whether this 'mobility' would end up in exit from the public sector. For months there was extensive bargaining and daily press reporting over the annual targets for job cuts and exits among the ministries on the one hand, and between the government (MAREG) and the EC-ECB-IMF on the other. Employees and sectors subject to exit risk were mobilized on a daily basis with protests and marches with the support of ADEDY and its federations. In mid-2014, EC- ECB-IMF reported that 'on public administration reform, the authorities are opposed to setting further quantitative targets for exits. They consider such targets as distracting attention from other reforms. With exits so far coming mostly from one-offs, staff's concern relates to whether the taboo on dismissals has fundamentally been broken and therefore whether the efforts are durable to rejuvenate a public sector with a legacy of patronage hiring' (IMF 2014: 13).

Public Sector Unions Against the Crisis and in Crisis

A Unitary Confederation With High Union Density

Civil servants with public law contracts and public sector employees with permanent private law contracts have the right to unionize. Greece has a model of unitary Confederations, split between the public sector and the private sector: ADEDY (the Supreme Administration of Civil Servants' Trade Unions) for civil servants, GSEE for private law contract employees. ADEDY, formed in 1947, throughout the post-war and the post civil war period suffered direct governmental interference and was subject to electoral malpractice. In 1983, it shifted to proportional representation for representative elections and was reorganized in a three-tier structure (Ioannou 2005). This structure is compatible with trade union law and comprises primary-level trade unions (by occupation or by ministry, of which there are more than 1,200 active in ADEDY at the end of 2014) that form secondary-level federations; secondary-level federations (of which there are 45 active in ADEDY at the end of 2014) can be organized to the tertiary-level confederation ADEDY (Table 2.4). There is no evidence of public service unions that are not members of the federations

Table 2.4 ADEDY Federations, Unions and Voting Members at Its Congresses, 1983–2013 (Greece)

Year	Number of Primary-Level Unions	Number of Federations	Voting Members	Average Size of Unions	Average Size of Federations	Union Density %
1983	n.a	25	96,000	n/a	3,840	26,9
1992	1,090	55	235,533	216	4,282	51,3
1998	1,264	52	240,709	190	4,629	49,4
2007	1,260	46	289,469	230	6,293	57,5
2010	1,250	41	315,000	252	7,683	47,2
2013	1,170	41	216,000	185	5,268	34,3

Source: 1983–1998: Ioannou 2005, 2007–2013: ADEDY register.

belonging to ADEDY, although some very small unions are not represented at the ADEDY Congress. There has been a distinctive group of public sector employees among those 150,000 that, at the end of 2009, were mostly under fixed-term and temporary private contracts, that may form their own trade unions which, in turn, have no right to be members of federations belonging to ADEDY. This restriction has been, since 2010, a contentious issue in intra-union debates at the ADEDY Congresses and of its constituent federations and unions. This stems from the widespread use of fixed-term and temporary contracts, which became the primary target for public sector job cuts.

The federations and the primary-level unions affiliated with ADEDY are mostly products of the 1970s and the 1980s. Union density has fluctuated from 26.9% in 1983 to 51.3% in 1992 and subsequently peaked at 57.5% in 2007. At the ADEDY Congress of 1992 (28th), a record 55 federations participated. The number of primary-level unions more than doubled from 607 primary level to 1,264 between 1986 and 1998 and remains at this level (see Table 2.4). Although four federations, DOE—the Federation of Primary School Teachers, OLME—the Federation of Secondary Education Teachers, POEDHN—Public Hospitals Personnel and POE OTA—Local Government Employees have been the most influential (in terms of membership) (Ioannou 2005), the structure of ADEDY at the primary and secondary levels has remained fragmented despite attempts at rationalization. Since the crisis, ADEDY union density has been falling from 47.2% in 2010 to 34.3% in 2013 but remained well above the national average of both private and public sectors, which was around 15–20% (EC 2013a: 106–107).

The crisis stimulated further consideration of ossified trade union structures, and this was considered during 2013–14, but there has been little consensus. Issues under consideration include: mergers of federations in public service subsectors, expansion to incorporate fixed-term and temporary public

Table 2.5 Main Adjustment Measures in Greece

Year	Month	Measures
2009	December	- Abolition of exceptions: all public sector recruitment should be through the Public Sector Hiring Authority.
2010	March	- A 12% cut from January 2010 in bonus payments (excluding family and child benefits and those related to length of service).
		- Christmas, Easter and holiday pay bonuses (13th and 14th salary) reduced by 30%.
		- Upper limits for overtime reduced from 60 to 40 hours per month per employee.
		- Pay caps of just under €6,000 per month.
		- All conflicting provisions in collective agreements were annulled.
		- Hiring freeze.
2010	May	- Further 8% reduction from June 2010 in bonus payments.
		- Christmas bonus/pay reduced to €500 and Easter and holiday pay/ bonuses reduced to €250. Abolished for employees with a monthly salary exceeding €3,000.
2010	December	- Across-the-board pay reduction of 10% from January 2011 for any pay package exceeding €21,600 a year.
		- Monthly public sector pay cap reduced to €4,000.
		- A threshold set so that the total pay cut since 2010 should not exceed 25%.
		- Lower limits for overtime (20 hours per month per employee from July 2011).
		- Reduction of 30–50% in allowances paid in sections of the public sector by ministerial decisions and court awards.
2011	January	- All new public employees subject to private sector social security fund IKA-ETAM. Existing public employees offered the option to join on a voluntary basis.
		- Target set for personnel reductions of 20% (i.e. 150,000) of public sector job by 2015. Decisions for non-renewal of existing short-term contracts.
		- Replacement rate for retiring public employees set at 10%.
2011	March	- Consolidation (from January 2012) of the public health service for civil servants and central administration employees (Organization for the Health Insurance of Public Sector employees) into the newly founded National Health Service Organization.
		- Introduction of special unemployment contribution (2% of the wage).
2011	June	- Weekly working time increased to 40 hours from 37.5 hours.
2011	November	- New pay system for the public sector to take effect from January 2012 for civil servants. It included a guideline for average monthly total pay of €1,900 per employee.

(Continued)

Table 2.5 (Continued)

Year	Month	Measures
2012	November	- Christmas, Easter and holiday bonuses completely abolished. - Average pay reduction of 12% in the 'special wage regimes' (covering judges, diplomats, political appointees, doctors, professors, police and armed forces).
2012	December	- 'Labor reserve' scheme redesigned and renamed as 'Availability' and 'Mobility' schemes to relaunch the restructuring and downsizing of the central public administration. Quantitative targets set for 25,000 employees in each scheme.
2013	December	- Two-year (2014–2015) administrative reform action plan adopted. Government Council of Reform established.
2014	May	- Transitional system of individual evaluations with a ceiling to the percentage of employees assigned top grade and a floor to those with low grade (not implemented). - New procedures for recruitment of top public sector managers, planned for December 2014. New system of individual performance evaluations, planned for 2015. (All postponed for 2016). - New revised pay system for civil servants to take effect from January 2015 (postponed for 2016).
2015	August	- Harmonization of pension rights requirements of civil servants to private sector employees.

Source: 2009–2012 Ioannou (2013), 2013–2015 see text.

sector employees working under private law contracts, to reconsider the merger with GSEE Confederation (an issue pending since the early 1990s), modernization of member participation, introduction of tenure limits in the elected bodies of the Confederation and new codes of practice relating to trade union funding. The congress to consider these issues has been postponed because of the many different perspectives and the inability to gain the necessary 75% support for change as well as the lack of financial resources for the congress.

The Militant Leanings of the Greek Civil Servants

The declining union density of civil servants since 2010 has been accompanied by increased militancy. At the 35th ADEDY Congress, the dominant factions, associated with the traditionally dominant political parties (i.e. the Socialist PASOK and the center right New Democracy) lost their majority in the 85-member ADEDY Confederation General Council and the control of its Executive Committee. Left-wing and militant fractions increased their

General Council presence from 23 seats in 2010 to 44 in 2013. This produced on the one hand a left militant relative majority at the public sector Confederation for civil servants, but also a divided leadership because of these different groupings.

Since 2010, ADEDY has shifted from being a bureaucratic structure towards becoming more of an umbrella for local-level movements. ADEDY has called numerous general strikes (more than 40), mobilizations, work stoppages, protests and marches. Although the strikes recorded rather low participation rates, ADEDY federations and primary-level unions have been prominent in disputes relating to the EC-ECB-IMF adjustment programs in general and specifically public sector pay and employment relations matters, including the 'availability' and 'mobility' schemes, mandatory exit policy and the transitional appraisal system. It is not possible to trace any occasion since 2010 where the ADEDY Confederation, its federations and unions have had the opportunity to consult or bargain on any matter with government representatives and reach any, even limited, area of agreement and mutual understanding. There has been an increasingly adversarial pattern of industrial relations coupled with more politicized conflict and, in parallel, many public sector reforms became the subject of appeals in the courts and before the Council of State, feeding into the well-known systemic legal formalism and adding to the existing backlog in the courts (Ioannou 2013: 301). Public sector protest movements were followed by a protest vote in the January 2015 parliamentary elections that brought into office a new coalition government led by the left-wing SYRIZA. The new government promised to re-establish the status quo ante in public sector employment relations and reinstate the public sector employees that lost their jobs because of the 'availability' and exit schemes. When after the September 2015 elections, the re-elected government made a U-turn by signing the MoU for the third bailout program, ADEDY reignited the war against their former political ally.

The Consequences of the Crisis: The Status Quo Ante for Public Sector Employment Relations Curtailed

The Severe Asymmetries That Led to the Crisis Have Been Preserved

A previous account (Ioannou 2013) on public sector adjustments in Greece made reference to a Gordian Knot. This metaphor refers to adopting bold decisions to address intractable problems, but its application to the public sector, in hindsight, seems over-optimistic. Instead, the notion of an odyssey looks more pertinent, representing the length of time needed to achieve reform (see Spanou and Sotiropoulos 2011). Consequently, like past administrative reform, fiscal consolidation and public sector reforms are lengthy processes. This is not only a question of the length of the journey; it is also a question of its direction. The standard rhetoric and narrative holds that, as part of two successive EC-ECB-IMF adjustment programs (with a third starting in late 2015), the public sector is subject to 'excessive austerity', but this account doesn't stand up to close scrutiny.

Greece is a unique case because between 2001–2009, it increased its share of general government expenditure as a percentage of GDP, only surpassed by Denmark, France, Finland and Belgium in the OECD ranking and remained at a similar level in 2011 despite the adjustment process and the 'austerity', above Sweden, and in all periods above the OECD average (OECD 2013: 75). Moreover, in Greece, the public sector primary expenditure as a share of GDP rose to 49% in 2013.

Since 2010, fiscal adjustment has been the cornerstone and lynchpin of the adjustment program and Greece emerged, and this is extraordinary by any international comparison, from having the weakest to the strongest cyclically adjusted fiscal balance in the euro zone. This affected radically pay determination, employment status, working conditions and the role of employers and trade unions in the public sector, through pay cuts, hiring restraint and job cuts (Ioannou 2013). But the reduction of public administration staff only partially had a net savings effect, as it pushed the exiting civil servants to another public budget line, that of pensions. The net savings came mainly from the non-renewal of contracts of fixed-term employees, who missed out on former opportunities for clientelistic and patronage hiring, i.e. by having their fixed-term contracts transformed into permanent contracts. The issue of the size of public sector employment in Greece and its fiscal impact is more a question of flows rather than stocks. In other words, labor flows out of the public sector have been encouraged by a relatively generous pension rights regime (shorter working life, lower pensionable age and higher pensions) compared to private sector employees, with direct repercussions for the sustainability of public sector expenditure.

It is also important to note that the mixture of unstable and discontinuous freezes, cuts and reforms encompassing every segment of the public sector in Greece since 2010 (see Ioannou 2013) did not address effectively the causes of fiscal destabilisation or contribute sufficiently to restoring fiscal balance. As Giannitsis and Zografakis (2015: 16) argue, 'government expenditure contributed by 77 % to the fiscal derailment of the period 2006–2009, while the subsequent governments refused to adjust expenditure to its previous level with respect to GDP. . . . instead of rebalancing rocketing public expenditure, policy chose to decrease the deficit by expanding the revenue side of the budget. From the very beginning of the crisis, increased taxes have been the preferential policy instrument and played a primary role in reducing the fiscal deficit . . . [which] between 2009 and 2013 was achieved largely because of the increase of the revenue/GDP ratio by 9.7 percentage points which represents 72.4 per cent of the total fiscal adjustment'.

The Public Sector Has Been Fighting for the Status Quo Ante . . .

Despite the standard rhetoric about 'austerity', the Greek public sector has not suffered the most from the Greek crisis and adjustment, in terms of employment levels, employment status and in terms of pay relativities compared to the private sector. Nonetheless, the special status of public employment has been weakened. This occurred in various ways: the public sector pension reform (2011) subjected all new public sector employees to the private sector social security fund IKA-ETAM, an increase from June 2011 of the weekly working time for public sector employees under public or private law contracts to 40 hours (from 37.5), the consolidation in 2011 of the public health service for civil servants in the National Health Service Organization and the introduction of special unemployment contributions, equal to 2% of the wage, for civil servants (Ioannou 2013). In addition, under the third adjustment program, pension rights for civil servants are being harmonized with the private sector, with the retirement age increasing over the next decade from 62 to 67. But despite these diminishing differences between public and private sector employment, the key difference with regard to tenure and seniority has been unaffected, as they are protected by the Constitution.

Outwardly, the Greek government has lacked ownership of the adjustment program or a strategy for dealing with the public sector financial crisis and reform of public sector management and employment relations. But this is only partially true. Six years on, while presenting any need for adjustment and reform as an imposition by the international creditors, there has been a de facto strategy to safeguard pre-existing public sector status and incomes and to avoid the implementation of reforms. Key stakeholders in the public management and public employment sphere appeared unwilling, and often resisted, the adoption and implementation of management principles, reorganization of the public sector and measures to repair public sector finances. This has been a common trait of successive governments since 2009 (PASOK socialist government in 2009, PASOK and ring-wing New Democracy and far right LAOS coalition government in 2011, New Democracy, PASOK and DHMAR Democratic Left coalition government led by New Democracy in 2012, and SYRIZA ANEL coalition government led by left SYRIZA in 2015). Once again, there has been a continuing failure of public sector reform and attempts to maintain a clientelistic and patronage-based state.

The rationalization and modernization of the public sector has been necessary but largely elusive. This process has been difficult because of the bargaining between the international creditors and national politicians who position themselves as opposed to 'neoliberal' and 'absurd' demands, and secondly because of traditional union responses against reforms, reinforced by protest and militant movements against any change and committed to preserving the status quo ante. Without the involvement of public sector employers and of (some) public sector unions, there was no scope for reforms to be implemented.

The Greek crisis has fiscal, structural and financial aspects with the public sector central to the crisis erupting and its adjustment process. The fiscal deficit has been in double digits since 2009, and public sector market access to sovereign debt was lost in 2010. In 2011–2012, there was widespread uncertainty about Greece's future in the euro zone and in 2015, these doubts re-emerged. From 2008–2013, the economy collapsed. More than 25% of the GDP was lost because the previous level of GDP was unsustainable without double-digit public sector deficits covered by unconditional access to new and rapidly expanding public debt. Annual growth turned slightly positive only in 2014, for the first time since 2007, to turn negative again in 2015–2016. Unemployment soared from 7.5% to 27% due to more than one million private sector job losses. In this context, the Greek public sector had to adjust and reform. The standard narrative describes this adjustment as austerity. In one sense, this is the case in a context of unsustainable public sector deficits that accumulated debt for the economy and future genera- tions. In another sense, however, it has not been austerity when considering national economic capacity and social justice in terms of the continuing dif- ferences in the consequences of the crisis for the public and private sectors.

In spite of these entrenched vulnerabilities (unsustainable public debt and deficits and inefficient service provision), instead of redirecting and modifying public sector employment relations in a more balanced direction, there has been fierce defense of long-standing trends. This took the form of protest movements and successive rounds of protest voting. It could be argued that there has been a pretense that an inclusive economy and society existed before the 2009–2014 economic collapse that granted all citizens equitable opportunities and entitlement to a fair share of common prosper- ity. The Greek political establishment has been struggling to preserve those norms and structures, but this stance is typical of a populist and clientelistic past which aimed to maintain pre-existing privileges. A side effect of these policies was the need for a continuous and rapid expansion of public sec- tor employment and expenditure, feeding into unsustainable public debt, even after the country joined the euro currency union. Greece confronted the crisis with a distorted economy, a protected non-tradable sector of the economy, the major constituent of which has been the public sector and a diminishing and weak tradable sector, confronting strong international competition.

Although the collapse in private sector and public sector incomes between 2009–2014 disrupted the pre-existing system of inefficient provision of pub- lic goods and services, there were no domestic reform actors with the capac- ity to establish and implement structural reforms of the public sector. This is why numerous measures have not delivered the anticipated results in terms of public sector efficiency and quality. The lack of national 'ownership' of the adjustment/reform programs, coupled with the particularistic influ- ence of interest groups, shaped policy design and outcomes with variations between subsectors (central government, local government, education and health). Central government and the health sector were the initial focus of reform because of their financial importance in curbing expenditure, while local government and education were put to one side and only subject to incremental budget cuts and horizontal cost restrictions. Only after 2013 were these sectors more subject to reform. It is not a coincidence that militant trade union behavior and adversarial employment relations in local government and education alongside very weak management performance has resulted in unmanaged growth.

In the context of the crisis, a fourth actor played an increasingly key role and became dominant in the traditional triangle of employment regulation between government, labor and management: the financial markets and institutional creditors (Cutcher-Gershenfeld *et al.* 2015). The public interest, traditionally represented by the government in consultation with labor and management, has been sidelined. The financial markets and institutional creditors have been used as an alibi for the responsibilities of the three national actors. In hindsight, it can be suggested that the public interest in government-labor-management relations is based on a strong (internationally) tradable sector and associated systems of employment relations that condition private and public sector pay and employment conditions. The reverse is visible in Greece's pay formation system with the public sector as the leader, less related to the precise model of employment regulation (predominantly a sovereign model tradition) and more to do with the protectionist cum clientelistic model that became entrenched between 1949–2009.

Conclusion: The Short-Termism of the Greek Public Sector in a Context of Structural Vulnerabilities

All the main actors: the EC-ECB-IMF Troika, successive national governments since 2009 and management and labor, including the public sector trade unions (and the opposition and protest movements) have failed to address the need for structural reforms (i.e. mainly rebalancing the protected and the open sectors). In addition to its debt challenge, Greece also confronts an aging society, increasing ecological problems and the pressure from accelerating massive illegal migration flows from Africa and Asia through Greece towards central Europe. It is therefore unclear which scenario (Lodge and Hood 2012) of state functions (directing, hollow, local communitarian, coping) is emerging in Greece. In the absence of national coalitions for effective public sector reform, the degree and direction of adjustment and reform intensity depends on the influence of particularistic interest groups. In different sectors, we observe different 'states'; e.g. 'local communitarian' in areas of social policy and social protection such as the Orthodox Church and NGOs addressing the needs of those unemployed and uninsured, or segments of the health sector, for instance, in mental health reform (characterised by slow deinstitutionalization of mental health patients). In education the state is 'coping', in central government 'directing' and it is 'hollow' in local government. Greece therefore has a rather long transition to overhaul the inefficient public sector of recent decades. Varvaressos's (1952: 203) conclusion from over 60 years ago is still valid: 'we must not expect any real improvement in the country's economic situation as long as we do not deal with this fundamental problem of the inadequacy of its administrative machinery'.

References

Argyriades, D. (2013) 'Greek Exit from the Crisis—A Pressing and Much-Needed Public Service Reform', *Social Sciences*, 2: 78–90. doi:10.3390/socsci2020078

Bach, S. and Bordogna, L. (2013) 'Reframing Public Service Employment Relations: The Impact of the Economic Crisis and the New EU Economic Governance', *European Journal of Industrial Relations*, 19(4): 279–294.

CGMA (2012) *Strategic Performance Management in the Public Sector*, CGMA Report, January 2012.

Christopoulou, R. and Monastiriotis, V. (2013) 'The Greek Public Sector Wage Premium before the Crisis: Size, Selection and Relative Valuation of Characteristics', *British Journal of Industrial Relations*. doi:10.1111/bjir.12023

Christopoulou, R. and Monastiriotis, V. (2014) 'The Public-Private Duality in Wage Reforms and Adjustment during the Greek Crisis', Research Paper No 9/2014 Hellenic Foundation for European and Foreign Policy (ELIAMEP).

Cutcher-Gershenfeld, J., Brooks, D., Cowell, N., Ioannou, C., Mulloy, M., Roberts D., Saunders, T. and Viemose, S. (2015) 'Financialization, Collective Bargaining, and the Public Interest', in Weller, C. E. (ed.) *Inequality, Uncertainty, and Opportunity, the Varied and Growing Role of Finance in Labor Relations*, LERA Research Volumes, ILR Press, 31–56.

Danopoulos, A. and Danopoulos, C. P. (2009) 'Greek Bureaucracy and Public Administration: The Persistent Failure of Reform', in Farazmand, A. (ed.) *Bureaucracy and Administration*, Boca Raton FL: CRC Press/Taylor and Francis Group, 395–408.

Drosou, S. (2003) *The Institution of Collective Bargaining in Public Administration*, Paper Presented at the Conference "State and Public Policy", National Kapodistrian University of Athens, 30 May 2003 (in Greek).

European Commission (2010) *The Economic Adjustment Programme for Greece*, DG Economic and Financial Affairs, Occasional Paper 61.

European Commission (2012) *The Second Economic Adjustment Programme for Greece*, DG Economic and Financial Affairs, Occasional Paper 94, March 2012.

European Commission (2013a) *Industrial Relations in Europe 2012*.

European Commission (2013b) *Study to Quantify and Analyse the VAT Gap in the EU-27 Member States*, TAXUD, July 2013.

European Commission (2013c) *Standard Eurobarometer 79*, Spring 2013.

European Commission (2014a) *The Second Economic Adjustment Programme for Greece Fourth Review—April 2014*, Directorate-General for Economic and Financial Affairs, EUROPEAN ECONOMY Occasional Papers 192.

European Commission (2014b) *Standard Eurobarometer 81*, Spring 2014.

European Commission (2015) Memorandum of Understanding between the European Commission Acting on Behalf of the European Stability Mechanism and the Hellenic Republic and the Bank of Greece, mimeo, 11. 8.2015.

Giannitsis, T. and Zografakis, St. (2015) *Greece: Solidarity and Adjustment in Times of Crisis*, IMK, Macroeconomic Policy Institute, Hans-Boeckler-Foundation, Study 38, March 2015.

Halásková, M. (2015) 'Public Administration in EU Countries: Selected Comparative Approaches', *Ekonomická revue—Central European Review of Economic Issues* 18, 45–58. doi:10.7327/cerei.2015.03.04

IMF (2014) Greece: Fifth Review Under the Extended Arrangement Under the Extended Fund Facility, and Request for Waiver of Nonobservance of Performance Criterion and Rephasing of Access; Staff Report; Press Release; and Statement by the Executive Director for Greece Series: Country Report No. 14/151.

Ioannou, C. (1996) *The Restructuring of Employment Relations in Greek Public Services*, Paper to the ARAN Workshop, 'The Restructuring of Employment Relations in the Public Services in Western Europe: a Comparative Analysis', Rome, January.

Ioannou, C. (2005) 'From Divided "Quangos" to Fragmented "Social Partners": The Lack of Trade Unions' Mergers in Greece', in Waddington, J. (ed.) *Restructuring Representation: The Merger Process and Trade Union Structural Development in Ten Countries*, Bruxelles: P.I.E-Peter Lang, 139–164.

Ioannou, C. (2010) ' "Odysseus or Sisyphus" Revisited: Failed Attempts to Conclude Social-Liberal Pacts in Greece', in Pochet, Ph., Keune, M. and Natali, D. (eds.) *After the Euro and Enlargement: Social Pacts in the European Union*, Brussels: Observatoire Social Europeen & ETUI, 83–108.

Ioannou, C. (2013) 'Greek Public Service Employment Relations: A Gordian Knot in the Era of Sovereign Default', *European Journal of Industrial Relations*, 19(4): 295–308.

Kyriopoulos, E., Mylona, K., Tsiantou, V. and Kyriopoulos J. (2011) ' "Troica" Health Care Economics in Greece', *Value in Health*, 14(7). doi:http://dx.doi.org/10.1016/j.jval.2011.08.691

Lodge, M. and Hood, C. (2012) 'Into an Age of Multiple Austerities? Public Management and Public Service Bargains Across OECD Countries', *Governance: An International Journal of Policy, Administration, and Institutions*, 25(1): 79–101.

Manesiotis, V. G. and Reischauer, R. D. (2001) 'Greek Fiscal and Budget Policy and EMU', in Bryant R. C., Garganas, N. C. and Tavlas, G. S. (eds.) *Greece's Economic Performance and Prospects*, Washington, DC and Athens: Brookings Institution and Bank of Greece, 103–152.

Ministry of Interior. (2008) *Public Administration in Greece*, Athens July 2008 (in Greek).

OECD (2007) *Education at a Glance 2007*, Paris: OECD Indicators, OECD Publishing.

OECD (2011) *Greece: Review of the Central Administration*, OECD Public Governance Reviews, OECD Publishing. http://dx.doi.org/10.1787/9789264102880-en

OECD (2013) Government at a Glance 2013, Paris: OECD Publishing. doi:http://dx.doi.org/10.1787/gov_glance-2013-en

OECD (2015a) *Taxing Wages 2015*, Paris: OECD Publishing. doi:http://dx.doi.org/10.1787/tax_wages-2015-en

OECD (2015b) Government at a Glance 2015, Paris: OECD Publishing. doi:10.1787/gov_glance-2015-en

Olson, M. (1973) 'Evaluating Performance in the Public Sector', in Moss, M. (ed.) *The Measurement of Economic and Social Performance*, Studies in Income and Wealth, Vol. 38, NBER, 355–409.

OMED (2010) *Report of Activities for the Period 1992–2010*, Organisation for Mediation and Arbitration, Athens (in Greek).

Papagaryfallou, P. (1973) *The High Council for Civil Service*, Athens (in Greek).

Spanou, C. (2008) 'State Reform in Greece: Responding to Old and New Challenges', *International Journal of Public Sector Management*, 21(2): 150–173. http://dx.doi.org/10.1108/09513550810855645

Spanou, C. and Sotiropoulos, D. (2011) 'The Odyssey of Administrative Reforms in Greece, 1981–2009: A Tale of Two Reform Paths', *Public Administration*, 89(3): 723–737.

Sotiropoulos, D. (2004) 'Southern European Public Bureaucracies in Comparative Perspective', *West European Politics*, 27(3): 405–422.

Stamati, F. and Baeten, R. (2014) *Health Care Reforms and the Crisis*, Brussels: ETUI, Report 134.

Varvaressos, Kyriakos. (1952) *Greece—Report on the Economic Problem*. Unnumbered series; no. UNN 18. Washington, DC: World Bank. http://documents.worldbank.org/curated/en/1952/02/1554071/greece-report-economic-problem

3   Spain: Rationalization Without Modernization

Public Service Employment Relations Under Austerity

Oscar Molina

Introduction

Changes since the transition to democracy have significantly re-shaped the boundaries of the Spanish public sector, understood as the activities and institutions that enable the executive arm of the government to implement laws. In particular, the 1978 Constitution opened the door to a process of asymmetric regional decentralization where Autonomous Communities (regions) have acquired increasing responsibility on issues that include education and health. Some authors have described this configuration in terms of 'imperfect federalism' where regions have acquired new competences and roles to different extents and following different paths (Moreno 1993). Moreover, the 1978 Constitution also established the local level of government that has gradually expanded its functions and policy responsibilities that nonetheless vary depending on the size of the municipality. However, as pointed out by Vallés and Brugué (2001), local government in Spain has not acquired the importance it has in other European countries. Nonetheless, the largest municipalities (over 50,000 inhabitants) manage issues that include public transport, social services, cleaning, environmental protection, libraries, food markets and fire protection.

This process of decentralization means that the central government's role within the public sector is increasingly limited to coordinating implementation at regional and local levels rather than delivering public services. This applies particularly to the two sectors discussed in more detail in this chapter, i.e., education and health. In both cases, there has been devolution of powers to the Autonomous Communities. In the case of the health sector, some autonomous communities created their own regional health systems in the 1980s (Catalonia, Andalusia, Basque Country, Valencia, Galicia and Navarre), and the remaining ones did so in 2001. The role of the central state in the case of the health sector is limited to coordinating the regional health services and maintaining quality standards across them. Regions have full autonomy in managing and organizing health activities. A similar process characterized the education sector, where some autonomous communities were given the resources and legal capacity to manage their education system (namely, Catalonia and the Basque Country). The remaining regions did so over the 1980s, and by 2000, all Autonomous Communities had acquired the competences allowed by the constitution regarding education at the graduate and undergraduate levels. The role of the central state in education has accordingly been limited to setting the structure of the different academic levels as well as the conditions to access and obtain the different academic titles.

The second long-term development consists of a significant increase in the private provision of these public services. This process started in the mid-1980s, but recent developments have accelerated both the privatization process as well as the contracting out of certain activities. The privatization of public companies started in the early 1990s, and by the early 2000s, most of them were in private hands. Moreover, there has been an increase in the contracting out of public education and health services that has further contributed to blur the boundaries between the public and private spheres. This process has been particularly intense in the health sector (Sánchez 2013).

Since the return to democracy, the public sector in Spain has undergone significant long-term transformations in employment relations (Jódar *et al.* 1999). These include the expansion in the number of public sector employees since the early 1980s and the decentralization towards regional and local levels of government in the 1990s and early 2000s. These two trends were accompanied by the gradual introduction of negotiation and collective bargaining as a mechanism to regulate working conditions of public employees. Moreover, since 1992, several attempts were made to flexibilize and modernize public sector employment relations along the lines of New Public Management (NPM) principles. In spite of these changes, public sector employment relations before the crisis were still characterized by the lack of a common regulatory framework for all public employees, severe coordination problems among the different levels of government and the limited implementation of key human resource policies and practices, including training, career development and effective performance assessment (Jódar *et al.* 1999: 194–195).

More recently, two main developments have marked the evolution and characteristics of public sector employment relations in Spain. The first was the approval in 2007 of the General Public Employment Statute (EBEP, *Estatuto Básico del Empleado Público*). The importance of the 2007 EBEP is twofold. On the one hand, it has consolidated and given coherence to several patchwork changes introduced since the mid-1980s that lacked coherence and left many regulatory gaps. In particular, it has regulated several aspects that were left ambiguous by previous laws and that had been subject to diverse interpretations in the courts (De la Villa 2007). Most importantly, the EBEP has contributed to further unify working conditions and rights of civil servants and workers with ordinary employment contracts in the public sector. Moreover, it has also expanded the collective rights of civil servants, and more specifically, it has opened up new spaces for collective bargaining in regulating the working conditions of this group of workers.

The second important policy development in this period has been the implementation of austerity policies aimed at fiscal consolidation which have triggered a moderate decrease in public employment levels and a deterioration in working conditions, including pay cuts, more working hours, easier dismissal etc. Moreover, these policies have also been accompanied by restructuring and rationalization in the public sector, and in particular, attempts at eliminating overlap in functions and services between different levels in the public administration, the 2013 law for the rationalization and sustainability of local government being a case in point. The impact of these policies has varied across levels of government, sectors and groups of employees. In particular, the local level has been more affected by the fall in public employment levels, while the regional level that manages services such as education and health has witnessed changes in the composition of the labor force. The adjustment of public sector employment in Spain has concentrated on workers with ordinary contracts, and more specifically, those with temporary or interim contracts (i.e., temporary appointments until the job position is assigned on open-ended basis). Finally, in addition to the pay cuts and hiring restrictions, reforms have been implemented in the education and health sectors that have opened the door to greater private provision.

As a consequence of the rationalization imposed by austerity measures since 2010, the modernizing and reformist character of the EBEP hasn't been fully developed. Some authors have even argued how this rationalization has gone in the opposite direction of the modernization envisaged by the 2007 EBEP. This would be the case of the gap between rights and career prospects of civil servants and salaried employees in the public sector that the EBEP tried to close, but that the austerity measures have widened again (Cuenca *et al.* 2013: 2). Similarly, the unilateral imposition of austerity measures on public sector employees have contrasted with the expansion of collective bargaining as a regulatory tool in the public sector since the mid-1980s. Moreover, the crisis and austerity measures have hindered the implementation of most of the mechanisms envisaged in the 2007 EBEP in order to promote more and better objective grounds for performance assessment or career guidance and development for public employees.

This chapter analyzes the development of public sector employment relations in Spain, paying particular attention to the impact of the recent financial and sovereign debt crisis and austerity measures implemented. This chapter assesses whether the policies implemented in the context of the crisis deviate from the previous reform path or have simply implied an impasse in a long-term process that will continue once the economy recovers its growth path. It is argued that the crisis and the rationalization imposed by austerity policies have hindered the implementation of the modernization agenda envisaged in the 2007 EBEP. Moreover, reforms since 2013 are introducing structural changes in the organization of public sector in Spain, the reform to rationalize local government being illustrative of these trends. As the principles enshrined in the 2007 EBEP have provided strong legal grounds for its modernization, we can expect post-crisis employment relations in Spain to follow this road.

Organization Structure and Employment

Workforce Structure and Trends

Before entering into the detailed analysis of workforce structure and trends in Spain, it is important to consider the three types of contracts that can be found in the public sector as laid out in the 2007 EBEP (De la Villa 2007). Firstly, civil servants *(funcionarios)* are appointed with open-ended contracts according to public sector rules and regulations. Secondly, there are those employees carrying out a paid professional service for the Public Administration but are employed following general labour law regulations laid down in the Workers' Statute, either with an open-ended or temporary contract *(personal laboral)*. Finally, there are those civil servants who are appointed for a certain period *(personal eventual)*, or occupy interim positions *(funcionarios interinos)*, but under public sector regulations. In the last two categories, employees enjoy similar job protection to a civil servant, meaning that they can't be dismissed until their contract expires *(personal eventual)* or the job position is announced and assigned *(funcionarios interinos)*. There is no rule determining the percentage of workers under these different contracts in each sector, but in parallel to what has happened in the private sector since the mid-1990s, some agreements and pacts include a maximum number of workers with a temporary contract. This was, for instance, the case of the last general agreement signed in 2009 for the period 2010–2012 that contained an 8% limit on temporary employment in the public sector. Each of these contractual arrangements differs in terms of recruitment rules, determination of working conditions and more importantly, job security. In this regard, the dualization that is very often used to characterize the labor market in Spain can also be found in the public sector. It is important to bear in mind these differences because, as we will see later on, the adjustment undertaken in public sector employment has mirrored this duality.

The EBEP regulates the following aspects of public employment: access to public employment under principles of equality, merit and ability, as well as transparency in the selection process; the specific right of civil servants to irrevocability, but conditional upon performance assessment; professional career and promotion under criteria of objectivity and transparency; functional and geographical mobility; continuous training; non-discrimination on reasons of birth, race or ethnic origin, gender, sex or sexual orientation, religion etc.; conciliation of personal, familial and work life; remuneration, including autonomy in the determination of complementary remunerations, which can vary by administration bodies and be related to professional career, specific occupation and performance; and right to social dialogue, representation and participation, including the role of collective agreements in establishing working conditions of all the public personnel.

Public employment as a percentage of total employment in Spain has historically been below the OECD average. In 2012, it was 13.2% compared

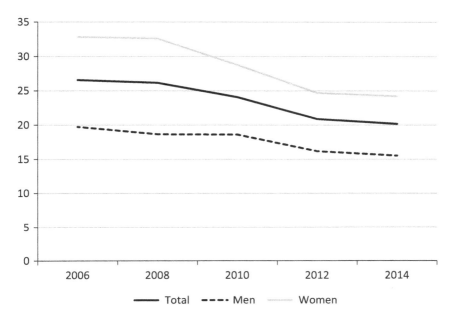

Figure 3.1 Evolution of Public Sector Employment by Gender as % of Total Public Sector Employment (2006–2014)

Source: INE, Encuesta de Población Activa (Labour Force Survey)

to the OECD average of 15.1%. Figure 3.1 and Table 3.1 show the distribution of public employees according to their contractual status and gender. In line with the private sector, women are more affected by temporary jobs in the public sector than men. Moreover, there has been a reduction in the number of employees with temporary contracts from a peak high of 26.5% in 2006 down to 20.2% in 2014. We accordingly observe that similarly to what has happened in the private sector of the economy, the lion's share of job losses in the public sector have occurred among workers under general labor law regulations and in particular, those with temporary contracts.

Each of the four subsectors analyzed exhibit different reliances upon the different contract types mentioned earlier (see Table 3.1). In the case of the local government, 55% of all employees are under general labor law regulations, which contrasts with only 3.4% in the health sector. Moreover, the health sector is characterized by a greater proportion of workers under general labor law regulations, with almost 33.5% of all employees.

The adjustment in public sector employment as a consequence of the crisis has had two characteristics. First, a fall in the number of public employees between 2008 and 2014 of around 2.7%. This decrease contrasts with the steady growth experienced since the transition to democracy.

Table 3.1 Distribution and Evolution of Public Employees by Level of Administration, Sector and Type of Contract (2009–2014) (Spain)

	2009				
	Civil Servants	Salaried Employees	Other (1)	Total	% Women
Central Government (Excl. Military)	309456	129075	7140	445671	34,5
Regional Government	876691	148222	307931	1332844	65,8
Education (Excl. Universities)	407442	36900	95013	539355	67,4
Health	298891	18254	167579	484724	70,3
Local Government	213985	371331	44189	629505	47,2
Total	1400132	648628	359260	2408020	55,1
	2014				
	Civil Servants	Salaried Employees	Other (1)	Total	% Women
Central Government (Excl. Military)	317577	92627	10402	420606	36,1
Regional Government	866993	134847	275102	1276942	67,8
Education (Excl. Universities)	394967	43209	83009	521185	69,9
Health	301038	16281	160018	477337	73,2
Local Government	211988	305052	38680	555720	46,0
Total	1396558	532526	324184	2253268	56,5
	2009–2014 Percentage change				
	Civil Servants	Salaried Employees	Other (1)	Total	
Central Government (Excl. Military)	2,6	−28,2	45,7	−5,6	
Regional Government	−1,1	−9,0	−10,7	−4,2	
Education (Excl. universities)	−3,1	17,1	−12,6	−3,4	
Health	0,7	−10,8	−4,5	−1,5	
Local Government	−0,9	−17,8	−12,5	−11,7	
Total	−0,3	−17,9	−9,8	−6,4	

Source: Ministerio de Hacienda y Administraciones Públicas, Boletín del Registro Central de Personal (Statistical Newsletter of Public Sector Employees). (1) In this category, there are workers with fixed-term contracts (*personal eventual*) and civil servants appointed temporarily (*funcionarios interinos*)

Notwithstanding the overall reduction in public employees during the 2009–2014 period, the impact of the 2008 crisis on public employment was not immediate. In the years 2008–2009, the neo-Keynesian response carried out by the socialist executive allowed small increases in public employment in a context of rapidly growing unemployment. However, the severe deterioration in the economic context and public finances led the government to implement the first austerity package in 2010, hence opening the door to public sector layoffs and the limitation in the replacement rate for retiring civil servants to 10%. The second characteristic of public sector adjustment has consisted in an accumulated decrease in the average wage of public employees of around 15–20% in the period 2008–2014. We can accordingly conclude that for the whole public sector, the adjustment has been more intense on the wage side. This notwithstanding, the public sector wage premium has experienced little variation during the crisis due to the decrease experienced also on private sector wages as a consequence of the internal devaluation process (Hospido and Moral-Benito 2014).

Job losses in the public sector have not been distributed evenly across the four sectors. In particular, the decrease in employment in the local government has been 11.7% compared to 5.6% in central governments and only 1.5% in the health sector (see Table 3.1). But we also find significant differences across the four subsectors in the extent to which this decrease has affected different categories of workers. Thus, in the case of the central and local governments, the reduction has been particularly important among employees under general labor law regulations, with a decrease of 28.2% and 17.8%, respectively.

Public Sector Employment Relations and Pay Determination

Main Features of Employment Regulation

The 1978 Spanish Constitution laid down a number of general principles to guide public sector employment. These included, among others, the need to hire according to objective and publicly known rules, access according to merit and qualifications, as well as equal opportunities. However, no mention was made of the regulatory instruments to be used; that depended on the legal status of public employees, i.e., whether they were civil servants, salaried employees under general labor law regulations or other personnel. For salaried employees, collective bargaining plays the same role as in the private sector. This means they have the right to sign collective agreements at any level (local, regional or state). However, this different legal status also generated uncertainty about whether those principles orienting employment of civil servants (including access and promotion rules) applied to salaried employees.

The constitution did not recognize the right of civil servants to collectively negotiate their working conditions, which were accordingly regulated unilaterally by the government. A first step in granting civil servants the possibility to bargain on working conditions and work organization came with the 1984 Civil Service Reform Act that for the first time included the collective bargaining principle for public sector employees. Later on, the 1987 Law on the Institutions of Representation and Determination of Working Conditions for Public Sector Employees regulated in more detail the right to negotiate civil servants' working conditions. In particular, this law provided for the creation of a centralized bargaining table and some sectoral tables, but the number of issues subject to collective regulation was limited. Subsequently, there was a gradual expansion of collective bargaining in establishing civil servants working conditions.

More recently, the 2007 EBEP established detailed regulation of collective bargaining in the public sector and opened up new opportunities for the collective regulation of working conditions for both civil servants and non-civil servants. In particular, rather than detailing the issues that can be negotiated, the law simply defined those issues that do not necessarily have to be negotiated, i.e., issues where the government retains its capacity to regulate unilaterally, but that could also be subject to negotiations and eventually be regulated through a collective agreement. These issues are, among others, the general organization of the Public Administrations, the determination of working conditions for public sector managers and the regulation of procedures for entry and promotion. Thus, as pointed out by De la Villa (2007: 3), since the early 1990s, there has been a twofold process of mutual influence between civil servants and salaried public employees whereby some of the principles that have traditionally characterized the civil servant employment relationship are increasingly applied to salaried employees. This process of upward harmonization has occurred on issues like pay scales and work organization. But at the same time, the right to collective bargaining, which applied only to salaried employees, has been gradually extended to civil servants.

Collective Bargaining Structure

In the case of salaried employees, collective bargaining is regulated by general labor laws and can take place at any level where worker representation structures exist. However, in the case of civil servants, the gradual opening of spaces to negotiate working conditions lacked legal support and has been characterized by ambiguity around the structure of collective bargaining. The EBEP established a series of common bargaining forums for both civil servants and salaried employees, but it also contains specific regulations of negotiation structures for civil servants. According to this law, the collective bargaining structure for public employees consists of three main levels (see Figure 3.2). At the peak level, there is a joint bargaining forum comprising public employees (civil servants as well as salaried employees) from any level of the public administration (general state administration, Autonomous Communities and the local level). These joint bargaining forums deal with

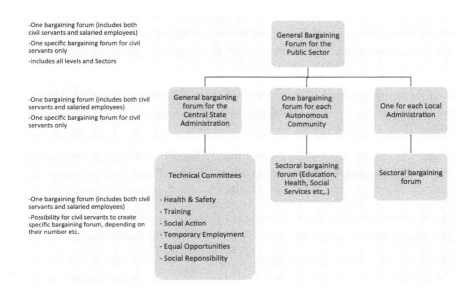

-One bargaining forum (includes both
civil servants and salaried employees)
-One specific bargaining forum for civil
servants only
-Includes all levels and Sectors

General Bargaining
Forum for the
Public Sector

-One bargaining forum (includes both civil
servants and salaried employees)
-One specific bargaining forum for civil
servants only

General bargaining
forum for the
Central State
Administration

One bargaining
forum for each
Autonomous
Community

One for each Local
Administration

Technical Committees

Sectoral bargaining
forum (Education,
Health, Social
Services etc,.)

Sectoral bargaining
forum

-One bargaining forum (includes both civil
servants and salaried employees)
-Possibility for civil servants to create
specific bargaining forum, depending on
their number etc.

- Health & Safety
- Training
- Social Action
- Temporary Employment
- Equal Opportunities
- Social Reponsibility

Figure 3.2 The Structure of Collective Bargaining in the Public Sector (Spain)

common issues for civil servants and salaried employees. Thus, for instance, general increases in salaries of public employees are set and then included in the budget law. Moreover, agreements reached on other issues like work organization or training are taken as a baseline for negotiations at lower levels. In the second level, there is a bargaining forum for each administration, i.e., one for the general administration, one for each of the Autonomous Communities and one for each local government. Finally, the third level consists of sectoral bargaining forums created by the general bargaining forums at the higher level. Collective bargaining in the sectoral bargaining forums will deal with any issue not covered by the general bargaining forums or that the general tables explicitly delegates to the sectoral bargaining forums. Finally, the EBEP also considers the existence of specific bargaining forums for civil servants only, that could be formed at state level (the general bargaining forum of the Public Administrations) as well as at the level of the Autonomous Communities and local government. In spite of the possibility to rely upon different bargaining forums, what we have seen in recent years is a trend consisting in a narrowing down of the gap in the conditions negotiated for civil servants and salaries of employees. In this vein, the negotiation in the general bargaining forum for civil servants plays the role of a pattern for negotiations in the joint general bargaining forum of salaried employees and civil servants. The coverage of collective regulation in the public sector is generally very high, if only because ultimately, employees are covered by the general principles laid down in the agreements reached at the general bargaining forum for the public administration or the ones in each autonomous community. However, where trade unions find more obstacles to create bargaining forums is at local level, and it is at this level where most coverage gaps exist. Despite EBEP, the unilateralism that has accompanied austerity policies has led to many collective agreements expiring without being renewed. As a consequence, and similar to developments in the private sector, where collective bargaining coverage has declined significantly, the number of workers covered by 'alive' collective agreements has declined.

The May 2008 Agreement for the Rationalization of Collective Bargaining in the Central Administration also establishes for civil servants the creation of several technical bargaining forums that are dependent on the general bargaining forum. These committees deal with specific issues and groups such health and safety at work, training, pensions and social benefits, equal opportunities, public employees with temporary contracts, social responsibility (i.e., the promotion of trust relations, cooperation and sustainable management in the public sector) etc.

Social dialogue and collective bargaining have delivered several agreements for civil servants as well as for salaried employees. The last general pact signed by trade unions and the government at the central level was the 2009 Social Pact for the Public Sector for 2010–12. Even though some of the contents of this pact have been implemented (for instance, the setting up of the Employment Observatory or the first gender equality plan), the economic crisis has hindered the implementation of most of them, particularly those with financial implications, as a consequence of the imposition of austerity measures between 2010–2014. In the context of technical committees, the most important agreements signed recently have been the 2013 Agreement for On-the-Job Training of Public Sector Employees.

Changes in public sector collective bargaining have paralleled those occurring in the private sector. First, a gradual decentralization of collective bargaining has occurred, with the number of issues negotiated by lower-level bargaining forums gradually increasing. This process has occurred in a coordinated way due to the strongly hierarchical character of public sector collective bargaining with issues that can be negotiated at lower level decided on at higher levels. Secondly, the scope for the collective regulation of working conditions has widened since the return to democracy. Particularly important in this regard has been the 2007 EBEP. Moreover, this law also reinforced the importance of local-level bargaining. This trend, however, has been reversed in the context of the crisis, where unilateral state regulation has gained new momentum, both in the private and public sector (Molina 2014). Finally, the creation of new voluntary bi-partite institutions to assist in dispute resolution has also characterized public sector collective bargaining developments. In this vein, the EBEP has regulated in detail the process to be followed in case of disagreement, including the extra-judiciary conflict resolution mechanisms and the cases of unilateral regulation by the state.

Public Employers

State Policy and Reforms of Public Sector Employment Regulation

Reforms in the organization and structure of the Spanish public sector have changed their focus, rationale and instruments since the return to democracy (Jódar *et al.* 1999). In the first half of the 1980s, the objective of these legal reforms consisted of reorganizing the public sector and the civil service after the dictatorship, and in particular, adapting the public sector to the new territorial organization of the state and the process of political and administrative decentralization. This was accompanied by an expansion in the number of public sector employees, but without paying much attention to performance, career development etc. Modernization in the 1980s was therefore associated with decentralization and a quantitative expansion in public employment. Since the early 1990s, reforms have moved in two directions: First, to introduce changes in the structure of public services, organizational change and the transformation of the traditional bureaucratic logic by introducing flexibility in management and NPM principles (Villoria 1996); and secondly, to develop and consolidate a coherent and well-defined personnel policy. Negotiations among the most representative trade unions and employers since the early 1990s attempted to remove some of the traditional characteristics of personnel policy, including the hierarchical authority principle. Particularly important in this regard was the 1992 Plan for the Modernization of the Central Government, which aimed at enhancing the efficiency, quality and effectiveness of the public administration by simplifying administrative procedures, extending the use of information technology and improving recruitment and training of public managers. In spite of its ambitious character, the reform fell short of expectations due to the impact of the early 1990s crisis and the resistance of some groups of civil servants to the introduction of NPM techniques and principles (Alonso and Clifton 2013).

The main events in the reform of public sector employment relations in Spain are, on the one hand, Law 30/1984 on the Reform of the Civil Service (*Medidas para la Reforma de la Función Pública*) and more recently, Law 7/2007 on the Public Employment Statute (EBEP). As pointed out by Jódar *et al.* (1999: 172), the 1984 law was aimed at defining the rights and working conditions of civil servants. However, it opened the door for the public administration to hire employees under general labor law regulations. Since then, several piecemeal reforms have been passed with the twofold objective of filling in gaps and legal loopholes while at the same time modernizing public sector employment and the personnel policy. With the objective of introducing more rational and modern criteria in the regulation of public sector employment as well as to fill regulation gaps, the 2007 EBEP was approved by the socialist government just months before the crisis started. The government highlighted how its intention was not to overhaul public sector employment, but to consolidate into a single piece of regulation some of the changes, either formal or informal, that had occurred since the early 1990s in the management of public sector personnel policies. However, the importance of this law does not stem only from this consolidation of existing practices that had developed in a rather unstructured way. This law also contained a very ambitious modernizing agenda, including: limiting an excessive reliance upon temporary employment, greater flexibility in managing human resources, simplification of recruitment procedures and a greater emphasis on training, performance appraisal and career development, consolidating some of the principles of NPM.

Notwithstanding its importance, the impact of the 2007 EBEP on public employment relations remains limited because the required implementation at both the central and regional levels has not yet occurred and many innovations remain potential rather than actual practice. This situation stems from the uncertain context characterized by austerity measures that have precluded the national and regional governments from enacting further administrative regulations based on the EBEP. Consequently, austerity policies have interrupted the modernization of public employment relations in Spain, but not necessarily led to its abandonment. This can be observed particularly in the case of individual performance assessment and appraisal practices, which was one of the key innovations introduced by the EBEP and that has been implemented to a very limited extent (Pablos and Biedma 2013). In particular, management by objectives was very loosely established in the law as the principle that should guide HRM practice in the Spanish public sector in the coming years. Some authors have accordingly criticized the fact that too much emphasis is placed on objectives, which contrasts with the lack of reference to skill acquisition and mechanisms to enhance individual performance (Villoria and Del Pino 2009).

Reforms in public sector organization have accelerated since 2012 under the ring-wing People's Party's government and linked to the 2012 National Reform Program. During 2012, the Commission to Reform the Public Administration (the so-called CORA, *Comisión para la Reforma de la Administración Pública*) was established with the objective of enhancing efficacy, efficiency and service quality. Four main lines of action were identified: avoid overlapping competencies among levels of administration, simplify administrative procedures, re-establish centralized management in those cases where there are common resources and gains to be achieved and finally, some reorganization and rationalization of the competencies and structures of public administration. In 2013, a report containing more than 200 specific recommendations and policy actions was published. In order to monitor the implementation of these recommendations, a number of specific technical commissions have been created. An OECD assessment of the characteristics of the plan and its potential impact pointed out that the objective of this plan is to move beyond the short-term cost savings imposed during the crisis towards a more ambitious modernization of the Spanish public administration (OECD 2014).

At present, the most important outcome made by CORA has been Law 27/2013 for the rationalization and sustainability of local government. This law has provided a new framework for the articulation of local government within the regional and central ones. In particular, this reform is based on four principles (Arenilla 2015). First is the need to better articulate the different levels of the public administration, and in particular, to avoid overlapping competences and duplication with the regional and central governments under 'the principle of one administration, one competence'. Second is the principle of putting the citizen at the center of public service delivery and guaranteeing equal access to these services. Thirdly is the principle of guaranteeing the financial sustainability of the services delivered at the local level. Finally, the law also addresses the issues of transparency and accountability as two sides of the same coin, which have become particularly important in the context of the crisis and the unveiling of several cases of corruption and misuse of public money. Summing up, the reform emphasizes the need to put the citizen back at the center of local government and enhance the efficiency of services delivered. The most important implication of this reform for public employment relations is that it sanctions the recentralization of selection processes by the National Public Administration Institute in the case of civil servants. The rationale of this reform has been diverse. It is expected to save financial resources, alleviating fiscal pressures in the context of adjustment provoked by the sovereign debt crisis; it also addresses some structural problems of public administration in Spain. However, the centripetal and recentralizing characters of some aspects of this reform are in line with the ideology of the ring-wing government in power since 2011.

Characteristics of Public Employers

One of the key aspects dealt with in the 2007 EBEP was the role and position of senior civil servants. A characteristic of the public sector in Spain was a sharp division between the political and the administrative levels. The lack of a well-defined professionalization path for senior civil servants and the excessive politicization of top positions in the public administration has been an ongoing concern of this group of public employees. Moreover, some studies (OECD 2010) have highlighted the absence of a strong focus on career development of civil servants that has been reflected in the small percentage of senior civil servants as a percentage of total employees, the lack of a specific HRM policy for this group (Blanco 2010) and continuing politicization (Catalá 2005). A recent survey carried out among senior civil servants in the public sector reinforced their perception that NPM reforms were weakly institutionalized and that fragmentation, coordination and politicization remained important problems (Alonso and Clifton 2013).

The EBEP does not explicitly distinguish senior civil servants as a specific category within public employees, though it dedicates a separate chapter to this group. The introduction to the EBEP acknowledges the importance of this group as a source of modernization in the public sector, as its role is subject to the principles of efficiency and efficacy and its performance is assessed according to objectives. However, the law did not provide for the detailed regulation of these matters, but only vague and general pointers for future action (Monereo *et al.* 2008). Rather, it has left open scope for further regulation by decree, and in particular, the possibility for lower levels (regional and local) to regulate the role and expectations of senior civil servants.

One of the most important consequences of the reforms and changes that have occurred over the crisis years has been a certain recentralization that contrasts with the long-running trend towards greater autonomy for subnational government, public agencies and autonomous public services. In its attempt to reduce the fiscal deficit and keep under control the wage bill, the central government has relied upon two main tools. First, it has imposed some measures on lower levels, including wage cuts as well as a ban on recruitment or a very low replacement rate. Secondly, it has imposed stringent budgetary constraints and has lowered the transfers from the central to the regional and local levels. The best example of this recentralization can be found in law 27/2013, which introduced new rules for local governments. Two aspects are particularly important regarding the role of public employers. The first is the limitation on their competences assumed by local governments in order to safeguard their financial and fiscal sustainability. As pointed out by Mellado (2015), the logic behind Law 27/2013 responds to the financial and fiscal imperatives imposed by central government rather than to an attempt to modernize and rationalize personnel policies at local level. Overall, the traditional subordination of local government to the central government and subsequently to the regional government remains. In this vein, the law establishes that the delivery of non-compulsory services by local governments to citizens is conditional upon the fulfilment of fiscal stability. As a result, a number of services that have been gradually assumed by local government will no longer be delivered at this level because of budgetary constraints. This includes social services in large municipalities that will from 2016 be delivered by regional governments.

Secondly, law 27/2013 has created the role of a nationally accredited local government civil servant (*funcionarios de administración local con habilitación de carácter nacional*). According to the text, this will enhance the autonomy of public employees at the local level and the quality of the services provided while at the same time increasing centralized control. In particular, the central administration regains the capacity to select, recruit and approve the candidates for civil servant positions at the local level. The stronger role attached to the local supervisor (*Interventor local*) together with the limits imposed by the central government on the number of employees at local level or their wages implies a recentralization of the public sector. This later measure is particularly important, as it has implied a 'de facto' loss of autonomy in personnel policies by local-level governments.

The public health system shares many of the features of these adjustments, including wage freezes and increases in working time. However, in 2012, the ring-wing People's Party's government enacted an urgent law for 'guaranteeing the sustainability of the national health system and enhance its quality' that not only implemented some cost-saving mechanisms (e.g. the centralized negotiation of certain medicines to benefit from economies of scale), but it also contained other rationalization measures, for example, the creation of a common professional scale for all Autonomous Communities to facilitate regional mobility and the creation of a central registry of health professionals, as well as the centralized setting of common standards for the compensation of public health workers.

Trade Unions

Composition: Structure and Membership in the Public Sector

The trade union landscape in the public sector is slightly more fragmented than it is in the private sector. There are, on the one hand, the federations of public services of the two largest trade union confederations in Spain, CCOO and UGT. The process of merger and internal restructuring within the confederations has implied changes in the representation of public employees (Jódar *et al.* 1999). In the case of CCOO, this representation is carried out by three different federations. First, there is the Federation of Citizens' Services (*Federación de Servicios a la Ciudadanía*), which is the first federation in terms of membership within CCOO, with 263,000 affiliates in 2014. This federation represents the interests of public employees of the central, regional and local governments and the services provided. Secondly, there is also the Federation of Health Activities (*Federación de Sanidad y Sectores Sociosanitarios*), which represents the interests of workers in health activities, both private and public. Finally, there is the Education Federation (*Federación de Enseñanza*) that represents the interests of teachers and workers in education centres, both private and public.

When it comes to the other large confederation, UGT, there is a specific organization for public sector employees, the Federation of Public Services (*Federación de Servicios Públicos*, FSP) that also includes those in the public health system. In addition to the FSP, there is an Education Federation (*Federación de Trabajadores de la Enseñanza*). Another important trade union in the Spanish public sector is the Civil Servants' Independent Confederation (CSIF—*Confederación Sindical Independiente de Funcionarios*), which was created in 1980 in order to become an alternative to the dominance of UGT and CCOO in the public sector. It represents public employees from all levels and sectors in the public administration and has become an important actor in the public sector, where it enjoys the status of most representative trade union, together with UGT and CCOO.

In addition to these confederations, there are other trade union organizations in the public sector. First, nationalist trade unions parties operating in regions like Galicia (the Federation of Public Administration of the Galician Interunion Confederation (CIG), *Administración*) and the Basque Country (Federation of Public Services of the Basque Workers' Solidarity (ELA-GIZALAN)) are also important. At the same time, there a number of professional trade unions such as SATSE and CEMSATSE for nurses and doctors, respectively. Finally, there are other smaller unions, including USO (*Unión Sindical Obrera*) that has a specific federation for public employees and CGT (*Confederación General del Trabajo*). These latter two trade unions have the status of most representatives, and as consequence, are legally empowered to participate in the bargaining forums and sign agreements, in some sectors.

Up-to-date and reliable information on trade union membership in Spain does not exist. Membership figures are not made publicly available by trade unions, and they do not use a common methodology in order to keep track of their members. As a consequence, we can only rely upon indirect sources in order to provide some insights on membership levels and trends. The largest union at national level in total membership was FSC-CCOO (257,635 members in 2011), followed by FSP-UGT (228,521) and CSI-CSIF (159,975) (Caprile and Sanz 2011). According to the 2011 wave of the Quality of Life at Work Survey, density in the private sector was 15.1%, while in the public sector, it reached 31% (Alós *et al.* 2015). However, membership is not the criteria used to determine trade union representativeness. Instead, an electoral audience criterion is used whereby those trade unions achieving a minimum of 10% representatives at the national level or 15% at the regional level are entitled to conclude collective agreements in a specific sector at national or regional level, respectively. Moreover, trade unions achieving these percentages can also participate in social dialogue and negotiations with government. CCOO, UGT and CSI-CSIF fulfil the criteria at national level, while ELA and CIG achieve these criteria at regional level. Some of the smaller trade unions like now USO may also reach the 10% at the national level or the 15% criteria at the regional level for some specific sectors.

Employee Voice and Representation Structures

The role of trade unions as representatives of public employees was regulated by two laws approved in 1984. The first is the Civil Service Reform Act (*Ley de Medidas para la Reforma de la Función Pública*). This law divided civil servants into three categories. The first category is made up of the armed forces and other military groups, which do not have the right to unionize or go on strike. Secondly, there are those groups of civil servants that have the right to associate in order to defend their corporate interests but cannot join trade unions. This category is composed of groups of the police and the judiciary. Finally, there is the remainder of civil servants who enjoy trade union rights like any other worker. The other regulation is the 1984 Organic Law for Trade Union Freedom (LOLS—*Ley Orgánica de Libertad Sindical*). As noted above, this law established a representativeness criteria based on the number of votes obtained in work councils' elections rather than levels of membership. This regulation defined the type of worker representation structures and the mechanisms to elect representatives as well as the criteria allowing trade unions to participate in negotiations and sign collective agreements.

Regarding worker representation structures, there is a difference between civil servants and salaried employees. In the latter case, the same representation structures found in the private sector apply, i.e. personnel delegates (*Delegados de Personal*) and work councils (*Comité de Empresa*). However, in the case of civil servants, these representative structures are personnel delegates (*Delegados de Personal*) and personnel assemblies (*Juntas de Personal*). Personnel delegates are elected in public sector units where the number of civil servants and/or salaried employees is equal or higher than six and below 50. By contrast, work councils or personnel assemblies are elected in those units with more than 50 employees. These rules apply to the national, regional, local and sectoral levels.

The first union elections in the public sector were held in 1978, but only for workers with employment contracts under general labor law regulations. Civil servants had to wait until the 1987 Law on Bodies of Representation, Determination of Working Conditions and Participation of Civil Servants in the Public Administration (*Ley de Órganos de Representación, Determinación de las Condiciones de Trabajo y Participación del Personal al Servicio de las Administraciones Públicas*) that implemented the principles orienting the 1984 LOLS for civil servants.

Recent analysis of the results of trade union elections in Spain confirms the dominance of CCOO, which in 2012 held 5,147 delegates amongst civil servants (22.3%), compared to 4,616 for UGT (19.9%) and 3,946 (17%) for CSIF (Alós *et al.* 2015). Finally, a particularly feature of the public sector is corporate trade unions, which obtained 6,671 delegates (28.8%). Other trade unions obtained fewer delegates: USO (779 delegates, 3.4%) and CGT (478 delegates, 2.1%) at the national level and ELA (555 delegates, 2.4%) and CIG (359 delegates 1.6%) at the regional level. Higher membership levels compared to the private sector, together with the institutionalization of representation structures at higher and lower levels as well as a relatively high mobilization capacity, make trade unions in the public sector stronger than in the private sector. Moreover, trade unions' bargaining power is stronger at higher and intermediate levels than at the local level.

The Consequences of the Crisis for Public Sector Employment Relations

Background: Drivers and Responses to the Crisis

Among the large Euro zone countries, Spain is, alongside Greece, the country where the financial and sovereign debt crisis have had a deeper and longer-lasting impact, given the confluence of several causes. First, Spain shares with other southern European economies low and stagnant productivity related to the production structure and the pattern of economic specialization of the economy (Mas *et al.* 2012). Second, it also (with Ireland) had a housing bubble leading to an unprecedented expansion of the construction sector and a steep rise in private indebtedness (López and Rodríguez 2011). Finally, the quasi-federal state structure based on the Autonomous Communities (*Comunidades Autónomas*) has led to the growth of overlapping institutions and competences and increasing public expenditure managed at the regional level. Evidence of a generalized waste of public resources and corruption as well as the failure of large investments such as airports or hospitals during the growth years are evident. This unique combination of problems distinguishes Spain from the other countries most affected by the sovereign debt crisis and has to be borne in mind when one considers the impact of the crisis on the public sector.

Before the financial and debt crisis, some commentators pointed to Spain as a success story owing to its employment creation record, increase in per capita GDP and low unemployment. But after four years of unprecedented job destruction, Spain has now become the 'sick man of Europe', with a sluggish economy and unemployment that is still increasing, hitting almost 6 million or 26% of the active population by the third quarter of 2013. Per capita GDP has decreased to 2002 levels, while inequalities have grown remarkably and are challenging social cohesion against a background of declining coverage of unemployment benefits and social spending cuts (Muñoz de Bustillo and Pérez 2011). Spain lost an opportunity in the pre-crisis years to overcome some of the historical problems that made the country lag behind in Europe and faces enormous difficulties in recovering its growth path and catching up with, especially, northern European countries.

Adjustment policies may share a diagnosis of the problems affecting Spain, but not how to deal with them. After an initial period of inaction under the socialist government led by Rodriguez Zapatero, the first phase in the response comprised a fiscal stimulus followed by a shift towards austerity. This switch, combining spending cuts and tax increases, only happened once the risks of contagion from the Greek sovereign debt crisis became apparent in early to mid-2010. Hence, there is continuity in economic policy over the late socialist (2008–2011) and People's Party (November 2011–) governments—the major shift was induced externally and did not stem from the change in governing party, although spending cuts have been more concentrated on education and health since the People's Party came to power.

Type of Austerity Measures Pursued

As a result of financial pressures, governments in Spain have approved austerity measures since 2010 until 2015 in order to reduce the public deficit. These packages have been imposed unilaterally by governments and have consisted of several measures, including cuts in social spending and policies, cuts in public sector employees pay, limits on hiring and replacement of retired workers, cuts in public investment, a freeze on pension benefits, increases in working time for public employees etc. Even though the intensity and type of measures included have varied, common to all austerity packages has been the use of public sector pay and employment as an important adjustment mechanism. In this vein, the adjustment in Spain has been more expenditure rather than revenue based (Dellepiane and Hardiman 2012).

The first austerity package was approved in 2010 by the left-wing Zapatero government (Royal Decree Law 8/2010 on extraordinary measures to reduce public deficit) and consisted of a 5% pay cut for public employees (between 8% and 15% pay cut for high-ranking officials), the removal of a €2,500 childbirth allowance, the imposition of savings on local and regional public spending and a reduction in public investment. This package implied that the Collective Agreement for Public Work 2010–2012 signed in 2009 was not fulfilled. Trade unions reacted by calling for a one-day public sector strike. Moreover, a few weeks later, the Zapatero government unilaterally reformed labor market regulation and announced a reform of the pension system that led to a general strike on September 2010. In spite of the confrontation with trade unions and under strong international pressure, the Zapatero government announced in July 2010 a new austerity budget for 2011 consisting of cuts in overall public spending amounting to 7.7%, a 5% cut in public employees' pay for 2011 and a rise in personal income tax for those at the top of the income distribution. In December 2010, new actions were announced, including a cutback to the unemployment benefit system, tax cuts for small businesses and an increase in the tobacco tax.

Just one month after being elected, the new government headed by Mr. Rajoy approved in December 2011 a number of austerity measures, including a freeze in public employees' salaries for 2012, an increase in working time for public employees and a 0% replacement rate in the public sector. In February 2012, the government passed a reform of the labor market that, among many other things, facilitated collective dismissals on economic grounds in the public sector for those employees with ordinary labor law contracts. But the most drastic austerity package was announced by the Rajoy government in March 2012. With this package, the Rajoy government aimed at reaching a €27.3bn of budget cuts and tax rises. Again, this package also contained a freeze on public sector pay as a well as the limits on the replacement of retiring public employees. The lion's share of savings and cuts related to the central administration, while another important part would be a reduction in the deficit of Autonomous Communities. Education and the health system were amongst the most affected departments by the cuts imposed on the Autonomous Communities. Trade unions reacted to this austerity package and the labor market reform approved by the government in February 2012 by calling for a general strike in March that same year.

Also in 2012, the government headed by Mr. Rajoy announced in July an austerity budget for 2013 that included an increase in value-added tax, a reduction in unemployment benefits after six months and a further cut in public employees' pay by eliminating the Christmas bonus payment for that year. Coinciding with the presentation of the budget for 2013, the government announced that for the third consecutive year, there would a freeze on public sector pay. Local government was the target of the first austerity package presented by the government in May 2013. In particular, the government announced a reform of local government (see below), which is considered inefficient, together with a reform in the benefits received by public employees at the local level that would also allow considerable savings.

Since 2014, no other austerity packages have been approved, though the budget remains austere and restrictive. Some of the austerity measures taken in previous years have been maintained, including the freeze on public sector pay. Others have been relaxed, such as the limit imposed on new appointments in the public sector and the elimination of the Christmas bonus payment. Moreover, a certain revitalization of collective bargaining in the public sector seems to have happened after five years of unilateral imposition of pay cuts, increases in working time and virtually no replacement of retiring employees. However, some of the measures adopted during the crisis and justified by the need to make more efficient the functioning of the public sector in the context of severe budget constraints have become long-lasting structural changes. This would be the case of the 2012 reform of collective dismissal regulation in the public sector that opened the door to the possibility to collectively dismiss in case of tighter budget constraints and the insolvency of the public administration unit. But probably more important was the reform of the local government, and in particular, the changes introduced in the remuneration and recruitment policies (see below).

Consequences

When analyzing the consequences of policies implemented during the economic crisis, it is important to distinguish between those that responded to short-term financial constraints and were aimed at reducing the budget deficit and that may be relaxed or removed once the economic context changes, and those policies with a more structural character and long-lasting impact. The former have mostly consisted of pay cuts and freezes and increases in working time as well as limits on new job offerings in the public sector. The aim of these measures was not to modernize public sector personnel policies or to equalize public and private sector working conditions, but simply to reduce the wage bill while at the same time, and as a side effect, to enhance productivity. Thus, for instance, in the case of pay cuts, they were justified as a way to share the costs of the adjustment, and in particular the internal devaluation carried out in the private sector, with workers in the public sector. As a matter of fact, a decline in real wages has occurred in both sectors of the economy and the gap between the two has not changed substantially. But these measures have certainly impacted upon the quality of employment in the public sector. Other measures, like the reduction in the replacement wage for temporary sickness, have been justified on the grounds that they will contribute to reduce absenteeism and hence improve productivity.

Table 3.2 Main Austerity Measures in Spain

Year	Month	Measures
2010	May	- Average 5% cut in public sector wages (between 6% and 15% for senior civil servants and officials; between 0,56% and 7% for those at the bottom of the pay scale) - Wage freeze for 2010 and 2011
2011	July	- Replacement rate for retiring public employees set at 10% - No new positions coming out
2011	December	- Increase in working time from 35 to 37,5 hours
2012	February	- Labor market reform 3/2012 (and its administrative development in October 2012) has opened the door for mass redundancies of salaried employees in the public sector. This procedure sets a maximum compensation of 20 days per year worked (with a maximum of 12 months) under the so-called objective reasons. These include public entities having a deficit or a reduction in their budget of at least 5% in relation to the previous year, or 7% in the last two years.
2012	May	- Elimination of the Christmas bonus payment
2012	July	- Reduction of additional (to holidays) paid leave days for personal reasons from 6 to 3 - Reduction of replacement wage in case of temporary sickness. Before it was 100% from the very first day, while it changed to 50% during the first three days; 75% between the 4th and the 20th day; after the 21st, they would get the whole salary
2013	March	- Wage freeze
2013	December	- Law for the Rationalization and Sustainability of Local Administration o Centralized setting of certain components of remuneration o National accreditation and selection process for local civil servants

However, some of these short-term shock measures are having an impact on the size and capacity of the public sector to deliver services (Muñoz and Antón 2013). This would be the case of the prohibition of new appointments that effectively has reduced the size of the public sector, particularly in the local governments, or the new regulation of collective dismissals in the public sector, which has had a similar impact. This means that the number and quality of services provided may have been eroded. This has certainly been the case in the health sector, although with differences across regions, as noted in a recent study by Cortès-Franch and González (2014). Moreover, this prohibition has also impacted on the composition of public employment, with an increase in interim civil servant positions, particularly in sectors like education, but also the health system. In the case of education, there has been an increase in the ratio of students per professor in most regions. In the case of the health system, many hospitals were forced to close entire branches to save on maintenance, but also because they lacked the necessary human resources to keep them fully operational. This has also translated into a decline in the number of beds per thousand persons.

Another impact of the crisis and austerity measures has been a move back towards unilateral state regulation of working conditions. In 2008 and 2009, wage increases for civil servants were agreed on in the general bargaining forum. For salaried employees, their wages and wage increases for 2008 and 2009 were negotiated in the 'Second Collective Agreement for Salaried Employees 2006–2008' and the 'Third Collective Agreement for Salaried Employees 2009'. These two agreements established that the same increases negotiated for civil servants should be applied to salaried employees. By contrast, between 2010–2015, pay increases for public sector employees have been imposed unilaterally.

In some regions, the crisis has been used as an excuse in order to impose both short-term and more structural reforms in those sectors where they have the capacity to regulate them. This, for instance, would be the case of education and health in the region of Madrid, where trade unions, opposition political parties and civil society organizations mobilized against spending cuts and the implications for service quality. But they also protested against the attempts by the regional government to further privatize the health system. Other measures introduced during the crisis were aimed at rationalizing the public sector while modernizing it and avoiding overlapped competencies and service delivery. This has particularly been the case of the regional and local governments. However, it has been pointed out that some components of local-level government reform reflect a downsizing rationale rather an attempt at modernization (Mellado 2015). In particular, this law contains limits on the number of employees, either civil servants or salaried, with open ended or temporary contracts, that can be hired. Particularly important is the limitation on the number of employees with fixed-term contracts, whose number had increased very rapidly at local level and who were hired at the margins of the law. This, together with an explicit preference for civil servant status of local-level public employees, suggests that the growth in the number of temporary workers experienced since the mid-1980s will slow down in coming years.

The reduction in the number of public employees has been particularly important at regional and local levels. This is due partly to the greater reliance upon temporary employment at this level compared to the regional and central levels of public administration. But it has also been suggested that there was a bubble in the public services delivered at the local level, reflected in the number of public employees (Cantero 2010). Political parties used the opportunities provided by the law in order to incorporate public employees at the local level with non-stable contracts as a way to enhance the operational capacity of municipalities, particularly those of large cities (Cuenca 2013).

Responses of Employers and Trade Unions

Union responses to the imposition of austerity measures, and in particular those affecting the public sector and public employees, have shifted between reliance on traditional strategies/resources and the use of new protest repertoires and tactics. In this vein, there have been several strikes called by trade unions against the impact of austerity on the public sector. In 2010, a general strike of all public workers was organized to protest against cuts in public employees' pay imposed by the Zapatero government. In 2012 and 2013, two general strikes of the education sector were organized by the most representative trade unions together with students' associations. Moreover, several strikes have been called at the regional level in sectors like education and health. Particularly important in this regard have been the strikes in the Autonomous Community of Madrid against cuts and attempts to further privatize the health system.

But trade unions in the public sector have also relied upon other tactics in order to enhance the efficacy of their action. One of the innovative aspects has been the unity of action amongst all trade unions and professional associations in the public sector. Thus, in 2012, the Joint Platform of Public Workers Trade Unions and Professional Associations (*Plataforma Sindical y de Asociaciones Profesionales de Empleadas y Empleados Públicos*) was created in order to enhance the impact of actions and mobilizations, including strikes, in the public sector. The fragmentation along ideological and corporatist lines that characterizes the union landscape was accordingly overcome in a context where the threat to all categories of public sector employees was becoming more intense.

Moreover, some of the mobilizations against the impact of austerity measures have enjoyed broad social support. This would be the case of the so-called Green and White Tides (*Marea Verde* and *Marea Blanca*, respectively), where trade unions have participated and have been an important actor but haven't directly led them, hence breaking with the traditional leadership role of trade unions in social aspects. Thus, for instance, in the case of education, the *Marea Verde* were a set of mobilizations, protests and strikes against cuts in the education system and their negative impact on the quality of public education in Spain (Rogero *et al.* 2014). This movement consisted of civil society organizations, including students' organizations, parents' associations and teachers, but also other groups not strictly related to education. Trade unions supported them and were one among other members of a coalition movement aimed at reversing decisions taken unilaterally by both central and regional governments.

Similarly to what happened in the education sector, the White Tide (*Marea Blanca*) has comprised a number of actions, including strikes and demonstrations, in the health sector. These actions have taken place at the regional level as health policy and hospitals are decentralized and have been particularly important in Madrid, Catalunya and to a lesser extent, Andalusia. In contrast to the case of education, the *Marea Blanca* doctors' and nurses' trade unions have been actively involved and have had a more important role, as the organization of two general strikes in 2012 and 2013 in Madrid showed. However, they have also tried to build a coalition with other civil society actors in order to gain visibility and social support.

In spite of the extremely negative context of austerity policies and the declining trust in trade unions, these public sector mobilization experiences have been effective in a double sense. First, in some cases (most notably in the case of healthcare in Madrid), they have managed to hinder the implementation of some of the most radical privatization decisions. More importantly, adopting a long-term effectiveness approach, these mobilizations have allowed trade unions to build broader social coalitions with other civil society actors and citizenship, sharing similar perceptions on these specific issues.

When it comes to employer organizations, they have on several occasions expressed the need to downsize the public sector wage bill and have recommended that the executive take advantage of the window of opportunity opened by the crisis in order to move in three directions. The first direction is to introduce new mechanisms enhancing the productivity and efficiency of the public sector. The second is to reduce the number of public employees. Finally, the third direction is to increase the participation of the private sector in the provision of services as a mechanism to lower costs and achieve additional efficiency gains, particularly in the education and health sectors.

Conclusions

Public sector employment relations in Spain have faced, since the 2008 crisis started, significant challenges that have led governments to implement a mix of short-term and long-term adjustments that will certainly have implications for its future trajectory. Governments' responses to these challenges under austerity have shifted from the implementation of short-term cost-cutting measures (2010–2012) characterized by state unilateralism towards a more structural long-term reform approach more recently (2013–2015). In the first phase, the response orchestrated by both left and ring-wing governments would fit into the coping state's response (Lodge and Hood 2012), although in some regions governed by ring-wing governments, this opened a window of opportunity for advancing a liberalizing and marketization strategy. In a second stage, the short-term saving measures have been maintained, but at the same time, the government has pushed for a more ambitious reform of public sector organization in Spain in order to enhance its efficiency. It is still difficult to assess the impact of this reform, as it is still underway in many aspects. However, some of the pieces of regulation already passed point towards a reversal of some of the long-running trends in the Spanish public sector and in particular, the process of decentralization. However, these reforms do not necessarily imply abandoning the principles of NPM that have oriented reforms of public sector employment relations over the last two decades. The underlying principles behind them respond more to a rationalization rather than a shift back to pre-NPM public sector employment relations principles. However, this does not mean either that these reforms imply a modernization of public sector employment relations, as their impact is expected to be limited.

The most important impulse towards the modernization of public sector employment relations came just before the crisis with the 2007 EBEP. Even though many aspects of this reform haven't been implemented because of austerity policies, it will certainly develop its full potential once the emergency situation generated by the crisis ends. This law contained several innovations with respect to previous regulations and included many of the principles behind NPM. Some of the most important aspects were the implementation of more significant performance appraisal mechanisms, training and career development policies; the role, position and policies towards senior civil servants; and finally, the articulation and rationalization of collective bargaining for public sector employees.

Finally, it is important to highlight the asymmetrical impact of austerity measures across sectors and/or levels of government. Even though there has been a generalized deterioration in public employees' working conditions and in the quality of public services delivered, public employees at the regional and more importantly, the local level have to a greater extent been affected by austerity measures. Moreover, the adjustment has been more intense for salaried employees than for civil servants because of their different regulations. In this regard, the dualization that characterizes public sector employment relations in Spain remains in spite of the attempts by the 2007 EBEP to close the gap between the two groups of employees.

References

Alonso, J. and Clifton, J. (2013) 'Public Sector Reform in Spain: Views and Experiences from Senior Executives', Report for the COCOPS FP7 Project.

Alós, R., Beneyto, P., Jódar, P., Molina, O. and Vidal, S. (2015) *La Representación Sindical en España*, Madrid: Fundación 1° de Mayo.

Arenilla, M. (2015) 'Génesis y finalidad de la reforma', *Revista de Estudios de la Administración Local y Autonómica*, January, 1–8.

Blanco, C. (2010) 'La figura del directivo público profesional: reclutamiento y estatuto', *Documentación Administrativa*, 286, 179–205.

Cantero, J. (2010) 'La incidencia del fenómeno de la externalización en la Administración General del Estado. ¿Existe algún límite?' *Documentación Administrativa*, 286, 297–334.

Caprile, M. and Sanz, P. (2011) *Spain: Representativeness Study of the European Social Partners Organisations—Public Administration Sector*, Dublin: Eurofound.

Catalá, R. (2005) 'Directivos Públicos', *Presupuesto y Gasto Público*, 41, 211–225.

Cortès-Franch, I. and González, B. (2014) 'Crisis económico-financiera y salud en España. Evidencia y perspectivas. Informe SESPAS 2014', *Gaceta Sanitaria*, 28, 1–6.

Cuenca, J. (2013) 'La planificación de recursos humanos: un instrumento necesario para afrontar la crisis en el empleo público local', in Boltaina, X., Cuenca, J., Jiménez, R., Mauri, J. and Palomar, A. (eds.) *El empleo público local ante la crisis*, Granada: CEMCI-Fundación Democracia y Gobierno Local, 89–124.

Cuenca, J., Cubas, J., Márquez, A., Tomás, J. and Orsini, A. (2013) 'El impacto de la crisis en el empleo público local: el caso del área metropolitana de Valencia', *Gestión y Análisis de Políticas Públicas*, 10, 43–54.

De la Villa, L. (2007) 'El Estatuto Básico del Empleado Público: Comentario de urgencia a los aspectos laborales de la Ley 7/2007', de 12 de abril, *Revista General de Derecho del Trabajo y de la Seguridad Social*, 14, 1–20.

Dellepiane, S. and Hardiman, N. (2012) *Fiscal Politics in Time: Pathways to Fiscal Consolidation, 1980–2012*, UCD Geary Institute DP Series 2012/28, Dublin: UCD.

Hospido, L. and Moral-Benito, E. (2014) *The Public Sector Wage Premium in Spain: Evidence from Longitudinal Administrative Data*, IZA Discussion Papers, No. 8315, Bonn: IZA.

Jódar, P., Jordana, J. and Alós, R. (1999) 'Spain. Public Service Employment Relations Since the Transition to Democracy', in Bach, S. and Bordogna, L. (eds.) *Public Service Employment Relations in Europe: Transformation, Modernization, or Inertia*, London: Routledge, 87–113.

Lodge, M. and Hood, C. (2012) 'Into an Age of Multiple Austerities? Public Management and Public Service Bargains Across OECD Countries', *Governance: An International Journal of Policy, Administration, and Institutions*, 25(1), 79–101.

Mellado, L. (2015) 'La situación del personal al servicio de la Administración Local', *Revista de Estudios de la Administración Local y Autonómica*, 1, 1–18.

Molina, O. (2014) 'Self-Regulation and the State in Industrial Relations in Southern Europe: Back to the Future?' *European Journal of Industrial Relations*, 20(1), 21–36.

Monereo, J., Molina, C., Olarte, S. and Rivas, P. (eds.) (2008) 'El estatuto básico del empleado público', Comentario sistemático de la ley 7/2007, de 12 de abril de 2008, Granada: Comares

Moreno, L. (1993) 'Ethnoterritorial Concurrence and Imperfect Federalism in Spain', Documentos de Trabajo—Unidad de Políticas Comparadas (CSIC) DT 93–10, Madrid: CSIC.

Muñoz de Bustillo, R. and Antón, J. I. (2013) 'Those Were the Days, My Friend: The Public Sector and the Economic Crisis in Spain', in Vaughan-Whitehead, Daniel (ed.) *Public Sector Shock: The Impact of Policy Retrenchment in Europe*, Cheltenham: Edward Elgar, 511–542.

Muñoz de Bustillo, R. and Pérez, A. (2011) 'From the Highest Employment Growth to the Deepest Fall: Economic Crisis and Labour Inequalities in Spain', in Vaughan-Whitehead, D. (eds.) *Work Inequalities in the Crisis: Evidence from Europe*, London: Edward Elgar, 393–444.

OECD (2010) *Spain: Human Resources Management Profile*, Paris: OECD.

OECD (2014) *Spain: From Administrative Reform to Continuous Improvement, OCDE Public Governance Reviews*, Paris: OCDE.

Pablos, J. and Biedma, J. M. (2013) 'La evaluación del rendimiento individual: Un instrumento válido para lograr la eficiencia en la gestión de los Recursos Humanos en las Administraciones Públicas', *Gestión y Análisis de Políticas Públicas*, 10, 1–18.

Rogero, J., Rodríguez, F. and Rojo, R. (2014) 'La "Marea Verde": Balance de una Movilización Inconclusa', *Revista de la Asociación de Sociología de la Educación*, 7(3): 567–586.

Sánchez, M. (2013) 'La contrarreforma sanitaria', *Papeles de Relaciones Ecosociales y Cambio Global*, 123: 63–72.

Vallés, J. M. and Brugué, Q. (2001) 'Gobierno Local', in Alcántara, M. and Martínez, A. (eds.) *Política y Gobierno en España*, Valencia: Tirant lo Blanch, 267–302.

Villoria, M. (1996) *La modernización de la administración como instrumento al servicio de la democracia*, Madrid: INAP-BOE.

Villoria, M. and Del Pino, E. (2009) *Dirección y gestión de recursos humanos en las administraciones públicas*, Madrid: Tecnos.

4 Italy: The Uncertainties of Endless Reform

Public Service Employment Relations Confronting Financial Sustainability Constraints

Lorenzo Bordogna

Introduction

Since the 1980s, public service employment relations in Italy have experienced a continuous process of reform within a wider design to restructure the public administration as a whole. The most important change occurred in 1992–93, just after the exit of Italy from the European Monetary System (September 1992), the strong devaluation of the national currency and the decision to prepare for participation in the Economic and Monetary Union (EMU) within the first group of countries, with the connected need to meet the Maastricht criteria for eligibility. Reducing or containing public expenditures, of which wages and salaries of public employees were and are a significant part, became a government imperative. This process coincided with the attempt to move the Italian public administration from a highly legalistic system, typical of the Napoleonic state tradition to which Italy belonged (Kickert 2007; Ongaro 2009, 2011), to a system closer to the private sector principles, to some extent along the guidelines of the New Public Management (NPM) approach, although with uncertainties and peculiarities. It was not a linear process of transformation, conditioned as it was by both economic pressures, further strengthened after the 2008 economic and sovereign debt crisis, and endogenous reasons for reform. After about three decades of change, different layers of administrative reform seem to coexist, not always in a consistent way. In the comparative public administration literature, it is debated whether Italy, once abandoned some features of the Napoleonic state tradition, is an example of NPM failure (Kickert 2007) or the 'least good fit' case of the neo-Weberian state prevailing in continental European countries (Pollitt 2007; Bordogna and Neri 2011; Pollitt and Bouckaert 2011).

The trajectory of public service employment relations reflects this wider and non-linear process of change. For about three decades after the end of World War II, the Italian public administration was associated with a professional corps of employees which, according to the Weberian idealtype of bureaucracy, entered the administration through selection procedures subject to universalistic criteria, were expected to serve impartially and exclusively the general interest of the nation, had formal and protected position with employment security and received a regular salary mostly based on seniority and on their rank in the organizational hierarchy (Bordogna and Pedersini 2013b). All public employees, not only civil servants, had a public law employment statute, subject to administrative tribunals in case of controversies. This implied the prevalence of the 'sovereign employer' model of employment relations (Beaumont 1992; Bach and Kessler 2007), according to which terms and conditions of employment were unilaterally determined by the government or public authorities through legislation and administrative acts. Public employees did not enjoy collective bargaining rights. But the right of association and the right to strike—the latter one to be practiced within the rules established by ordinary law, never approved until 1990—were affirmed by the 1948 Constitution without distinction between private and public sector employees, with few exceptions (such as armed forces and, to a lesser extent, the police). As usual in the sovereign employer model, the denial of collective bargaining rights was associated with special prerogatives attached to the public law employment statute, to begin with job security, but including also other internal labor market issues, like mobility, career and remuneration systems, disciplinary matters, retirement rules and pension treatments.

Following a more general trend (Treu 1987; Bordogna and Winchester 2001), the unilateralism of this model started to be eroded in the late 1960s and early 1970s, with the partial recognition of forms of joint regulation and even collective bargaining, subsector after subsector, to be extended to the large majority of public employees by legislation in 1983, despite some restrictions. Some matters were excluded from negotiations, and agreements, to be effective, had to be transposed into a decree of the President of the Republic. This law (No. 93/1983), however, while recognizing collective bargaining rights, did not abolish the special prerogatives attached to the public employment statute. This gave rise to a regime of 'double protection'—collective bargaining rights *plus* special prerogatives of the public law statute (Giugni 1992)—which in a few years led to wage increases notably higher than in the private sector. Destabilizing effects followed on the entire Italian industrial relations system as well as on public finances (Bordogna *et al.* 1999).

The inconsistencies of this regime have been addressed by the major 1993 reform, with the privatization of the employment relationship of the large majority of public employees and, at least formally, the abolition of the special prerogatives attached to the public law employment statute. Within this new framework, other reform waves followed until 2015.

After presenting the structure and size of the public sector, this chapter analyzes the evolution of employment relations since the early 1990s, including the role of the employers and trade unions, and then focuses on the consequences of the 2008 crisis and austerity policies for public sector working conditions and employment relations.

Organization Structure and Employment

Italy is a unitary state comprising twenty regions and one hundred and ten provinces; five regions and two provinces have a special autonomy statute. There are also about eight thousand municipalities. Since the early 1970s, a process of decentralization started that gave the decentralized levels of government, especially the regions, strong administrative and regulatory powers, further strengthened by a 2001 constitutional reform. The autonomous power to levy taxes is, however, limited. The president and council of the regions and provinces, as well as the mayor and council of the municipalities, are elected every five years by universal suffrage, with a majority system since the mid-1990s. Since 2012, this move towards decentralization has been partly reversed, with the decision to reduce and then suppress the provinces and with a constitutional reform, approved in 2015 and subject to a referendum in 2016, which to some extent reduces the powers of the regions *vis-á-vis* those of the central state.

Public functions are carried out at different administrative levels. The central government includes ministries and agencies to which some government functions have been devolved (mainly the internal revenue agency), the police and armed forces, compulsory social security and the education of all grades with the exception of vocational training, which is provided at regional and local government level. Public universities enjoy administrative autonomy, although they are mostly financed by central government. The national health service, created in 1978, is financed and coordinated at national level, but since the early 1990s, the regional level of government has had strong regulatory powers. Social services are mostly provided at the regional and local government levels.

Compared with the EU28 or the Euro zone 19, Italy has a comparatively large public sector in terms of government revenue and spending, with 48.2 and 51.2% of the GDP, respectively, in 2014. However, in terms of public sector employment share on total employment or total population, Italy holds an intermediate position, above Germany but significantly lower than France, the Nordic countries and, to a lesser extent, the UK.

At the end of 2014, all Italian public administrations, as defined by legislative decree No. 165/2001, employed 3.219 million persons with permanent employment contracts, including about 149,000 school teachers with one-year contracts, plus 104,000 employees with fixed-term and flexible contracts. This amounted to a little less than 15% of total employment, and to about 5.5% of total population (Table 4.1). The state railways and postal service are not considered in this chapter since these services, once included within the boundaries of the public administration, were converted into joint-stock companies between the mid-1980s and mid-1990s, although the state remains the main or sole shareholder; their employees have been moved from a public law statute to private employment contracts. Nor are local public services (garbage collection, water, energy, public transport)

Table 4.1 Public Sector Employment Levels and Wage Bill, 2001–2014 (000s)

	2001	2007	2008	2009	2010	2011	2012	2013	2014[***]
Public sector employment—Total	3656	3584	3579	3503	3438	3395	3344	3337	3323
Permanent employees[*]	3504	3429	3437	3376	3316	3284	3239	3233	3219
Employees with flexible contracts[**]	152	154	142	127	122	112	105	104	104
% of total employment	16.6%	15.5%	15.6%	15.5%	15.2%	15.1%	14.9%	15.0%	14.9%
Public sector wage bill (billion euros)	132.29	157.81	167.84	169.09	166.73	165.18	160.32	158.21	156.56
% of GDP	10.2%	9.8%	10.3%	10.7%	10.4%	10.1%	9.9%	9.8%	9.8%
Public deficit (%GDP)	-3.1	-1.5	-2.7	-5.3	-4.2	-3.5	-3.0	-2.9	-3.0
Public debt (%GDP)	104.7	99.7	102.3	112.5	115.3	116.4	123.2	128.8	132.3

[*]Including schoolteachers with one-year contracts and some groups of non-permanent employees of police corps and armed forces and other minor groups (in total, 304,000 employees in 2007 and 204,000 in 2014).

[**]Flexible contracts include: fixed-term (the largest group), trainee and agency contracts, and 'socially useful' work. The latter two groups are not strictly dependent employees of the public administration.

[***]Provisional data (excluding employees of few administrations not previously surveyed). I am grateful to Dr. A. Patassini (MEF) for providing these data.

Source: Ministero dell'Economia e delle Finanze (2014); Eurostat for the last two lines.

included, since their employees are under private employment contracts, despite these services being mostly owned and financed by municipalities.

The public sector as a whole comprises several subsectors, the largest of which in terms of number of (civilian) employees are education, the national health service, regions and local authorities, and the central government (ministries and agencies). All together, these four subsectors account for 77% of total permanent employees and 92% of civilian employees (Table 4.2). This chapter mostly focuses on them, although occasionally, other subsectors are mentioned.

Public employees differ also by employment statute. Since the major 1993 reform, the employment relationship of the large majority of them (more than 80%) has been 'privatized', and their terms and conditions of employment are determined *via* collective bargaining. Armed forces and the police are the largest groups excluded from privatization, in addition to other minor groups like teaching staff in universities (about 50,000), top-level state managers (until 1998), the judiciary, diplomatic and prefecture personnel, prison personnel and, since 2005, the national corps of firemen. Parts of these groups, however, enjoy some special negotiation procedures, different and separate from those of privatized personnel.

Employment levels have overall decreased since 2001, and especially after the 2008 economic crisis, due to cuts in the replacement ratios both of permanent and temporary employees, whose contracts were not renewed. From 2007 to 2014, total employment diminished by 7.3%, permanent employees by 6.1% and employees with flexible contracts by 33%. The decrease was actually larger, because since the year 2011, a few administrative units with about 24,000 employees, not previously surveyed, have been included in the official statistics. As a proportion of total population, it diminished from 6.14% in 2007 to 5.5% in 2014, and from 15.5% to 14.9% as a proportion of total employment, despite overall employment levels decreasing significantly as well.

With regard to the sectoral composition, the decrease has been larger in central government and in public schools, and lower in the national health service and in the regions and local authorities (regions with special autonomy statute actually recorded a notable increase), with the police and armed forces in between.

Women made up about 56% of permanent employees at the end of 2013, notably increased from 49.3% in 2001. As expected, this percentage is much higher in the education sector and in the national health service, respectively 79% and 65% in 2013, lower in the central government and the local government (around 53%) and very low in the armed forces and the police. In all subsectors, however, women's employment share has notably increased since 2001, even in the armed forces and the police.

Overall, the share of part-time workers on permanent employment is rather low, around 5.4% in 2013, up from 3.1% in 2001, lower than in the private sector. It is generally higher among women, in the national health

Table 4.2 Permanent Employees: Contractualized and Non-Contractualized Subsectors, 2007–2014 (000s)

	2007	2008	2009	2010	2011	2012	2013	2014**
Permanent employees—Total	3429	3437	3376	3316	3284	3239	3233	3219
Central government[1]	243	241	236	231	224	219	216	213
Non-economic public bodies[2]	59	56	54	52	50	49	47	46
Regions and Local Authorities[3]	586	595	594	589	597	584	578	566
National health service	682	690	694	689	683	673	670	664
Public schools[4]	1145	1140	1084	1053	1025	1022	1037	1048
Public universities[5]	117	120	116	111	109	106	104	101
Research institutes	16	17	18	18	21	21	21	21
Police*	334	331	329	324	324	320	317	314
Armed forces*	192	192	197	195	193	187	185	187
Firemen*	32	32	32	32	33	32	32	33
Judiciary*	10	10	11	10	10	10	10	11
Diplomatic personnel*	0.970	0.935	0.919	0.909	0.919	0.923	0.933	0.910
Prefect personnel*	1.5	1.5	1.4	1.4	1.4	1.3	1.2	1.3
Prison Personnel*	0.494	0.473	0.456	0.432	0.397	0.370	0.356	0.349
Others	11	11	11	11	13	13	13	13

*Subsectors under public law statute; employment conditions are not determined through collective negotiations with ARAN (the bargaining agent for all public administrations in national level negotiations, created by the 1993 reform).

**Provisional data (excluding employees of few administrations not previously surveyed).

[1]Ministries + Internal revenue agencies + Presidency of the Council of Ministers (PCM).

[2]Mostly compulsory social security organizations.

[3]Regions (including those with special autonomy statute), provinces, municipalities, chambers of commerce.

[4]Art and music schools included; teaching personnel with one-year contract included (235,000 in 2007, 149,000 in 2013).

[5]Both teaching and non-teaching personnel; teaching personnel (about 50,000 units) have no collective bargaining right.

Source: Ministero dell'Economia e delle Finanze (2014).

service and in the regional and local government. Finally, public employees are on average notably older than their private sector colleagues, with the partial exception of armed forces and the police (Bordogna and Pedersini 2013a; ARAN 2013b).

Public Sector Employment Relations and Pay Determination

As anticipated, since the early 1990s, public sector employment relations have shifted from the unilateralism of the sovereign employer model prevailing in previous decades associated with the public law employment statute, to forms of joint regulation of terms and conditions of employment typical of the model employer approach. Four reform waves took place. The first and most important one in 1992–1993, the second one in 1997–1998, the third one in 2009, and the last one in 2014–2015, partly to be implemented in 2016.

In the wake of the monetary and financial crisis of 1992, the major 1992–1993 reform (law no. 421/1992 and legislative decree no. 29/1993, followed by several integrations during the decade), aimed at a general redesign of the principles regulating the Italian public administration. This included the separation of the responsibilities of political authorities in charge of defining overall goals, assigning resources and evaluating results, from those of professional managers, in charge of realizing programs with operational autonomy; the establishment of tight budgetary rules and controls; the introduction of performance appraisal systems at all levels. The reform of employment relations was part of this broader design. The separation between political and managerial responsibilities implied the creation of a central agency, ARAN, for the compulsory and monopolistic representation of all public administrations in national-level negotiations; the aim was to insulate collective negotiations from party politics, remedying the invasion of political parties into the public sector employment relations arena widely experienced in the 1980s. The inconsistencies of the regime of double protection introduced ten years earlier (collective bargaining rights *plus* the special prerogatives of the public law statute) were addressed, on the one hand confirming, and even strengthening, collective bargaining rights of the large majority of public employees but, on the other hand, abolishing their public law employment statute. This reform was therefore labeled 'first privatization', or also 'contractualization', of the employment relationship of public employees. Compared with the previous regime, the scope of negotiable matters was enlarged to almost all terms and conditions of employment, collective bargaining became the exclusive method of determination of pay issues and agreements were made immediately effective with no need to be transposed into a decree of the President of the Republic, although the bargaining procedure still required some control and authorization by the central government and the state Court of Accounts. A two-tier bargaining system was introduced, close to the model of 'organized decentralization'

(Traxler 1995) adopted in the private sector in the same year, with the sectoral national level as the main pillar, and, as a second pillar, a decentralized level of negotiations on matters and within constraints defined by the higher level. At the same time, the employment relationship of the large majority of public employees, with the above-mentioned exceptions, was 'privatized', its public law statute abolished, the special prerogatives attached to it reduced or cut and its jurisdiction moved from administrative law and tribunals to civil law and ordinary tribunals. Managerial prerogatives and responsibilities on organizational as well as on personnel and employment relations matters were strengthened, and some market-type, selective and discretionary incentives were introduced in the pay and career systems of all staff, replacing automatic and 'collectivist' mechanisms based on seniority (every two years with regard to pay). Annual performance appraisal procedures were introduced both for managerial and non-managerial staff, with some forms of performance-related pay.

In summary, within the broader program to abandon or weaken the Weberian ideal-type of bureaucracy, the regulation of public sector employment relations shifted from a sovereign employer model to a private sector-style approach, embedded, at least in theory, within a more 'voluntarist' context, more open to some market, or market-type, constraints (Bordogna *et al.* 1999).

This major shift away from unilateralism was strengthened by the so-called 'second privatization' reform of 1997–1998, the closest to NPM prescriptions, which further moved the regulation of the public sector employment relations toward the private sector model. In particular, the greater emphasis on the regulatory role of collective bargaining took on three main features. First, the privatization and contractualization of the employment relationship was enlarged also to top-level state managers, who lost their previous public law employment statute. Their terms and conditions of appointment, especially on pay matters, previously unilaterally set by legislation, were now determined through a double process of negotiation: collective agreements between ARAN and representative trade unions with regard to the basic salary, and individual negotiations with the pertinent political authority (minister) with regard to the variable component linked to the type of assignment and to performance. Second, the role of the decentralized level of bargaining was strengthened. The scope of decentralized negotiations was enlarged to cover, at least *de facto*, organizational and HRM matters previously reserved to managerial responsibilities, and individual employers were allowed, under certain (rather loose) conditions, greater autonomy in pay negotiations, increasing the financial resources beyond the limits set by higher-level collective agreements. Third, the centralized controls by the government and the state Court of Accounts on collective agreements, before their final approval, both at the national and decentralized levels, were significantly relaxed.

These changes aimed to bring the public sector bargaining structure and process even closer to those of the private sector, with the expectation to obtain similar outcomes in terms of wage dynamics. However, some of these changes generated unexpected and even perverse effects, partly due to a problem of design and partly due to a failure of implementation (Zoppoli 2008). Two features, in particular, turned out to be problematic. First, the greater negotiating autonomy at the decentralized level, not accompanied by the appropriate institutional and financial arrangements to strengthen actors' responsibility, made collective bargaining 'a sham' (Clegg 1975), promoting actors' collusive behavior to the detriment of third parties (higher levels of public administration, taxpayers) rather than a genuine conflict of interests with beneficial systemic effects (Bordogna 2007, 2008). Despite some qualification (Carrieri and Ricciardi 2006), the two-tier bargaining system shifted from an organized toward a disorganized decentralization model (Traxler 1995), and this was particularly relevant given that in the public sector the lower level of negotiation is almost universally practiced quite differently from the private sector. The overall outcomes were wage increases at the decentralized level between 2000 and 2007 from 10 to 15 percentage points higher than in the private sector (Dell'Aringa and Della Rocca 2007; Dell'Aringa 2007; Vignocchi 2007; ARAN 2009, 2011, 2012) and encroachment on managerial prerogatives on work organization and HRM issues by trade unions and workplace employee representatives. Second, the contractualization of the employment relations of top-level state managers weakened their position both *vis-á-vis* trade unions, on which they depended for their basic salary, and political authorities, which were in charge of appointing them in their position, evaluating their performance (with the connected variable salary) and renewing or denying their (re) appointment. This had also negative effects both on the wage dynamics of this group, three to four times higher than the average in this period, and on the effectiveness of the appraisal system of the entire personnel (Talamo 2007).

The third reform wave, the so-called 2009 Brunetta reform from the name of the Minister of Public Function of the Berlusconi government, intended to respond to these difficulties. Although it had endogenous reasons rooted in previous employment relations developments, the implementation of the reform was affected by government responses to the economic crisis.

The Brunetta reform did not repeal the basic features of the 1992–1993 legislation, the privatization and contractualization of the employment relationship of public employees, but introduced important amendments and integrations. The role of collective bargaining was reduced and embedded within a stricter web of rules and constraints, which weakened also the role of trade unions (Ricciardi 2009). Employment relations, especially at the decentralized level, and HRM practices were partially re-juridified, to the detriment of the autonomy of collective negotiations but, to some extent, also of managerial discretion. The two-tier bargaining structure was preserved, but with a strong reduction of the number of bargaining areas at the national level (from twelve to a maximum of four) and a tighter hierarchical relationship between the two levels of negotiation, downplaying the autonomy of the lower level. The scope of negotiable matters was limited, especially at the decentralized level, excluding those related to organizational and HRM issues. Wage increases and career promotions were made conditional on stricter performance appraisal systems, with a view to avoid the generalized, non-selective practices previously utilized, and stricter legal liabilities of individual employers and managers in case of violation of these principles were introduced. The powers of the central government and of the state Court of Accounts on bargaining procedures and outcomes were re-established after their relaxation in the second privatization reform to control not only the financial compatibility of agreements with the public budget, but also their conformity with the basic reform principles (meritocracy, selectivity, transparency). A new central authority was created (CIVIT) to promote performance management and performance appraisal systems within each individual administration and to monitor their operation. The reform aimed also to activate forms of social control by the consumers and local communities, introducing principles of transparency and accountability in relation to the costs and the effects of agreements at the decentralized level on service provision. Other measures included a firmer attempt to reduce the absenteeism of public employees, which was, and still is, notably higher than in the private sector.

Because of the economic crisis, however, the implementation of the Brunetta reform proved very problematic, in particular with regard to employment relations (Bordogna and Pedersini 2013b). In spring 2010, a government decree suspended national-level negotiations for the entire 2010–2012 bargaining round and froze wages and salaries of all public employees, including the non-contractualized groups, to the 2010 level. This freeze was extended for several years directly cancelling two entire bargaining rounds at the national level and indirectly preventing decentralized negotiations on wage issues, until in summer 2015 a judgment of the Constitutional Court declared unconstitutional its further extension. Other parts of the reform met difficulties as well, especially with regard to the implementation of the complicated architecture of the performance management and performance assessment system.

The last reform under the center left Renzi government (the so-called Madia reform, from the name of the Minister of Public Function) comprises a group of measures approved in 2014, immediately effective, and a larger set of principles approved in 2015, whose specification and implementation are expected in 2016. The first group includes measures aimed to progressively relax turnover cuts over the 2014–2018 period, to facilitate compulsory and voluntary mobility of personnel from one to another administration, to cut the amount of working time off and paid leave for union activities, which had already been reduced by the Brunetta reform, and to simplify the procedures regarding performance management and performance assessment systems. In particular, the special authority (CIVIT) created for this purpose by the previous reform was suppressed and the related functions transferred partly to the Department of Public Function and partly to the national anti-corruption authority (ANAC). The second piece of legislation includes, among others, important guidelines to redesign the managerial role in the central as well as in local government and in the health sector, to be implemented in 2016.

All three of the largest trade union confederations supported the approval of the first and second privatization reforms, but they split with regard to the Brunetta reform. CGIL (Italian General Confederation of Work) fiercely opposed it, while CISL (Italian Confederation of Workers' Unions) and UIL (Italian Union of Work)[1] partly accepted it, although rejecting the anti-public and anti-state rhetoric that surrounded it, and criticizing the cuts in working time off and paid leaves for union activities. Approximately the same positions are observable with regard to the 2015 reform, with UIL probably closer to CGIL than to CISL.

Public Employers

State Policies

Policies of privatization and marketization in a strict sense, that is, the transfer of parts of public services and public administrations from public ownership to private hands, and their exposure to market competition have been, in Italy, less radical than in other European countries. Between the mid-1980s and mid-1990s, policies of privatization in this sense were pursued with regard to several state-owned companies and banks (Italian Telecom, three major state-owned banks and others) and to some local public services, but their employees did not have public employment status. Different are the already-mentioned cases of state railways and the postal service. Their transformation into joint-stock companies implied for the employees the loss of their public employment status, which facilitated large redundancies.

These policies of privatization, however, were part of a broader reform process, stimulated by the increasing financial difficulties of the state, which affected the context in which employment relations takes place, and the characteristics of the state as an employer. Relevant in this sense were the government adoption, also with a view to the participation to the economic and monetary union (EMU), of tighter budgetary rules aimed at increasing the accountability and financial responsibility of all public administrations and at partially opening them to market pressures. These reforms have been more pronounced in the health service and in local government, linked to the process of administrative decentralization, and less marked in the central government and in the education sector.

The universal national health service, created in 1978 in substitution of the previous Social Health Insurance system, was the object of an important reform in 1992–1993, followed by some amendments in 1999, which gave the regions wide responsibilities in terms of the planning, organization and monitoring of services. Despite some variation across regions, this reform reorganized the public health sector in local health enterprises (LHEs) and hospital enterprises (HEs); introduced elements of managed competition based on quasi-market mechanisms and a partial purchaser-provider split; replaced the previous financing system based on the number of days of recovery with the DRG system (Diagnosis-related group, based on a classification of hospital costs/products); empowered the role of users' choice; and strengthened managerial autonomy (Maino and Neri 2011). The reform created also the role of a general manager at the head of the LHEs and HEs, appointed by the regional government and chosen from a national (then regional, and lately again national) list of candidates and employed on a five-year private contract. General managers have great autonomy within the constraints of the budget assigned by the regional authority, with incentives to rationalize activities and contain expenditures, subject to the control of the state Court of Accounts.

The municipalities and provinces as well received by the legislation of the 1990s a degree of autonomy in deciding on the services to provide to citizens and in defining their organizational structures, together with the possibility to create the role of a general manager under a private contract, in cases with more than 15,000 inhabitants (more than 100,000 since 2010). The financial autonomy of local governments was increased as well, with the possibility to raise taxes within nationally defined thresholds, although to a significant extent they are still dependent on financial transfers from the central government, diminishing since the 2008 economic crisis. Since the early 2000s, moreover, their expenditures are subject to the strict constraints of the so-called 'Domestic Stability Pact', instrumental to the requirements of the EU Stability and Growth Pact, with important effects on personnel policies and the provision of services. The number of provinces was reduced in 2012, and they were abolished in 2015, part of their functions and personnel being transferred to regions and partly to the municipalities.

Finally, also the school sector, traditionally characterized by a highly centralized hierarchical organization under the tight control of the central, regional and provincial offices of the Ministry of Education, received some financial and operational autonomy within the process of administrative decentralization of the late 1990s and early 2000s. The about-10,000 school heads, with both didactic and administrative responsibilities, progressively reduced to about 7,000 thanks to processes of aggregation, obtained a qualification as school managers, with a national collective agreement separate from that of the remaining personnel. However, these changes only marginally concerned human resource management matters. The entire teaching and non-teaching staff remained directly employed by the Ministry of

Education and appointed, distributed and transferred by central and peripheral ministerial offices, according to national rules, with no power of choice by the individual school manager. Only a 2015 reform, effective from the academic year 2015–2016, strengthened the managing powers of the school heads, partially increased the financial resources at their disposal and gave them some discretion in hiring part of the teachers and in assigning annual bonuses upon the decision of an appraisal committee chaired by the school manager and composed of representatives of teachers, students (in high schools), parents and one external member.

The Role of Managers

As already seen, the role and functions of the managerial staff in relation to public employers and political authorities, on the one hand, and to trade unions and employees, on the other hand, has been one of the main issues addressed by all the reform waves since 1992–1993. A distinct managerial role, with a separate career from that of the remaining personnel, was introduced in the state/central government sector in 1972, later extended also to the territorial authorities, with some differences. The control of political authorities remained, however, quite strong and pervasive. The principle of distinction of responsibilities between political authorities and managerial staff was clearly affirmed by the major 1992–1993 reform, as mentioned above. The managerial role was distinguished in two hierarchical levels. The employment relationship of the lower level, similar to that of the remaining personnel, was privatized and contractualized, while the employment relationship of top-level state managers remained under public law statute until the second privatization reform of 1998, when it was privatized as well. As above underlined, this change created a double dependence of top-level managers from both trade unions and political authorities, to the detriment of their autonomy (Rusciano 2005, 2008; Talamo 2007; Zoppoli 2009). Moreover, the fact that they could individually negotiate with political authorities the variable component of their salary, on top of the basic salary resulting from collective agreements, allowed an uplift of the salaries of this group between 2000 and 2007; it was three to four times higher than that of all the rest of employees, lower managerial staff included. The 2008 Brunetta reform increased significantly the weight of the variable component of compensation for all managerial staff linked to performance and strengthened their appraisal procedures and the system of responsibilities, but did not address the above-mentioned problem. This was partly addressed by the 2015 reform of the center left government, which contains important principles that widely redesign the managerial role in all public administrations (state, regional and local government). Among others, the reform envisages the creation of three semi-autonomous national commissions, one for each level of government, that to some extent mediate the relationship between political authorities and top-level managers with regard to their appointment and the appraisal of their performance. Moreover, the reform establishes general criteria for the compensation of managers that should avoid the excessive dynamic and differentiation of previous experience. The specification and implementation of these general principles, however, need further legislation, expected in 2016.

The managerial role in the Italian public administration to a large extent corresponds to a career-based system, in which staff are hired through a public contest with a permanent contract and progression occurs from within. However, the 1993 reform opened the possibility also in the central government sector to recruit managerial personnel from outside with a fixed-term employment contract. This possibility was later reaffirmed by all the reform waves, and is currently quantified in 8–10% of the managerial staff of each individual administration. Thus, since 1993, Italy belongs to the group of countries with a mixed system, career-based and position-based, at least to some extent. The number of managers (medical doctors excluded), until recently quite high, even more than three per 100 employees in some subsectors, has decreased since 2008, as an effect of government policies that cut the replacement ratio.

Employers Associations

Since the major 1993 reform, all Italian public administrations, with the exceptions of the five regions and two provinces with a special autonomy statute, are compulsorily and monopolistically represented by ARAN in all national-level negotiations. This legal provision implies that national-level collective agreements apply to all of the about 2.6 million contractualized public employees, with an *erga omnes* effect, differently from the private sector. The purpose of creation of this agency was to 'depoliticize' the collective bargaining process, increase its autonomy and strengthen its transparency, insulating it from the political and parliamentary arenas. The multiplicity of actors that previously used to intervene in the bargaining process and in the management of personnel matters—ministers, political parties, individual parliamentary members—was replaced by a 'technical' agency, endowed with an autonomous legal status. However, the insulation from the political arena can only be limited, for obvious reasons. The financial resources for collective negotiations are decided by the budget law of the state, on government proposal and parliamentary approval, both exposed to party politics. Secondly, the five members of ARAN's executive committee, one of which designated by the Conference of the Regions and another one by the national association of municipalities, are nominated by the government, and their activity is subject to the supervision of the Minister of Public Function. Thirdly, with regard to the general criteria and main aims of negotiations, ARAN has to follow the directives of employers. The role of employers in negotiations was strengthened by the second privatization reform through the creation of the so-called 'sector committees' with the power to send directives to ARAN before the start of the bargaining round, to be informed during the negotiation process and to evaluate the draft agreement before final approval. Four sector committees were created, one for the central government and the school sector, operated by the government itself; one for the regions and the health sector, operated by the conference of the presidents of the regions; one for the local government, operated by the national association of municipalities and provinces; and one for the universities, operated by the conference of the rectors. Such sector committees, by their very nature, are more sensitive to political considerations than ARAN, encouraging trade unions to overcome potential stalemates in negotiations through a direct pressure on them, bypassing ARAN and delegitimizing its authority. The 2009 Brunetta reform tried to address this problem by reducing the number of the sector committees, increasing the control of central government on all of them, strengthening the authority of the president of ARAN, now nominated by a decree of the President of the Republic, and making ARAN's executive committee members incompatible with previous political and trade union responsibilities. However, the effectiveness of these changes is still to be proved, given the freeze of bargaining activity since 2010.

Trade Unions

Since the end of World War II, trade unions and interest associations have always had a large and influential presence in the public sector. Even when the right to collective bargaining was not recognized, they were able to play a pervasive role in the regulation of internal labor market issues (recruitment, careers, mobility, disciplinary matters etc.). After a partial decline in the 1950s, within a general decreasing trend, the membership of public sector unions affiliated to the three main confederations (CGIL, CISL and UIL) started to increase almost constantly through the early 1980s. Public sector members as a proportion of the total membership of the three largest confederations (pensioners excluded) increased from about 10% to 26% in the same period and remains at around 25% in 2014 despite the privatization processes of the previous decades—the stronghold of the Italian trade union movement. As in most advanced economies (Clegg 1976; Visser 2006; Bordogna and Pedersini 2013a; Pedersini 2014), the density rate has always been notably higher than in the private sector, around 50% in the second decade of the 2000s, including also the unions not affiliated with the largest confederations, and is even higher among managerial staff.

An important feature of Italian public sector trade unionism, quite distinct from the private sector, is the high fragmentation of the representation system, particularly intensified in the mid-1980s under the regime of 'double protection' (Bordogna 1989; Cella 1991). This is linked to the strong presence of 'independent' organizations, often craft or professional/occupational unions not affiliated with the largest confederations, which follow the logic of action of special interest groups (Olson 1965), capable of representing in a radical way the interests of their often small membership and to feed disruptive disputes in the public services.

To limit the potential effects of this fragmentation, the second privatization reform introduced precise quantitative criteria of trade union representativeness in order to select the unions admitted to national negotiations and entitled to sign collective agreements with general validity. In each national-level bargaining unit or area, representative unions are those that reach a threshold of at least a 5% average between the percentage of their members on total membership in that bargaining area and the percentage of votes on total votes cast in the elections for the workplace employee representation bodies. Moreover, before signing collective agreements with general validity, ARAN has to ascertain that the signatory unions have together obtained a representativeness of at least 51%. Since the two largest confederations, CGIL and CISL, have a representativeness around 30% each, depending on the sector, the combination of these two rules has proved effective not only in simplifying the bargaining tables, but also in facilitating a certain coordination of union bargaining strategies. The pursuit of very narrow, special interest objectives has been discouraged, and free riding and leapfrogging behaviors have been limited, at least to some extent.

The same legislation established the right to elect every three years, by secret ballot and universal suffrage, employee representation bodies (*RSU—rappresentanze unitarie del personale*) in each administrative unit with more than 15 employees. This means there are more than 70,000 *RSU* representatives, which testifies to the extent to which unions are rooted in Italian public administrations. They have collective bargaining rights at the decentralized level and a pervasive voice in the management of internal labor market issues, widely practiced after the second privatization reform and partly reduced by the Brunetta reform. Since 1998, *RSU* elections were regularly held with a very high participation rate, although partly declining from the initial 80% and more, depending on the sector. The most recent elections for which data are available were held in spring 2012 (data from the 2015 election have not been certified yet by ARAN).

Tables 4.3 and 4.4 confirm three features of public sector trade unionism. First, there is a high union membership, although declining in some sectors in recent years, and there is even higher participation in the *RSU* elections, which contrasts with trends in political elections. Second, there is the great organizational fragmentation, well beyond the traditional divisions along political and ideological lines between the three largest confederations, testified to by the extremely high number of independent unions. Albeit fragmented, all together these unions cover a share of total membership and *RSU* votes, which in some sectors reaches almost 40%. Third, Table 4.4 confirms the effectiveness of the rules for trade union representativeness

Table 4.3 Union Members* and Rsu Votes in Main Subsectors, 2007 and 2012 (Employees Only, Managerial Staff Excluded)

	Ministries**		Regions and Local Authorities***		NHS		Schools****	
	Members	RSU votes	Members	RSU votes	Members	RSU votes	Members	RSU votes
2007	113,243	197,298	242,258	394,489	287,345	376,464	539,617	888,287
2012	97,597	178,595	201,901	397,836	278,810	371,286	550,443	783,703
% change	−13.82	−9.48	−16.66	0.85	−2.97	−1.38	2.01	−11.77

*Data refer to *deleghe*, written notifications undersigned by employees to check off union dues from their monthly pay. The validity of this subscription lasts until the employee formally revokes it.

**Ministries + government agencies + PCM.

***Regions and provinces with special autonomy statute excluded.

****Arts and music schools included.

Source: ARAN.

Table 4.4 Union Representativeness by Main Organizations, 2012 (Employees Only, Managerial Staff Excluded)

	Ministries**		Regions and Local Authorities***		NHS		Schools****	
	Members	RSU votes	Members	RSU votes	Members	RSU votes	Members	RSU votes
CGIL	21.29%	25.53%	36.53%	37.84%	26.64%	28.80%	23.43%	33.14%
CISL	25.10%	22.71%	28.38%	28.84%	25.67%	25.40%	28.18%	24.65%
UIL	19.43%	18.99%	16.25%	17.31%	16.83%	18.03%	13.18%	15.37%
Independent I	13.84%	11.75%	6.13%	5.26%	9.47%	8.99%	18.17%	14.87%
Independent II	8.53%	6.90%			5.26%	5.21%	9.13%	6.34%
Independent III	6.01%	7.02%			5.31%	4.77%		
Independent IV	4.00%	6.65%						
Others independent, not representative	1.82%	0.45%	12.72%	10.75%	10.83%	8.82%	7.90%	5.64%
Total members, total RSU votes	73,486	132,309	201,901	397,836	278,810	371,286	574,158	776,793
Union density, participation rate	45.9%	82.6%	42.2%	83.1%	51.6%	68.7%	54.4%	77.2%
Total number of unions	67		133		100		89	

*Data refer to *deleghe*.
**Ministries only; government agencies and presidency of the council of ministers excluded.
***Regions and provinces with special autonomy statute excluded.
**** Arts and music schools excluded.

Source: ARAN.

introduced in 1997. The 5% threshold is capable of selecting, depending on the sector, four to seven representative unions admitted to the national level negotiation tables, out of a number that is fifteen to twenty times higher (4 out of 139 in the regional and local authorities sector). An inter-confederal agreement between the three largest trade union confederations and the main employers' association, CONFINDUSTRIA, has decided in 2014 to extend this system also to the private sector, including the majority rule for the general validity of collective agreements.

Figure 4.1 summarizes the bargaining structure and the negotiating parties on both sides. The national sector-level bargaining units, initially eight, rose to twelve during the second privatization period and were reduced to at most four by the Brunetta reform. Their boundaries are negotiated by ARAN and the representative confederations before a new bargaining round starts. Cutting them down from twelve to four implies also changes in the list of representative unions.

According to the 2009 rules, which resemble those introduced in the private sector in the same year, the two-tier wage-setting system envisages increases determined in a uniform way every three years by national, industry-level negotiations, taking as reference the inflation rate predicted by an EU source for the relevant period, controlled by imported inflation (energy and food prices). Gaps between actual and predicted inflation are recovered in the following bargaining round. At the lower, single-employer level, there is room for additional wage increases negotiated within guidelines and limits set at a higher level, in principle linked to productivity and to collective and individual performance. However, since 2010, this bargaining machinery has been frozen for five years.

Public sector labor disputes strongly intensified in the second part of the 1980s, related to the fragmentation of trade unions. In 1990, four decades after the enactment of the constitutional law, the Parliament approved a law on the exercise of the right to strike in essential public services, amended in 2000. Essential public services are those instrumental to the fruition of the rights of the person protected by the constitution, part of which are provided by public administrations, and part, like public transports, delivered by private providers with employees under private employment contracts. This legislation found an effective way, based on a mix of legal rules and collective agreements between the relevant parties, under the supervision of an independent authority (*Commissione di Garanzia*), to reconcile the rights of service users and citizens at large with the right to go on strike of public employees, equally protected by the constitution (Treu 2000). Among the legal rules, there is the obligation of at least ten days' advance notice before strike action, and the obligation for the social partners to reach collective agreements, subject to the validation of the Commissione di Garanzia, regarding the provision of minimum services even in the case of a strike. Public service conflict decreased significantly, with the notable exception of the transport sector, like in many countries.

Figure 4.1 Bargaining Levels and Bargaining Agents[a]

Bargaining level and type of agreement	Bargaining agents Employers	Bargaining agents Employees
1. National multi-industry level: - national framework agreements to define bargaining sectors or areas (*comparti* for employees; *area* for managerial staff); - national framework agreements on issues common to two or more sectors or areas	ARAN	'Representative' trade union confederations[b]
2. National industry level (or *comparto*): - sectoral agreements at national level (or CCNL) for non-managerial staff (three-year validity); - area agreements at national level (or CCNL) for managerial staff (three-year validity)	ARAN	- National sectoral trade union organizations (*sindacati di categoria*) which are 'representative' within the sector or bargaining unit/area; - Confederations with which representative trade union organizations within the sector or bargaining unit/area are affiliated
3. Decentralized, single employer level: 'integrative' agreements at single administration unit (a municipality, a region; a hospital etc.).	Head of the administrative unit (or its representatives), with possibility of ARAN assistance	- Unitary workplace employee representation bodies-RSU (legally based and elected every three years in any administrative unit with more than 15 employees); - Other representatives, according to the provisions of national collective agreements (representatives of each territorial structure of union organizations that have signed the national collective agreement)

[a]Trade union representativeness criteria have been defined by the legislative decree no. 369/1997.
[b]Trade union confederations to which, in at least two sectors or bargaining areas, representative sectoral union organizations (*sindacati di categoria*) are affiliated.
[c]Sectoral union organizations with no less than 5% representativeness in their sector or bargaining area, as the average of the percentage of members on total membership and percentage of RSU votes on total votes cast.

Economic Crisis and Public Service Employment Relations

The government measures in response to the 2008 financial and economic crisis have had a direct and heavy impact on public sector employment levels, wages, working conditions and pension arrangements. The link with the reform of employment relations is, however, less direct. On the one hand, the Brunetta reform to some extent predated the crisis and, as noted above, had endogenous reasons, rooted in the weaknesses and unexpected outcomes of the second privatization, although the interactions between the implementation of the reform and government responses to the crisis have been frequent and important. On the other hand, the Renzi government reform arrived when the crisis is declining or is over, and in a sense tried both to amend the most controversial features of the Brunetta reform and to take stock of the transformations induced by the crisis.

Government Responses to the Crisis and Impact on Public Sector Working Conditions

Italy has never been under the financial program of the Troika (European Commission, European Central Bank and International Monetary Fund). However, with a public debt always around or above 100% of the GDP since the advent of the euro (see Chapter 1), not only there was no room for a fiscal stimulus when the crisis arrived, but its financial vulnerability rapidly worsened in the following years, reaching a dramatic peak in summer and autumn 2011. At the beginning of August, a confidential letter to the Italian government by the president of the European Central Bank urgently pressed for 'immediate and bold measures' to ensure fiscal sustainability, among which were 'significantly reducing the cost of public employees, by strengthening turnover rules and, if necessary, by reducing wages'. Some of these measures, often under emergency conditions, had already been adopted by the Berlusconi government in summer 2008, spring 2010 and twice in 2011. Others, in line with the ECB requests, were decided by the Monti government at the end of 2011 and in 2012, among which a major reform of the pension system and the introduction in the constitutional law of the principle of structural balance of the public budget, in accordance with the new EU economic governance (the Europlus Pact and the so-called Fiscal Compact—*Treaty on Stability, Coordination and Governance in the Economic and Monetary Union*). These policies were substantially confirmed by the Letta coalition government (April 2013–February 2014), and (only) partially relaxed under the Renzi government, thanks also to slightly improved economic conditions and a more flexible interpretation of the rules of the Stability and Growth Pact by the European Commission (2015).

Some of these measures were later partially repealed by judgements of the Constitutional Court, but in the meantime, their effects were apparent. All in all, at the end of the crisis, the Italian public administration was to an appreciable extent leaner and less expensive than seven years earlier

(Table 4.1). Total public sector employment at the end of 2014 was 7.3% lower than in 2007, and the public sector pay bill 7.4% lower than in 2009.

Three main sets of measures were adopted, targeted at public sector employment levels, the wages and salaries of public employees and the pension system (Bordogna and Pedersini 2013b). In many cases, they have been of the 'cheese-slicing' type (Pollitt 2010), that is, uniform, across-the-board measures. In other cases, they had a sector- or group-specific character, like specific savings programs devoted to the health or school sectors, or cuts in financial transfers from the central to the local government, or cuts in expenditure for personnel with flexible employment contracts.

Replacement ratios, both of managerial and non-managerial staff, were restricted to 10% in 2009; this percentage was increased to 20% in 2010 and 2011 and 50% in 2012, with some variation across subsectors. In the following years, these measures have been partially relaxed and are expected to be cancelled in 2018. Special measures regarded both teaching and non-teaching staff of the school sector, whose employment levels decreased significantly in the first years of the crisis, only partly compensated by the stabilization policies of temporary staff, notably intensified in 2015. Regions and local authorities were affected by cuts in financial transfers from central government, as well as by the restrictions of the Domestic Stability Pact, introduced in 1998 and severely tightened during the crisis. These cuts had indirect effects not only on employment levels but also, in some cases, on externalization processes and on the quantity and quality of services provided (Bordogna and Neri 2014). Expenditure for temporary staff was cut to half of the 2009 level.

As effect of these measures, the decrease in employment levels has affected the entire public sector, although in an uneven way: it has been more pronounced in the central government and the school sector and less marked in regions and territorial authorities and in the national health service. An indirect effect of the restrictions in replacement ratios has also been an increase in the average age of public employees, already comparatively high, which in turn might negatively affect the quality of public services.

The second set of measures, first adopted in 2008 and then tightened since 2010, regarded the dynamic of wages and salaries of public employees. The 2008 legislation already imposed moderate increases in the 2008–2009 national level bargaining round, about half of the increases agreed upon in previous rounds. But a government decree in May 2010 simply suspended the entire bargaining machinery at the national level, however reformed by the Brunetta legislation, canceling the 2010–2012 bargaining round, with no possibility of recovery in the following rounds. Wages and salaries of all managerial and non-managerial staff, including the non-contractualized groups, were frozen at their 2010 level, with the partial exception of the variable component linked to merit or performance. Later measures extended the suspension of national level collective bargaining and the wage freeze to 2013, 2014 and 2015, with no possibility of recovery and with effect on future pension payments, until a sentence of the Constitutional Court in summer 2015 declared unconstitutional the further extension of these measures. However, at the end of 2015, no negotiation has started yet. Collective negotiations at the decentralized, single-employer level, the main source of wage drift in previous rounds, were not frozen, but highly discouraged by very tight financial constraints. The only possibility left to the bargaining parties was to use a limited proportion of efficiency savings, after certification at the central level. The end-of-service allowance for all public employees was significantly reduced from January 2011. Further measures approved in 2010 affected higher-level salaries, with cuts of 5% and 10% of gross salaries exceeding respectively 90,000 and 150,000 euros a year; but these measures were repealed by the Constitutional Court at the end of 2012, on the grounds that they implied a discrimination between public and private sector employees. Finally, other expenditures were reduced, among which those for the personnel training activities, restricted to no more than 50% of the 2009 amount. Also, spending review procedures have been repeatedly revived, although generally with few effects.

Overall, this wide set of measures has proved effective. The wide gap with the increases of the private sector over the 2000–2007 period has been, first, significantly reduced, and then reversed in the following years (ARAN 2012, 2013a). Also, the total public sector pay bill has to some extent decreased since 2009 (Table 4.1).

The third set of measures, concerning the pension system, related to both private and public employees, although with some provisions targeted at the latter group. Among these was the increase of the standard retirement age for female public employees from 61 to 66, in line with that of male employees, following a 2008 sentence of the European Court of Justice and a recommendation of the European Commission. But the most important measures had a general character, regarding all the employees, private and public, males and females. In particular, the standard pension age was linked to changes in life expectancy, with a prospect to reach at least 67 by January 2021, and the value of pensions was reduced by lowering the protection from inflation and by shifting all employees from an earnings-related to a contributions-related system, including the cohorts of elder workers, previously excluded (Jessoula and Pavolini 2012). Most of the preceding measures have been unilaterally taken by the government without negotiations with trade unions and in some cases, explicitly against trade union protests.

Consequences for Employment Relations

As already noticed, both in the case of the Brunetta and the Renzi-Madia reform, there has been a certain decoupling between measures affecting the institutions of public sector employment relations and austerity policies in response to the crisis, but also important interactions.

Although initially unrelated to the economic crisis, the general logic of the Brunetta reform and the government austerity measures in response to the crisis moved in a convergent direction, at least in the first phase (Bordogna and Pedersini 2013b). In the wake of a vociferous campaign against the alleged privileges of public sector employees and the unjustified power of public sector trade unions, the purpose of the Brunetta reform to restore the responsibility of public sector employers and to redraw the boundaries between unilateralism and joint regulation of employment relations was consistent with the government need to cut the total public sector pay bill. However, as the crisis deteriorated and the urgent need arose to achieve results in the short run, the government found it easier to utilize its peculiar position in public sector employment relations to fully restore unilateralism and get rid entirely of any form of joint regulation, however weakened by the Brunetta legislation. This, incidentally, was also to the detriment of the implementation of other features of the reform, in particular those related to the performance management and performance appraisal system. In a sense, with the suspension of the bargaining machinery, also a large part of the Brunetta reform was frozen.

At the end of the crisis, the bargaining machinery is still suspended and wages and salaries of public employees are still frozen, despite the judgement of the Constitutional Court. The challenge for the Renzi-Madia reform, still framed within the principles of privatization and contractualization of the employment relationship of public employees, is to find a way out from unilateralism, reconfiguring at the same time employment relations institutions capable of avoiding the problematic outcomes of the second privatization reform.

Responses of Employers and Trade Unions

The main trade union confederations had different positions against austerity policies, partly resembling the reactions to the Brunetta reform. The CGIL fiercely opposed them, compared to a more conciliatory attitude adopted by the CISL and UIL. But what is more noteworthy is the overall moderate level of trade union protest. There have been strikes against austerity packages, like those against the measures of May 2010 and of August 2011. But they were mainly called for only by the CGIL, and in any case remained more moderate than on previous occasions or in other European countries. Most surprising is perhaps, especially if compared with previous occasions, the moderate protest against the radical reform of the pension system adopted by the Monti government in December 2011. Probably the same sense of national emergency that justified or supported the unilateralism of the government dampened trade union protest.

Despite the unfavorable context, the elections for the renewal of workplace employee representative bodies have been regularly held in March 2012 and in March 2015 with a high participation rate, although slightly lower than in previous elections. On the employers' side, there were protests against government policies, especially on the part of regions, municipalities and universities against the combination of cuts in financial transfers from the central government with the constraints of the Domestic Stability Pact. On some occasions, the trade union protests seemed to join those of territorial authorities, but in no case were they able to change the substance of austerity policies beyond minor adjustments.

Conclusions

Since the early 1990s, Italian public service employment relations have been experiencing a continuous process of change within a broader restructuring of public administration as a whole. Coming from a Napoleonic state tradition with a Weberian type of bureaucracy and an employment relations system inspired by the sovereign employer model, the major 1992–1993 NPM-inspired reform moved a resolute step towards a private sector model of employment relations. This model is distant from the unilateralism and the special prerogatives of the public law employment statute and firmly based on 'free' collective bargaining and, at least in principle, on business-type HRM practices combined with market, or market-type, incentives. A further, even more resolute step in the same direction was moved by the second privatization reform, the closest to NPM prescriptions, with the expectation that mimicking the private sector rules would produce the same behaviors and the same outcomes. The evidence revealed the fallacy of this expectation, and highlighted the theoretical weaknesses of a design that programmatically ignored the peculiarities of the public sector employer.

The Brunetta reform tried to address these problems in contradictory ways, mainly pursuing a retrenchment of collective bargaining and union prerogatives and building an exceedingly complicated and baroque performance management and performance appraisal system, but leaving without a solution the crucial issue of the role of managers.

The arrival of the crisis, with its emergencies in a country with the second-highest public debt in the EU, opened the way to a full return to unilateralism for more than five years, without any consultation with trade unions. Despite any rhetoric on privatization and contractualization, the government responses to the crisis highlighted once again the irreducible political nature of public service employment relations. This step back toward unilateralism is bound to finish, also by virtue of the 2015 sentence of the Constitutional Court, although it is not clear which directions the Italian employment relations institutions will take after the end of the crisis.

What is clear is that the Italian experience, with all its oscillations, is an instructive example of how difficult in advanced democracies it is to reconcile fully developed union prerogatives and collective bargaining practices with economic and financial sustainability, in a context where market constraints are absent or structurally weak. The uncertain trajectory of public service employment relations reforms in Italy testifies to the theoretical importance of this problem as well as to the practical difficulties of its solution.

Note

1. Over the entire post-WWII period, CGIL, CISL and UIL have been the three largest trade union confederations, traditionally linked, respectively, to the Communist and Socialist Party, to the Christian Democratic Party and to other parties of the center left-wing of the political spectrum (socialist, social democratic and republican parties). Since the mid-1960s, these linkages with political parties have weakened, and the unity of action between the confederations has generally increased, although with periods of harsh contrasts.

References

ARAN (2009) *Rapporto trimestrale sulle retribuzioni dei dipendenti pubblici*, Rome, December.

ARAN (2011) *Rapporto semestrale sulle retribuzioni dei dipendenti pubblici*, Rome, December.

ARAN (2012) *Rapporto semestrale sulle retribuzioni dei dipendenti pubblici*, Rome, June.

ARAN (2013a) *Rapporto semestrale sulle retribuzioni dei dipendenti pubblici*, Rome, June.

ARAN (2013b) *Anzianità ed età del personale pubblico*, Occasional Paper, Rome: n. 3.

Bach, S. and Kessler, I. (2007) 'Human Resource Management and the New Public Management', in Boxall, P., Purcell, J. and Wright, P. (eds.) *The Oxford Handbook of Human Resource Management*, Oxford: Oxford University Press, 469–488.

Beaumont, P. (1992) *Public Sector Industrial Relations*, London: Routledge.

Bordogna, L. (1989) 'The COBAS: Fragmentation of Trade Union Representation and Conflict', in Leonardi, R. and Corbetta, P. (eds.) *Italian Politics*, London: Pinter Publishers, 50–65.

Bordogna, L. (2007) 'La contrattazione collettiva: un nuovo equilibrio tra centralizzazione e decentramento', in Dell'Aringa and Della Rocca (eds.), 63–91.

Bordogna, L. (2008) 'Moral Hazard, Transaction Costs and the Reform of Public Service Employment Relations', *European Journal of Industrial Relations*, 14(4): 381–400.

Bordogna, L., Dell'Aringa, C. and Della Rocca, G. (1999) 'Italy: A Case of Co-Ordinated Decentralization', in Bach, S., Bordogna, L., Della Rocca, G. and Winchester, D. (eds.) *Public Service Employment Relations in Europe. Transformation, Modernisation or Inertia?* London: Routledge, 94–129.

Bordogna, L. and Neri, S. (2011) 'Convergence Towards an NPM Programme or Different Models? Public Service Employment Relations in Italy and France', *The International Journal of Human Resource Management*, 22(11): 2311–2330.

Bordogna, L. and Neri, S. (2014) 'Austerity Policies, Social Dialogue and Public Services in Italian Local Government', *Transfer*, 20(3): 357–371.

Bordogna, L. and Pedersini, R. (2013a) 'Public Sector Industrial Relations in Transition', in European Commission, Directorate-General for Employment, Social Affairs and Inclusion (ed.) *Industrial Relations in Europe 2012*, Luxembourg: Publication Office of the European Union, 93–128.

Bordogna, L. and Pedersini, R. (2013b) 'Economic Crisis and the Politics of Public Service Employment Relations in Italy and France', *European Journal of Industrial Relations*, 19(4): 325–340.

Bordogna, L. and Winchester, D. (2001) 'Collective Bargaining in Western Europe', in Dell'Aringa, C., Della Rocca, G. and Keller, B. (eds.) *Strategic Choices in Reforming Public Service Employment*, New York: Palgrave, 48–70.

Carrieri, M. and Ricciardi, M. (eds) (2006) *L'innovazione imperfetta. Casi di contrattazione integrativa negli enti locali*, Bologna: Il Mulino.

Cella, G. P. (ed) (1991) *Nuovi attori nelle relazioni industriali*, Milano: F. Angeli.

Clegg, H. A. (1975) 'Pluralism in Industrial Relations', *British Journal of Industrial Relations*, 13(3): 309–316.

Clegg, H. A. (1976) *Trade Unionism under Collective Bargaining*, Oxford: Basil Blackwell.

Dell'Aringa, C. (2007) 'Contrattazione collettiva e costo del lavoro', in Dell'Aringa and Della Rocca (eds.), 3–32.

Dell'Aringa, C. and Della Rocca, G. (eds.) (2007) *Pubblici dipendenti: una nuova riforma?*, Soveria Mannelli: Rubbettino.

European Commission (2015) *Communication from the Commission to the European Parliament, the Council, the European Central Bank, the Economic and Social Committee, the Committee of the Regions and the European Investment Bank: Making the Best Use of the Flexibility within the Existing Rules of the Stability and Growth Pact*, Brussels, 13.1.2015: COM(2015) 12 final provisional.

Giugni, G. (1992) 'La privatizzazione del rapporto di lavoro nel settore pubblico', *Lavoro Informazione*, 11: 5–8.

Jessoula, M. and Pavolini, E. (2012) 'Pensions, Healthcare and Long-Term Care in Italy', Asisp Annual National Report.

Kickert, W. (2007) 'Public Management Reforms in Countries with a Napoleonic State Model: France, Italy and Spain', in Pollitt, Ch., van Thiel, S. and Homburg, V. (eds.) *New Public Management in Europe. Adaptation and Alternatives*, London: Palgrave McMillan, 26–51.

Maino, F. and Neri, S. (2011) 'Explaining Welfare Reforms in Italy between Economy and Politics: External Constraints and Endogenous Dynamics', *Social Policy & Administration*, 4: 445–464.

Ministero dell'Economia e delle Finanze-Ragioneria Generale dello Stato (2014) *Analisi di alcuni dati del Conto Annuale 2007–13*, Roma.

Olson, M. (1965) *The Logic of Collective Action*, Cambridge: Harvard University Press.

Ongaro, E. (2009) *Public Management Reform and Modernization: Trajectories of Administrative Change in Italy, France, Greece, Portugal and Spain*, Cheltenham: Edward Elgar.

Ongaro, E. (2011) 'The Role of Politics and Institutions in the Italian Administrative Reform Trajectory', *Public Administration*, 89(3): 738–755.

Pedersini, R. (2014) 'European Industrial Relations between Old and New Trends', *Stato e Mercato*, 3: 341–368.

Pollitt, C. (2007) 'Convergence or Divergence: What Has Been Happening in Europe?', in Pollitt, C., van Thiel, S. and Homburg, V. (eds.) *New Public Management in Europe. Adaptation and Alternatives*, New York: Palgrave McMillan, 10–25.

Pollitt, C. (2010) 'Cuts and Reforms: Public Services as We Move into a New Era', *Society and Economy*, 32(1): 17–31.

Pollitt, C. and Bouckaert, G. (2011) *Public Management Reform: A Comparative Analysis. New Public Management, Governance and the Neo-Weberian State*, Oxford: Oxford University Press.

Ricciardi, M. (2009) 'La contrattazione nel pubblico impiego', in Mascini, M. (ed.) *L'Annuario del lavoro 2009*, Roma: il diariodellavoro, 163–173.

Rusciano, M. (2005) 'Contro la privatizzazione dell'alta dirigenza pubblica', *Diritti, Lavori, Mercati*, 3: 621–632.

Rusciano, M. (2008) 'Contrattazione collettiva e relazioni sindacali nelle pubbliche amministrazioni', in Tursi, A. and Periti, E. (eds.) *Lavoro, cambiamento organizzativo e contrattazione collettiva nelle università*, Bologna: Il Mulino, 21–43.

Talamo, V. (2007) 'Per una dirigenza pubblica riformata', in Dell'Aringa and Della Rocca (eds.) 119–166.

Traxler, F. (1995) 'Farewell to Labour Market Associations? Organized versus Disorganized Decentralization as a Map for Industrial Relations', in Crouch, C. and Traxler, F. (eds.), *Organized Industrial Relations in Europe: What Future?* Aldershot: Avebury, 1–19.

Treu, T. (ed.) (1987) *Public Sector Labour Relations*, Geneva: International Labour Organization.

Treu, T. (2000) 'Il conflitto e le regole', *Giornale di diritto del lavoro e di relazioni industriali*, 86(2): 285–328.

Vignocchi, C. (2007) 'Tre tornate di contrattazione negli enti locali: cosa salvare di un'esperienza controversa', in Dell'Aringa and Della Rocca (eds.) 33–61.

Visser, J. (2006) 'Union Membership Statistics in 24 Countries', *Monthly Labor Review*, January: 38–49.

Zoppoli, L. (2008) 'A dieci anni dalla riforma Bassanini: dirigenza e personale', *Il lavoro nelle pubbliche amministrazioni*, XI: 1–36.

Zoppoli, L. (2009) 'La valutazione delle prestazioni della dirigenza pubblica: nuovi scenari, vecchi problemi, percorsi di "apprendimento istituzionale"', *Quaderni di diritto del lavoro e delle relazioni industriali*, 31: 149–175.

5   France: The Crisis Speeds Up Public Service Reform and Adjustment

Catherine Vincent

Introduction

For the last twenty-five years, successive French governments have been interested in reforming the state. However, the political will to modernize the public service has been accelerating since 2008, a trend further strengthened by the sovereign debt crisis in the euro zone. While the objective of modernization policies has been twofold from the outset—improving the quality and efficiency of public services and curbing public spending—the latter objective has been a priority since 2010. All public officials are certain that modernization can only be achieved through social dialogue and employees' agreeing to state reforms. It might also be because unions have been a key, hence unavoidable, force in public services: until recently, few reforms have been implemented through frontal attacks on trade unions.

From the 2000s, the modernization of the public sector has introduced management by objectives applied to state spending. This new principle of governance—deemed as the only tool able to introduce an efficiency rationale (Lacaze 2005)—has been combined with the priority, as of 2007, to reduce drastically public spending. An overhaul of state service organizational structures has been implemented to improve performance and allow for downsizing. Meanwhile, in the context of austerity that followed, the central government increased the drive to decentralize public services at the local level. The 2010 crisis amplified these policies. After the arrival of a left-wing government in 2012, the only variation in this pattern has been to slow down staff streamlining in several subsectors.

These transformations are accompanied by profound changes in human resource management, inspired by private sector management forms that concretely change workers' situations: developing service projects and employees' empowerment on objectives, attempts to develop a professional public service rather than a statutory one, decentralization of staff management and reform of rating and evaluation procedures (2002) as well as staff mobility (2009). They are also accompanied by a change in the rules of social dialogue: decentralizing consultation bodies, introducing new criteria for trade union representativeness and generalizing collective bargaining (2010). Unions' strategies and the type of role they perform are challenged by these reforms. The model of employment relations in the public sector is being transformed, and unions are struggling to maintain or renew the compromises that had established their legitimacy.

Definition of the Public Sector

In France, the public sector includes three public service branches (hospital, territorial and state) and utilities, mainly in transport and energy. This chapter focuses on the public service that brings together all the organizations subject to administrative law (i.e. the employer's legal category) and where recruitment is based on public law (i.e. the employee's status).

The State Civil Service (*la Fonction publique d'Etat*, FPE) includes central government departments and their decentralized administrations across the territory as well as public administrative institutions (EPA), for example, *Pôle emploi* (the agency in charge of monitoring the unemployed) or the National Centre for Scientific Research (*Centre national de la recherche scientifique*). It employs about 2.4 million workers (see Table 5.1). With just over one million workers, the Ministry of Education (primary and secondary) is the largest public employer. In France, education services are provided by public institutions but also by private ones. The vast majority are partly financed by public funds (these institutions are under contract with the Ministry of Education). Private education, mainly religious-based education, comprises about 30% of pupils and students. Public funding to private schools is used to pay teachers who, therefore, are counted as public servants. There are 840,000 teachers in primary and secondary education, of which just over 700,000 teach in state-run schools, representing 35% of the entire state civil service workforce.

Local authorities (*la Fonction publique Territoriale*, FPT) share areas of intervention at three geographical levels: a) the regions in charge of economic development, transport, vocational training and maintenance of high school buildings; b) the *départements* (counties) in charge of road maintenance and maintaining junior high schools as well as of welfare. The latter represents a growing share of their expenditure; and c) municipalities, in charge of urban planning, environment, maintenance of primary schools and, on a voluntary basis, many local services (kindergartens, libraries, sports facilities etc.). There are nearly 1.9 million local authorities' employees, including 1.5 million at municipal level.

The public hospital service (*Fonction publique hospitalière*, FPH) includes public health and medico-social institutions. Healthcare supply is provided in establishments of three types: state-owned, non-profit private and profit-making private. The public sector covers nearly 65% of hospital capacity. FPH employs 1.1 million employees, with the exception of their medical staff (physicians, hospital pharmacists and orthodontists do not belong to the civil service but have their own status). Healthcare workers account for two-thirds of the workforce of FPH: nurses, orderlies and rehabilitation staff.

Table 5.1 Public Service Employment in France (000s), 1990–2014

	1990	1995	2000	2005	2008	2009	2010	2011	2012	2013	2014
Total	4485.7	4710.1	4831	5273.9	5363.9	5386	5379.4	5358.8	5372.6	5416.9	5431.1
FPE	2357.5	2422.4	2572.3	2658.8	2509.3	2483.7	2457.8	2398.7	2373.2	2385.5	2375.3
Of which:											
Ministries	2169	2214.4	2382	2422.8	2213.7	2135.2	2030.1	1965.9	1922.3	1853	1913.6
EPA	188.5	208	190.3	236	295.6	348.5	427.7	432.8	450.9	532.5	562
FPT	1326.4	1447.5	1328	1562.8	1769.8	1806.5	1811	1830.7	1862.4	1878.7	1894.7
FPH	801.8	840.2	930.7	1052.3	1084.8	1095.8	1110.6	1129.4	1137	1152.7	1161.1

Scope: all staff, tenured and non-tenured employees, excluding subsidized contracts

Source: DGAFP, Insee

Employment Structure and Evolution of the Public Service

Working in public services is strongly identified with servicing the state, which itself embodies the general interest. Since the general interest is identified with the state, the latter has unilaterally granted a status detailing its public servants' rights and duties (Supiot 2000). In the long-standing administrative and legal culture in France, employment in the civil service is characterized by a separate status. This categorization and separation differs from employment in the private sector, which allegedly serves its own special interests, and therefore is regulated and embodied in private law contract.

Despite these differences, there are no clear-cut and precise criteria to establish civil service status. The decision to allocate and categorize a service as state employment reflects historical, social and institutional legacies (Rosenvallon 1990). Though employment relations in the civil service are specific to it, this is not irreversible, as shown, for example, by the privatization of telecommunications activities, historically provided by a central administration and turned into a privately owned company in the late 1990s.

Public Service Employment Trends: A Clear Shift in Staffing Since the Mid-2000s

Public employment is a broad economic concept, referring to all staff working in public bodies or agencies mainly financed by mandatory contributions (social security or private educational institutions, for example). Employment in the public service comprises all employees working for one of the three branches of the public service, regardless of their types of employment: tenured public servants, contract employees on a permanent or a fixed-term contract, on subsidized contracts (one of the key measures of French employment policies) or temporary workers. In 2013, 5.5 million people were working in the three public service branches (not counting subsidized contracts). Among them, nearly 17% (915,000) were public employees without a public servant status. Over the last 10 years, the number of non-tenured staff has increased by 2.8% on average, while the total number has been increasing by 1.3%. Despite many agreements signed on this subject with trade unions, reducing precariousness has not actually happened. In France, public employment still accounts for about a quarter of the total workforce and the public service itself almost 20%.

Public servants are divided into three categories: A (supervisors and highly qualified professionals), B (middle management and qualified professionals) and C (operational personnel). Almost three in ten public servants belong to Category A, but distribution by hierarchical categories differs substantially according to the various branches of the public service. It is in the state administration that most skilled jobs are found, explained by the size of the teaching profession within this category. This results in 49.6% of state administration comprising Category A, compared to 15% of the public hospital service and 8% in local authorities. The latter, however, is largely made up of operational employees (76.1% are Category C).

Women are in the majority in public services (52%). They account for about three-quarters of hospital staff; in particular, nurses, midwives and caregivers are highly feminized occupations. By contrast, maintenance and associated jobs are dominated by men (71%). Gender specialization of tasks remains high and no significant developments in this area seem to be emerging. The proportion of women in Category A is increasing steadily (62% across all public services), but is slightly lower (60%) in the state civil service branch (FPE), and if teachers are excluded, this figure would be even lower at 44%. Women are still under-represented in senior management and executive jobs. Nonetheless, public employers are more progressive than private sector employers: a real effort towards women's advancement has been made since 2013, supported by agreements negotiated with the trade unions.

In the public service as a whole, employment has almost been stable since 2004, quite a departure from the upward trends typical of previous decades. In more recent years, a slight downtrend has been observed. The growth of state civil service staff has posted a real downward trend since the mid-2000s. Between 2006 and 2011, FPE staffing decreased by 16.5%. Shifts in FPE employment result from two types of adjustment: net job losses per se, owing to non-replacement of departing staff, and staffing cuts from the redeployment of people to other public service branches, mainly local authorities in recent years. Excluding staff transfers, between 2006 and 2011, ministries (a combination of central and decentralized administrations) downsized staffing by 5.3%. Reductions in the recruitment of state tenured staff was initiated in the early 2000s and led in 2003 to strict regulation of recruitment following retirement. After Nicolas Sarkozy's election to the French Presidency in mid-2007, the rule of not replacing one retiring civil servant out of two was passed. This rule applies only to the FPE. Ultimately, declining recruitment in central government is close to what was observed in the 1990s in countries that deeply restructured their state apparatus (Sweden and Canada).

An analysis of workforce trends indicates that until 2008, the net destruction caused by ministries was more than compensated for by job growth in local authorities and the public hospital service, even excluding outside transfers. Employment growth has not stopped, but has significantly slowed down since the end of 2004.

Resizing the state has serious consequences in terms of the reorganization of state structures and productivity issues that accompany this process. It has led to an employment consolidation trend and the redefinition of management methods.

Public Service Employment Relations: Hybridizing the Public Model of Industrial Relations

The general structures of employment relations in the public and private sectors differ from each other. Despite a hybridization of the two models (initiated as early on as the creation of the civil service status in 1946), representing employees' interests remains specific in the public sector. The characterization of public employment by status—as opposed to private employment, which is ruled by contract—corresponds to a system of specific industrial relations. The state unilaterally decides on terms and conditions of employment, though not without consulting employee representatives to inform its decision-making. In the private sector's collective bargaining model, it is the agreement between parties that underpins the validity of the employment rules (Saglio 2001).

The Creation of a Civil Service Status

The adoption of a protective status dates back to 1946, but the creation of a general status common to all three branches of the public service only goes back to 1983. This status defines public servants' rights and obligations, including: permanent jobs occupied by tenured permanent public servants, recruitment by competitive examinations and a right to a career that defines procedures for minimum promotion in line with seniority (length of service).

Public servants are recruited in hierarchically categorized (A, B, C) groups called *corps* (body). Career advancement takes place within each *corps*, itself divided into grades.[1] Within a grade, promotion is mainly based on seniority. Promotion to a higher grade is never automatic but occurs in various ways: at the administration's discretion, after consultation with employee representatives; via professional examinations or competitive examinations. Transition from one grade to another is framed by statute but also budgetary requirements; the rate of promotions is prescribed by the Finance Act (*loi de finances*). Mobility between categories is high: for example, one category B agent in two is promoted to category A during their careers. The practice of promotion and career paths varies and is far from uniform across different bodies (*corps*). What appears as a highly uniform and centralized structure conceals branches and departments that are managed very differently on the basis of opaque practices. Mobility between the three branches of the public service is rare.

Conditions of employment are much more differentiated within local authorities (FPT) or the public hospital service (FPH). On one hand, employees that have passed the competitive exams (at national or territorial level) must be recruited by their local employers (the hospital director or the mayor, for example). On the other hand, a larger share of highly qualified contractors is employed there as well: managers hired on political criteria (a spoils system) into local authorities, doctors working both in public hospitals and the private sector and others. Mobility between the private and public sector is higher in both these branches of the public service.

The public service status is unique in that it involves employee representatives in the management of individual careers sitting on joint administrative committees (*commissions administrative paritaires*, CAP) and organizes departments through advisory committees. Before reforms in 2010, employer-appointed representatives and employee representatives elected by all employees, but based on trade union lists, had equal representation, but subsequent to the 2010 reforms, this position has been modified.

The consultation bodies dealing with departments' organization—the Technical Committees (*comités techniques*, CT)—are consulted on organizational changes (budgetary rules, staffing trends etc.) and on the collective elements of working conditions. They are set up at all levels of administrative structures with, at the top, a council for every public service (FPE, FPT, FPH) plus a board common to all three. Until 2010, CTs were joint bodies. Their performance results were mixed (Fournier 2002), and they used to play a rather formal role: the administrative hierarchy acting as dormant representatives, except for the most senior one; union representatives clinging to their positions. In order to revitalize this institution, its functioning was made more akin to that of works councils (*comités d'entreprise*) in the private sector. In 1991, the Establishment Technical Committees (*comités techniques d'établissement*) were introduced in the hospital sector and, in the rest of the public service, the *comités techniques* were established after 2010.

CAPs are consulted on individual elements of employment relations (recruitment, rating, assignment, promotion, disciplinary action and so on). Commissions are set up for each public servants' *corps*. Since the early 2000s, CAPs have been decentralized in some services. In hospitals, for instance, a CAP can legally be set up if four employees belonging to one category or another work in the institution. In others, like the Ministry of Finance, a collective agreement set up the decentralization. There is no equivalent body in the private sector. CAPs are the basic institution of public sector employment relations. Trade unions have used these legally based employee representative bodies to provide visibility and legitimacy for their actions. From a legal point of view, they are purely advisory bodies where workers, speaking through their elected representatives, make their views known to their supervisors, who are not required to act on these views. In many state departments, CAPs stick more or less strictly to this advisory role, and unions just restrict themselves to informing—or enlightening, as one might say—the decisions made by the administration by telling them what employees think. The work undertaken by employee representatives in these joint bodies, however, is not unimportant. In other state departments, as is the case in the Ministry of Finance but especially of Education, CAPs are a real instrument for unions' involvement in the drafting of statutory rules and internal labour market management. Unions have imposed a genuine co-determination of collective criteria for employees' individual career management (Tallard and Vincent 2009). Public sector unions have built their strength and ability to protest based on their links to the shop floor through CAPs.

Collective Rights: The Right to Strike and Collective Bargaining

In terms of collective rights, the full right of association (except for armed forces) and the right to strike are constitutionally protected. All public employees (except military personnel, police, magistrates and prison guards) enjoy the right to strike with special regulations: advance notice by unions before taking industrial action and compulsory negotiations between administrative employers and trade unions during the period of notice. In addition, the provision of minimum service is laid down for those providing essential public services, such as health and transport services. By contrast, until recently, there was no scope for collective bargaining, despite some partial recognition in a 1983 law (see below). In the absence of negotiations, trade unions can only challenge the employer's decision by exercising the right to strike. Conflict is therefore an inherent component of the system of social rules in the public service. The emergence of the recognition of bargaining in the public service has been concomitant, over the last decades, with a decline in conflict proneness. Bargaining practices have gradually established themselves and have been legally acknowledged since 2010. However, bargaining rights remain rather weak and, regarding wages, embedded in specific procedures (Bordogna and Neri 2011).

In France, the 1981 political shift (the election of a socialist president after more than twenty years of right-wing presidents and governments) put on the agenda a new positioning of the state, in which it tried to get the whole of society mobilized to combine economic development and social progress. In this dynamic, wage earners' rights were to be transformed in the 1980s, and this agenda had major implications for public servants as well.

While, at the time, their status still made no reference to bargaining, the 1983 Act homogenizing the three public services recognized the possibility for public sector unions to conduct, together with the government, 'negotiations prior to the determination of remuneration and talks with the authorities responsible for managing the various levels', issues relating to working conditions and organization'. The agreement had no independent legal value and was only morally and politically binding on signatories, but this was beneficial for the unions, as the administration had hitherto always honored its commitments by translating the content of agreements into legislative or regulatory form. A degree of ambiguity in the 1983 act enabled bargaining to extend beyond the intent of the law and extended into many new fields. Although unions had, in theory at least, only the right to 'discuss' the following topics, agreements included: the 1989 protocol to renovate the public service wage grid, the 1989, 1992 and 1996 framework agreements on vocational training and the 1996 protocol that created the end of career leave, as well as the 1996 and 2000 agreements on precarious employment.

Regarding wages, the wage-setting system is still highly centralized. Even if some room for negotiations was recognized in 1983, the government has never been obliged to open negotiations, much less to reach an agreement. The government has kept the ability to set or freeze wage rates unilaterally. Even when an agreement has been reached, it cannot be implemented without being confirmed by the Parliament. Public servants in each grade are classified in a wage grid: according to their position, they are assigned a number of index points. Their base wage (excluding bonuses and benefits) is reckoned by multiplying this figure by the value of the index point. Traditionally, it is the value of the index point that is the subject of annual wage bargaining. Despite staunch union opposition, the automatic link to inflation of this index was discontinued in1983 and replaced by a yearly increase target in public service payroll. By signing an agreement in 1985, most of the public service unions agreed the new method of calculation. Since then and up to 1999 (except for 1996 and 1997), agreements were reached each year, rarely on an across-the-board wage increases, but related to structural changes or targeted at specific groups (special measures for low-paid employees, specific increases for categories of public servants, redesign of the wage grid (1989), incentive plans etc.). However, since the 2000s, in contrast to what happened in the private sector, the deployment of bargaining has resulted in a deadlock in the wage area, due to rising pressure to contain the wage bill (with the exception of the 2006 and 2008 agreements). Bargaining on working time was also unsuccessful, as the introduction of the 35-hour working week modeled on the private sector proved complicated in a context of stable staffing levels. Nonetheless, social dialogue did have some influence on wage fixing up to 2010.

In this context, the civil hospital service looks exceptional. Agreements, often innovative in content, have been concluded since the early 2000s. The introduction of reduced working time (a 35-hour week) with no job creation became a source of conflict, in a context already marked by health expenditure controls. The magnitude of the social movement, and the negotiations that ensued, have embedded bargaining and assisted the development of social dialogue. The March 14, 2000 agreement concerned 'the modernization of the public hospital sector, organized enrolment growth and forward-looking employment and skills management' (GPEC, *Gestion prévisionnelle des emplois et des compétences*). Strong emphasis was also placed on the development of social dialogue at all levels, particularly in hospitals (Tallard and Vincent 2010).

The need to renew industrial relations and provide a legal basis and stable bargaining procedures was felt by all players but was not formalized until the 2010 law, which established collective bargaining procedures. The new legislation does not change wage bargaining.

Reforming Social Dialogue

The reform of social dialogue in the public service results from a long reflection and consultation process. This led to a series of agreements signed on June 2, 2008, by all trade union federations' officials, with the exception of the FO Union (*Force ouvrière*) and the French Confederation of Christian Workers (*Confédération française des travailleurs chrétiens*, CFTC), and later, their transposition into law in the July 5, 2010 law on the renewal of social dialogue. Such agreements were innovative in that they were the first to have been concluded on such a topic since the creation of the public service, and they were signed by many trade unions.

The 2010 reform enshrined the hybridization of the private and public models by introducing new representativeness criteria based on those found in the private sector;[2] bargaining rights at all levels, except on wage issues; the devolution of advisory bodies and the removal of the parity principle in CTs. Signatory unions therefore accepted this dilution of the specific features of the public service model of employment relations. Opposition to this dilution and distancing from a distinctive public service model of employment regulation led to two trade unions refusing to sign the agreement.

The most significant changes relate to CTs. The 2010 reform introduced elections for employee representatives rather than being appointed by trade unions; their powers were also extended. The law made them the central forum for employee representation, at the expense of CAPs. CAPs have also been decentralized to the local level. Unions were initially very much opposed to the aim of decentralizing CAPs to the local level, because they believed that multiplying decision-making places might increase variability in approach and result in a loss of equity guarantees in terms of staff mobility and careers. A compromise was finally struck when the government gave up on removing the parity principle of representation (as had occurred in relation to CTs) in CAPs.

In terms of representativeness, because of the shifting role of CAPs, the election of CTs has become decisive. CTs are organized on the basis of broader organizational constituencies amongst all staff categories, including contractors, rather than specific occupational groups. These different electoral criteria impact the outcomes of elections, benefiting trade unions with a broader appeal. The representativeness criterion adopted by the law has no minimum threshold, as in the private sector, but is based on the union obtaining a sufficient percentage to have at least one seat on the CT of the level of interest. The representation threshold depends directly on the number of seats provided in the relevant body, and that number is in turn determined at the administration's discretion. The reform also defines more specifically the conditions to stand for elections: the union must have existed for two years and abide by republican values. The impact of the reform at the local level has therefore been quite different from the way it has affected the private sector, including maintaining the representativeness of many autonomous unions (not affiliated with the main trade union confederations).

Finally, regarding collective bargaining, renewal remains incomplete. It is generalized down to the local level, but the law does not confer on agreements legally binding status, as only their legislative or regulatory implementation grants them normative scope. Changes have occurred, but remain within the existing framework. However, agreements' validity conditions have been defined with great precision. Only representative organizations may take part in negotiations, and agreements must have been signed by unions that are representative of the majority as indicated by votes cast.

The 2008 agreements are remarkable for the willingness that unions demonstrated to reform employment relations rules—together with the government—despite the conflictual context. Downsizing, budget constraints and large-scale, imposed organizational change was hardly conducive to effective dialogue. It is mainly this difficult context that explains the conclusion of few agreements, especially at the ministerial and local levels. In 2015, at the three public services branches level, only three agreements have been signed: the 2011 agreement on precarious employment, the 2013 agreement on gender professional equality and the 2015 agreement on work-life quality.

The Evolutions of the Model in a Context of New Public Management

In conventional analysis, employment relations in the private sector form a system resulting from the interactions between employees, employers and government. Transposing the analysis into the public service immediately raises the issue of the lack of separation between the role of the state as employer and the role of the state as regulator and custodian of the system of employment relations. This is evident in the State Civil Service where, despite the recent introduction of bargaining procedures, rules governing employment relationships are determined by the state authority. This confusion of roles is less marked in the hospital and local authority public services because of their decentralized organization. Despite centralization elements derived from the 1983 common status (national competitive exams, wages determined by national rules), some leeway still exists in staff management (working time, bonuses, promotions). Local authorities' autonomy has also been reinforced by the February 19, 2007, law, which removes promotion quotas and leaves local councilors more choice in promotion matters. At hospital level, the figure of the employer, embodied by the hospital director, approximates to that of the employer in the private sector, due to its relative autonomy both in the allocation of the budget and in the management of non-medical staff, making the director 'a local entrepreneur in the hospital public service' (Schweyer 2001).

Consequently, the introductions of new forms of staff management have differed between the three branches of the public service both in terms of type and timescale.

Budgetary Control Designed to Foster Public Services Modernization

The development in Europe of New Public Management (NPM) Policies has directed a lot of interest at encouraging modernization in France by reference to policies implemented in the private sector and in other countries (Bach and Bordogna 2011; Bezes and Jeannot 2011). In the 1990s and 2000s, with some time lag, under the impetus of the so-called Rocard circular,[3] practices inspired from the private sector and traditionally little used in the French public service—such as collective bargaining, GPEC devices— were disseminated in specific forms. Because of resistance to change, as much from staff as from the administrative hierarchy, changes were initially minimal, except in the public hospital service (see below).

A decade later, in 1998, the Jospin circular[4] followed the same reform agenda, but implementation deadlines were more coercive. It adopted the same objectives, but provided more impetus to state reform by the use of multi-year 3-to-5-year modernization programs developed by each ministry, jointly with the Finance Ministry. In early 2000, the LOLF (*Loi organique relative aux lois de finances*), supported by the socialist Finance Minister, Laurent Fabius, and passed unanimously, introduced genuine expenditure control by implementing budgetary control mechanisms at all levels of state administration.

Anxious to preserve local councilors' autonomy, MPs have until very recently left local government services outside the scope of budgetary control. In contrast, changes happened earlier and more significantly in the public hospital service. Initiated in 1991 (Evin law) and intended to reduce Social Security's chronic deficits while curbing health spending, it was reinforced in 1996 (Juppé law). The hospital system reorganization affected both healthcare provision methods and funding allocation mechanisms that encouraged hospitals—whether public or private—to compete amongst themselves. Optimal resource allocation is based on the health administration taking over skills previously held by social partners in the health insurance system (*Assurance-maladie*). The development of health maps/planning tools and hospital financing arrangements are overseen by regional agencies (*Agences régionales de santé*) that are a decentralized administrative level of the Health Ministry rather than an executive agency in the English-speaking countries' sense of the term. Due to its own governance arrangements and the specific management/employee relations that arise from the autonomy of hospitals, the hospital sector has changed rapidly. It has refocused on its core business through a policy of systematically outsourcing activities that are not directly related to healthcare (catering, laundry, maintenance etc), and hospitals have therefore embraced many aspects of NPM.

An NPM Within the Status

The renewal philosophy of the public service is based on two pillars: improving relations with users by bringing the administration closer to citizens, and getting public servants involved in change by turning them into active stakeholders of change. The implementation of new HRM forms belongs to the second pillar. The approach is to maintain the framework of the public servants' status but adapt it to changing requirements, techniques and skills and as a result, 'move from a purely statutory management to a more trade and skills-centered management' (Rocard circular). This new HRM is based on classic tools in this respect: training executives in management and in team leadership and increased effort in vocational training, while encouraging mobility and facilitating career paths.

The desire to 'promote a results culture' is reflected in a more managerial approach, characterized by greater proximity to staff and individualization. Thus, the establishment of local HR correspondents in each department aims to develop a local human resources policy, thereby pulling the rug from under unions, which used to undertake this role. This new form of HRM was affirmed by the reform of assessment and scoring procedures (2002 Decree, April 29).

In the state civil service, assessing employees' professional value includes a general judgment and a numerical score that determines the rate of advance to the next level. The previous rating process seemed transparent and fair to civil servants' unions, because a joint consensus was reached that implied providing acceptable career paths for all staff. In addition, a national equalization mechanism in each grade limited managers' flexibility and prevented employees in the same department from comparing their respective marks. The new procedure disrupted these patterns: objectives have been set from one year to the next and are used as a basis for assessing and achieving greater differentiation of individuals' progression, conferring greater discretion and authority to department heads. It introduced the concept of a yearly contract (appraisal) concluded individually with each civil servant, designed to enable the administrative hierarchy to discern and identify an elite's outstanding performance; however, unions believe this process only results in employees competing with each other.

The reform of the rating process was opposed by unions and triggered sporadic conflicts, including at the Ministry of Finance, which had made a radical interpretation of it (Tallard and Vincent 2009). These reactions did not prevent the implementation of the law but only limited its effects in terms of individualization, enhancing the possibilities of challenging a rating in the CAP.

It is especially in the area of performance management that changes have been most important, with major consequences for middle management's working conditions as management responsibility is pushed down throughout the management hierarchy. A 'management dialogue' in which managers at all levels agree on objectives, how to achieve them and success criteria, aimed to modify existing top-down management methods. The main lever for such performance-based steering relates to constantly increasing quantitative indicators throughout ministries. However, in a context of budgetary constraints, this control mode increases pressure on local managers and is a source of diffuse but nonetheless real malaise (Brière *et al.* 2012).

This individualization process is also manifest in wage setting. Variable pay components have increased in all public servants' compensation, but for managers, they are granted mainly on the grounds of performance. In 2008, the share of awards and bonuses in total compensation (including overtime) was 15.5% in FPE, 17.4% in FPT and 23.4% in FPH. If we look at how these awards are shared out by professional categories, for top managers, 65% of total compensation comprises variable pay and bonuses, compared to 37% for police officers; for teachers, the proportion falls to 10% (mainly comprising overtime).

Since the late 1980s, the methods to reform the state have involved managerial techniques borrowed from private enterprises. Establishing a more managerial staff management approach was carried out by developing a bargaining rationale over public servants' working conditions but without calling into question the existence of the public service status. Nevertheless, the overhaul of many aspects of this status allows changes in the way employment relations are managed (see below).

Influential But Divided Unions

As noted earlier, transposing the usual analysis on employment relations into the public service raises complex issues, i.e., the lack of separation between the role of employer and regulator, but also in relation to the role of trade unions as collective stakeholders in this environment. Unions established their legitimacy by specific forms of relationship with management leaders, but also in their privileged links with staff. The role of trade unions in both the public and private sectors is to defend workers' interests, but public sector unions sought to balance defending public servants' interests while supporting the overall mission of public services and affirming their role in the implementation of public policies (Vincent *et al.* 2005). The links between union officials and staff have been developed on the basis of a common understanding of the public service's missions that unions seek to advocate because they stem from legitimate political decision-making. Grounded in the visibility and legitimacy of their action in CAPs as well as the trust-based relationships they have with the staff, unions obtained strong representational influence in dealing with senior managers.

Unionism in the public sector is characterized by both the relative numerical strength of its members—the average unionization rate in all three public services ranges from 15 to 20%, as against 5% in the private sector—and the multiplicity of organizations. Although the right to organize was granted to public servants in 1946—alongside many professional associations that switched to becoming autonomous unions—major trade union confederations were tolerated by political authorities from the 1920s. Public service unions were therefore established on a corporate basis (by department) and included middle managers, designed to assert their own rights over the political and administrative elite that directs the state.

Within the CGT, state civil service unions are grouped in the public servants' General Union Federation (*Union générale des fédérations de fonctionnaires*). Major federations belong to the finance and infrastructure ministries. In the hospital sector, the health and social welfare is particularly well established among category C employees. CGT has been weakened by the decline in the relative weight of this category among all public servants.

The weight of the public service is considerable in *Force Ouvrière*, which is less well established in the private sector than the CGT. The General Federation of Civil Servants (*Fédération générale des fonctionnaires*) consists primarily of the finance, police and national defense federations. *Force Ouvrière* became the first state civil service union in 2011. Staff in the other two public branches are grouped within the Federation of public services and Health Services (*fédération des Services publics et de santé*). The latter remains the largest of *Force Ouvrière*'s federations, especially due to its very extensive presence in local government.

Within the CFDT, the Union of Public Servants' Federations and Related Staff (*Union des fédérations des fonctionnaires et assimilés*), founded in 1973, is an umbrella organization for all three public services. The most important federations are the General Trade Union of Education (*Syndicat général de l'Education nationale*), *Interco*, which includes local authority staff and the Social and Health Federation (*Fédération santé-sociaux*) which, like the CGT, includes hospital and social care staff. Due to its isolation when supporting pension reform in 2003, the CFDT is in decline in terms of membership and influence.

The last two representative confederations in the private sector, the CFTC and the CFE-CGC (managers and professional staff), are very poorly represented in the public service. The latter is only present in very few ministries, such as finance and the police.

Unlike the private sector, powerful autonomous unions (that is, not affiliated with the main trade union confederations) exist in the public service. When the CGT and *Force Ouvriere* split in 1948, some federations chose to preserve their unity by declaring they were autonomous—the main example being the National Federation of Education (Fédération de l'Education nationale, FEN). National education is the only public sector where unions are structured on the basis of trades/occupations (teachers in general education, technical education, management staff, administrative staff etc.). Long enjoying hegemony in this area, FEN is paying an expensive price for splitting in 1993 (see below). Established in 1945, the Autonomous Federation of Territorial Public Service (*Fédération autonome de la Fonction publique territorial*, FA-FPT) is a union comprising more than 250 local government employees' trade unions. In a world where elected politicians act as their employers, it boasts staunch independence vis-à-vis local political power.

During the year 1993, a new wave of fragmentation of union representation occurred in the public service, with the creation of new independent unions and the restructuring of existing clusters. Autonomous unionism has since been polarized between a reformist movement and an antagonistic one. Within the reformist movement, a new group has emerged: the National Union of Autonomous Unions (*Union nationale des syndicats autonomes*, UNSA). Created in 1993 by FEN, it includes a number of independent unions, among then education, the police and the defense department. UNSA has taken some hold in the private sector but has so far failed to achieve representative status in this area. In the protest pole, we first find the Unitary Union Federation of Teachers (*Fédération syndicale unitaire de l'enseignement*, FSU), after FEN splintered in 1993. The FSU remains the leading organization in national education, but their attempts to gain a foothold in other departments have not yet been successful. The second component is the Federation of Solidarity unions (*Union Syndicale Solidaires*). *Solidaires* mainly results from the grouping of SUD (solidarity, union, democracy) following a series of splits to the left of the CFDT. One of the trade union founders of *Solidaires* is the SUD health sector union, relatively well established in hospitals.

As in the private sector, trade union presence in the public service is difficult to assess, both in terms of membership and location. Although participation has been declining steadily for two decades, professional elections are a good indicator in assessing unions' respective influence. The December 2014 elections were the first to take place simultaneously in all three branches of the public service since the adoption of the new rules on representativeness. Although nine organizations are recognized as representative of the whole public service, the election results grouped around the three main trade union confederations in the private sector (CGT, CFDT, FO), plus the FSU and UNSA in the state civil service. The elections confirmed trends previously identified: a steady erosion of the CGT, the growth of FO and UNSA and the stagnation of the CFDT.

In summary, a fragmented and often divided unionism confronted the state's reform policies, but trade unions remain influential.

Table 5.2 CT Election Results in the Public Services (in %) (France)

	Public services		FPE		FPT		FPH	
	2008/2010/2011*	2014	2011	2014	2008	2014	2011	2014
Participation rate	54.6	52.8	53.0	52.3	60.9	54.9	51.0	50.1
CGT	25.3	23.1	15.8	13.4	33.0	29.5	33.6	32.1
CFDT	19.2	19.2	14.6	14.0	21.9	22.3	24.4	24.8
FO	18.2	18.6	16.6	17.0	17.4	17.7	22.8	23.8
UNSA	9.2	10.3	14.0	14.8	6.3	8.2	4.3	4.6
FSU	8.2	8.0	15.8	15.6	3.1	3.3	-	-
Solidaires	6.6	6.8	8.6	9.0	2.9	3.5	8.9	8.5
CFTC	4.0	3.3	3.9	3.3	4.7	3.5	2.9	2.9
CGC	2.9	2.9	5.2	5.4	1.3	1.4	0.4	0.5
Divers	6.4	7.8	5.5	-	9.4**	10.7**	2.7	2.8

*The elections took place on the same day for the 3 branches of public services in 2014. The previous election was in November 2011 for the FPE, in 2010 for the FPH and in 2008 for CAP in the FPT.
**mainly FA-FPT

Source: DGAFP, Ministry of Public services.

A Delayed Impact of the Crisis

From 2007 onwards, with the election of President Nicolas Sarkozy—whose electoral platform included significantly reducing public deficits by lower public spending—the reform movement has accelerated. In the state administration (FPE), pressures to implement quantitative adjustments have been intensifying, with a drive to maintain strict wage moderation and increased downsizing (Bordogna and Pedersini 2013). The new policy is especially remarkable in terms of the implementation of large-scale structural reform. The economic crisis coincided with the acceleration of reforms: it is therefore difficult to distinguish between measures resulting from a political shift from those induced by the crisis. However, from 2010 onwards, it has become clear that the desire to meet European commitments to budget moderation has become the main driver of change. Nonetheless, when a socialist government took office in 2012, it modified this stance, allowing more recruitment, but only in education (for teachers) and justice (for judges). Overall, wage moderation and the objective of controlling the number of public sector jobs have been maintained. By the end of 2013, pressures from the European Commission have been pushing for the adoption of drastic public spending reduction policies. The extension to local authorities of the austerity policy is now officially linked to a commitment to reduce the public account deficit.

*An Ambitious Structural Reorganization Amid
Increased Demands*

The new policy—approved in 2007 and reinforced in 2009—consists of an analysis of all public service missions in order to better link activities to users' needs and thus reduce public spending. Dubbed the General Review of Public Policies (*Révision générale des politiques publiques*, RGPP), its content is close to policies implemented in other countries such as Canada between 1994 and 1998, called the Program Review, or in Sweden. Although, in France, the RGPP did not have as great organizational consequences as has been noted in these two countries, this reform is unprecedented in terms of administrative organization and public spending. The reorganization unfolds along three axes. First, some measures aim to influence the scope of public intervention: the deletion of measures considered obsolete and transferring to the private sector activities deemed too expensive (e.g., mountain rescue services etc). Second, some measures change the ways organizations are managed: development of public-private partnerships for large investments (building hospitals and stadiums) and outsourcing of peripheral functions. Finally, the most significant measures seek to improve efficiency in the provision of public services:[5] the creation of a central agency to manage young teachers to assist in filling vacancies and the establishment of a single tax service by merging the two main branches of the Ministry of Finance (taxes and public accounting), as well as pooling the support functions of state services devolved to the regional level.

One of the objectives of RGPP, if not the main one, has been to restore the public finances, and the key measure taken since 2008 was the decision not to replace one in two staff that retire. By maximizing the prospects of a significant number of retirements between 2009 and 2012, the implementation of this accounting rule had important effects in terms of declining recruitment in the state civil service. Since 2008, this has contributed to 40% of the decline in state civil service employment—this translates into an average annual decline of 1.5% in the workforce in this area. In ministries, employment declined by 2.3% in 2012 compared with 2011 and by 0.3% in 2013 but increased in public institutions (+ 0.4% in 2012 and + 1.9% in 2013). As mentioned earlier, these changes can be explained in part by the continued transfers from the former to the latter. However, by neutralizing this effect, the increase in public institutions' staffing remains at above 2% in 2012 and, in each state department, particularly in defense, declining recruitment has finally been achieved (INSEE 2014).

However, the contribution of each ministry to this overall downsizing effort differs substantially. Indeed, policy makers adjust replacement rates to their political priorities. Over the 2008–2011 period, the education, security, justice and social ministries were relatively spared. Conversely, other departments applied harsher alternative replacement standards, namely finance, defense, culture, infrastructure and ecology (CAS 2011). The cumulative decline between

2006 and 2011 in recruitment in these departments was 9%. Trade-offs have also been made between different categories. The decrease in recruitment is particularly noticeable in Category C, where the non-replacement of retirees is more than twice as high as Category A employees and nearly three times that of Category B. The continuation of these trends until 2020 would lead to the dominance of Category A staff; they would account for two-thirds of the state civil service.

Throughout the public service, overall recruitment has kept increasing slightly (+ 0.3% in 2012 and + 0.7% in 2013), the other two branches off-setting the decline recorded in the FPE: still in local government, + 1.7% in 2012 and + 0.9% in 2013 and in the public hospital sector, + 0.7% in 2012 and +1.4% in 2013. The local civil service (FPT) remains the main engine of job creation. In ten years (2002–2012), its workforce has grown by 33.4%, in a context of some tasks being increasingly allocated to local government, especially with continued decentralization and employee transfers.

A Restructuring of Status and Compensation

The scale of reorganization and job cuts has generated strong tensions in terms of human resource reallocation. In a context of workforce contraction, only internal or external mobility could reduce these tensions and manage the likely short staffing in essential functions. The development of a public service based on employment contract rather than status has been one of the cornerstones of ongoing reforms (Silicani 2008). This strategic issue, however, was associated with few concrete measures other than civil servant mobility.

The 2009 law on public servants' mobility promoted and organized mobility within the public service. It allows public servants to take a new position in another department and harmonizes dismissal practices between the three public branches. It also regulates job mobility in case of state administration restructuring. There was no job security enshrined into the public service status. Even if it was rare, economic redundancies unilaterally decided by the government had already been used to reduce staffing (in the defense ministry and public hospitals, for example). The status only imposed an obligation to propose three alternative public employment job offers to the affected public servants. In a way, the new law includes more protective provisions (Rouban 2014). Henceforth, those 'at risk' employees can be placed in a situation of career transition and benefit from personalized professional development designed by their ministry in order to make sure they can continue in employment. If they refuse three successive offers of public employment corresponding to their grade, they can be placed on 'temporary leave of absence' (without compensation) or, where appropriate, allowed to retire. Trade unions have, of course, unanimously denounced this part of the law as 'a clause allowing the mass dismissal of employees through administrative restructuring' (CGT), or putting 'an end to civil servants' tenure and guaranteed employment' (FO). Unions did not mobilize, however, as they would have been hard put to stage a protest against the law. So far, provisions on reclassification have not been used for collective reallocations.

Unions have been increasingly concerned about sluggish wage bargaining, which has stalled for several years. Since mid-2010, public servants' salaries have been frozen. In order to offset this impact in terms of a loss of purchasing power, a specific premium was set up in the 2008 wage agreement: the individual purchasing-power guarantee (*Garantie individuelle de pouvoir d'achat*). Any public servant whose compensation (this does not refer to their base wage, but takes into account all increases related to seniority and career development) has increased less than inflation over the previous four years receives a compensatory premium to make up the difference. Despite this measure, average wages have declined since 2010: in 2012, for example, the average net wage in constant euros fell by 0.8% in the FPE, 0.6% in the FPH and 0.5% in FPT. With the freezing of the index point, increasing pension contributions, which was voted on in 2010, and re-evaluating the minimum wage, the impact of flattening the wage range has been growing over the last few years (Gautié 2013). The lack of an overall wage policy reinforces the development of more or less individualized compensation schemes. Successive governments have restricted bargaining over compensation to the bonus component.

Pay for performance has been possible in the civil service since 1959, but it used to be restricted to top officials. An additional step in wage individualization was achieved in 2007 with the introduction of a unified system of bonuses based on two criteria: the functions held by employees and their individual performance. This new system now applies to all supervisory staff to enhance 'management dialogue'. It has, however, been seldom used to date and concerned about 100,000 people in early 2015.

Public service unions have denounced the entire wage policy and demanded a return to general increases to protect purchasing power. However, in the early years of the crisis, they have been reluctant to commit themselves to this issue, certainly hampered by the scale of redundancies in the private sector, which highlighted public employees' more privileged situation. Breaking with that restraint, all unions, with the exception of CFE-CGC, called for a day of action on jobs and wages in May 2014—a unique occasion under a left-wing government, as the last general strike dates back to 2007. The demonstrations staged throughout France were massive, but did not have an impact on government decisions.

More generally, after massive movements in the public sector against the 2003 and 2009 pension reforms (which have not, however, led to significant amendments to the initial plans), unions have not managed to mobilize against the establishment of an accounting logic governing workforce management. However, resizing the state has already had significant consequences. The productivity and organization challenges that accompany this process have had a direct impact on employee's working conditions.

In a context of declining recruitment, work-life issues have become a priority. Having somehow lost the 'war on safeguarding jobs' in the context of budgetary restrictions, unions have been concentrating on working condition issues.

Beyond the arrangements and timetables—frantic, according to unions—along which ongoing reforms are being pushed forward, social tensions express a deeper malaise linked to the overall dynamics of state modernization. Indeed, the redefinition of state functions supported by the RGPP as well as the ongoing introduction of NPM practices—but not in contradiction with the general status of the public service—affects the view employees have of their professional identities (introduction of measurable standards of performance, managerial forms of management that oppose and override professional expertise) (Bezes and Lodge 2015). Since the defense of this identity is also the basis of the relationship between trade unions and workers, the very cornerstone of the public service employment relations system has been shaken. This weakening is all the more extensive as the other pillar of the system—the weight of trade unions in career management—is being challenged by the new HRM policies. Finally, the contradiction between the prospect of new guarantees for social dialogue and the lack of consultation that governs decision-making increases unions' distrust and leads them to return to a more direct confrontational strategy, but one that involves more local, hence less universal, issues. A case in point is that of the Ministry of Finance, where two national strikes took place to challenge the merger of both major administrative functions: one in May 2010, supported by 35% of agents, and another in February 2012, when 27% took part.

Austerity Measures Are Affecting the Whole Public Service

After 2008, the crisis severely affected public finances, both due to lower tax revenues and counter-cyclical stimulus policies in the first two years. Between 2007 and 2009, the government deficit almost tripled, up from 2.7% to 7.1%, which shows the limited effects of spending reduction policies. Since 2011, France has been among the countries where fiscal consolidation has become imperative (OECD 2011). Numerous austerity measures have been implemented several times in a row, initially rather modest, then with more teeth. Additional savings are also planned in healthcare services.

Since François Hollande was elected in 2012, the Modernization of Public Action succeeded RGPP, but its content has remained essentially identical, with the notable exception of some departments easing staff reduction targets. A 'dispensation' replacement rate was established in the Ministry of Education. Yet, since the overall objective remains keeping staffing as it currently is, more stringent targets are being applied to other departments. The evolution of staffing figures in the Ministry of Education clearly illustrates such continuity. The change in employees belonging to the public and private sectors of state-financed education fell by 120,000 between 2002 and

2013, half of whom were teachers. Over the 2010–2013 period, the number of teachers dropped by only 4,000, but by nearly 55,000 regarding other staff (Concialdi 2014).

Previously spared from budget cuts, local authorities have, since 2014, been required to contribute to the recovery of the public finances (Jeannot 2014). Non-earmarked financial transfers from the state (about a quarter of local authorities' resources) and their own specific tax rules have afforded them greater scope for choice, which they have mobilized to expand their range of services to the population, as evidenced by increased recruitment in recent years. The recent limitation of taxes on companies, established in 2010—with a view to reducing labor costs more than cutting local government's revenues—has led to gradually reducing this freedom. Transfers from the state, already frozen since 2011, have been experiencing a significant decline since 2014: after a reduction in 2014, the 2015 appropriation fell by 6.5%. In addition, a national objective about local authorities' spending (not binding, at least initially) is enshrined in the 2015–2017 public finance-programming bill. Finally, regions merging and reorganizations at the 'department' (county) level should lead to declines in staffing.

Conclusion

Substantial reforms affecting both the size and organization of public services have been launched since the late 1990s. For some politicians and senior policy makers, these reforms should be part of a long-term neoliberal objective: privatization and outsourcing of non-sovereign functions and the introduction of NPM accompanied with challenging the status of public service careers. This political stream was not a dominant trend, partly also because of employees' and influential trade unions' resistance to these changes. Therefore, a middle way has been found: reorganizing the government and multiplying the provision of services' delegations along with assignment and staff transfers at the local level. The introduction of HRM inspired by private sector practices has slightly transformed employment relationships somewhat, without changing the framework of the general status: career-based system for managerial staff partially amended, performance-related pay for managers, individualized staff management and measurable standards of performance. Even if these changes have had a real impact on public service employees' working conditions, they were implemented within the public service status. Despite the government's aim to strengthen social dialogue, collective bargaining remains weak and under the unilateral power of administrative law.

In this context of structural reforms, the sovereign debt crisis precipitated quantitative adjustments. The reduction of public spending has been conducted based on strict payroll control and even, at least within the scope of central government, some downsizing has been achieved. The arrival to power of a socialist government in 2012 inflected a number of choices (tax burden increases, recruitment in priority ministries etc.) without giving up on the two former objectives. The issue of narrowing the scope of government intervention has been extended to local authorities, who have to comply with an accounting logic in the same way as the central government has had to since 2008.

France has been, in recent years, a good example of long-term structural reform implementation, introduced rather cautiously, but they have been on a collision course with the imperative of short-term quantitative adjustments, unilaterally implemented without consultation or planning.

Notes

1. The Labour Inspectorate *corps* (Category A), for example, comprises three grades: labor inspectors, labor deputy directors and labor directors.
2. In the private sector, trade union representativeness rules were changed markedly by the June 2008 act, which introduced electoral criteria: to be representative, a union must have obtained a 10% threshold of support at work council elections and an 8% threshold at sector and inter-professional levels. Trade unions representativeness at the national level was previously granted by the Ministry of Labour.
3. The February 23, 1989, circular on reviewing the civil service. Michel Rocard was the socialist prime minister from 1988 to 1992.
4. The June 3, 1998, circular on the preparation of multi-year modernization schemes in administrations. Lionel Jospin was socialist prime minister from 1997 to 2002.
5. *'Faire mieux avec moins'* (Doing more with less): this is the motto conferred to the RGPP by President Sarkozy on announcing the launch of that policy.

References

Bach, S. and Bordogna, L. (2011) 'Varieties of New Public Management or Alternative Models? The Reform of Public Service Employment Relations in Industrialized Democracies', *International Journal of Human Resource Management*, 22(11): 2281–2294.

Bezes, P. and Jeannot, G. (2011) 'The Development and Current Features of the French Civil Service System', in Van der Meer, F. (ed.) *Civil Service System in Western Europe*. 2nd ed., Cheltenham: Edward Elgar, 185–216.

Bezes, P. and Lodge, M. (2015) 'Civil Service Reforms, Public Service Bargains and Dynamics of Institutional Change', in Van der Meer, F., Raadschelders, J.-C.and Toonen, T. A. J. (eds.) *Comparative Civil Service Systems in the 21st Century*, London, Palgrave Macmillan, 136–161.

Bordogna, L. and Neri, S. (2011) 'Convergence towards an NPM Program or Different Models? Public Service Employment Relations in Italy and France', *International Journal of Human Resource Management*, 11: 2311–2330.

Bordogna, L. and Pedersini, R. (2013) 'Economic Crisis and the Policies of Public Service Employment Relations in Italy and France', *European Journal of Industrial Relations*, 19(4): 325–340.

Brière, B., Lecomte, E., Lochard, Y., Meilland, C., Piney, C. and Vincent, C. (2012) *Cadres de proximité, construire un environnement «capacitant»: le cas de la DGFIP*, Paris: DGFIP.

CAS (2011) 'Tendance de l'emploi public: où en est-on ?', *La note de synthèse*, 214.

Concialdi, P. (2014) 'L'éducation n'est pas épargnée', in Concialdi, P. and Math, A. (eds.) *Santé, éducation: services publics dans la tourmente, Chronique Internationale de l'IRES*, 148, 5–21.

Fournier, J. (2002) *Livre blanc: Le dialogue social dans la fonction publique*, Paris: Ministère de la Fonction publique.

Gautié, J. (2013) 'France: The Public Service under Pressure', in Vaughan-Whitehead, D. (ed.) *Public Sector Shock. The Impact of Policy Retrenchement in Europe*, Cheltenham: Edward Elgar, 174–213.

INSEE (2014) 'L'emploi dans la fonction publique en 2012', *Insee Première*, 1496.

Jeannot, G. (2014) 'Austerity and Social Dialogue in French Local Government', *Transfer: European Review of Labour and Research*, 20(3): 373–386.

Lacaze, A. (2005) 'La LOLF: simple outil de management ou dogme écrasant ?', *Gérer et comprendre*, 81: 5–13.

Rosenvallon, P. (1990) *L'Etat en France de 1789 à nos jours*, Paris: Le Seuil.

Rouban, L. (2014) *La fonction publique en débat*, Paris: La Documentation Française, coll. Les études.

Saglio, J. (2001) 'Les relations professionnelles entre négociation et consultation', in Pouchet, A. (ed.) *Sociologie du travail 40 ans après*, Paris: Elsevier, 233–247.

Schweyer, F.-X. (2001) 'Les directeurs d'hôpital: des entrepreneurs locaux du service public hospitalier', *Revue Française des Affaires Sociales*, 4, 115–121.

Silicani, J.-L. (2008) *Livre blanc sur l'avenir de la fonction publique*, Paris: Conseil d'Etat.

Supiot, A. (2000) 'Introduction', in Bodiguel, J.-L., Garbar, C. and Supiot, A. (eds.) *Servir l'intérêt général*, Paris: PUF, 13–32.

Tallard, M. and Vincent, C. (2009) 'L'action syndicale au défi de la gestion locale des personnels: Tensions à l'administration fiscale', *Sociologies pratiques*, 19: 55–67.

Tallard, M. and Vincent, C. (2010) 'Entre expertise et partenariat: Les syndicats face aux nouvelles formes de gestion du personnel à l'hôpital', *Economies et* Sociétés, série «Socio-économie du travail», AB, 1157–1183.

Vincent, C., Rehfeldt, U. and Tallard, M. (2005) *Formes de syndicalisme et formes de représentation dans la fonction publique*, Noisy: IRES/CGP.

6 Britain: Contracting the State

Public Service Employment Relations in a Period of Crisis

Stephen Bach

Introduction

The 2008 financial crisis precipitated the deepest recession in Britain since the 1930s, and the state is contracting in two main ways. Successive governments have used the financial crisis to reduce the size and ambition of the state, using austerity as a means to curb social rights and curtail the provision of public services. Secondly, trends towards a contract state have accelerated, with the state overseeing a network of private and voluntary sector providers and community provision, distancing itself from a responsibility to finance, provide and ensure decent employment standards for its workforce. These trends build on extensive reorganization of the public sector over recent decades that developed detailed systems of performance management, diversified service provision and shifted away from a model employer tradition. Reforms of collective bargaining and trade union representation proceeded in a more cautious manner, but the unexpected election of a Conservative government in 2015 unleashed new measures to undermine trade union representation.

The 2008 financial crisis had major implications for the Britain economy because of the disproportionate size of financial services in the economy. Eliminating the deficit has been central to a strategy to restore public finances and part of a larger ambition to permanently reduce the size of the public sector, with strong reliance on employment and wage reductions to achieve this goal. Britain is shifting from a public sector that was comparable in scope and expenditure to parts of continental Europe towards a smaller public sector that is much closer to public spending patterns in countries such as the US and Japan (Taylor-Gooby 2012). These ambitions were advanced between 2010–2015 with little disagreement within the Coalition government about the centrality of fiscal consolidation (Johnson and Chandler 2015). Poor economic growth, however, led to continual extension of timelines for deficit reduction. The Conservative government elected in 2015 has reiterated its ambition that the share of government spending should reduce to 36.5% of national income by 2019–20, close to a historical low for the post-1945 period.

Elements of Hood and Lodge's (2012) multiple scenarios are visible in the British case. There has been public policy support but rather less tangible results in terms of a communitarian state, with voluntary sector providers becoming more prominent in public discourse, but frequently in a subsidiary role to large private sector providers. These developments have also proceeded alongside state withdrawal as the government has redefined its role and curtailed its ambition in areas of social policy. This has occurred by the introduction of charges, reducing entitlement to social care, benefit restrictions and withdrawing child benefits from more affluent families (Lupton *et al.* 2015). There has been a tendency towards the hollowing out of the state, and this shift has a strong ideological component, with more emphasis on self-reliance through paid employment and voluntary provision rather than the state providing a safety net for all citizens.

This chapter focuses on the continuous restructuring of the public sector over recent decades and considers the implications of the economic crisis for employment relations. It examines workforce trends, reforms of public sector pay determination and the challenges for employers and trade unions, before considering the consequences of austerity in which the Conservative-led Coalition government of 2010–15 had an ambition to permanently reduce the size and scope of the public sector, substituting civil society for big government (Bach 2012; Grimshaw and Rubery 2012; Scott and Williams 2014). Substantial steps were taken along this path, with the share of public employment reducing as a proportion of total employment from 19.4% to 17.2% between 2010–2015 (ONS 2015). The policy program of the current Conservative government includes continuing austerity, further marketization and privatization and limiting trade union influence.

Organization Structure and Employment

There are two significant features of governance that have influenced the structure and functions of the public sector and shaped public sector employment relations. The first is that Britain is a unitary state with certain responsibilities devolved to the Scottish government and Welsh Assembly since 1999. Devolution has extended furthest in the case of Scotland, and consequently, some departments, notably education and health, are England-only departments. The dominant governance model remains parliamentary sovereignty, in which a government that has a majority in parliament has an electoral mandate that is very difficult to challenge. This constitutional settlement has facilitated 'strong' government that has pursued wide-ranging restructuring of the state including privatization and the abolition, merger and reorganization of government departments. This constitutional position was not fundamentally changed by the growth of judicial review and a period of Coalition government between 2010–2015.

The second important characteristic is that in contrast to most countries, Britain does not have a clear demarcation between public and private sector employment, reflecting a common law tradition. Public sector employees are covered by the same legal provisions, including issues such as dismissal and redundancy, although collective agreements may enhance these statutory provisions. Civil servants are not defined by a separate legal statute, but instead, the term reflects the relatively small proportion of public sector employees that work in the central government in the ministries and executive agencies, undertaking work led by government ministers. Civil servants are employed under contracts of employment and do not have the special status of civil servants that is evident in many countries.

Nevertheless, distinctive responsibilities and attributes are required of civil servants, and these have been formalized in the 2010 Constitutional Reform and Governance Act, which was prompted by concerns about the politicization of the civil service and about standards in public life. For the first time, statutory provision was made for a Civil Service Code that forms part of the terms and conditions of employment of all civil servants and requires civil servants to adhere to core values of 'integrity, honesty, objectivity and impartiality' (House of Commons 2010: paragraph 3). The statutory position of the code represents a departure from a tradition that has rarely emphasized the distinctive constitutional responsibilities and norms of civil servants.

The civil service is one component of the public sector that in the national accounts includes general government activities (split between central and local government) and market activities (public sector corporations, itself sub-divided into financial and non-financial public corporations). These classifications are based on government control rather than ownership, using indicators such as the ability of government to close the organization, and results in three main categories. The first main component is *central government*, which includes all organizations that are controlled and mainly financed by central government. These include government departments, executive agencies and other public bodies, such as the armed services, national museums, NHS (National Health Service) trusts and academy schools. One of the biggest changes in this category since 2010 relates to the more than 4,600 academy schools that control their own staff, curriculum and budget, but are funded and accountable directly to the central government rather than forming part of the local government.

Local government comprises local authorities that cover a specific locality and have the power to raise some taxes locally and to charge for specific services. Unlike most public bodies, they are governed by elected politicians. In comparative terms, the local government has been a large component of the public sector workforce because there is no tradition of the central government developing area offices to provide local services (with the exception of services for the unemployed). The local government has responsibility for a wide range of services, of which the largest element (more than half its expenditure) is adult's and children's services (NAO 2013a: 11). The local government also includes: environmental services, cultural and leisure services, highways, housing, planning and a diminishing portfolio of directly managed schools. Local government autonomy has fluctuated over time, and conflict with the central government in the 1980s led to tight control over their finances and functions. The Coalition government's espousal of 'localism' and the extent to which local authorities have responded imaginatively despite deep cuts in their budgets (Grant Thornton 2014) has led to some rehabilitation of local government, but not in relation to school provision. Increased responsibilities, however, have occurred in a context in which their capacity to address these increased duties has contracted sharply (Lupton *et al.* 2015: 34).

Public corporations are market organizations originally associated with nationalized industries, prior to wholesale privatization from the 1980s. This category now comprises organizations controlled by government, but with substantial freedom to conduct their activities along commercial lines such as London Underground and the BBC. This category has been subject to large workforce fluctuations after 2008 because many banks were redefined as public financial corporations when the government took temporary control of many banks in response to the financial crisis. In addition, the Royal Mail was privatized in 2013, but its branch structure—the Post Office—remains in public hands.

Workforce Structure and Trends

The public sector is a sizeable and distinctive employer, and at its high point in 2009, it employed around 6.3 million workers, approximately 20% of the workforce. Workforce trends are detailed in Table 6.1. The public sector has been subject to significant fluctuations in employment over the last half century. In the three decades after 1945, there was substantial growth in public sector employment, with rapid expansion of employment in education, health and social services. From the mid-late 1970s, heightened concerns about Britain's economic performance was capitalized on by the incoming 1979 Conservative government of Mrs. Thatcher to undertake a sustained period of public sector reform. Privatization led to reductions in public corporations' workforce from two million workers in 1979 to 600,000 by 1991 (Cribb *et al.* 2014a). Core areas of the public sector were relatively stable during this period, with the partial exception of the civil service, and in some cases (e.g. the police), employment increased during the 1980s. In the early 1990s, recession re-emerged and general government declined in this period (Winchester and Bach 1995).

The election of the Labour government in 1997 marked an important juncture for public sector employment trends. The Labour government

Table 6.1 Public Sector Employment 1991–2015 by Sector (000s) (UK)

Headcount, not seasonally adjusted, thousands	Central Gov (incl. NHS) [A]	Local Gov [B]	Total General Gov [A + B]	Total Public Corporations	Total Public Sector	Of which: Civil Service
1991	2333	3075	5408	582	5990	593
1992	2348	3021	5369	544	5913	609
1993	2529	2788	5317	515	5831	601
1994	2470	2752	5222	446	5668	578
1995	2417	2757	5174	433	5607	555
1996	2379	2732	5111	395	5506	538
1997	2338	2726	5064	348	5412	516
1998	2342	2708	5050	350	5400	505
1999	2346	2744	5090	359	5449	504
2000	2384	2779	5163	367	5531	516
2001	2462	2781	5242	379	5643	522
2002	2553	2798	5351	377	5728	538
2003	2663	2841	5504	387	5891	560
2004	2749	2895	5644	378	6022	570
2005	2808	2925	5733	383	6117	571
2006	2785	2935	5720	362	6082	558
2007	2745	2943	5687	356	6044	539
2008	2750	2923	5672	361	6033	523
2009	2852	2910	5763	566	6329	527
2010	2868	2907	5775	540	6315	522
2011	2839	2760	5599	507	6106	488
2012	2731	2559	5289	475	5764	458
2013	2822	2423	5245	454	5699	450
2014	2881	2353	5233	183	5416	442
2015*	2909	2271	5181	178	5359	431
% change						
1991–1997	0.2	−11.3	−6.4	−40.2	−9.6	−13.0
1997–2010	22.7	6.6	14.0	55.2	16.7	1.2
2010–2015*	1.4	−21.9	−10.3	−67	−15.1	−17.4

*excluding Quarter 3 and Quarter 4

Source: http://www.ons.gov.uk/ons/rel/pse/public-sector-employment/q2–2015/tsd-pse-q2–2015.html

was elected on a platform that pledged significant investment in the public services to address staff shortages and service quality concerns, targeted on priority areas of education and health. Health was the largest gainer, with the NHS spending almost doubling in real terms in the decade up to 2010, accompanied by a rapid scaling up of employment. This investment, fueled by the profitability of financial services in the City of London, made a substantial difference in remedying decades of under-investment, but in the aftermath of the financial crisis enabled the

Table 6.2 Characteristics of the Public and Private Sector Workforces (UK)

	Public	Private
Occupation		
'Managers, Directors and Senior Officials'	12.4%	4.7%
'Professional Occupations'	13.7%	39.3%
'Associate Professional And Technical Occupations'	13.1%	15.2%
'Administrative and Secretarial Occupations'	10.1%	14.8%
'Skilled Trades Occupations'	13.3%	2.2%
'Caring, Leisure And Other Service Occupations'	8.1%	14.8%
'Elementary Occupations'	11.8%	6.6%
Other	17.4%	2.3%
TOTAL	100.0%	100.0%
Age, Gender, Hours, Temporary		
Under 25 years old	5.4%	11.6%
Over 50 years old	35.8%	32.8%
Female	67.3%	43.2%
Part time	30.0%	27.5%
Temporary*	7.7%	5.3%

Source: Quarterly Labour Force Survey, January—March 2015, available at: http://discover. ukdataservice.ac.uk/

*Not permanent in some way

Coalition government to portray the public sector as profligate in developing its austerity program.

Public sector employment has certain characteristics that differentiate it from private sector employment. According to LFS (Labor Force Survey) data, and like other EU countries, the workforce is highly gendered, with over 67% of the workforce comprised of women, compared with 43% in the private sector (see Table 6.2). This proportion has been gradually increasing because the female-dominated sectors of education and health expanded steadily. Almost three-quarters of women in the public sector are employed in health or education, while men are more likely to be employed in public administration or defense, which are more prone to expenditure cuts (Cribb *et al.* 2014a). However, in absolute terms, women have been more affected by austerity measures because they constitute a higher proportion of the workforce (Fawcett Society 2012). The importance of the professions within the workforce is evident and in addition, a higher proportion of workers in the public sector had a higher education qualification (57%) compared with 37% of private sector workers; the gap was almost double in relation to postgraduate degrees (Cribb *et al.* 2014a). The public sector employs an older workforce: almost 36% are over 50, compared with around 33% in the private sector and far fewer young workers (Table 6.2).

There are also some differences in relation to part-time work, with 30% of the public sector employed part time compared to 27.5% in the private sector. The public sector also makes some use of temporary employment, but less than other EU countries, with 7.7% of staff employed on temporary contracts (around two-thirds are employed on fixed-term contracts). The main motives for the use of temporary employment relate to budgetary uncertainties and staff shortages, but some professional staff, such as nurses and social workers, seek temporary employment to avoid administrative burdens and value the increased flexibility and higher pay (Cornes *et al.* 2013). Staff shortages and budgetary restrictions haves encouraged the use of agency nursing and medical staff, with the NHS spending £2.6 billion between 2012–13 and 2013–14 on temporary medical staff (Department of Health 2015: 9).

Public Sector Employment Relations and Pay Determination

Overview

In the 1999 predecessor of this book, it was stated that in the previous twenty years, reforms of pay determination had been more limited than the radical restructuring of public services. This was despite Conservative government exhortations in favor of devolved bargaining (Winchester and Bach 1999: 53). This analysis has been confirmed by developments since 1999 because despite important reforms of pay determination, national structures of collective bargaining have remained largely intact, and the gulf with private sector pay determination practice has widened (van Wanrooy *et al.* 2013). One irony is that the resilience of centralized systems of national pay determination has facilitated paybill control during a period of austerity.

National collective bargaining on an industry-wide basis has been the most important method for determining terms and conditions of public sector employment, with separate arrangements for the civil service, NHS, local government and schools (see Table 6.3 for details). Collective bargaining occurs on an annual basis, although in particular economic or political circumstances, two- or three-year deals are sometimes concluded. The scope of collective bargaining is fairly wide, and its coverage is very extensive, although coverage is affected by the existence of the system of independent pay review (see below). For many decades, collective agreements typically established national wage and salary structures and specified a wide range of terms and conditions of employment, often in a detailed and prescriptive manner (Beaumont 1992).

Despite this institutionalized system of collective bargaining, there is no legal obligation on employers to negotiate over pay and conditions unless statutory union recognition has been obtained under the 1999 Employment Relations Act. In the public sector, the statute has little relevance because in 2011, 92% of public sector workplaces with more than 5 employees

Table 6.3 Structures of Pay Determination in the Public Sector* (UK)

Sector	Institutional structure	Employer representation	Trade union representation
Civil service	Each department, executive agency and other non-departmental public body negotiates its own pay and conditions for all civil servants, except senior civil servants, after its pay remit is agreed with HM Treasury. Senior civil servants are covered by the Senior Salaries Review Body (SSRB). Around two-thirds of civil servants are employed in the four largest departments that lead on work and pensions, justice, taxation and defense.	Department and executive agency specific. The Cabinet Office submits evidence to the SSRB.	The main civil service trade unions recognized for pay bargaining purposes are the Public and Commercial Services Union (PCS), Prospect and the First Division Association (FDA). Some departments and agencies recognize in-house staff federations.
NHS	The NHS staff council is responsible for core NHS conditions of service (Agenda for Change), and this agreement covers all staff directly employed by the NHS, except senior managers and doctors and dentists covered by the remit of the Doctors' and Dentists' Review Body (DDRB). The NHS Pay Review Body (NHSPRB) makes recommendations on pay and related matters for its remit groups. The DDRB makes recommendations on pay and related matters for its remit groups.	UK Health Departments, NHS Confederation and other employer representatives. Employer organizations submit evidence to the NHSPRB. Employer organizations submit evidence to the DDRB.	There are 15 recognized staff organizations. These include large, general trade unions (Unison, Unite, GMB) and specialist professional trade unions including the Royal College of Nursing (RCN), Royal College of Midwives (RCM), the Chartered Society of Physiotherapy (CSP) and the Society of Radiographers (SoR). Staff side organizations submit evidence to the NHSPRB. The British Medical Association (BMA) and the British Dental Association (BDA) submit evidence to the DDRB.

(Continued)

Table 6.3 (Continued)

Sector	Institutional structure	Employer representation	Trade union representation
Local government	The national joint council for local government services—the single-status agreement.	Local government association.	Unite, Unison, GMB.
Schools	The School Teachers' Review Body (STRB) is a statutory body that makes recommendations on pay and conditions for school teachers in England and Wales.	The Department for Education, the National Employers' Organisation for School Teachers and other organizations submit evidence to the STRB	The head teacher and teacher trade unions submit evidence to the STRB. These include the Association of School and College Leaders (ASCL), the Association of Teachers and Lecturers (ATL), the National Association of Head Teachers (NAHT), the National Association of School-teachers Union of Women Teachers (NASUWT) and the National Union of Teachers (NUT)

ªThese arrangements have different geographical coverage. The dominant pattern is that pay determination arrangements cover England, Wales and Northern Ireland but not Scotland. Most review bodies have a UK-wide remit and receive evidence from the devolved administrations in Northern Ireland, Wales and Scotland. For the first time, in 2015, the NHS Pay Review Body reported for Scotland only because the NHSPRB was asked not to make a recommendation for England.

Sources: NHS Agenda for Change handbook; Office of Manpower Economics; Local Government Association

recognized trade unions (van Wanrooy *et al.* 2013: 59). Collective agreements are not legally binding between the parties; they are recommendations to the central government or public employers and once accepted, the terms of the collective agreement are incorporated into individual contracts of employment. Governments promoted and endorsed collective bargaining as a crucial element in the ideal of the state as a 'good employer' in the sixty years from 1919 to 1979 (Fredman and Morris 1989: 142).

The deteriorating economic and industrial relations context at the end of the 1970s precipitated widespread public sector strike action in 1978/79. This 'winter of discontent' paved the way for a decisive shift in government policy on public services' collective bargaining. The Conservative government emphasized the importance of affordability in pay settlements and devolved responsibility to local employers where possible. It also removed groups from direct collective bargaining as opportunities arose (White and Hatchett 2003).

The System of Independent Pay Review Bodies

An unusual feature of the British approach to public sector pay determination has been the existence of a separate system of independent pay review. Originally covering distinctive groups of employees, including senior civil servants and doctors and dentists, the system was transformed during the 1980s with its extension to half a million nurses, midwives and other health professionals and a decade later to teachers. The system has continued to expand to include the whole NHS workforce, prison staff and the police, and by 2015, there were eight Pay Review Bodies (PRBs). Each PRB has a distinctive remit, but they all make pay recommendations to government for 2.5 million workers—around 45% of public sector staff and a paybill of £100 billion (OME 2015). All of the review bodies have a small group of members appointed by the government and they take evidence from interested parties and visit workplaces. The reports assess conflicting arguments on affordability and recruitment and retention and consider evidence on employees' motivation, morale and workloads. They make recommendations on pay increases—and other matters in their terms of reference—that are not binding on the government.

For critics, which include both trade unions and employers, the system of pay review represents a form of unilateral government pay determination that is far removed from collective bargaining. Government ministers' are in control because they appoint PRB members, determine their terms of reference and can choose to delay, stage or reject recommendations. Moreover, the PRB system provides a veneer of rationality that disguises hidden political bargaining within government (Seifert 1992: 276–280). Employers have also been wary of a system that generates paybill commitments but without employers having sufficient influence to determine these outcomes (White and Hatchett 2003). The main beneficiary is the government because the review body process distances ministers from direct pay negotiations with trade unions while exerting a very powerful influence over their deliberations. In contrast to the risk of industrial action that is an intrinsic part of collective bargaining, the PRB process has discouraged industrial action: for example, the establishment of the prison service review body in 2001 was accompanied by a voluntary agreement precluding strike action.

Industry Developments

Looking back over the period from 1979, the reform of collective bargaining arrangements progressed most rapidly and extensively in the civil service, mainly because government ministers were able to exercise more direct control than in other parts of the sector. Following the creation of semi-autonomous executive agencies from the end of the 1980s, the Treasury delegated its direct responsibility for negotiating pay and conditions to individual departments and agencies. This was followed in 1996 by the abolition of civil service-wide pay except for the 3,600 most senior civil servants, whose pay is determined by the system of independent pay review. In place of a handful of national agreements, over 150 new bargaining units were created, subsequently reduced by reorganizations. Each department and executive agency established their own pay and grading structures, leading to variation in pay structures. Despite this process of delegation, the bargaining process is tightly controlled. The Treasury issues detailed guidance to departments and approves planned pay awards (Treasury 2015).

In the NHS, national bargaining between many trade unions and NHS employers on employment conditions with some scope for local trust-level agreements coexists alongside review body recommendations on pay matters. The most concerted attempt to develop trust-level bargaining occurred during the 1990s as part of attempts to develop market competition in the NHS. This experiment failed because of managerial reluctance to antagonize the workforce in a context of forceful union opposition, limited managerial skills and potentially high transaction costs (Bach and Winchester 1994). The Labour government took note of this failure but also favored more local flexibility within coherent national frameworks. It encouraged trade unions and employers to work in partnership to devise reforms acceptable to both parties and that dealt with an increase in equal pay litigation (Perkins and White 2010).

Local authorities are independent employers, but they are voluntarily covered by national level pay bargaining—the national joint council for local government services—that decides on pay and core national conditions while providing local authorities with considerable local flexibility and, if they so wish, the scope to opt out of national pay bargaining. Employer and trade union negotiating bodies comprise the Local Government Association (LGA) and the main local government trade unions—Unison, GMB and

Unite. The LGA coordinates and lobbies on behalf of local government, but it is not the employer and elected councilors, representative of LGA membership, lead negotiations (Bach and Stroleny 2014).

Pressure on national bargaining emerged because by the mid-2000s, it was abundantly clear that local authorities confronted a huge pay bill increase to ensure compliance with equal pay law. This stemmed from male-dominated occupations like refuse collectors receiving substantial bonus payments denied to mainly female workers, such as school lunch supervisors. Ultimately, these pressures resulted in local government being covered by one collective agreement—the 1997 single-status agreement—that influenced subsequent NHS pay reform. This landmark agreement between trade unions and employers harmonized terms and conditions and preserved national bargaining, but provided for each local authority to implement local pay and grading structures underpinned by job evaluation (McLaughlin 2015).

These reforms have contributed to the resilience of national systems of pay determination, as the Workplace Employment Relations Survey (WERS) indicates. Of public sector employees, 96% are employed in workplaces that recognize trade unions, and 92% of workplaces recognize trade unions for pay bargaining (Van Wanrooy *et al.* 2013). Moreover, although the expansion of the system of pay review removes formal collective bargaining over annual pay awards, in the NHS, trade union and employer influence over employment conditions is institutionalized via the NHS staff council. Consequently, the contrast between pay setting in the public and private sector has widened substantially, and in 2011, almost 90% of private sector employees worked in workplaces where management unilaterally set pay (van Wanrooy *et al.* 2013). This contrast has been noted by commentators critical of the alleged inflexibility and unwillingness of trade unions to accept the reform of national arrangements (Wolf 2010).

It is noteworthy, however, that when employers have been granted opportunities to opt out of national bargaining, few have done so. In the NHS, foundation trusts have additional freedoms to set their own local pay and conditions, but this has only occurred in only one case (during the 1990s), reflecting local recruitment difficulties. Academy schools have also not chosen to utilize their increased discretion, and academy chains have recognized trade unions for bargaining purposes. While 53 councils, around 15% of local authorities, have opted out of the national agreement, this occurred mainly in the 1990s for recruitment and retention reasons. Employers are cautious about embracing local pay determination and at present, use the flexibility within national pay structures to tailor pay and conditions to local circumstances. However, the combination of increased diversity of public service provision, competition for service contracts and budgetary restrictions points to a continued erosion of the regulatory influence of national agreements.

Public Employers

State Policies

The central government has combined a high level of influence over the funding and management of public services, with an emphasis on devolving authority to managers within separate employer units in the civil service, hospitals and schools. Managers have been held accountable for organizational performance by a mixture of targets and the establishment of competitive mechanisms to challenge the incumbent provider. New Public Management (NPM) has cast a long shadow over this restructuring process with the fragmentation and commercialization of the public sector, with the ultimate goal of replacing rule-bound behavior with incentive structures that encourage managers and the workforce to be responsive to market pressures, performance standards and service users (Pollitt and Bouckaert 2014).

This reform agenda has been pursued in a relatively consistent manner since the early 1980s, albeit with different governments overlaying their own interpretation and political priorities on a core template of state modernization (Bach and Kessler 2012). The role of the public sector has shifted from the provision of public services as a right and expectation of citizenship towards the targeted delivery of services that enables citizens to thrive in a global economy. International benchmarking has become more influential, as the preoccupation of government with comparative Programme for International Student Assessment results testifies. This process commenced in earnest in 1979 with the Conservative governments' emphasis on the superiority of market relations, competition and private sector management expertise. Nationalized industries and public utilities were privatized, and the remaining public services were subject to a process of compulsory competitive tendering that started in support services such as hospital cleaning and refuse collection and was subsequently extended into administrative functions (Smith Institute 2014).

This process of shifting from direct to indirect service provision has been accompanied by market making. The state has increasingly focused on commissioning rather than directly providing services with service standards and labor conditions regulated indirectly through contracts, backed up by regulation and inspection. These oversight regimes have simultaneously proved to be intrusive in terms of the disruption and anxiety they engender in staff, but also frequently ineffective in finding and remedying poor standards of practice that may continue unchecked for many years (Gash *et al.* 2013). These reforms have fostered the growth of large service corporations that specialize in outsourcing and whose expertise resides in their ability to win government contracts. This has led to the entanglement of government and business with at least £1 in every £3 that government spends on public services channeled to independent providers (Julius 2008; Crouch 2013).

After 1997, the Labour Prime Minister concluded that 'public service reform needed major structural change, including a much closer relationship with the private sector' (Blair 2010: 313–314). One of the most controversial components of this agenda was the private finance initiative (PFI), in which a private sector consortium financed, built and operated hospitals for around a twenty-five year period. Trade unions campaigned successfully for safeguards on pay and conditions when workers were transferred to private contractors, but the abolition of these arrangements in England in 2010 has led to new starters being employed on inferior rates of pay, reinforcing the erosion of labor standards associated with public sector outsourcing (Smith Institute 2014). Moreover, PFI schemes also saddled NHS trusts with large annual payments that substantially increased their deficits (Committee of Public Accounts 2015).

These trends have been underpinned by managerial and organizational restructuring that has increased the authority of managers with incentive structures and sanctions to ensure adherence to overall government policy. Separating policy from delivery was fashionable and went furthest in the civil service with the establishment of executive agencies, headed by a chief executive, intended to focus on delivery and results rather than the Whitehall preoccupation with policy. By 1998, 139 agencies had been established, employing three-quarters of all civil servants, but subsequently, there has been a modest cull in the number of agencies (James *et al.* 2012). The model remains intact, but concerns emerged about the fragmentation of public services and criticism that individual agencies, foundation hospitals and academy schools were preoccupied with delivering their own results to the detriment of collaboration across organizational boundaries. Moreover, the distancing of policy and delivery meant that policy was devised without any certainty that it could be delivered by the frontline. Encouraging collaboration within and across sectors and strengthening networks was a partial if incomplete response to these criticisms (Bach and Kessler 2012).

Status and Pay of Senior Managers

The scale of organizational change over recent decades has raised the profile, status and pay of senior managers and increased mobility between the public and private sectors. In the NHS, reforms from the 1980s were initially underpinned by a relatively crude assumption that the increased influence of general managers could be used to undermine the power of professional staff, leading to strained relations between managerial and professional staff (Bach 2004). Increasingly, medical and other professionals have been encouraged to take up managerial roles and manage performance rather than act as representatives of staff concerns, a role that has not always proved comfortable for clinicians (Walshe and Chambers 2010).

Within the civil service, more emphasis has been placed on specialist rather than generalist roles and external recruitment used particularly to source commercial skills. On average, just under a quarter of senior civil servants were recruited externally in the years up to the start of austerity measures in 2010, concentrated in specialist roles such as finance and information technology (NAO 2013b). The proportion of external appointments declined to 12% in 2011, attributed to internal redeployment to avoid redundancies, a pay freeze and a subsequent pay cap that discouraged external applicants (Agboniahor 2014). External appointments have exacerbated the anomalies that stem from pay delegation, resulting in significant pay variations in the senior civil service (SCS) for similar roles. In 2012, civil servants that joined the SCS from outside the civil service earned on average 24% more than internal appointments (NAO 2013b: 42).

In a climate of increased attention and analysis of pay inequality in the private sector, more attention has focused on top management pay in the public sector. In the decade up to 2009, local authority chief executive pay increased by 75% and NHS chief executive pay doubled, and these increases far outstripped pay increases to other public sector employees (Communities and Local Government Committee 2014). These trends have been justified in terms of the increased responsibilities placed on public sector top managers and their lower earnings compared to similar roles in the private sector, although non-pay benefits such as historically higher levels of job security also require consideration (Hutton 2011). Unease remains about high pay packages of top public sector managers, but there is also a recognition that few people want to take on demanding and risky leadership roles in a context of intensive scrutiny and accountability for performance. Austerity measures, by simultaneously increasing the demands on senior managers and by curbing their pay, have reinforced recruitment and retention difficulties amongst top managers (Deloitte/Reform 2015).

Trade Union Organization

The extent of trade union organization has been a distinguishing feature of the public sector, and the current Conservative government has tried to prevent opposition to its public sector agenda by limiting trade union influence. In 2015, the Conservative government published a Trade Union Bill that makes it more difficult to take strike action in essential public services by raising thresholds for strike action. It also makes it easier to hire agency workers to replace those on strike. In conjunction with the removal of automatic deduction of trade union membership fees, these measures have raised concerns that partnership working will be jeopardized (Neville and 0'Connor 2015).

Table 6.4 Trade Union Membership Levels and Density by Sector, 1995 to 2014 (UK)

	Trade union membership levels, thousands		Trade union density, %	
	Private Sector	Public Sector	Private Sector	Public Sector
	All employees	All employees	All employees	All employees
1995	3,391	3,722	21.4	61.3
1996	3,297	3,664	20.5	60.7
1997	3,265	3,635	19.8	61.2
1998	3,352	3,579	19.5	60.4
1999	3,311	3,667	19.0	59.9
2000	3,308	3,810	18.8	60.3
2001	3,276	3,767	18.4	59.7
2002	3,193	3,837	17.7	59.8
2003	3,216	3,903	18.2	59.4
2004	3,063	4,017	17.3	58.8
2005	3,008	4,075	16.9	58.2
2006	2,984	4,075	16.6	58.7
2007	2,933	4,118	16.1	59.0
2008	2,805	4,124	15.5	57.1
2009	2,628	4,143	15.1	56.6
2010	2,486	4,103	14.2	56.3
2011	2,525	3,923	14.2	56.6
2012	2,589	3,917	14.4	56.3
2013	2,643	3,843	14.4	55.4
2014	2,681	3,764	14.2	54.3

[1]Year-on-year changes are subject to rounding errors

Source: Labour Force Survey, Office for National Statistics

Trade union membership has been in long-term decline and declined from its 1979 historic high point of 13.2 million to under 11 million in 1985 and stood at 9.8 million in 1990. More recently, membership has stabilized. Membership has become concentrated into a smaller number of large trade unions with a series of ongoing amalgamations and mergers. Public sector trade union membership increased slightly during the mid-2000s, followed by some decline as austerity took hold after 2010 (Table 6.4). Trade union density has exhibited a more consistent decline, but it is notable that the gap between public and private sector trade union density has continued to widen.

Trade Union Structure

The structure of trade unionism has evolved incrementally overseen by a single national union confederation (the TUC), but with limited author-ity to prevent inter-union rivalry and multi-union representation in many workplaces. The mid-nineteenth century craft unions of skilled workers offered a partial model for the later growth of occupational (professional) unions, but these have coexisted alongside the growth of general unions with more open membership criteria. In the public sector, a myriad of large and small trade unions exist that often compete for members and reflect distinctive ideological positions. These differences, however, are not associated with support for different political parties. The trade union movement established the Labour Party and trade unions remain a key source of funding, but the ties between the Labour Party and trade unions have weakened.

Overall, the largest general trade unions, such as Unite and the GMB, have a strong presence in the public sector. Unison has representation across the public services, but the largest proportion of its membership is in local government, and it has a substantial membership in health. PCS is centered in the civil service and is especially well represented amongst lower-grade staff, while Prospect is concentrated in professional and technical grades. There are also a number of influential trade unions representing the most senior managers in the civil service (the FDA) and education (ALCS and the NAHT). Many of the largest trade unions are occupational unions representing educational professionals, mainly but not exclusively classroom teachers, (i.e., the rival NUT and NASUWT and the ATL) and in health, there is the RCN, representing nurses, and the BMA, representing doctors.

Data from individual membership reports of trade unions[1] indicates large variations in recent membership trends between individual trade unions. Trade unions with strong professional membership in health and education have continued to build membership. For example, the British Medical Association increased its membership by 43% between 1999–2013 and the National Union of Teachers by 35% in the same period. These trends are in marked contrast to the general trade unions that despite merger activity, have been subject to membership losses. In part, these different trajectories reflect the growth of key occupational groups during the 2000s. Doctors, nurses and teachers followed the example of their peers and continued to join trade unions in high numbers, reflecting the identity of these trade unions in combining professional and trade union activities (Kessler and Heron 2001). By contrast, the large general unions often represent groups that are more exposed to privatization and outsourcing and confront financial difficulties associated with membership decline (Bryson and Forth 2011).

Public sector employee voice systems have been subject to less institutional change. The implementation of the Information and Consultation of Employees 2004 regulations had little impact on workplace consultation arrangements, with even fewer consequences for the public sector (Hall and Purcell 2012). Although WERS data indicate that a small proportion of non-union representatives exist in the public sector, trade unions retain an almost complete monopoly of representation in consultation arrangements. These take the form of joint consultative committees (JCC), established on a voluntary basis, comprising employer and employee representatives that act as a forum for employers to communicate their plans and to consult with trade unions and are widespread in the public sector. What is less certain is how much JCCs influence management decision-making and how much effort managers expend on these arrangements compared to forms of direct communication with the workforce. The 2011 WERS data indicate a further increase in public sector direct communication and involvement mechanisms, while the presence of JCCs is in decline (Van Wanrooy *et al.* 2013).

Trade Union Responses

There has been a long-standing debate as to how trade unions should respond to these membership challenges. The dominant response has been to focus on improved organizing, which takes different forms in different unions but is centered on recruiting and retaining members alongside strengthening workplace organization and activism. This strategy has been approached in different ways, but the TUC Organizing Academy that trains young organizers has been central to these endeavors, and many unions have increased the number of organizers they employ. Overall, however, a detailed analysis of union organizing strategies in Britain concludes that 'the impact of organizing initiatives is very mixed and presents few reasons for optimism' (Simms *et al.* 2013: 171).

An integral component of the organizing approach is an attempt to develop effective workplace organization and build membership in outsourced and private sector workplaces, often using membership targets to monitor progress. Unison has combined gaining recognition agreements with major public service contractors alongside membership recruitment. This has resulted in the recruitment of over 100,000 private contractor members, although the union does not underestimate the difficulties of recruiting and servicing union members in dispersed workplaces with limited HR expertise (Unison 2014). Some of the criticisms of organizing initiatives have suggested that they fail because they do not encourage participation, and one response has been to develop alliances with service users and local communities, hence the term community unionism, to resist cuts in services (Tattersall 2010). Despite attracting considerable interest within the union movement, support for local campaigns has not always been translated into a concerted commitment towards community unionism.

Austerity Measures and Consequences

In 2010, the Conservative-led coalition government entered office committed to eliminating the deficit. This had reached a post-war high because of the unprecedented financial support provided to the disproportionately large banking sector in the aftermath of the 2008 financial crisis. The coalition agreement placed deficit reduction at the center of its policy program, but the government's ambition was to use fiscal consolidation to reduce the size and scope of the state. In the 2010 spending review, a target was set to reduce the deficit from 8.4% of the GDP in 2009 to 0.4% by 2015, with three-quarters of deficit reduction linked to public spending cuts of £81 billion (total government expenditure in 2010–11 was £697 billion) (Treasury 2010). It was envisaged that the current account would be back in balance by 2015–16, but the depth of the recession, weak growth and lower than expected tax receipts led to further deterioration in the public finances, leading the government to extend the time period for deficit reduction. Instead of eliminating the deficit between 2010 and 2015, it was reduced by half as a share of the GDP and public sector net debt increased from 68.7% of the GDP to 80.4% in 2014–15 (OBR 2015).

The scale of real-term expenditure cuts has been unprecedented, and these cuts have been distributed very unevenly between departments. The government pledged to increase real spending on the NHS and non-capital spending on schools, but this has not prevented health and education spending falling as a proportion of GDP. The relative protection for health and education was accompanied by larger cuts for unprotected departments that meant an overall 9.5% real cut in departmental spending (2010–2015) was translated into a 20% cut for unprotected departments (IFS 2015: 158). In terms of major areas of public employment, local government has been hard hit, reflected in large employment reductions (Table 6.1). Central government funding to local authorities has declined by around 37% and factoring in their own tax raising powers, this amounts to a reduction of 25% in their spending power between 2010–2015 (NAO 2014).

The political ideology and underlying economic assumptions of the Conservative-led Coalition government constituted important drivers of public expenditure reductions. The starting point was sustained criticism of the previous Labour government's expansion of public services and assertions that government spending had jeopardized the public finances, an argument repeated in the 2015 election campaign (Conservative Party 2015). Large-scale privatization was revived with the (partial) privatization of the Royal Mail and the probation service. There has also been an acceleration of the pace of outsourcing, especially in areas of justice, welfare and defense. The number of outsourced contracts increased by 125% from 526 under the last Labour government to 1,185; government expenditure on outsourced services doubled, increasing from £64 billion to £120 billion between 2010–2015 (Plimmer 2015). Although outsourcing has been the dominant trend, some local authorities and NHS trusts have brought services back in-house because internal service provision facilitates work reorganization and generates higher levels of saving (Grant Thornton 2014).

Provider diversity continued to evolve with more emphasis on social enterprise and voluntary sector provision. The most high-profile and controversial attempt to diversify provision has been the growth of free schools that have been established by parents, teachers and academy chains and are intended to increase local choice and stimulate innovation. More important in terms of scale and impact has been encouragement for more schools to become academies and leave local authority control. Academies and free schools often have industry sponsors and are not bound by national terms and conditions of employment. A major concern to staff and trade unions has been the deregulation of the teacher workforce that allows the use of non-qualified teachers in classrooms.

Coalition policy also envisaged a reduction of the public domain. Planned expenditure cuts were intended to reduce the public sector workforce to its lowest level as a share of total employment since at least 1971 (OBR 2014). Scaling back the state put pressure on public services to curtail services, often combined with shifting services to social enterprises and volunteers, with the latter celebrated as examples of civic activism and strong communities. Reductions of statutory services in the provision of libraries, day centers and other services used by the vulnerable alongside tightening eligibility criteria have been widely reported (House of Commons 2013; National Coalition for Independent Action 2015).

Wage Restraint and Pay Reform

The Coalition government stated in its 2010 spending review that 'the overall value of the public sector reward package, including pension provision, has remained generous in recent years' (Treasury 2010: 37). A public sector wage premium exists, but although earnings are typically higher in the public sector, this in part reflects the workforce characteristics described earlier (differences in education, age, gender), and the results are sensitive to differences between full-time and part-time workers, men and women and job size (Dolton and Makepeace 2011; Muller and Schulten 2015). The government suggested that not only was wage restraint essential to reduce the public sector paybill, but it would also ensure fewer job losses. Wage restraint was accompanied by changes in pension rules that increased contributions and raised the pension age in a phased manner. The government restrained public sector pay (with some measures to protect the lowest paid) by a combination of a two-year pay freeze followed by three years in which pay settlements were limited to an average of 1%. The 1% pay cap has been extended to cover the 2015–2020 parliament. Local government pay awards are not directly controlled by the central government, but as local government has experienced the deepest expenditure cuts, pay restraint has been severe, although some local authorities have attempted to cushion wage reductions for the lowest paid (IDS 2013). The result of these policies is that compensation of government employees as a share of GDP decreased by 1.1 percentage points between 2009 and 2013 (OECD 2015). Public sector workers have confronted reductions in real pay, and public sector pay is well below the long-term average relative to the private sector, raising longer-term recruitment and retention issues (see Cribb *et al.* 2014b).

The government's pay agenda comprised much more than a public sector income policy because austerity measures have been used to weaken national pay bargaining. The government favoured regional pay and proposed more local or what it termed 'market-facing' pay in the expectation that public sector pay rates would be reduced, especially in poorer parts of the country. The government's consultation, however, found little favor with employers or trade unions, cognizant of the failed experiments with local pay in the 1990s and unconvinced that public sector pay rates 'crowded out' private sector employment.

The system of independent pay review has been expanded and the scope for manoeuvre of the existing pay review bodies has been reduced. The Police Negotiating Board was abolished, and in 2014, the Police Remuneration Review Body was established. Its remit followed closely the recommendations of the Winsor review that proposed fundamental changes in police pay and conditions that were rejected by the Police Federation. Overall, prescriptive remits and government incomes policy has severely curtailed the independence of the pay review bodies, and they have also been sidelined in key disputes, for example, the dispute over new contracts for junior doctors during 2015. The independence and role of the pay review bodies has therefore been subject to increased criticism, especially from trade unions, during a period of austerity.

The government also encouraged the individualization of pay by strengthening performance management at the local level and downgrading the role of national pay structures. One prominent target of these efforts has been the elimination of progression pay in which staff move up an incremental pay point (linked to experience), which the government regards as an 'automatic' pay increase regardless of performance. In the NHS, negotiations between employers and trade unions led to a 2013 agreement that made progression through all pay points conditional on meeting locally agreed performance criteria. The School Teachers' Review Body had their proposal for a system of performance-based pay linked to the achievement of appraisal objectives accepted, and it commenced in September 2014. Any performance increases awarded do not need to be linked to existing pay points, and the pay structure could potentially 'wither on the vine' with more emphasis placed on the school-level pay policy. Similarly, the government in its remit to the civil service has required the removal of progression pay by 2015. Consequently, the turn away from seniority-based increments has increased the importance of linking pay to performance in the public sector.

The coverage of national pay structures has also been reduced a variety of ways. Not only has the government presided over the expansion of NHS foundation trusts, academies and free schools that can set their own pay, but it also does not require private prisons to follow review body recommendations. An important development has been the withdrawal of protection (termed the Two-Tier Codes of Practice) introduced by the Labour government that prevented new recruits in outsourced public services being employed on inferior terms and conditions than equivalent staff transferred from the public sector.

Finally, there has been an erosion of the capacity of trade unions to defend their membership. The government criticized the tradition of workplace trade union representatives being provided with time in their working week to deal with employment relations matters, termed 'facilities time'. The civil service has been required to reduce facilities time, initially to a target of 0.1% of the paybill, and the default position is that trade union activities will not attract paid time off. In addition, the government is working towards ending trade union subscriptions being deducted by the employer at source 'check off' starting in the civil service. This requires trade unions to re-recruit members and although PCS has been active in signing up members to direct debit (PCS 2015), reductions in union membership seem inevitable.

Consequences

The main consequence of austerity measures has been employment reductions that have varied widely between sector and geographical location. These reductions are in a context in which the Office of Budget Responsibility (OBR) estimates that only 40% of cuts in day-to-day public spending have been completed, with the remainder due in the 2015–2020 parliament (OBR 2014: 148). In particular, the pace of austerity decelerated towards the end of the parliament as the 2015 general elections approached, but austerity measures will continue unabated in the 2015–2020 parliament (OBR 2015).

The impact of the financial crisis on the public sector workforce did not take effect until 2010, but subsequently there has been a rapid decline in employment targeted at specific parts of the public sector. It is expected that this trend will continue until the end of the decade, and the OBR has forecast that between 2011–2019, general government employment will fall by 1.1 million, around 20% in the overall headcount (OBR 2015: 77). Leaving aside public corporations, affected especially by bank reclassifications, local government has experienced the largest employment reductions since 2010, shedding almost one in five of its workforce (Table 6.1).

The limited change in the central government category reflects in large part the stability of NHS employment. In the NHS between 2010–2015, there was less emphasis on headcount reduction of frontline staff despite worsening financial and service pressures because NHS employers' requirement to achieve high-profile wait time and service targets was highly dependent on adequate staffing levels. A series of hospital scandals and inquiries identified inadequate numbers of registered nursing staff as an important contributory factor that bolstered investment in nursing staff, at least in the short term

(Public Accounts Committee 2015). This relative workforce stability in the NHS is not sustainable without significant injections of resources along-side major shifts in working patterns over the coming years (NHS England 2014). In schools, the teacher workforce has also been fairly stable since 2010 (DfE 2015), but other parts of the education workforce (e.g. further education) have experienced falls in employment.

In the case of the civil service, the Coalition government, without prior consultation, announced the abolition or merger of 262 government organizations in its 'bonfire of the quangos' and implemented a recruitment freeze on permanent civil servants, fixed-term appointments and temporary staff, alongside a moratorium on employing consultants. In 2012, the Civil Service Reform Plan committed the Coalition to reducing the size of the civil service by 23% between 2010–2015 (Cabinet Office 2012). In this period, civil service employment declined by over 17%, taking civil service employment to its lowest level for 75 years, with further significant cuts in employment planned between 2015–2020.

There has been considerable opposition to austerity measures with many local campaigns, but the response from mainstream trade unions has been cautious because of uncertainty about the willingness of members to take industrial action. Trends in striker days have not been markedly different from overall patterns over the last decade, but there has been a discernible increase in striker days (working days lost) since 2012. Table 6.5 indicates that strike action remains centered on the public sector, and the number of striker days in the public sector more than quadrupled from around 200,000 per annum in 2012 to around 850,000 in 2015. These trends raise questions about the continuation of relatively quiescent employment relations. As private sector wage growth recovers, the sustainability of a public sector pay squeeze becomes less certain, and these pressures are exacerbated by staff shortages and low morale in many parts of the public sector (Deloitte 2015).

Conclusions

Britain has been in the vanguard of restructuring the public sector, and there has been a continuous thread in government policy from Thatcher to Blair that emphasized market-based governance and a ratcheting up of individual and organizational performance requirements. This policy agenda was translated into increased work intensity that rose faster in the public sector than the private sector in the period 2001–2012 and was accompanied by an increased gap; jobs requiring public sector workers to work very hard were more prevalent than in the private sector (Felstead *et al.* 2013). Despite continuous organizational restructuring until the financial crisis, employers maintained aspects of the model employer tradition with well-established systems of employee voice, progressive HR policies in areas such as equality and diversity and an expectation of employment

Table 6.5 Strike Action (Total) (UK)

Total	Working days lost in the public sector (thousands)	Working days lost in the private sector (thousands)	Number of stoppages in the public sector	Number of stoppages in the private sector
1997	72	164	116	178
1998	117	163	128	122
1999	71	171	122	134
2000	363	135	138	132
2001	395	128	145	114
2002	1125	201	93	131
2003	369	129	79	106
2004	743	165	99	94
2005	99	61	77	87
2006	656	96	112	97
2007	1002	36	127	66
2008	711	48	86	82
2009	368	90	68	62
2010	314	53	66	61
2011	1276	115	114	80
2012	198	51	85	96
2013	362	80	79	80
2014	716	74	90	121
2015	850	141	187	200

Source: ONS Labour Disputes Survey

[1]Due to rounding, the working days lost for the public and private sector may not add up to the total working days lost.

security. This employment settlement was underpinned by an acceptance that the state would provide, directly or indirectly, a certain level of protection for its citizens.

The economic and financial crisis has created opportunities for the government to advance structural changes that are altering the size and role of the public sector. A constant refrain that public expenditure has been excessive combined with a judicious use of examples of public sector failure has been used to intensify and redirect earlier patterns of restructuring (Scott and Williams 2014). Previous governments concentrated on organizational and managerial restructuring in the expectation that employers with increased responsibilities and confronting competition from other public and private sector providers would reshape employment relations. These expectations were partially fulfilled, but national systems of pay determination remained largely intact, trade union and workforce voice remained prominent and shifting political interventions made employers concentrate on incremental adaptations to changes to workforce structure and roles.

What is distinctive about the experience of the Coalition government has been that its mantra of deficit reduction has been converted into a series of step-by-step policy interventions that have impacted directly on the pay, conditions and levels of employment in the public sector. To date, five years of income policies have led to reductions in real earnings in the public sector, and this trajectory continues because of the suggestion that public sector pay and conditions remain generous. Widespread reviews of public sector employment conditions are leading to reductions in other components of remuneration, including pensions and allowances. Employment reductions have been most pronounced in local government and the civil service, and these trends are set to continue over the 2015–2020 parliament, with differences in the scale of cuts between protected and unprotected departments. Overall, the coalition has achieved its main short-term objective of 'deprivileging' public sector workforce conditions in a context in which protest has been limited. The 2015 Conservative government is seeking to forestall more concerted opposition by returning to a more Thatcherite agenda that involves further restrictions on strike action by more stringent ballot thresholds on lawful industrial action and by curbing the capacity of trade unions to operate effectively by the reduction of facilities time and the ending of check off arrangements. The economic and financial crisis has therefore been used to advance an agenda in which a threadbare and highly conditional set of social and welfare rights are serviced by a workforce that is scattered between a mixture of public, private and voluntary sector providers that are employed on downgraded employment terms and conditions.

Note

1. https://www.gov.uk/government/organisations/certification-officer

References

Agboniahor, W. (2014) 'Special Report: Senior Civil Service Recruitment', *Civil Service World*, 24 November.
Bach, S. (2004) *Employment Relations and the Health Service: The Management of Reforms*, London: Routledge.
Bach, S. (2012) 'Shrinking the State or the Big Society? Public Service Employment Relations in an Era of Austerity', *Industrial Relations Journal*, 43(5): 399–415.
Bach, S. and Kessler, I. (2012) *The Modernisation of Public Services and Employee Relations: Targeted Change*, Basingstoke: Palgrave-Macmillan.
Bach, S. and Stroleny, A. (2014) 'Restructuring UK Local Government Employment Relations: Pay Determination and Employee Participation in Tough Times', *Transfer*, 20(3): 343–356.
Beaumont, P. (1992) *Public Sector Industrial Relations*, London: Routledge.
Blair, T. (2010) *A Journey*, London: Hutchinson.
Bryson, A. and Forth, J. (2011) 'Trade Unions', in Gregg, P. and Wadsworth, J. (eds.) *The Labour Market in Winter: The State of Working Britain*, Oxford: Oxford University Press, 254–271.
Cabinet Office (2012) *Civil Service Reform Plan*, London: Cabinet Office.
Committee of Public Accounts (2015) *Financial Sustainability of NHS Bodies*.

Communities and Local Government Committee (2014) *Local Government Chief Officers' Remuneration*, London: House of Commons.

Conservative Party (2015) *The Conservative Party Manifesto 2015.*

Cornes, M., Manthorpe, J., Moroarty, J., Blendi-Mahota, S. and Hussein, S. (2013) 'Assessing the Effectiveness of Policy Interventions to Reduce the Use of Agency or Temporary Social Workers in England', *Health and Social Care*, 21(3): 236–244.

Cribb, J., Disney, R. and Sibieta, L. (2014a) *The Public Sector Workforce: Past, Present and Future*, London: Institute for Fiscal Studies.

Cribb, J., Emmerson, C. and Sibieta, L. (2014b) *Public Sector Pay in the UK*, London: Institute for Fiscal Studies.

Crouch, C. (2013) 'From Markets vs States to Corporations vs Civil Society', in Schafer, A. and Streeck, W. (eds.) *Politics in the Age of Austerity*, Cambridge: Polity.

Deloitte/Reform (2015) *The State of the State 2015–16: Recalibrating Government*, London: Deloitte.

Department for Education (2015) *School Workforce in England: November 2013*, London: DfE.

Dolton, P. and Makepeace, G. (2011) 'Public and Private Sector Labour Markets', in Gregg, P. and Wadsworth, J. (eds.) *The Labour Market in Winter: The State of Working Britain*, Oxford: Oxford University Press, 272–288.

Fawcett Society (2012) *The Impact of Austerity on Women*, London: Fawcett Society.

Fredman, S. and Morris, G. (1989) *The State as Employer: Labour Law in the Public Services*, London: Mansell.

Gash, T., Panchamia, N., Sims, S. and Hotson, L. (2013) *Making Public Service Markets Work*, London: Institute for Government.

Grant Thornton (2014) *Rising to the Challenge: The Evolution of Local Government.* London: Grant Thornton.

Grimshaw, D. and Rubery, J. (2012) 'The End of the UKs Liberal Collectivist Social Model? The Implications of the Coalition Government's Policy during the Austerity Crisis', *Cambridge Journal of Economics*, 36(1): 105–126.

Hall, M. and Purcell, J. (2012) *Consultation at Work: Regulation and Practice*, Oxford: Oxford University Press.

House of Commons (2010) *The Civil Service Code.* https://www.gov.uk/government/publications/civil-service-code/the-civil-service-code

House of Commons (2013) *Library Closures, Third Report of Session 2012–13, Volume 1*, London: House of Commons.

Hutton, W. (2011) *Fair Pay in the Public Sector*, London: Treasury.

IDS (Income Data Services) (2013) *Pay and Conditions in Local Government 2013*, IDS Pay Report, 16 July, London: IDS.

IFS (2015) *Green Budget 2015*, London: IFS.

James, O., Mosley, A., Petrovsky, N. and Boyne, G. (2012) 'United Kingdom', in Verhoest, K., Van Thiel, S., Bouckaert, G. and Laegreid, P. (eds.) *Government Agencies: Practices and Lessons from 30 Countries*, Basingstoke: PalgraveMacmillan, 57–68.

Johnson, P. and Chandler, D. (2015) 'The Coalition and the Economy', in Seldon, A. and Finn, M. (eds.) *The Coalition Effect 2010–2015*, Cambridge: Cambridge University Press, 159–193.

Julius, D. (2008) *Public Services Industry Review*, London: BIS.

162   *Stephen Bach*

Kessler, I. and Heron, P. (2001) 'Steward Organization in a Professional Union: The Case of the Royal College of Nursing', *British Journal of Industrial Relations*, 39(3): 367–391.

Lodge, M. and Hood, C. (2012) 'Into an Age of Multiple Austerities? Public Management and Public Service Bargains across OECD Countries', *Governance*, 25(1): 79–101.

Lupton, R. with Burchardt, T., Fitzgerald, A., Hills, J., McKnight, A., Obolenskaya, P., Stewart, K., Thomson, S., Tunstall, R. and Vizard, P. (2015) *The Coalition's Social Policy Record: Policy, Spending and Outcomes 2010–2015*. London: Joseph Rowntree Foundation.

McClaughlin, C. (2014) 'Equal Pay, Litigation and Reflexive Regulation: The Case of the UK Local Authority Sector', *Industrial Law Journal*, 43(1): 410–456.

Muller, T. and Schulten, T. (2015) *The Public-private Sector Pay Debate in Europe*, Brussels: ETUI.

NAO (National Audit Office) (2013a) *Financial Sustainability of Local Authorities*, London: NAO.

NAO (National Audit Office) (2013b) *Building Senior Capability in the Senior Civil Service to Meet Today's Challenges*, London: NAO.

NAO (National Audit Office) (2014) *The Impact of Funding Reductions on Local Authorities*, London: NAO.

National Coalition for Independent Action (2015) *Fight or Fright: Voluntary Services in 2015*. London: NCIA.

Neville, S. and O'Connor, D. (2015) 'NHS Managers Warn of Impact of Trades Union Reforms', *Financial Times*, 15 October.

NHS England (2014) *Five Year Forward View*, London: NHS England.

OBR (2014) *Economic and Fiscal Outlook, November 2014*, London: OBR.

OBR (2015) *Economic and Fiscal Outlook, March 2015*, London: OBR.

OECD (2015) *Government at a Glance 2015: Country Fact Sheet UK*, Paris: OECD.

OME (Office of Manpower Economics) (2015) *About Us*. https://www.gov.uk/government/organisations/office-of-manpower-economics/about

ONS (2015) *Public Sector Employment, Q4 2014*, London: ONS.

PCS (2015) *National Organising Strategy*, London: PCS.

Perkins, S. and White, G. (2010) 'Modernising Pay in the UK Public Services: Trends and Implications', *Human Resource Management Journal*, 20(3): 244–257.

Plimmer, G. (2015) 'Public Service Outsourcing Jumps under Coalition', *Financial Times*, 30 April 2015.

Pollitt, C. and Bouckaert, G. (2014) *Public Management Reform: A Comparative Analysis*, Oxford: Oxford University Press.

Scott, P. and Williams, S. (2014) 'The Coalition Government and Employment Relations: Accelerated Neo-Liberalism and the Rise of Employer-Dominated Voluntarism', *Obervatoire de la Société Britannique*, 15: 145–164.

Seifert, R. (1992) *Industrial Relations in the NHS*, London: Chapman and Hall.

Simms, M., Holgate, J. and Heery, E. (2013) *Union Voices: Tactics and Tensions in UK Organizing*, Cornell; Cornell University Press.

Smith Institute (2014) *Outsourcing the Cuts: Pay and Employment Effects of Contracting Out*, London: The Smith Institute.

Tattersall, A. (2010) *Power in Coalition: Strategies for Strong Unions and Social Change*, Cornell: Cornell University Press.

Taylor-Gooby, P. (2012) 'Root and Branch Restructuring to Achieve Major Cuts: The Social Policy Programme of the 2010 UK Coalition Government', *Social Policy and Administration*, 46(1): 61–82.

Treasury (2010) *Spending Review 2010*, London: The Treasury.

Treasury (2015) *Civil Service Pay Guidance 2015 to 2016*, London: The Treasury.

Unison (2014) *Private Contractors and the Fragmented Workforce: Committing to the Future*, London: Unison.

Van Wanrooy, B., Bewley, H., Bryson, A., Forth, J., Stokes, L. and Wood, S. (2013) *Employment Relations in the Shadow of Recession: Findings from the 2011 Workplace Employment Relations Study*, London: PalgraveMacmillan.

Walshe, K. and Chambers, N. (2010) 'Healthcare Reform and Leadership', in Brookes, S. and Grint, K. (ed.) *The New Public Leadership Challenge*, Basingstoke: PalgraveMacmillan.

White, G. and Hatchett, A. (2003) 'The Pay Review Bodies in Britain under the Labour Government', *Public Money and Management*, October, 237–244.

Winchester, D. and Bach, S. (1995) 'The State: The Public Sector', in Edwards, P. (ed.) *Industrial Relations: Theory and Practice in Britain*, Oxford: Blackwell, 304–334.

Winchester, D. and Bach, S. (1999) 'The Transformation of Public Service Employment Relations in Britain', in Bach, S., Bordogna, L., Della Rocca, G. and Winchester, D. (eds.) *Public Service Employment Relations in Western Europe: Transformation, Modernisation or Inertia?* London: Routledge, 1–21.

Wolf, A. (2010) *More Than We Bargained for: The Social and Economic Costs of National Wage Bargaining*, London: CentreForum.

7 The Netherlands: The Economic Crisis Spurs Public Service and Employment Relations Reform

Peter Leisink

Introduction

Since the 1980s, successive governments in the Netherlands have engaged in policies to reform public services. These reform policies have in part been inspired by New Public Management (NPM) ideas, as they combine a drive for efficiency and effectiveness, less bureaucracy and better services for citizens and businesses (Hood 1991). Some reform decisions were explicitly motivated by NPM ideas as in the 1980s, when efficiency operations went along with privatization, the creation of agencies and targets for personnel reduction. Also, performance management gained influence through performance measurement and results-oriented budgeting. Since the late 1990s, government interest in efficiency fluctuated, but interest in raising the effectiveness of government and the quality of public services remained. A prominent example is healthcare, where neoliberal ideas led the government in 2006 to introduce market-like mechanisms, hoping that competition would improve efficiency and innovation. However, because governments in the Netherlands are coalition governments, often consisting of three parties, there is a tendency for consensus and compromise, and government policies are less extremely ideological compared to the anti-government ideologies underlying the Thatcher and Reagan reform policies (Pollitt *et al.* 2007; Noordegraaf 2009). In addition, reforms are incremental and less disruptive, as they tend to be in majoritarian political systems (Pollitt and Bouckaert 2011).

Public service reforms obviously affected employment relations (Leisink and Steijn 2005; Steijn and Leisink 2007). In general, the reform policies were oriented at the 'normalization' of public sector employment relations by bringing them more in line with private sector employment relations. These were particularly prominent in the 1990s and included such decisions as the privatization of the general pension fund for public employees (1992), the breaking up of the comprehensive public sector wage system into separate wage systems for fourteen subsectors (1993) and the introduction of employee participation through the works council (1995). The normalization process incited initiatives by members of parliament from 1997 onwards to end the employment statute of public sector employees.

Thus, public service reform in the Netherlands can be characterized as an ongoing and incremental process, based on ideas about modernization of public services. However, one might expect that the fiscal and economic crisis since 2008 has ended this kind of incremental modernization process and forced a drastic reform program (Bach and Bordogna 2013). Moreover, the economic crisis combined with other challenges, such as demographic changes impacting the labor market and welfare state provisions. Scoring a medium degree of financial and demographic vulnerability (Lodge and Hood 2011), the viability of the Dutch government's modernization path might be questioned. On the other hand, given the Netherlands' historical reform path, one may wonder whether a change of state response would take the form of one of the types of state response distinguished by Lodge and Hood: the directing state, the hollow state, the local communitarian state and the (barely) coping state. This chapter will examine the nature of recent public service reform in the Netherlands by addressing two questions. First, what are the trends in the organization and management of public services in the Netherlands? The focus is on the changes following the economic crisis since 2008, but placing these in the longer time frame of public service reforms since the 1980s. The second question is: what do the public service reforms imply for public sector employment relations and the traditional idea of the public employer as a model employer?

The Public Sector

For the purpose of this chapter, it is necessary to explain what is understood by the concept of 'public sector' in the Netherlands. Formal characteristics—public law regulation and government funding—and the public goal of organizations are the basis for establishing the public sector in the Netherlands. Public sector organizations are mostly regulated by public law. The 'public statute' of public sector workers was established in 1929 by the *Ambtenarenwet* (civil servants law) as a consequence of Article 109 of the constitution, similar to other countries with a *Rechtsstaat* tradition (Bordogna 2013). The public employment statute goes along with distinctive employment conditions, which today include the unilateral appointment of public employees, appeal procedures in the case of employer decisions such as disciplinary measures and dismissal and the unilateral binding determination of employment conditions by the employer (BZK 2008). The public statute holds today for about 900.000 employees in the central, provincial and municipal governments, the police, the armed forces, the judiciary, the water districts and a large part of employees in education.

Traditionally, the state has depended on private, not-for-profit organizations for services like education, health and housing (Noordegraaf 2009). In primary and secondary education, most schools are entities with a statutory task and have a legal personality based on either public or private law

(Yesilkagit and Van Thiel 2012: 181). All schools are government funded and are held accountable by the school inspectorate. As they serve a public goal, they are regarded as part of the public sector.

The healthcare sector consists of academic medical centers, which are also legal entities which are appointed by law to carry out a particular public task for which they receive funding from the government (Yesilkagit and Van Thiel 2012: 181), and general hospitals, which usually have the legal status of a foundation or a private corporation for which public law does not hold. All hospitals are government and collectively funded and are legally not allowed to make a profit and to pay dividends to stockholders. Because hospitals are regarded as private organizations with a public goal, they are denoted as semi-public organizations (VWS 2013).

For the purpose of comparison, this chapter will concentrate on:

a.   government, including the central, provincial and municipal governments;
b.   education, focusing on primary and secondary education;
c.   healthcare, focusing on academic medical centers and general hospitals.

This focus means that other parts of what is understood by the concept of 'public sector' will not be included in the analysis. These are parts of government employment—the police, the judiciary, prisons, armed forces, water districts—education—vocational and higher education—and the care sector—mental care, childcare, youth care, elder care and other designated care institutions.

Employment Structure and Trends

Before concentrating on the main sectors of government, education and healthcare, this section will first describe the general trends in public employment since 1990. Over the full period under review, employment has declined because of public service reforms aimed at more efficiency, privatization and the creation of agencies. However, the pattern of change is different between the sectors and fluctuates over the years.

Between 1982 and 2000, the number of public employees[1] declined from 615.200 to 456.900 employees (Van der Meer and Dijkstra 2013). This was primarily achieved through privatizing public organizations and additionally by a gradual reduction of employment, particularly in the armed forces, municipalities, public agencies and ministries. This latter gradual reduction amounts to about 20% of the total loss of public sector employment between 1980 and 2000.

However, when the economy recovered by the end of the 1990s, governments relaxed the reform policies aimed at cutting public employment. Over the period 2000–2010, employment expanded again from 456.900 to 486.400 employees, but there were fluctuations between years (Van der Meer and Dijkstra 2013: 16–19). In some years, such as the 2003–2005 period, employment declined modestly by gradual reductions and the privatization of the Netherlands Central Bureau for Statistics. However, in the 2006–2009 period, modest growth occurred particularly because of a growth of about 10.000 employees in public safety, including the police, the judiciary and the intelligence service.

Table 7.1[2] (BZK 2014: 12) presents the public sector workforce trends from 2003 to 2013.

Concentrating on this period, we can detect the influence of the economic and fiscal crisis. Over the 2003–2013 period, public sector employment (in headcount) declined from 12.3% of the total labor force in 2003 to 11.3% in 2013.[3] The pattern differs for the subsectors, however. The number of employees in the central government declines from 2003 until 2005, then rises modestly from 2006 through to 2009 and then declines every year until 2013. The number of employees in the provincial and municipal governments declines every year over the full period, the only exception being 2009, when a slight increase can be noted. In both primary and secondary education, the number of employees rises until 2009, although fluctuating slightly in secondary education, and then declines modestly but steadily from 2009 onwards. By contrast, the number of employees in healthcare, both academic medical centers and general hospitals, increases steadily over the whole period, but fluctuates somewhat since 2009. Focusing on the period since 2009, employment has declined in all subsectors with the exception of healthcare, which has seen a slight increase.

The share of female employees is highest in education and lowest in government, with healthcare taking the intermediate position (BZK 2014: 16). Since 2009, the percentage of women in the four subsectors has remained stable in healthcare and has increased slightly in education and government. In other words, women have not suffered disproportionally from the decline of public sector jobs. The proportion of part-time jobs differs between the subsectors in a pattern similar to the proportion of female employees. Education has the highest proportion of part-time employees, government the lowest and health takes the intermediate position. Since 2009, the proportion of part-time employees has remained stable in government and healthcare, and has increased slightly in education.

The percentage of employees having a flexible contract (temporary work, call contract) has shown a steady increase since 2008. However, the average percentage of employees having a flexible contract over the period 2005–2012 is 12% in the public sector versus 19% in all other sectors. Within the public sector, the percentages of employees having a flexible contract vary, for instance, from 2% in the police, 5% of provincial and municipal employees to 7% of central government employees. However, the chance of employees having a flexible contract to get a permanent job is smaller in the government sector than in other sectors (Smulders and Houtman 2012; Pot and Smulders 2013). The legal construction of employing employees on a payroll basis has grown in central government as a means to evade the

Table 7.1 Number of Employees in Specific Public Subsectors (The Netherlands)

	1995	2000	2003	2004	2005	2006	2007	2008	2009	2010	2011	2012	2013
Central* Government	98.400	116.000	125.393	119.630	116.615	120.287	123.171	123.335	123.599	122.537	119.064	116.997	116.413
Provincial Government	11.700	13.000	14.019	13.686	13.341	13.337	13.180	13.003	13.285	13.217	12.625	12.179	11.494
Municipal Government	172.100	177.000	191.727	187.731	180.329	177.618	171.353	171.189	177.133	175.176	168.051	163.115	155.140
Primary Education	n/a	n/a	178.934	180.147	180.676	180.708	184.790	187.072	189.586	186.587	182.793	177.193	177.921
Secondary Education	n/a	n/a	100.779	102.027	100.283	100.984	106.429	105.051	108.324	106.093	106.002	105.991	105.920
Academic Medical Centers	30.000	45.000	55.663	56.614	56.478	57.661	60.391	62.121	64.252	65.196	66.718	65.297	67.336
General Hospitals**	n/a	n/a	169.275	170.894	176.022	176.142	178.397	178.786	188.365	185.648	185.491	188.348	n/a

*Central government, excluding the police, the judiciary and military personnel
**Source: retrieved from http://www.dutchhospitaldata.nl/kengetallen/Paginas/default.aspx

costs that accompany workforce cuts (Verhulp 2013). A payroll construction involves that the employee works for government but has a formal employment contract with a private agency that takes care of the administrative employer obligations, such as paying taxes. Despite criticism of this type of contingent work, it appears that about 18% of the total number of 150,000 employees employed on a payroll basis work for a government organization and another 8% in education (Verhulp 2013). An example is the Ministry of Economic Affairs, which employs 600 employees on a payroll basis. When central government ministries attempted to cut their workforce by ending payroll contracts, union protests forced the government to make severance payments according to the collective labor agreement for government employees.

The decline of employment in the four sectors under consideration is the result of an outflow of employees, which is at the same or only slightly lower level as the outflow in 2008 when the economic crisis began, and an inflow, which is much lower than in 2008 because of government policies to reduce public sector employment (BZK 2014: 22). These reductions were not affected by fixed replacement ratios as in other countries, but mostly by coalition agreements on reduction targets or overall cutbacks on the budget of ministries. As a consequence, the government sectors have an aging workforce, with almost half of all employees being 50 years or older and with the annual inflow of 9,000 young employees in 2008 now reduced to about 3,000 employees. These trends are largely in line with the analyses made by the federations of government employers and unions in 2010 (VSO *et al.* 2010). As a result, the government foresaw no quantitative labor market problems but emphasized the need for a workforce policy concentrating on internal mobility, flexibility and quality.

The workforce trends over the period since 2008 have not been caused by any major changes in public sector labor market rules such as those regarding recruitment, job security and dismissal, with one exception: namely, the government's decision in 2004 to end the fiscal subsidy of early retirement and subsequent decisions to raise the retirement age. Workforce trends have taken place within the existing regulatory framework. Thus, given the demographic trend of a declining number of childbirths, schools have been less willing to offer a permanent job to job seekers, usually young teachers.

Public Sector Employment Relations and Pay Determination

Since the 1950s, labor relations in The Netherlands have involved a two-tier system (Visser 1992). At the national sectoral level, trade unions represent workers' interests through collective bargaining with employer organizations, resulting in collective agreements that are mainly multi-employer, industry-wide agreements. The legal framework for collective bargaining involves that collective agreements that are concluded by representative employer and employee organizations are generally binding for the sector (extension clause). The coverage of collective agreements is very high, with more than 80% of all workers having their employment conditions determined by collective agreements.

At the company level, every employer who employs fifty or more employees is obliged to have a works council. This obligation is laid down in the Works Council Act. Works councils consist of elected employee representatives. They have legal rights of information, advice and approval (co-determination) through which they can influence company policies and represent workers' interests regarding issues in health and safety, personnel policies and so on. The Works Council Act provides for frequent consultations between the works council and the employer.

This institutional framework is a feature of today's labor relations system in the Netherlands, which now also holds for the public sector because of the normalization and decentralization developments since the 1990s (Leisink and Steijn 2005; Steijn and Leisink 2007). Normalization had two faces from the perspective of public sector employees. On the one hand, some employment conditions worsened, such as the legal protection against redundancy and social security benefits. However, the restriction of the legal protection against redundancy had little impact in practice for older government employees because the so-called LIFO principle still holds. LIFO stands for 'last in, first out', which means that those who have joined government employment last will be the first to go if redundancies occur. Practically, when government employees are declared redundant because of reorganization, older employees have the first right to be placed in a vacancy that occurs in the same employing unit. On the other hand, the prohibition to strike, which existed until the 1980s, was lifted and employee participation was strengthened through the extension of the Works Council Act in 1995, which gave works councils in the public sector the same legal rights as works councils in the private sector have. However, the works councils' powers in the government sector differ from the private sector in one important respect. In order to protect the principle of the primacy of politics, a clause was added to Article 46 of the Works Council Act 1995, stating that neither 'decisions concerning the tasks of public bodies nor the policies concerning the execution of these tasks can be subjected to the right of consultation of the works council, with the exception of the consequences for the job activities of staff in this organization'. This governmental exception has periodically created conflict. A survey in 2011 showed that 15% of government works council members have the experience that the works council is occasionally/frequently not consulted on issues because of the 'primacy of politics', but only 3% of government employer representatives claim that this is the case (A + O fonds Rijk 2011). Apart from this exception, public sector works councils have the legal rights that works councils generally have, including the right of approval in the field of personnel and social policies, the right of advice in the field of economic and financial issues and the right of information.

Decentralization gave a major impetus to collective bargaining in the public sector. Until 1993, terms of employment for all public sector employees were centrally determined by the government. Although unions were consulted, the government formally determined the terms of employment unilaterally. Since 1993, real negotiations between the public sector employer and the unions take place at the level of the 14 subsectors, which correspond with the specific parts of the government, education and healthcare sectors that were mentioned in the introduction to this chapter. The government was in favor of decentralization because it recognized that there were important differences between the labor market situations of the 14 subsectors. The unions initially opposed the decentralization because from their perspective, this would put an end to the solidarity between all public sector workers. However, unions later accepted decentralization because they obtained the so-called 'agreement requisite', which means that changes in the existing terms of employment of government employees cannot be imposed unilaterally by government but need the approval of half of the unions represented in the negotiation process.

Since 1993, collective bargaining takes place at the level of the sector between the respective sector associations of employers and unions. For some sectors, such as primary and secondary education, decentralization implied that associations that had so far represented schools in consultations with the ministry over government educational policies had to assume a new role as employer. In addition, some sectors, notably the central government and primary and secondary education, are fully dependent on government funding and have no independent sources of income, which means that central government ministers have a major influence on the budget that is available for wages.

Collective bargaining on the union side brings between 3 and 5 unions to the table. Fragmentation is not a feature of union organization in the Netherlands. In addition, it is usual for unions to coordinate their policies, with the largest union taking the lead, which is the union associated with the Federatie Nederlandse Vakbeweging (FNV; Dutch Federation of Trade Unions). Table 7.2 provides an overview of employer and union organizations per sector.

The length of collective agreements varies but is usually between 1 and 2 years. The institutional framework regulating collective agreements provides that the existing collective agreement is automatically extended if no new collective agreement has been concluded before the old one expires. All employees in a particular sector are covered by the collective agreement, which is generally binding when it is concluded by representative organizations. Only some specific categories of employees are excluded, such as top managers, but also medical specialists in general hospitals who are self-employed.

Table 7.2 Overview of Employer and Trade Union Organizations for Each Sector (The Netherlands)

Sector	Employer	Trade unions
Central government	Ministry of Home Affairs	4 unions: ACOP (associated with FNV), CCOOP (associated with CNV), Ambtenarencentrum, CMHF
Provincial government	IPO = Association for InterProvincial Consultation	4 unions: ACOP (associated with FNV), CCOOP (associated with CNV), Ambtenarencentrum, CMHF
Municipalities	VNG = Association of Dutch Municipalities	3 unions: Abvakabo FNV, CNV Publieke Zaak, CMHF
Primary education	PO Raad = Council for Primary Education	5 unions: Abvakabo and AOb (both associated with FNV), CNV Onderwijs, FvO, AVS
Secondary education	VO Raad = Council for Secondary Education	4 unions: Abvakabo and AOb (both associated with FNV), CNV Onderwijs, FvO
Academic medical centers	NFU = Netherlands Federation of University Medical Centres	4 unions: ACOP (associated with FNV), CCOOP (associated with CNV), Ambtenarencentrum, CMHF
General hospitals	NVZ = Association of Hospitals	4 unions: FNV, CNV Zorg en Welzijn, FBZ, NU'91

Public Employers

This section provides an overview of government reform policies from the 1980s until the mid-2000s. The following section examines what these reform policies implied for the role and responsibilities of employers in the central government, municipalities and education.

Government Public Sector Reform Policies

Public service reform policies of successive governments since the 1980s have been characterized by an agenda aimed at increasing efficiency and flexibility, reducing bureaucracy and improving services to citizens and businesses. Governments decided on concrete reform agendas with titles such as 'Better government for citizens and businesses', 'Different government' or 'Compact government', and some even had specific state secretaries or ministers charged with the reform. There are minor differences between these reform agendas, indicated by shifting emphases on efficiency (1980s), innovation and quality (1990s) and accountability (early 2000s) (Noordegraaf 2009). The present reform agenda aims at a smaller government by emphasizing the active role that citizens and businesses should play in society and the restricted supplementary responsibility that the government has in providing additional professional services through nonprofit service organizations when citizens are unable to provide for work and welfare themselves.

Initially, in the 1980s, NPM ideas were articulated explicitly. Reform operations focused on efficiency, cutbacks and privatization. An example is the privatization of the postal services in 1989. Municipalities privatized many municipal organizations, such as hospitals, elderly homes, slaughterhouses, housing corporations, utilities and transport companies (Van der Meer and Dijkstra 2013: 20). Public sector unions strongly opposed these privatizations. However, NPM ideas had a strong hold on politicians in the 1980s, partly as a backlash to the previous decades of an expanding welfare state favored by social democratic politicians. Given this ideological climate, public sector unions concentrated on protecting employment conditions in the transition from public to private employment. Government's 'Great efficiency operations' also aimed at job reductions and rationalizing management by the introduction of contract management. Planning and control cycles and performance management were introduced in the central government as well as in many municipalities (Noordegraaf 2009).

Privatization was a less-favored reform option during the period from 1989 to 2002, when there were coalition governments in which the Social Democrats participated. During that period, the focus of reform policies shifted to quality of service, reduction of bureaucracy and the creation of semi-autonomous agencies. The service quality interest resulted in initiatives to benchmark service delivery in an increasing number of sectors, including municipalities, the police, schools and elderly homes. Increasing service quality and efficiency was also the basis of an agreement in 1992 between the central and local governments to transfer tasks to the local government. An example is public housing, where the central government restricted its task to deciding policy goals while their implementation was left to municipalities and housing corporations, as a consequence of which, the central government unit for public housing was halved to about 1,250 employees (Rosenthal *et al.* 1996: 39).

From the early 1980s, agencies were created, operating at arm's length of the government and carrying out public tasks such as regulation, service delivery and policy implementation. Such agencies are semi-autonomous organizations that have no legal independence or which are legally independent organizations, based on public or private law. Government's interest in agencies as an instrument of reform policies derives from the fact that, compared to government bureaucracies, agencies face less hierarchical and political influence on their operations and have more managerial freedom (Van Thiel 2012: 18). This managerial freedom includes the formal autonomy to conduct negotiations over a collective labor agreement, either as an individual agency, as holds, for example for the Netherlands Central Bank, or as a collection of similar agencies, as is the case for five designated research agencies. The number of semi-autonomous agencies (in Dutch: *Zelfstandig BestuursOrgaan*) increased rapidly in the 1980s and 1990s, totaling 630 by 2004. The number of employees they employ is estimated at about 120,000, equalling the number of employees employed by the central government. Examples of semi-autonomous agencies are the Central Agency for the reception of asylum-seekers, the Netherlands Central Bank, the Chamber of Commerce and the Netherlands Broadcasting Company. In line with their managerial autonomy, semi-autonomous agencies report on average once a year to the parent ministry about their performance, but they also have to report to their board and are audited by others such as the ministry or accountants hired by the agency and/or ministry. Yesilkagit and Van Thiel (2012: 188) report that semi-autonomous agencies have on average up to 10 performance indicators. As a result of critical evaluations of their lack of democratic accountability, legal requirements were tightened for these agencies in 2006.

The continuing rise of the costs of healthcare was a permanent worry of governments from the 1980s onwards. Successive ministers introduced measures to improve cost efficiency. Policies in the 1990s included cost-control measures, the cooperation between healthcare providers, patient involvement and network management, which included activating pressure groups, advisory bodies, patient organizations and politicians to get involved in policy development, based on the idea that a critical counterforce would result in lower costs for treatments (Trappenburg 2008). The introduction of market-like mechanisms, marked by the 2006 law on market regulation of healthcare was the most distinctive reform inspired by NPM ideas. In the new system, insurance companies are given the power to contract services from healthcare providers on behalf of their clients. As citizens are free to select their own insurance company, the idea is that insurance companies will compete for clients by offering the best healthcare package against the lowest costs, which in turn incentivizes insurance companies to conclude cost-effective contracts with hospitals for providing these services. This system generated public criticism, first concerning the dominance of insurance companies, the four largest ones of which are presumed to form an oligopoly, disrupting the mechanisms of the free market, and secondly concerning the declining power of medical professionals in deciding what is best for the patient. Notwithstanding these criticisms, the system has succeeded in containing costs better than any measure before and a recent international survey of healthcare systems declared the Dutch system the best (Health Consumer Powerhouse 2015).

Implications of Reform Policies for Public Sector Employers

Central Government

The coalition agreements of new cabinets usually laid down governmental reform policies and often combined a general reform policy agenda with specific plans for the central government. The central government employer, represented by the Minister of Interior Affairs, was bound by these coalition agreements and had little room in negotiating agreements regarding the reform consequences with the trade unions. On the one hand, the minister benefitted from the 'primacy of politics' when reorganizations were decided, and on the other hand, the minister was not always in the position to impose the specific implementation plan when the unions obstructed this by making use of the existing institutional framework.

An interesting example is the creation of shared service centers (SSCs). In the early 2000s, reform plans involved the creation of SSCs for a variety of support services, such as ICT, finance, HRM and housing. These SSCs were meant to improve quality of service and to raise efficiency, the latter being illustrated by a future reduction of about 1,000 jobs in the case of P-Direkt, the SSC for HRM. The departmental works councils felt bypassed by the cabinet decision to create the SSCs without asking their advice and decided in 2003 to go to court in order to get their legal right of advice recognized. However, the court rejected the works councils' claim on the grounds of the principle of the primacy of politics (Leisink and Steijn 2005).

On the other hand, the reorganizations accompanying the reforms were regulated by the existing institutional framework, and one element of this was the LIFO principle. As a consequence of this principle, the redeployment of staff who had been made redundant by the reorganizations favored employees with more seniority over younger ones. This consequence was unattractive for the employer, who attempted to negotiate a social plan that did not prioritize seniority, but quality. However, the unions viewed the procedural guarantees offered by the employer as insufficient. Their worries about the consequences for older employees were compounded by the governmental decision to stop fiscal subsidy for early retirement schemes. The unions then decided not to give up the LIFO principle and, given the 'agreement requisite' obtained by the unions in 1993 in exchange for the government's decision to decentralize the regulation of employment conditions, the central government employer was unable to impose a social plan based on the employer's objective to guarantee quality and the employment opportunities for young employees (Steijn and Leisink 2007).

Ongoing job reductions have been instigated ministries to introduce greater job flexibility. One example was the Ministry of Education, which was characterized as a compartmentalized department and which decided in 2005 to introduce a policy to rotate employees over policy fields. In other respects, standardization increased. A new reform program in 2007 announced a cut of 12.800 jobs and a structural saving of €630 million, which was to be achieved by centralization and standardization and giving ministries less freedom in hiring, housing and ICT. Parallel to this reform program, a new collective agreement was concluded for the 2007–2010 period. While the previous years had seen very modest annual wage increases of no more than 1%, this new collective agreement granted a wage increase of 13.2% for the 4-year period as well as a guarantee against forced redundancies.

Municipalities

Municipal employers are formally autonomous, yet the central government exerts considerable influence because it provides more than half the budget for the municipalities. However, municipalities are sensitive to being kept on a leash by the central government, as was demonstrated in 2012 when they concluded a collective agreement allowing municipal employees a wage increase despite central government pressure to stick by the general policy of a wage freeze. This employer autonomy is also manifest in employment relations policies, which partly responded to municipal reform policies—involving privatizations, efficiency programs, outsourcing and public-private partnerships—and partly reflected a proactive labor market and employment policy view. The 2000–2002 collective agreement stands out as one that illustrates this prominently. The agreement introduced several new employer instruments. One was the decision to introduce employee competencies as a basis for job performance interviews and plans for training and development. Every employee would have the right and the facilities to agree a personal development plan to keep up to date. Another measure was the introduction of results-based pay, which makes a small portion of wages flexible and dependent on outstanding performance results. By 2003, 1 in 5 municipalities had introduced this scheme. However, municipal employers did not as a rule aim at mutual gains agreements. In 2005, municipalities were the scene of enduring industrial conflicts because municipal employers wanted to abolish early retirement schemes.

Education

Although schools in primary and secondary education gained formal autonomy more than 20 years ago, the Minister of Education still has much influence on employer policies. In fact, the ministry made use of its funding authority to initiate specific employment policies which the ministry deemed necessary as part of its policy to incentivize quality (Leisink and Boselie 2014). Thus, the minister had direct influence on the employer policies of schools. For instance, in early 2000, the Minister of Education decided that schools would have to implement a specific form of integral personnel policies that prioritize professional development of teachers because this would strengthen the labor market position of schools. For the same reason in 2008, the ministry concluded a covenant with the employer and union organizations, imposing detailed rules for the quota of teachers that schools had to promote to higher salary scales in recognition of superior performance.

Trade Unions

Union Structure and Membership in the Public Sector

There are three main confederations of unions in the Netherlands, which are represented in the national tripartite Socio-Economic Council. The largest is the FNV, which has a predominantly social democrat/socialist political orientation, the second largest is the Christian CNV and the third is the confederation of middle and higher employees, the MHP. Unions affiliated with the same confederation coordinate their collective bargaining policies through their confederation.

Unions in the Netherlands are mostly structured on the basis of sector; they organize employees in all occupations in a particular sector of industry. Thus, the largest confederation FNV has a member parliament representing 26 sectors. The sectoral structure is related to what unions regard as their primary function, namely negotiating collective agreements, which in the Netherlands are sectoral or company agreements. For collective bargaining purposes, there is no structure at the regional level. The local/regional level has always been weakly developed in the trade union structure, although recently with the decentralization of social services to the local level and the coordination of labor market policies at the regional level, new initiatives have been taken to reinvigorate some form of local union activity.

The overall unionization rate has declined steadily in the Netherlands from 28% of the labor force in 1995 to 20% in 2011. In October 2013, almost 1.8 million employees were union members. The decline of union membership is comparatively large among employees aged 25–45 years. Currently, union membership among employees younger than 25 years is 6%, is 16% among employees 25–44 years old, and is 29% among 44–64 years old. About 23% of male employees are unionized compared to 17% of female employees. Union membership among employees with a permanent job is 21% compared to 9% for employees with a flexible job.

Union membership in the public sector is higher than in the private sector. Table 7.3 provides statistical information on the unionization rates for 3 aggregate sectors, namely government, education, health and social care. The data from 2006 onwards are included in order to monitor the effect of the economic crisis. The data show that unionization rates in all three sectors declined steadily from 1995 to 2008–09 and then stabilized.

The decline of union membership is a general trend in the Netherlands, for which a variety of structural explanations have been suggested (Bryson *et al.* 2011; Visser 2013). These include the decline of employment in the

Table 7.3 Unionization Rates in Government, Education, Health and Social Care

	1995	2000	2006	2007	2008	2009	2010	2011
Government[*]	46	43	40	39	36	36	34	34
Education[**]	42	40	34	32	30	32	30	30
Health and social care[***]	24	25	22	21	20	20	18	19

[*]Central, provincial and municipal governments; military personnel; police and judiciary
[**]Primary, secondary, vocational and higher professional education, universities
[***]Hospitals, mental health, childcare, youth care, care for the elderly, home care

construction and manufacturing industries where union membership was traditionally high and the increase of employees with flexible contracts and self-employed employees. Union membership is increasingly less prevalent among young employees. This holds for the public sector as well, where union policies had less attraction for young employees as a consequence of their focus on older workers' interests through, for instance, holding on to the LIFO principle and industrial action to block the end of early retirement schemes and the rise of the retirement age.

Representation of Employee Voice

The two-tier system of labor relations that the Netherlands has holds for the public sector as well. At the national sectoral level, unions represent workers' interests, while at the company level, works councils provide a channel for employee voice. In the public sector, all employers facilitate employee voice through works councils.

A collective agreement typically consists of rules concerning wages, working hours, social security arrangements and pension schemes. These are regarded as the primary terms of employment. Usually, collective agreements also deal with secondary terms of employment, including traveling allowances, holidays, training facilities and older worker policies.

Traditionally, a division of labor has existed, with unions concentrating on collective bargaining over pay and conditions. Although unions have broadened their scope of activities to include issues such as training, employability and job mobility, sectoral collective agreements tend to restrict themselves to framework arrangements on these broader issues, delegating their operationalization to the decentralized level, usually the works council. Union organization at the workplace level is mostly absent, but collective agreements typically provide facilities and paid time off for union representatives. There is an indirect union influence at the company level because the majority of works council members are of union members.

The Consequences of the Economic Crisis for Public Sector Employment Relations

This section provides an overview of the measures that successive government coalitions decided on since the outbreak of the economic crisis in 2008. The banking crisis, the bailout of the banks, the ensuing fiscal crisis and the economic crisis prompted government action. The institutional requirements of the European Stability and Growth Pact were a major factor prompting the austerity measures decided by successive governments. After an initial period of negative economic growth from mid-2008 to mid-2009, another period of negative economic growth hit the Netherlands in 2011 and 2012. This is reflected in multiple packages of austerity measures succeeding each other; see Table 7.4. This section will describe the measures

Table 7.4 Austerity Measures in the Netherlands

Time period	Coalition government	Planned austerity packages	Austerity measures affecting public services (selected instances)
2007–2010	*Balkenende IV* Christian democrats, social democrats, Christian union	Funding freeze on municipalities 2009–2011 €3.2 billion austerity package (2010)	Reduction of central government by 10,000 jobs €600 million wage restraint €231 million efficiency cuts in government €310 million savings on childcare
2010	*Rutte I* conservative liberals, Christian democrats	€18.3 billion austerity package up to 2015	€1.5 billion cuts in central government €870 million wage restraint public sector €500 million cuts on defense €300 million reorganization education for children with special needs
2012	*Rutte I + Parliament*	€12 billion austerity package	€1.6 billion wage freeze public sector 2012 + 2013 Pension age to 66 in 2019 and 67 in 2024
2012–2015	*Rutte II* conservative liberals, social democrats	€16 billion austerity package	€1 billion efficiency cuts on central government Harmonization of dismissal law Pension age to 66 in 2018 and 67 in 2021

and their impact on the public sector workforce. Subsequently, attention will focus on how employers and unions responded to these austerity measures, notably as regards employment conditions and the organization of public service provision.

Austerity Measures, Their Drivers and Consequences

Early 2010 austerity measures were presented that for the first time were explicitly connected to the fiscal and economic crisis. Indeed, the initial government response to the financial crisis of 2008–2009 consisted of emergency capital injections in the banking sector, Keynesian demand management and labor market protection instead of immediate welfare state retrenchment (Vis *et al.* 2011). But by 2010 the Balkenende IV government, which was in office from February 2007 until February 2010, decided on austerity measures amounting to €3.2 billion. This coalition government had decided on cutbacks before 2010, however. The Balkenende IV government carried out a reform program that planned to reduce the government workforce by 12,000 jobs. Also in April 2009, the Balkenende IV government decided to freeze central government funding to local government for the 2009–2011 period. The austerity measures that were announced by the Balkenende IV government included various measures that affected the public sector directly, such as wage restraint (€600 million) and efficiency cuts in the government (€231 million), as well as savings on childcare that affected employment indirectly (€310 million) (Algemene Rekenkamer 2011: 15–17).

In September 2010, the Rutte I government took office. This consisted of conservative liberals and Christian democrats and had a marginal majority because the populist Partij voor de Vrijheid (PVV; Party for Freedom) was willing to support it. Their Coalition Agreement referred to the credit crisis as well as to demographic developments as the reason for announcing austerity measures: 'Because of the ageing population, the credit crisis and the European debt crisis reconstruction measures of government finances are a sore need'. The continuity with earlier reform policies is apparent from the government's aim to create 'a strong, small and service-oriented government that costs less taxpayers' money, has less employees, less rules and less governors' (Coalition Agreement 2010: 5). They proposed 105 austerity measures that should save €18.3 billion in 2015. These measures addressed specific subsectors directly: for instance, cuts in the central government by €1.5 billion, wages in the collective sector by €870 million and defense by €500 million (Algemene Rekenkamer 2011: 12–13). Another specific measure was the reorganization of education for children with special needs (*Passend Onderwijs*), which should save €300 million. In addition, management functions were centralized, such as ICT, procurement, housing, audit and facility services.

There was a difference between the cutback measures of the Balkenende and the Rutte I governments. Whereas the Balkenende government—and previous governments—specified the number of government jobs that would have to be reduced—and always failed to achieve that specific target—the Rutte I government specified a financial target for each department and left it to the department's management how this target would be achieved. In practice, however, cutting jobs remained the major way in which departments intended to achieve their target. A 2011 survey of cutback measures of the ministries and the organizations under their authority, such as the police, defense and Inland Revenue, showed job cuts amounting to almost 10% of total government jobs.

The aim of the austerity measures decided by the Rutte I government was to comply with the requirements of the European Stability and Growth pact by 2013, more specifically, a national debt of no more than 3% in 2014. However, the economic crisis affected government finances more than foreseen and extra austerity measures were required by the European Commission before April 30, 2012. Because the Rutte I government had fallen by this time, an ad hoc parliamentary majority agreed upon a package of measures totalling €12 billion in order to meet EU requirements. The new cutback decisions included a wage freeze for public sector employees for 2 years, which should result in €1.6 billion savings in 2012 and 2013. Healthcare employees were excluded from this measure because of the sector's labor market problems and the expected future growth in demand for healthcare related to the aging population. Another measure in the parliamentary package included the withdrawal of the earlier cutback measure on education for children with special needs as a response to protests from unions, schools and parents. Apart from cutback measures, this 2012 parliamentary agreement included other types of measures as well, notably the decision to raise the pension age to 66 in 2019 and to 67 by 2024. The aim of this measure, benefitting the public budget, was to ensure that employees work longer and pay taxes instead of receiving a pension.

After the September 2012 elections, a new coalition cabinet took office in November 2012, this time consisting of conservative liberals and social democrats. New austerity measures were announced, topping earlier measures with an extra €16 billion. New measures included efficiency cuts on central government by about €1 billion, the harmonization of legislation concerning the dismissal of public sector employees with regulations for private sector employees, a cap on dismissal compensation and another speeding up of the rise of the pension age to the age of 66 in 2018 and to the age of 67 in 2021.

Building on plans for structural reform prepared by earlier governments, this government decided to further decentralize the provision of specific welfare arrangements to municipalities, notably the provision of sheltered workplaces, home care and youth care. This structural reform took effect from 2015 and went along with efficiency cuts up to 20% for providing these services, based on the argument that local government can provide these more efficiently. As such, the decentralization of these welfare arrangements was similar to earlier reforms like the 1990s decentralization of public housing. The decentralization of these services requires municipalities to network with a multitude of other organizations: private and public employers for providing sheltered workplaces to handicapped people; schools, welfare, police and youth care organizations for providing care to young people; home care organizations, general practitioners, and volunteers for organizing home care for the elderly and disabled. The quality of these social services will be dependent on the successful collaboration of these networks. A new feature of the current reform is the government's ideology of reversing the state's role in providing welfare services by prioritizing the individual citizen's responsibility.

This is particularly salient in home care; only if and when the citizen and his/her network of relatives, neighbors and friends is unable to provide for these services, which is to be determined by municipal employees, will state-funded professionals provide supplementary services.

The overview provided in Table 7.4 lists a variety of austerity measures in absolute terms. It is difficult to give a sense of the proportionate cuts in percentage terms. This is related to the fact that measures aim at achieving a structural cutback in expenditure but the time periods over which this is to be achieved vary between measures. However, a sense of their impact may be illustrated by the austerity package of €18.3 billion decided on by the Rutte I government in 2010. This austerity package, which covered the period 2010–2015, represented about 7.5% of total planned net government expenditure in 2010 (€ 244.1 billion)[4]. This overview of austerity measures shows that these measures have quantitative as well as structural goals, as in other countries (Vaughan-Whitehead 2013). The quantitative goals are evident from measures to achieve more efficiency, for instance, through outsourcing and the creation of shared service centers, and from measures cutting employment and wages. Structural reforms aim at 'service-oriented government' and resemble previous governments' reform programs.

Apart from the economic crisis, demographic changes are another important driver of change. Demographic trends have been a factor influencing public sector employment policy for more than a decade. In government and education, which have a workforce that is comparatively old, employers and unions initially developed age-related policies to support and retain older workers in order to deal with expected labor market shortages and the loss of knowledge as a consequence of the outflow of older employees. Subsequently, the combined consequence of demographic changes and the economic crisis manifested itself by the decision of successive governments to raise the retirement age.

The Differential Impact of Austerity Measures and Employer and Trade Union Responses

The overview of austerity measures taken by successive governments illustrates that the public sector was not affected uniformly by these measures. The 'closeness' of sectors to government and the autonomy which public sector employers have vis-à-vis government help to explain the differential impact of austerity measures. That is not to say that political concerns about the importance of specific public services were absent, but these were ambivalent, as illustrated by the initial decision to cut back on education for children with special needs, which was later repealed, versus the decision to exempt healthcare from wage restraint because of existing labor market shortages. Concentrating on some of these subsectors, this section will examine the consequences of austerity for public sector employment in relation to the policies that employers and unions pursued.

Central Government

Since the 2007–2010 collective labor agreement expired, there was no new collective labor agreement for the central government. The central government unilaterally imposed a wage freeze. The exceptionally long suspension of collective bargaining was the consequence of opposing positions taken by the employer and the unions. In 2010, unions demanded no forced redundancies, a 2% wage rise and no removal of the public employment status of civil servants. By contrast, the employer wanted to cut 10,000 jobs, a 2-year wage freeze and a 'normalization' of the status of civil servants. Ultimatums and union demonstrations did not have any effect on the employer and resulted in a prolonged period of a unilaterally imposed wage freeze. The specific situation of the central government sector can be explained by the position of the employer. The Minister of the Interior, who represents the employer, is bound by an agreement of the political parties that make up the coalition government. In this sector, the central government is in a position to impose budget cuts that were decided by the coalition parties. Union responses consisted of strategies to defend employment security and wages and of proposals on new issues such as strategic personnel planning, new ways of working and external mobility. The unions were too weak to organize mass protests and force the government to compromise. Despite the conflict between the employer and the unions, the employment relations as such were not affected. Employer and union representatives met each other informally and negotiated other issues besides the collective labor agreement. One result of this was the agreement on work-to-work support in 2013 (Leisink 2013). In early 2015, the government allocated a modest budget that enables the central government employer to begin negotiations over a new collective labor agreement, but employer proposals and unions demands are wide apart. Protests and minor strikes organized by the unions have not been successful in breaking the deadlock.

Municipalities

Municipalities are highly dependent on the central government for their income (Weske *et al.* 2014). In addition, municipalities can generate incomes with shrewd financial management and the exploitation of land. However, these sources of income are hard to enlarge, and incomes from land exploitation decreased due to the economic crisis. As a result, municipalities were heavily influenced by the budget cuts of the central government and insufficient compensation for social assistance payments by municipalities, which by itself resulted in a deficit of €396 million in 2010 and €650 million in 2011 (VNG 2011). Because of their budget constraints, municipal employers felt the need to restrain spending on employment conditions. Another issue impacting their spending decisions was the large uncertainty about financial prospects beyond the 4-year period of local politicians in office, which discouraged longer-term commitments to employment conditions.

On the other hand, the increasing importance of municipalities as 'nearby government' illustrated by their new responsibility for organizing core social services stimulated many to aspire to being an employer of choice.

Since 2008, three collective agreements were concluded, one covering 2009–2011, one covering 2011–2012 and one covering 2013–2015. The first agreement offered about a 1% annual wage increase, the second about 2% and the third one 1%, reflecting a compromise between the unions' traditional demands regarding pay compensating for inflation and employers' proposals for wage restraint. The second agreement also involved flexibility of opening hours without overtime payment or extra compensation. Negotiations regarding employment security concentrated on the length of the period in which the employee would have a right to job-to-job support while still on the local government's pay list after having been made redundant. In the end, the 2011–2012 agreement offered a 2-year period of job-to-job support on the local government pay list for employees declared redundant, as well as employability support for all employees in the form of a personal career budget of €1,500 for 3 years. The importance of this latter agreement must be assessed with a view to the cutbacks on public services, which went along with a steady decline of municipal employment, as Table 7.1 indicated.

Education

The economic crisis prompted the central government to introduce austerity measures that affected education. Apart from the wage freeze imposed by the government on primary and secondary education, the budget allocated by the Minister of Education for personnel costs was insufficient to meet the actual rise in costs, such as those due to the aging workforce. Primary schools' budgets for teaching assistants were also cut. In addition, many primary schools suffered a decrease in subsidies from municipalities for the maintenance of buildings. These austerity measures caused severe financial problems for primary schools, resulting in larger classes and job cuts for caretakers, cleaners and teacher assistants.

In primary education, a coalition of unions, employers and parents was successful in opposing the government's planned €300 million cut on education for children with special needs. The unions organized a strike. The PO-raad, the employer council, sympathized with the demands of the unions, and both parties presented a letter to the minister in which they argued against these cutbacks. These protests as well as the protest from parents resulted in parliament rejecting the planned budget reduction in April 2012.

Since 2010, the Minister of Education did not allow a wage increase, while the unions demanded a wage increase and employment security. As a consequence, there was no collective agreement from 2010 until 2014. The wage freeze lasted until the Minister of Education recognized that she needed the cooperation of schools and unions for achieving the goals of the ministry's educational policies. The Minister of Education used the tripartite platform of the Foundation of Education to discuss a National Education Agreement and commit the social partners to her educational agenda in return for lifting the pay freeze and allocating the budget for a wage rise to be negotiated by the employers' associations and trade unions. This national Education Agreement was concluded in 2013, but the two unions affiliated with the FNV (Abvakabo FNV and AOb) refused to sign the National Education Agreement. They criticized the ministerial approach as blackmail and insisted that the wage freeze should be lifted immediately. They also criticized the vagueness of the government's educational plans. However, based on the budget released by the ministry, the employer association and all unions concluded a collective agreement in 2014, offering a structural wage rise of slightly more than 1%.

Hospitals

In healthcare, demographic developments are the main driver of change: the aging of the workforce and of the population in general are resulting in an increasing demand for healthcare. Another driver is the labor market problem of attracting and retaining sufficient numbers of qualified employees. Yet another driver is the gradual introduction of market-like mechanisms giving a prominent role to health insurance companies, which attach increasingly strict cost and quality requirements to contracting with hospitals.

Hospital employers are autonomous, and the government is not in a position to impose a wage freeze. Thus, collective bargaining has been the normal routine. Union demands over the past years concerned wage rises, training and development, voluntary night shifts for employees older than 55 and improvements for students and interns. Employers wanted more flexibility at the local level, including a system of pay for performance. Collective agreements were concluded, one covering 2009–2010 and one covering 2011–2014. The first agreement offered employees a structural pay rise of 1% per year plus some other financial benefits and a new life-stage budget. The agreement for the 2011–2014 period offered employees a structural pay rise of 2% per year plus some other financial benefits and agreements on schooling. Both agreements were generally binding.

Because the economic crisis had a very limited impact on the hospital sector, employment relations are not under pressure. In the negotiations, there was the 'traditional' trade-off between employers and unions. Demographic developments gave rise to what employers and unions regard as innovative employment conditions, such as the life-stage budget, which offers all employees 35 hours per year of extra leave, which can be used at the discretion of employees. While previously, only older employees had the benefit of extra hours of leave, now also employees with young children or older relatives to care for have this benefit.

Conclusions

The economic crisis that hit the Netherlands in 2008 and went along with recessionary periods until 2011 has caused major reforms of public services and public service employment. These reforms resemble earlier reform policies, particularly those of the 1980s and 1990s. The policy objectives, which are central to today's reform program, echo the first NPM-inspired policies of the 1980s: increasing efficiency and flexibility, reducing bureaucracy and improving the quality of public service. The 2008 economic crisis prompted austerity measures that spurred the ongoing reform aimed at the modernization of public service management and employment relations.

The continuity between today's reform programs and the 1980s tradition is apparent from the structural and quantitative measures that make up the austerity packages in the Netherlands. Structural reforms decided by governments in the 1980s and 1990s favored privatization and the creation of semi-autonomous agencies. From the 2000s on, government organizations pursued similar aims through the creation of shared service centers for back office services in personnel, ICT, housing and finance, and through the creation of joint entities between municipalities for local levies and the provision of social services such as sheltered workplaces and youth care. Larger structural reforms today, notably the decentralization of social care from the central government to municipalities, are similar to those in the 1990s involving public housing. All these structural measures go along with quantitative goals of raising efficiency. There is also a continuity of measures with mainly quantitative goals, such as efficiency cuts leading to job reductions and wage restraints, although the latter's duration has no precedent.

The pattern of reform policies with their structural and quantitative measures does not fit neatly with the types of state responses to austerity offered by Lodge and Hood (2012). The influence of NPM policies and their attendant emphasis on cutting staff and conditions, which Lodge and Hood associate with the hollow state style, can be recognized in the decentralization of and cuts in social care, but this is not a hollow state style understood as government transfer of public services to the private sector. Rather, the decentralization of social care involves the transfer of government responsibility from the central to the local government. The simultaneous appeal to citizens' and corporations' private responsibility draws to some extent on features that Lodge and Hood ascribe to as a local communitarian state style. For instance, municipalities are required to ask elderly citizens dependent on social care first of all what kind of unpaid care relatives, neighbors, friends and charities can provide, and only then will municipal street-level bureaucrats decide what additional care will be provided by professional care workers employed by non-profit organizations. So, the Netherlands' state response style resembles neither a hollow state nor a local communitarian state style as described by Lodge and Hood (2012), but incorporates elements of the styles described under those two labels.

The reform of public employment conditions also demonstrates continuity. Normalization was the dominant trend throughout the entire period, and the employment conditions of public sector employees became almost similar to those of private sector employees, with the exception of those related to the public employment statute. Benefits that public sector employees still have compared to private sector employees are few and modest. Overall, they include slightly better compensation in the case of reorganization and slightly less working hours per year. However, the unilaterally imposed wage freeze resulted in wages that are increasingly worse than those for workers with similar jobs in the private sector.

The reform policies of successive governments since 2010 have generated much opposition and attempts to stop them. For instance, municipalities, although willing to accept a stronger position as 'nearby government' by taking responsibility for social care services, refused for a long time to conclude an agreement with the central government over the transfer of these services because of the drastic cutbacks. In the end, their acceptance was bought by central government by offering a transition phase softened by extra financial resources. Unions criticized and tried to stop the austerity policies, but overall, they were not very successful. This can be explained, first, by the absence of a wider social movement opposing the cutbacks on public services. Over the entire period, the Socialist Party was the only big party in parliament that opposed the austerity measures and joined forces with the unions. All other parties, from Conservatives through Liberals and Christian Democrats to Social Democrats, participated one or more times in coalition governments that decided on austerity measures (see Table 7.4). One rare example of a widely supported protest movement was the successful opposition against the cutbacks on education for children with special needs, in which unions, school employers, parents and political parties joined forces. Second, union membership has continued to decline since the 1980s, and this has contributed to the traditional lack of militancy of Dutch unions. One indicator is the number of days lost because of strikes, which amounts to an average of 9 days per 1,000 employees over the 2009–2013 period versus 66 days in Belgium over the same period. Rather than through militant opposition, Dutch unions take a pragmatic approach to protecting workers' interests. Next to holding on to traditional means such as the LIFO principle and dismissal compensation, public sector unions have come up with new agreements regarding employability, life-stage budgets and job-to-job support measures in order to support employees proactively for the future versatile labor market. Finally, the biggest trade union confederation, the FNV, suffered from serious internal conflicts that undermined joint resistance to government austerity policies. In 2011, the president of the FNV confederation, Agnes Jongerius, signed a tri-partite agreement that included a pension reform and a rise in the pension age. The two biggest unions, representing more than half the FNV membership, refused to accept the agreement. The ensuing conflict widened to include the structure and division of power within the FNV. The refusal of the biggest unions to accept proposals for a new structure occasioned the president to resign. As internal conflicts persisted, the FNV was virtually absent from the political arena, where austerity policies were decided. It took several interim presidents and external advisors to mediate and reform the internal structure and decision-making processes before the FNV was internally united again by choosing a new president (2013) and deciding on the new structure to take effect as of 2015.

The consequences of the public service reforms for citizens are daily news items. Media report poignant examples of elderly people deprived of elementary social care and municipalities that fail to organize home care and youth care. The consequences of reform for public service employees attract less media attention. The public sector employer continues to be distinctive (Bach and Bordogna 2013), although increasingly 'normal'. But does this discourage employees from seeking a job in the public sector? It is true that there are qualitative labor market problems: schools have difficulty attracting qualified teachers for core subjects like the sciences and public sector employers have problems finding ICT experts, and wages certainly factor among the causes. However, for the majority of public sector employees, intrinsic motives and their public service motivation are the main reason for looking for a public sector job (Leisink and Steijn 2008). These motives will continue to attract employees to public service employment, but it would serve both employees and citizens if public employers and unions would act on the basis of a vision of sustainable public services, having in mind the interests of both citizens and professional employees.

Notes

1. These are public employees employed by the central and local governments, the police, armed forces, water districts, judiciary and public corporations.
2. The official government database www.arbeidenoverheid.nl provides systematic data on public sector employment from 2003 onwards. The available data on 1995 and 2000 are added for comparative purposes, but should be seen only as indicative of employment trends; the criteria underlying these data differ from those of 2003 onwards.
3. Total employment in the general government sector is reported as representing 12.3% of the Netherlands' labor force in 2010 by the OECD Human Resource Country Profiles. This is a comparatively low percentage, as general government employment' share of the total labour force ranges from 6 to 30% between OECD countries. See http://www.oecd.org/gov/pem/hrpractices.htm
4. http://www.rijksbegroting.nl/2010/voorbereiding/miljoenennota

References

Algemene Rekenkamer (2011) *Bezuinigingsmonitor 2011*. Tweede Kamer der Staten Generaal, vergaderjaar 2010–2011, 32 758, nr.1. 's-Gravenhage.
A + O fonds Rijk (2011) *Medezeggenschap bij de overheid*. Den Haag: A + O fonds Rijk.

Bach, S. and Bordogna, L. (2013) 'Reframing Public Service Employment Relations: The Impact of the Crisis and the New EU Economic Governance', *European Journal of Industrial Relations*, 19(4): 279–294.

Bordogna, L. and Pedersini, R. (2013) 'Public Sector Industrial Relations in Transition', in *European Commission Staff Working Document: Industrial Relations in Europe 2012*, Brussels, 119–161.

Bryson, A., Ebbinghaus, B. and Visser, J. (2011) 'Introduction: Causes, Consequences and Cures of Union Decline', *European Journal of Industrial Relations*, 17(2): 97–105.

BZK (2008) *Bijzondere (rechts)positie van de ambtenaar*, Den Haag: Brief aan de Tweede Kamer (30 oktober 2008).

BZK (2014) *Werken in de publieke sector 2014. Trends and Cijfers. Deel: Cijfers*, Den Haag: BZK.

Health Consumer Powerhouse (2015) *Euro Health Consumer Index 2014 Report*. www.healthpowerhouse.com/files/EHCI_2014_report.pdf

Hood, C. (1991) 'A Public Management for All Seasons', *Public Administration*, 69(1): 3–19.

Leisink, P. (2013) 'Arbeidsverhoudingen bij de overheid : bezuinigingen als kans voor vernieuwing?' in *Staat van de ambtelijke dienst: Hoe staan de ambtenaren er anno 2013 voor?* Den Haag: CAOP, 130–134.

Leisink, P. and Boselie, P. (2014) *Strategisch HRM voor beter onderwijs*, Utrecht: Utrecht University.

Leisink, P. and Steijn, B. (2005) 'The Netherlands: Modernization, Participation and Strategic Choice', in Farnham, D., Hondeghem, A. and Horton, S. (eds.) *Staff Participation and Public Management Reform*, Houndmills: Palgrave Macmillan, 199–213.

Leisink, P. and Steijn, B. (2008) 'Recruitment, Attraction and Selection', in Perry, J. and Hondeghem, A. (eds.) *Motivation in Public Management: The Call of Public Service*, Oxford: Oxford University Press, 118–135.

Lodge, M. and Hood, C. (2012) 'Into an Age of Multiple Austerities? Public Management and Public Service Bargains Across OECD Countries', *Governance: An International Journal of Policy, Administration and Institutions*, 25(1): 79–101.

Noordegraaf, M. (2009) 'Dynamic Conservatism: The Rise and Evolution of Public Management Reforms in the Netherlands', in Goldfinch, S. and Wallis, J. (eds.) *International Handbook of Public Management Reform*, Cheltenham, UK/Northampton, MA, USA: Edward Elgar, 262–278.

Pollitt, C. and Bouckaert, G. (2011) *Public Management Reform: A Comparative Analysis*, Oxford: Oxford University Press.

Pollitt, C., Van Thiel, S. and Homburg, V. (2007) 'New Public Management in Europe', *Management Online Review*, 1–6.

Pot, F. and Smulders, P. (2013) 'Vaste en flexibele contracten en kwaliteit van de arbeid in het openbaar bestuur', in *Staat van de ambtelijke dienst: Hoe staan de ambtenaren er anno 2013 voor?* Den Haag: CAOP, 40–43.

Rosenthal, U., Ringeling, A., Bovens, M., t Hart, P. and Van Twist, M. (1996) *Openbaar bestuur: Beleid, organisatie en politiek*, 5e druk. Alphen aan den Rijn: Samson Tjeenk Willink.

Smulders, P. and Houtman, I. (2012) 'Arbeid in publieke en private sectoren vergeleken', *Tijdschrift voor Arbeidsvraagstukken*, 28(3): 268–287.

Steijn, B. and Leisink, P. (2007) 'Public Management Reforms and Public Sector Employment Relations in the Netherlands', *International Journal of Public Sector Management*, 20(1): 34–47.

Trappenburg, M. (2008) *Genoeg is genoeg: Over gezondheidszorg en democratie*, Amsterdam: Amsterdam University Press.

Van der Meer, F. and Dijkstra, G. (2013) 'Het regeerakkoord c.a. en de omvang van de ambtelijke dienst', in *Staat van de ambtelijke dienst: Hoe staan de ambtenaren er anno 2013 voor?* Den Haag: CAOP, 16–21.

Van Thiel, S. (2012) 'Comparing Agencies across Countries', in Verhoest, K., Van Thiel, S., Bouckaert, G. and Laegreid, P. (eds.) *Government Agencies: Practices and Lessons from 30 Countries*, Houndmills: Palgrave Macmillan, 18–26.

Vaughan-Whitehead, D. (2013) *Public Sector Shock: The Impact of Policy Retrenchment in Europe*, Cheltenham, UK/Northampton, MA, USA: Edward Elgar.

Verhulp, E. (2013) 'Geeft de overheid als werkgever het goede voorbeeld?' in *Staat van de ambtelijke dienst: Hoe staan de ambtenaren er anno 2013 voor?* Den Haag: CAOP, 36–39.

Vis, B., Van Kersbergen, K. and Hylands, T. (2011) 'To What Extent Did the Financial Crisis Intensify the Pressure to Reform the Welfare State?' *Social Policy and Administration*, 45(4): 338–353.

Visser, J. (1992) 'The Netherlands: The End of an Era and the End of a System', in Ferner, A. and Hyman, R. (eds.) *Industrial Relations in the New Europe*, Oxford: Blackwell, pp. 323–356.

Visser, J. (2013) 'Flexibility and Security in Post-Standard Employment Relations: The Case of the Netherlands', in Arthurs, H. and Stone, K. (eds.) *Rethinking Workplace Regulation. Beyond the Standard Contract of Employment*, New York: Russell Sage, pp. 135–154.

VNG (2011) VNG-reactie gemeentefondsbegroting 2012. http://www.vng.nl/files/vng/vng/Documenten/actueel/brieven/parlement/2011/20111111_Parlement_ECGF-U201101838.pdf on 14–10–2012

VSO, SCO and BZK (2010) *De grote uittocht. Vier toekomstbeelden van de arbeidsmarkt van onderwijs- en overheidssectoren*, Den Haag.

VWS (2013) *Kamerbrief: Goed bestuur in de zorg*, Den Haag: Ministerie van VWS.

Weske, U., Leisink, P. and Knies, E. (2014) 'Local Government Austerity Policies in the Netherlands: The Effectiveness of Social Dialogue in Preserving Public Service Employment', *Transfer: European review of Labour and Research*, 20(3): 403–416.

Yesilkagit, K. and Van Thiel, S. (2012) 'The Netherlands', in Verhoest, K., Van Thiel, S., Bouckaert, G. and Laegreid, P. (eds.) *Government Agencies: Practices and Lessons from 30 Countries*, Houndmills: Palgrave Macmillan, 179–190.

8 Germany: Retrenchment Before the Great Recession and Its Lasting Consequences

Berndt Keller

Introduction

Germany is a strictly federal, not a unitary, polity. Therefore, the public sector consists not of two but of three layers that are legally independent but empirically interrelated. The basic division of powers and functions between the federal, state and local/municipal levels is defined in the constitution, the Basic Law (*Grundgesetz* 1949). The federal government has exclusive legislative powers in traditional policy areas, such as foreign affairs and armed forces, and shares concurrent powers with the states that are exclusively in charge of areas such as police, education in an encompassing sense and cultural affairs. Municipalities have mandatory as well as voluntary tasks; they possess a high degree of autonomy, and their responsibilities include waste disposal, maintenance of public buildings and fire protection. Education is, with few exceptions, a public task, whereas healthcare is divided between the private and the public sectors and is more decentralized.

The strictly federal structure of the polity does not only determine a specific distribution of public tasks, but leads to a specific distribution of personnel. The states are the most important employers (about 51%), followed by the municipalities (30%) and the federal level (about 11%, plus 8% in social insurance, a German peculiarity).

The fundamental legal distinction of public employees is not only between private industry and the public sector, but within the latter between civil servants (*Beamte*) and employees (*Tarifbeschäftigte*). According to the Basic Law (Article 33), civil servants 'exercise sovereign authority' and therefore hold a unique public law status that includes guarantees of life-long employment in exchange for long-term service and permanent loyalty. They are, because of these 'traditional principles of the professional civil service', not allowed to bargain collectively or to go on strike. This prohibition refers to the status of the whole group, not to individual functions or essential tasks (Federal Ministry of the Interior 2009). In contrast, all employees have a private law status and therefore the same rights to bargain collectively and to go on strike as their counterparts in private industry. All members of both status groups have the basic right to form and to join unions or interest associations. In quantitative terms: in comparison with their functional equivalents in other countries, the percentage of civil servants in Germany (about 37%, including judges) constitutes an average figure (Demmke and Moilanen 2010).

As far as employment relations are concerned, this traditional 'legal dualism' has far-reaching consequences for procedures of interest representation. In a comparative perspective, three principles are to be distinguished: collective bargaining as the sole or prime method, more or less unilateral decision-making by public authorities and mixed forms (Traxler *et al.* 2001). Germany traditionally belongs to the third group of hybrid governance. In an empirical perspective, the continuing legal differences between both status groups are less important than they used to be; in a long-term perspective, adjustments of the working conditions of both groups have taken place.

Privatization measures played a role in the cutbacks in the number of employees, to be mentioned later, and account for about half of the reductions. They took place at the federal (especially postal and telecommunication service (*Bundespost*) and railways (*Bundesbahn*) in the 1990s) as well as at municipal level (among others, social and health service, refuse disposal, public facilities and utilities). These 'contracting out' measures resulted in the deterioration of working conditions (Flecker *et al.* 2014); furthermore, it cannot be assumed that supposed long-term cost savings resulted (Warner 2012). Public-private partnerships, new forms of cooperation and financing have also been occasionally introduced but, at least so far, have been of limited importance. Overall, there are around 200 projects concerning different parts of the infrastructure, such as roads and tunnels, motorways, schools and waste disposal.

Organization Structure and Employment

Long-Term Developments

To comprehend the long-term development of employment, our analysis needs a specific time frame. We have to move beyond the economic and financial crisis in 2008/2009 back to 1990, the date of German unification. The sudden and unexpected integration of the centrally planned economy of the German Democratic Republic into the social market economy of the Federal Republic of Germany (FRG) caused major problems of adaptation and had lasting consequences. In the new states, the oversized public sector had not only to be rigorously trimmed, but also to be completely reorganized (Keller and Henneberger 1992).

Throughout the 1990s and early 2000s, Germany was frequently considered 'the sick man of Europe' because it suffered from sluggish growth rates and persistently high rates of unemployment. These unfavorable macroeconomic circumstances created additional pressure for retrenchment measures in the public sector. These conditions changed only in the mid-2000s; overall employment reached its highest historical level and unemployment decreased substantially. Furthermore, throughout the 1990s, the more or less ambitious convergence criteria of the Stability and Growth Pact that preceded European Monetary Union had to be fulfilled (deficit of less than 3% of GDP, debt of less than 60% of GDP)—and were supposed to require the introduction of strict austerity measures.

In quantitative terms, in the early 1990s, there were about 6.7 million public sector employees. This number has considerably declined, especially but not only throughout the 1990s, to 4.6 million at present (about 12% of the labor force). It is rather low in comparison with other OECD countries (OECD 2011, 2013) and indicates the lasting trend towards a medium-sized public sector within a 'lean state' (Vesper 2012, European Commission 2013). This drastic decline is almost without parallel not only in comparison with Scandinavian countries, but even in the EU. If one selects another indicator, government compensation as a share of GDP, the results are very similar (Dewan 2012, DGB 2014a).

The new states in the east were hit harder than those in the west, and civil servants were affected less than employees because of their guaranteed life-long employment. All three levels of government were affected, but the municipal level was hit hardest. As already mentioned, privatization measures played a major role. Furthermore, there were schemes of voluntary early retirement. The number of 'entrants' was much lower than in previous decades.

The official figures provide only the total headcount and do not take into account the increasing percentage of part timers (about 32%). If full time equivalents instead of overall employment are calculated, the present overall total is about 4 million employees (DGB 2014a). This means that downsizing measures have continued, although in a less visible form. Cutbacks have been even more severe, with lasting consequences not only for working conditions, but also because of the creation of negative externalities. In particular, the provision of goods and services for consumers has deteriorated (such as the closure of public libraries and swimming pools, changes in timetables of public transport and changes in opening hours).

Cutbacks and austerity measures of various kinds (among others, low salary increases, reduction of social benefits and longer weekly working hours) did take place much earlier than in the majority of other EU member states and had lasting consequences for working conditions; in the long term, they have substantially changed not only the size but also the character of public sector employment. They were definitely not initiated because of the financial and debt crisis; interventions of the Troika (of the International Monetary Fund, the European Central Bank and the European Commission) had, in contrast to the 'program countries', did not take place. Recently, Council recommendations on the National Reform Program of Germany did not include specific recommendations for the public sector.

Table 8.1 Development of Public Sector Employment in Germany 1960–2013

Year	Federal Republic	Federal States	Local Authorities and Local Bodies	Federal Railways[2]	Federal Mail (Deutsche Bundespost)[1]	Indirect public services	Total	Change in comparison with previous year (in %)
1960	0.214	1.004	0.734	0.496	0.407	0.148	3.002	
1965	0.292	1.153	0.852	0.462	0.431	0.162	3.351	+1.76
1970	0.312	1.334	0.947	0.409	0.457	0.183	3.644	+3.79
1975	0.333	1.624	1.097	0.422	0.489	0.218	4.184	+1.60
1980	0.330	1.823	1.200	0.341	0.501	0.227	4.420	+1.17
1985	0.330	1.915	1.269	0.297	0.536	0.245	4.594	+0.88
1990	0.332	1.935	1.358	0.250	0.537	0.264	4.676	+1.28
1991	0.652	2.572	2.051	0.474	0.663	0.325	6.738	+43.03
1992	0.625	2.531	2.074	0.434	0.642	0.352	6.657	−0.81
1993	0.603	2.511	1.947	0.418	0.637	0.388	6.503	−1.97
1994	0.578	2.482	1.873	0.129	0.605	0.428	6.094	−6.29
1995	0.546	2.453	1.802	0.120	0.000	0.450	5.371	−11.86
1996	0.533	2.430	1.739	0.112	0.000	0.463	5.276	−1.77
1997	0.526	2.402	1.683	0.102	0.000	0.450	5.164	−2.12
1998	0.516	2.363	1.648	0.092	0.000	0.449	5.069	−1.84
1999	0.510	2.314	1.610	0.078	0.000	0.457	4.969	−1.97
2000	0.598	2.391	1.572	0.074	0.000	0.488	4.909	−1.21
2001	0.583	2.352	1.536	0.066	0.000	0.545	4.821	−1.79
2002	0.574	2.369	1.513	0.062	0.000	0.588	4.809	−0.25
2003	0.573	2.373	1.480	0.058	0.000	0.595	4.779	−0.60
2004	0.569	2.348	1.410	0.055	0.000	0.614	4.670	−0.83
2005	0.561	2.298	1.373	0.051	0.000	0.652	4.599	−1.52
2006	0.555	2.287	1.358	0.050	0.000	0.678	4.576	−0.50

2007	0.551	2.273	1.341	0.048	0.000	0.779	4.540	-0.79
2008	0.537	2.263	1.331	0.047	0.000	0.790	4.505	-0.77
2009	0.534	2.284	1.350	0.046	0.000	0.827	4.547	+0.93
2010	0.530	2.317	1.355	0.045	0.000	0.844	4.586	+0.86
2011	0.525	2.337	1.367	n/a	0.000	n/a	4.602	+0.34
2012	0.514	2.347	1.386	n/a	0.000	n/a	4.617	+0.32
2013	0.504	2.354	1.406	n/a	0.000	n/a	4.635	+0.39

- Figures are in millions and refer to June 30th of the corresp. year.
- Until 1990: West Germany. From 1991: Germany.
- From 2000: change in concept of calculating indirect public service.
- Rounding-off differences are possible.
- [1]From 1995: no longer public service due to privatization.
- [2]From 1994: Federal Rail Funds.

Source: Statistisches Bundesamt, Fachserie 14 Reihe 6, several volumes.

In contrast to other EU member states, a clear-cut distinction between the pre- and post-crisis employment situation cannot be constructed. Since 2008, there have even been some unexpected and, especially in the comparative perspective, remarkable countervailing tendencies that are to be explained by urgent needs in some widely neglected areas—and not as stimulus packages for public sector job creation in the Keynesian sense. Some small increases, however, the first since the early 1990s, in the number of employees have taken place in selected areas mainly at the municipal level (especially in preschool education and Kindergartens, but also in universities).

Female Employment

Equal rights and equal treatment of men and women are regulated by legal provisions and prevailing disadvantages are supposed to be eliminated. The first efforts to promote equality date back to the 1980s. In long-term comparison, the public sector initiated these measures earlier and more strictly than private industry; some progress has been made. Since the early 2000s, more vigorous plans for 'mainstreaming gender equality' have been introduced at all levels. The percentage of women has slowly increased despite the significant decline of the number of employees—reflecting their increasing overall participation rate in the labor force. At present, they constitute more than half (55%) of public sector employees, an average figure in the comparison of OECD countries (OECD 2013).

However, there still exists gender segregation *within* the highly segmented public sector labor market. Women are underrepresented in the upper career groups and higher ranks, especially in top-level executive positions, and the corresponding income groups and career opportunities. Due to a gender-specific division of employment as well as responsibilities for work and family, women are overrepresented among part timers, in the lower and middle ranks and in specific areas (such as social security, Kindergarten and education), as well as in various forms of atypical employment (such as fixed-term contracts). They are underrepresented in other areas such as police and defense.

Consequently, only a segmented integration of women into the employment model of the welfare state has been achieved (Kroos and Gottschall 2012). In contrast to some other countries (Karamessini and Rubery 2013; Rubery 2013), the financial and debt crisis and its austerity measures seem not to have had major detrimental effects because there were no recent reductions in public sector employment and no increase in unemployment.

Changes in the Composition of Employment

The traditional public sector labor force of the post-WWII decades was dominated by the uncontested norm of the so-called normal employment relationship (among others, male, full time and permanent employment with steady income, complete integration into systems of social security, especially health and pension). This structure has gradually but substantially changed towards a more heterogeneous composition including various forms of atypical (or contingent) work:

  a. Less than two-thirds are full-time employees (Statistisches Bundesamt 2008).
  b. Since the 1960s, the percentage of part-time employment has gradually but permanently increased. Since the early 1990s, it has even doubled (from 16 to 32%) and is even higher than in private industry. The vast majority (more than 80%) are women.
  c. There are regular as well as additional sector-specific legal opportunities for public employers to conclude fixed-term contracts (Keller and Seifert 2014). These specific contracts are automatically terminated after a fixed period, and employees have no rights of dismissal protection. These broad options are frequently used, especially at the municipal and state levels. About 9% of all employees (or about 15% of non-civil servants) have fixed-term contracts only. Younger age groups are overrepresented. Thus, a specific form of intergenerational inequality has come into existence: The opportunities of being transferred to the normal, more protected employment status are low—and even considerably lower than in private industry. This specific form of fixed-term employment is unevenly spread across areas of the public sector and contributes to collective closure. It does not constitute a new phenomenon but has substantially increased because of permanent budget constraints and consolidation measures (Altis and Koufen 2011).
  d. Furthermore, a small number of employees (about 200,000) are exclusively in marginal employment (or so-called mini-jobs, a German peculiarity and a form of restricted part-time employment, with monthly salaries of less than 450 euros). Their percentage is much smaller than in private industry.

The common feature of these employment forms is that they are more widespread in lower-level positions. Gender segregation matters again, and women are overrepresented in all atypical forms. Combinations, such as part-time and temporary contracts, occur frequently. Due to their special legal status, civil servants are less often affected than employees. From the employees' perspective, these contracts increase various short-term as well as long-term social risks. Their consequences (for income, employment stability, employability, integration into systems of social security) need to be better balanced with employers' interests in more flexibility in monetary, temporal as well as functional regards.

The extent of individual atypical forms differs between private industry and the public sector. Amazingly enough, however, their overall percentage is almost the same. The frequent assumption that the public sector constitutes a tightly regulated labor market with 'good' or 'model employers' is no longer valid (Keller and Seifert 2014). The impact of the statutory minimum wage that was introduced in 2015 is rather limited in the public sector because average salaries are higher than in private industry.

These shifts towards various atypical forms and, therefore, more heterogeneous employment patterns constitute long-term developments (Warsewa *et al.* 1996); they are definitely not recent reactions caused by the financial and sovereign debt crisis. These strategies of internal (part-time) as well as external (fixed-term) 'flexibilization' of employment structures existed already throughout the 1980s. Since the early 1990s, they have accelerated because of the poor macroeconomic and financial conditions public managers have confronted even in periods of economic recovery. In respect of 'flexibilization', the public sector does not constitute an outlier. In a comparative perspective, even the distribution across forms and areas of employment shows some striking similarities between countries (Morgan *et al.* 2000).

Overall, public sector labor markets are more segmented horizontally as well as vertically than they used to be, if not even dualized between protected 'insiders' and peripheral 'outsiders'. There is no longer an area that is sheltered from economic pressure and transformation. The public sector as a whole definitely does not constitute a 'protected' or 'rigid' labor market. The consequence is an increase of inequality within the public sector or to be more precise, between different segments of its workforce.

Two Forms of Employment Relations

Germany is known for its 'dual' system of employment relations that is characterized by the explicit legal distinction between the enterprise and the sectoral level (Keller and Kirsch 2015). This general pattern exists not only in private industry but also in the public sector, although partly on sector-specific legal foundations: at the organizational level, staff councils (*Personalräte*) are institutionalized and constitute functional equivalents of works councils in private industry. At the sectoral level, the traditional distinction between civil servants and employees is the rationale for the existence of two different forms of interest representation. About 37% of public employees are civil servants and 63% are employees. This distribution has been fairly stable over time.

Co-Determination

There are legally different but simillionar Staff Representation Acts (*Personalvertretungsgesetze*) at the federal and state levels that date back to the mid-1950s. Despite the fact that the production of public services has significantly changed, among others, by the introduction of IT, they were not amended in the recent past. Staff councils are proportionally composed in order to represent the heterogeneous interests of both groups of employees;

there are, however, certain restrictions for civil servants due to their specific legal status. Staff councils are formally independent from trade unions as well as interest associations, but informal cooperation takes place. Their size as well their impact increase with the number of employees. Coverage rates are exceptionally high (at more than 90%) (Keller and Schnell 2003, 2005) and have, in contrast to private industry, not significantly declined in the recent past. In contrast to works councils, their establishment is legally required in all parts of the public sector.

These institutions of 'collective voice' possess legally provided rights that range from pure information to participation and strict co-determination (exclusively in selected social matters, not in financial ones) (Altvater *et al.* 2011). These detailed rights constitute their primary power resource. Staff councils are strictly obliged to practice 'peaceful cooperation' with management, and are, in contrast to trade unions, not allowed to go on strike.

These legal preconditions restrain what has been termed 'management prerogatives' in other national contexts and prevent the evolution of conflictual or adversarial relations. Open conflicts with management are rare. Staff councils contribute to the development of 'cooperative' employment relations by concluding with management establishment agreements (*Dienstvereinbarungen*), the equivalent of works agreements in private industry. The impact of staff councils has increased because of emerging trends of decentralization and the increase of establishment agreements (e.g., on the introduction of performance-related pay) that have changed the former balance between the levels of the 'dual system'.

Collective Bargaining for Employees: The Traditional Pattern

In contrast to other federal states, collective bargaining takes place at the highly centralized national level. For several decades, bargaining coalitions existed on both sides and contributed to the maintenance of this unusual structure. On the employees' side, there were bargaining coalitions whose composition changed over time (Keller 1993). The Unified Service Sector Union (*Vereinte Dienstleistungsgewerkschaft—ver.di*), a member of the German Trade Union Federation (*Deutscher Gewerkschaftsbund—DGB*), is the most important union. Since 2007, ver.di has maintained a bargaining coalition with the German Civil Servants Association (*Beamtenbund und Tarifunion—DBB*) and internally taken the lead because of its size and superior capacity to strike (Keller 2010a). This bargaining coalition is unusual, and at least in the historical perspective unexpected, because both are members of different federations, the (general) DGB and the (specialized, public sector-specific) DBB.

On the employers' side, structures of interest representation have traditionally followed the organization of the federal state and thus established the largest bargaining domain. From the 1960s until the mid-2000s, the employers from all three levels formed an encompassing bargaining coalition, strictly coordinated their strategies and signed identical collective contracts (Keller 2010b). The key consequence of this three-layer structure of 'joint bargaining' was the conclusion and continued existence of a remarkably small number of collective contracts (especially *Bundes-Angestelltentarifvertrag* for white-collar employees and *Manteltarifvertrag für Arbeiter* for blue-collar workers). Thus, the working conditions (first of all, salaries but also working hours and social benefits) remained comparatively homogeneous and independent of the level, status and location of employment. For decades, this far-reaching similarity, if not even unity of highly standardized working and, therefore, living conditions constituted a political priority that was, in contrast to other countries, shared by all corporate actors.

After unification, the new federal states were integrated into this stable structure. In 1991, salaries were fixed at 60% of the corresponding level in the west. Since then, these levels have been gradually adjusted and, in contrast to private industry, are fully aligned.

Collective Bargaining for Employees: Recent Changes

Internal conflicts between representatives of the three governmental levels frequently occurred before as well as during bargaining rounds because of heterogeneous interests. However, these conflicts were always mediated by strategies and procedures of intra-organizational bargaining (Walton and McKersie 1991): unity and unanimity constituted the priorities of all participants. In the mid-2000s, the states terminated the employers' bargaining coalition after more than four decades because of accumulating dissatisfaction with its procedures and outcomes. The states insisted on independent negotiations of their own in order to reach more favorable results and more flexibility (among others, in term of weekly working hours and special bonuses). Since then, two collective contracts have been concluded, one for the federal and municipal level (*Tarifvertrag für den öffentlichen Dienst—*TVöD, since 2005), the other for the state level (*Tarifvertrag für den öffentlichen Dienst der Länder-*TV-L, since 2006 with the exception of Hesse and, until 2013, Berlin). Thus, decentralization pressures were stronger than expected and terminated the existing coalition.

These two collective contracts are formally independent from each other. In reality, however, they have led to similar but not identical outcomes. It remains to be seen if emerging trends towards more heterogeneity (probably not in salaries, but, among others, in the length of formerly uniform weekly working hours) will increase.

These major changes resulted in less vertical coordination and less centralization, but they remain limited rather than substantial changes. The bargaining structures remain fairly centralized, especially in comparison with other federal states. Australia, Canada and the US are characterized by rather decentralized structures and, therefore, more heterogeneity of various outcomes. In contrast

Table 8.2 Salary Increases in the German Public Sector 2005–2014

	Public sector[1]	Federal and municipal levels	State level[2]
2005	0.9	0.9	0.2
2006	0.4	0.4	0.4
2007	0.7	0.4	1.3
2008	4.4	4.7	3.9
2009	3.9	3.8	4.0
2010	0.8	0.4	1.6
2011	1.9	1.6	2.4
2012	2.2	2.4	1.9
2013	2.6	2.6	2.7
2014	3.4	3.7	3.0

[1]2005: without state level
[2]Without Berlin (until 2012) and Hesse (since 2004) (non-members of the Bargaining Association of German States (*Tarifgemeinschaft deutscher Länder*))
Source: DGB

to other countries, changes in the legal infrastructure did not take place. Coverage rates have always been considerably higher in the public sector than in private industry and have remained at an extraordinary level (of more than 95%) despite the transformation of 'joint bargaining'.

Trends of erosion, disintegration, fragmentation or even the collapse of existing bargaining structures that are to be observed in the public sector in other EU member states (Vaughan-Whitehead 2013) do not occur. Furthermore, 'tacit escape from collective bargaining', the non-compliance with agreed standards despite remaining a member of an employers' association and therefore being legally required to do so exists exclusively in private industry.

Extension clauses (or erga omnes clauses, in legal terms) exist on a legal basis (Collective Agreement Act/*Tarifvertragsgesetz*); since the early 1990s, they have only rarely been used in private industry. They are of no importance in the public sector because of the almost complete coverage rates. Opening clauses of a different nature (*Öffnungsklauseln*) that allow, at the level of the individual enterprise, for variation or deviation from arrangements concluded in sector-specific contracts have been agreed in collective contracts; they are of some importance also in the public sector (among others, for the introduction of performance-related pay). They increase the impact of staff councils and broaden their scope of action.

Industrial Disputes

Germany has never been a 'strike-prone' country. The public sector fits into this general pattern (Keller 2013b). Strikes are, in contrast to some other countries, rare events and happen only occasionally. More recently, there has been no major increase of industrial unrest, probably due to the fact that Germany was less seriously affected by the financial and debt crisis than other EU member states. Throughout the history of the FRG, there were only three major strikes (1974, 1992 and 2006). The first two were rather short, whereas the third was more protracted. They took place at the municipal level (among others, in public transport and waste disposal) because of its greater strike sensitivity and higher density ratios. Due to the highly centralized bargaining structures, they resulted in improvements for employees at all three levels. Short warning strikes are more frequent than regular strikes and take place shortly before or during bargaining rounds as an almost ritualized measure.

During the period of valid contracts, there is a strict peace obligation that has been observed. Traditionally, civil servants do not violate their group-specific prohibition to go on strike; in the recent past, it has been contested by some DGB-affiliated unions but not changed. Employers are not allowed to use civil servants as strikebreakers. There are no special provisions for conflict resolution in 'essential services'. Any kind of active outside interference does not take place. Lockouts have never happened in the public sector. In contrast to conflicts of interest, all conflicts of rights are settled by peaceful means, i.e., by negotiations between staff councils and management or by labor courts for employees and administrative courts for civil servants.

Since the mid-1970s, the bargaining partners have concluded mediation agreements (*Schlichtungsvereinbarungen*) as the only dispute settlement procedures on a purely voluntary base. More recently, these procedural arrangements have been more frequently used; they seem to have a certain 'narcotic' effect. In contrast to other countries, there are no other instruments for the resolution of collective conflicts of interest, such as various forms of arbitration.

Unilateral Regulation for Civil Servants: The Traditional Pattern

A different, highly legalized system of interest representation exists for civil servants. Its analysis requires a broader political science perspective. It consists primarily of unilateral decision-making authority of the legislature (*Bundestag*) but includes also certain consultation and hearing rights that are guaranteed in civil servant laws (Federal Civil Service Act/*Bundesbeamtengesetz* and, more recently, Civil Service Status Act/*Beamtenstatusgesetz*). These participation rights can be considered as partial compensation or, until the mid-2000s, even substitution for their missing rights of collective bargaining and to strike. Principally, the two federations, DBB and DGB, not their individual member associations, are to exploit these rights that are exerted already in the early, preparatory phase of all legislative provisions. Unilateralism as a sector-specific mode of governance has existed since the foundation of the FRG.

Between the early/mid-1970s and the mid-2000s, this sector-specific subsystem was also highly centralized. The legislature had the exclusive authority to decide on all framework conditions for civil servants at all three levels. The originally intended and later on obtained outcomes of this specific form of vertical 'harmonization' were very similar if not even uniform employment conditions across the territory of the FRG. The general pattern, which was never reversed, was that collective bargaining took place first. After its conclusion, the legislature decided to transfer all substantive results to civil servants on a one-to-one basis without any reductions or delays of a general or group-specific nature. Thus, both status groups were treated equally, and their working conditions changed in the same direction (Keller 2010a).

Surprisingly, this sector-specific sequence of 'pattern setting' and 'pattern following' proved to be stable for several decades despite the missing rights of civil servants to bargain collectively or to go on strike. The explanation was that both federations, the DBB and the DGB, managed to develop and to utilize informal instruments of interest representation, first of all lobbying activities, but also means of political pressure. Thus, these instruments developed into quasi-negotiation rights and constituted almost functional equivalents of collective bargaining rights (Keller 2010a).

Unilateral Regulation for Civil Servants: Recent Changes

In 2006, a major constitutional reform (*Föderalismusreform I*) took place in order to modernize governmental structures at the federal and state levels (Federal Ministry of the Interior 2009). It meant a politically motivated transformation from 'cooperative' towards 'competitive federalism'. It was definitely not caused by the financial and debt crisis, but by much earlier political decisions. As a by-product, this encompassing reallocation of political powers transferred the regulatory competence for setting the 'terms and conditions of employment' for those civil servants who are employed by the states from the federal to the state level. The major consequence was that states were granted autonomy to regulate all major employment conditions of their civil servants (first of all, salaries and pensions as well as status rights) by their own independent legislation.

This transformation initiated the emergence and then increasing differentiation of working conditions (i.e., salaries as well as weekly working hours, extended wait times for promotion, less opportunities for career progression and changed categories of job classification) between individual states. These include differences between east and west, richer (southern) and poorer (northern) states (Schneider 2014). The consequence of this gradual transformation towards more 'flexible' forms of regulation is the emergence of regional variation that did not exist before. The formerly prioritized principles of 'equal pay for equal work' and 'equality of working and living conditions' are no longer valid.

The assessment of this increased diversity depends on the perspective adopted. From a national point of view, it could be regarded as a violation of established and widely accepted principles; from a comparative perspective (of other federal states), emerging differences are not especially surprising. Furthermore, the constitutional reform has also introduced some formerly unknown although, at least so far, limited competition between public employers at state level, especially for young labor market 'entrants' (e.g. for teachers or IT experts).

In the recent past, there have been various attempts to treat civil servants worse than employees (such as delays of salary increases, smaller increases for some higher than for lower grades, introduction of longer weekly working hours). Thus, disparities between both status groups have increased and recently, these efforts have intensified. A decreasing number of states have transferred the collective bargaining results without any changes and substantive delays to their civil servants (DGB 2014b). Until the early/mid-2000s, such differences hardly existed. They indicate a qualitative change in 'strategic choice' of public policy making about employment relations and working conditions.

The former balance of power has been reversed. Interest organizations are no longer able to prevent a transformation of outcomes that result in disadvantages for their members. The parameters of the power relationship have shifted towards a sector-specific form of 'concession bargaining'. Formerly, trade unions and interest associations demanded and achieved improvements; instead, employers and their associations take the initiative and impose worse working conditions. Employers have used the opportunities that unilateralism essentially provides more widely than in the past.

Interest associations have complained about this deterioration in working conditions and have organized demonstrations and other forms of public protest. However, the range of their options is limited due to legal restrictions. Most recently, they sued some employers, and some constitutional courts at the state level (*Landesverfassungsgerichte*) defined certain future limits in altering working conditions.

Public Employers and Their Organizations

In contrast to other EU member states, there are employers' associations that represent their members' collective interests in bargaining. These associations date back to the post-WWII period when employment relations were re-established (Keller 1993). There are no special, quasi-independent agencies for coordination purposes.

At the municipal level, there exist, as in major parts of private industry, conventional employers' associations in all 16 states. They founded a peak association, the Federation of Local Employers Associations (*Vereinigung der kommunalen Arbeitgeberverbände*), which bargains on their behalf (Keller 2010b; Keller 2013a). Density ratios are high, at about 90%. The rare exceptions are some smaller municipalities and (semi-)privatized companies.

At state level, the Bargaining Association of German States (*Tarifgemein-schaft deutscher Länder*) exists. With the only exception of Hesse (and between 1994–2012, Berlin), it represents all states and acts as their only bargaining agent. Interests of individual states are coordinated by their ministers of the interior or of finance. At the federal level, the Minister of the Interior has traditionally been in charge of all employment issues, including collective bargaining; the Minister of Finance also takes part in processes of decision-making.

It is important to realize that the expenditure on salaries and social benefits as a percentage of overall expenditure differs significantly between the three levels (federal: about 10%, states: about 37%, municipal: about 26%) (Keller 2011). These percentages have remained relatively stable over time. This skewed distribution is the result of the specific distribution of public tasks and responsibilities as strictly defined in the Basic Law. It indicates that the outcomes of collective bargaining, especially of salary increases, for public budgets are more significant at the state than at the municipal and federal levels. Furthermore, it explains why the states were interested in more autonomy of the decision-making in personal matters that they finally achieved in the mid-2000s.

The traditional differences between private and public employers have gradually disappeared (Briken *et al.* 2014). Both use similar strategies and instruments (among others, increase of atypical forms of employment). Public sector employers no longer accept any special responsibility for the development of the general labor market (Tepe and Kroos 2010). They do not constitute distinctive employers 'of last resort' or 'model employers' for private industry anymore. In this regard, public employers in Germany are similar to their counterparts in other EU and OECD countries (Bach and Kessler 2007).

Trade Unions and Interest Organizations

In a comparative perspective, the overall number of public sector unions has always been small, reinforcing the high degree of bargaining centralization. Furthermore, there were no new unions established during the financial and debt crisis. The public sector is, as in other countries, the stronghold of unions. From their perspective, the problem of 'free-riding' exists but is of less importance than in private industry.

The Unified Service Sector Union, ver.di, was founded in 2001 as the result of a merger of five formerly independent unions (Keller 2005). After significant losses, this multi-industry union is the second largest union with, at present, about 2 million members. Ver.di organizes not only all three levels of the public sector and all levels of qualification, but also private service sectors. Ver.di cooperates closely on an informal base with the other DGB-affiliated professional unions: first of all, the Police Union

Table 8.3 Germany: Development of Ver.Di Membership 2001–2014

Year	Number of members (in thousands)			
	Overall	Civil servants	White collar*	Blue collar*
2001	2,806.5	245.0	1.690.1	871,3
2002	2,740.1	229.5	1.553.7	853,1
2003	2,614.1	218.6	1.467.7	834,0
2004	2,464.5	121.4	1.072.7	574,6
2005	2,359.4	n/a	n/a	
2006	2,274.7	187.2	2.011.0	
2007	2,205.1	180.2	1.951.5	
2008	2,180.2	173.3	1.936.6	
2009	2,138.2	166.9	1.903.4	
2010	2,094.5	161.5	1.867.0	
2011	2,071.0	156.6	1.849.6	
2012	2,061.2	151.9	1.847.5	
2013	2,064.5	146.7	1.857,6	
2014	2,039.9	n/a	n/a	

*from 2005: white-collar workers and blue-collar workers are summarized in the category 'employees'
Figures are rounded and correspond to December 31st of the corresponding year.
Detailed figures for 2014 not yet available.

Source: DGB-Mitgliederstatistik.

(*Gewerkschaft der Polizei*) with about 173.000 members, and the Union for Education and Science (*Gewerkschaft Erziehung und Wissenschaft*), with about 266.000 members. All in all, the DGB affiliates organize more employees than civil servants (about 450,000). The massive reductions of employees since the early 1990s mean the loss of (potential) members and resources.

The traditional focus of DBB as a 'status organization' was on civil servants and the representation of their specific interests. DBB affiliates have however expanded their traditional organizational domains and strengthened their 'collective bargaining wing'. They organize almost 370,000 employees in the public sector and its former, now privatized parts. Since the early/mid-1990s, DBB member organizations have kept growing, whereas DGB affiliates have suffered from losses due in part to privatization measures and workforce decline.

For decades, the relationship between the DGB and the DBB was characterized by political and ideological differences. It has improved, at least in a formal sense, because of cutbacks and retrenchments, towards more pragmatism and mutual recognition. However, both still compete for members; the principle of industrial ('one union per industry') and unitary

Table 8.4 Germany: Development of DBB Membership 1990–2014

Year	No. of members (in 1,000)			
	Total	Civil servants	White collar	Blue collar
1990	**997.7**	704.4	74.1	20,5
1991	**1,053.0**	712.6	292.8	47,6
1992	**1,095.4**	747.4	305.3	42,6
1993	**1,078.8**	758.8	297.8	22,2
1994	**1,089.2**	769.8	299.3	20,1
1995	**1,075.7**	777.4	279.9	18,3
1996	**1,101.6**	781.6	299.0	21,0
1997	**1,116.7**	798.6	298.7	19,4
1998	**1,184.1**	850.6	309.2	24,2
1999	**1,201.9**	867.5	302.2	32,2
2000	**1,205.2**	870.3	302.6	32,3
2001	**1,211.1**	878.2	299.9	33,0
2002	**1,223.7**	879.9	299.5	44,3
2003	**1,258.0**	910.8	305.2	42,0
2004	**1,269.8**	919.7	308.1	42,0
2005	**1,275.4**	918.8	314.6	42,1
2006	**1,276.3**	919.1	357.2	
2007	**1,278.4**	919.5	358.9	
2008	**1,280.8**	920.4	360.5	
2009	**1,282.6**	921.1	361.5	
2010	**1,261.0**	905.7	355.2	
2011	**1,265.7**	907.6	358.1	
2012	**1,271.6**	906.8	364.7	
2013	**1,276.4**	908.1	368.3	
2014	**1,282.8**	912.0	370.8	

˙from 2006: white-collar workers and blue-collar workers are summarized in the category 'employees'
Figures are rounded and correspond to December 1st of the corresponding year.

Sources: www.dbb.de (from 1999); Schroeder/Weßels 2003, 641 (until 1998).

unionism that (still) rules in private industry has never dominated in the public sector.

As in the majority of other EU member states (Bordogna 2008, European Commission 2011, 2013), density ratios 'on both sides of industry' have always been significantly higher than in private industry. At present, they are at about 60% on the employees' and even higher on the employers' side. The unusually high level of bargaining coverage (of more than 90%) (Ellguth and Kohaut 2011) is the result of high-density ratios and multi-employer bargaining. In contrast to private industry, it has not deteriorated in the recent past, despite major changes of bargaining arrangements and limited trends towards decentralization. It still constitutes the cornerstone of sector-specific employment regulation. Single-employer bargaining has always constituted a rare exception and has, in contrast to private industry, not developed.

Recent Changes and Their Consequences: Towards the Explanation of an Exceptional Case

Preliminary analysis shows that the public sectors of EU member states have been differently affected by the financial crisis that turned into a sovereign debt crisis (Bach and Bordogna 2013a, European Commission 2013, Vaughan-Whitehead 2013). First, the 'Great Recession' hit private industry, but, in its second stage and aftermath, its consequences spread to the public sector (Lewin 2012).

Formerly existing diversity and trends towards more divergence (between northern and southern as well as western and eastern countries) have been widening. Not exclusively Mediterranean but also eastern EU member states (European Commission 2013) have experienced substantial losses. In the case of Germany, there have been, in contrast to many other countries, few immediate consequences for public services and employment relations. The German economy suffered substantially from the crisis, and the GDP plummeted by more than 5% in 2008/2009. However, in contrast to other countries, due to measures of active labor market policy, unemployment did not rise (Möller 2010). The economy recovered quickly and kept growing. As a consequence, tax revenues and overall employment kept increasing. Germany turned into the frequently quoted 'economic miracle'.

Therefore, there are no characteristic features of a specific 'post-crisis public sector' to be detected. There seem to be, at least for the time being, no urgent need for immediate public sector initiatives aiming at long-term structural change (OECD 2012). Retrenchment measures as part of austerity packages would be difficult to explain to the public and to implement against citizens' preferences because the overall economic situation is comparatively favorable. Furthermore, one has to consider that the public sector provides major parts of the infrastructure as well as necessary services for the functioning of private industry.

Recent Changes

Trends towards limited decentralization occurred, although for different reasons, not only for employees but also for civil servants. After extended periods of institutional stability, transformations in both subsectors materialized within a remarkably short period of time. They are definitely of an organized and controlled and not of disorganized or fragmented nature (adapting Traxler's (1998) private sector typology). In contrast to other EU member states, especially the Mediterranean ones, unions and employers' associations remain in charge of procedural and substantive regulation of all employment conditions.

In a comparative perspective, trends towards decentralization that result from the abandonment of strict vertical coordination across government levels are limited and have not resulted in a significant increase in bargaining units (Casale and Tenkorang 2008, Keller 2013b). In terms of decentralization, the public sector in Germany has been a latecomer and has moved closer to the conditions already existing in other federal states (OECD 1997).

Long-term developments have led to the deterioration of the working conditions of the remaining workforce (Keller 2013a). The workload of individuals as well as their work intensity has increased because fewer employees have to accomplish the same number and amount of tasks. The obvious indicators are, of course, wages and salaries, whose increases were lower than in major sectors of private industry. Some fringe benefits (among others, Christmas and vacation bonuses) were curtailed or even abolished, weekly working hours were extended as well as working time further flexibilized; existing opportunities for early retirement were restricted and the age of statutory retirement was gradually increased (from 65 to 67 years for men as well as women). In contrast to frequent popular assumptions, if one controls for the usual characteristics, there is definitely no general 'wage premium' in the public sector. In other words, due to the specificity of tasks, the average human capital requirements are higher than in private industry. Furthermore, the wage structure is more egalitarian than in private industry.

These measures constitute a long-term trend (Keller 2013a). Their evaluation depends on the point of view: they are quite remarkable from a purely national-historical position but less so from a comparative, especially Mediterranean countries', perspective (Glassner 2010). They were not strategically planned in a long-term political perspective but incrementally introduced and constituted more or less accidental attempts of 'muddling through' in difficult times. They do not constitute a paradigm shift in employment relations. More recently, unions managed to resist employers' demands to extend weekly working hours to a considerable extent.

Public Sector Reform: NPM and Beyond

For more than two decades, the 'modernization' and 'reform' of the public sector and its labor force constituted a controversial topic in almost all European countries (Pollitt and Bouckaert 2011). Concepts of New Public Management (NPM) were supposed to bridge the gap between public and private sector employment models and to introduce market-related strategies and instruments to save scarce public funds and to increase efficiency and effectiveness. However, the overall results differ significantly across countries. They are at least mixed and include various unintended consequences (Bach and Bordogna 2013b).

In this regard, Germany was definitely a 'latecomer' among OECD countries. NPM was a certain reform narrative but in contrast to other countries, especially the Anglo-Saxon ones (Burke *et al.* 2013), never constituted the dominant paradigm. There is no broad legacy of NPM, and Germany belongs to 'a low NPM group' (Hebdon and Kirkpatrick 2005: 547). The specific German version of NPM, '*Neues Steuerungsmodell*' (Naschold and Bogumil 2000), had some impact especially at the municipal but less at the state and federal levels. Selective implementation of issues and instruments dominated. Its overall results towards more efficiency and 'marketization' are mixed and of a limited nature only (Kuhlmann *et al.* 2008). Holistic programs with vertically coordinated, standardized instruments do not exist; measures of consolidation and savings dominate (Bogumil 2014). They would be difficult to implement because of the high degree of decentralized autonomy government levels have within the federal structure that is enshrined in the Basic Law.

For the time being, there is no other general and more or less homogeneous reform concept or paradigm, such as a neo-Weberian one. Strategic HRM is difficult to detect. Existing efforts, such as 'the government program "Focused on the Future: Innovations for Administration" including the E-Government 2.0 program' (Federal Ministry of the Interior 2009), are of limited scope and do not present consistent concepts. Actions of muddling through and measures of incremental range (like 'reducing unnecessary bureaucracy and administrative burdens') dominate strategic planning for modernization (at the federal level, Federal Ministry of the Interior 2009).

Major transformations took place well *before*, not *because* of the financial and sovereign debt crisis—with lasting consequences. They were introduced by the fundamentally altered collective contracts TVöD and TV-L (for a list of changes, see Keller 2011). All long-standing legal differences between blue and white-collar workers (*Arbeiter and Angestellte*) were abolished, following the example of key private sector industries such as chemicals and metalworking. The bargaining parties introduced the unified status of employees (*Tarifbeschäftigte*) with uniform descriptions of job classification and 15 integrated salary groups instead of different salaries for employees and wages for workers. Each pay group has six steps from initial to final salary; progression is based on individual experience and performance instead of seniority/length of service, number of children and marital status. Furthermore, the introduction of a low wage band for most basic tasks was supposed to prevent further measures of privatization and/or outsourcing. It is valid exclusively for 'entrants' and to date, it has been of rather limited impact (Keller and Seifert 2014).

However, the special legal status of civil servants, whose maintenance and protection has been frequently criticized since the late 1960s (Bull 2006), was not substantially changed—or even abolished—by political decisions. It has proven to be quite flexible and able to adapt to changing economic as well as political circumstances. Exact lines of demarcation are difficult to draw and sometimes arbitrary (as in the case of teachers, who can be civil servants or employees).

Furthermore, the renewed collective contracts abolished the traditional grading principles and introduced new forms of performance-related pay (PRP) for all categories of employees; variable performance bonuses and allowances are to be based on performance assessment instead of seniority and to be rewarded on a temporary or permanent base. The goals of this management instrument are to increase flexibility and efficiency as well as to strengthen and reward individual performance and merit criteria.

In empirical terms, PRP is of less importance at the federal than at the municipal level. The amount of variable pay has remained strictly limited at 2% and has not been increased (up to the originally intended 8%). It creates additional tasks as well as major and protracted problems of uneven implementation for staff councils, the institutions of 'collective voice' at the decentralized shop floor level; it has had only limited and moderate overall effects (Schmidt and Müller 2013). The states introduced this new form of extrinsic performance rewards at about the same time in their independent collective contract. Later on, the states, in contrast to municipalities, decided to abandon it completely. In the mid-200s, PRP was on the bargaining agenda for both sides and at all three levels. At present, it constitutes a controversial issue, not only for unions, but also for local employers that do not act strategically during the implementation process.

The recent experience with PRP in Germany confirms major existing reservations (Matiaske and Holtmann 2007) and fits well into the general results of limited overall impact reached in comparative analysis (OECD 1997, 2005). The introduction of PRP would have been easier in more prosperous times; but at present, the incentive of labor cost savings generates severe implementation problems.

The Municipal Level

Public budgets have suffered from growing deficits and the almost permanent necessity of introducing consolidation measures. Because of the federal character of the polity, various public employers possess high degrees of autonomy and maneuver for strategic action. Their HRM policies are neither standardized nor strictly coordinated on a horizontal or vertical axis. The consequences of the financial and debt crisis vary not only *between* EU member states, but also *within* countries according to their levels of government. Furthermore, there is immense variation not only *between* these three levels but also *at* the municipal level (Leisink and Bach 2014 for a comparative overview). It deserves special attention because of its quantitative impact on overall employment and its qualitative importance for the supply of specific services.

In Germany, local authorities possess a high degree of decentralized autonomy and self-government that is enshrined in the Basic Law (Article 28). At present, the financial preconditions for their performance are extremely uneven. For a limited number, concentrated in certain regions in the west, extremely poor financial conditions exist. Their long-term debts as well as short-term bridging loans (*Kassenkredite*) have kept growing for years (overall as well as per capita), even before the financial and sovereign debt crisis. Their expenses for their mandatory tasks, such as social benefits and childcare (*Sozialausgaben*), have increased to a considerable degree; the responsibility for the execution of these tasks is delegated from the federal and state levels and can hardly be reduced for legal reasons. Their voluntary tasks that allow for some strategic options (among others, for cultural affairs and social work for specific groups), have already been substantially curtailed or even withdrawn.

These municipalities will not be able to solve these problems themselves (Deutscher Städtetag 2014). Transfers and subsidies from the upper levels do exist but remain limited and therefore insufficient; they have hardly increased, despite the recent growth of overall tax revenues (Keller 2014). It is, however, to be expected that, in the long run, the federal government will not be able to distance itself from more financial contributions for the solution of these urging difficulties. (Certain redistribution measures at the local level, from richer to poorer municipalities, could provide an additional option.)

The opportunities of municipalities to levy taxes in order to keep revenues at an equal level are legally constrained. Therefore, their strategic political choice is quite limited. Furthermore, because of their financial difficulties, they can scarcely afford any urgently necessary investment in their parts of the public infrastructure, such as public buildings, streets and bridges (Rietzler 2014). The existing legal framework has not been deregulated, but existing 'customs and practices' have been significantly changed. Salaries have not been cut or frozen, but have only moderately been increased. In the long run, employment and, therefore, working conditions at the municipal level have deteriorated and, despite some recent small increases, service provision has worsened. Municipalities have to implement all parts of their collective contracts without 'exit' options.

The percentage of civil servants is much smaller and, therefore, unilateralism of regulation is less important than at the state and federal levels. In contrast to other EU member states, especially some 'program countries', already existing forms of unilateralism have not been extended. A return to centralization of collective bargaining, as has happened in some other EU member states (Della Rocca 2013), has not taken place (Keller 2014).

Conclusion

In contrast to some other EU Member States, the financial and debt crisis was only a short-term event. All of the more recent institutional changes within both forms of interest representation took place *before* and not *because* of this external shock: the structure of collective bargaining has not been transformed *because* of but *before* the Great Depression. Unilateralism, a sector-specific mode of regulation has a long tradition and has, in contrast to more recent developments in some other EU member states (European Commission 2013), not been introduced or formally extended during and/or because of the crisis.

(Some) employers and political majorities were the driving forces of the limited decentralization of collective bargaining as well as the constitutional reform of federalism. They have transformed differing former 'customs and practices' to a significant degree so that equal treatment of both groups, employees and civil servants, is not the outcome anymore. Unions and interest organizations opposed these changes in both subsectors but could not prevent them.

Major forthcoming problems that have not been discussed are twofold. The first is more of a national, the second more of a general European nature. The increasingly unfavorable average age of staff (Altis and Koufen 2011) has been caused by the high number of 'entrants' throughout the 1960s and 1970s who are about to retire. In this frequently quoted 'golden age' of the public sector, the social and welfare state and therefore the number of its employees expanded considerably in almost all industrialized countries, including Germany. The changing age structure has two major consequences in terms of the recruitment of new personnel and the growing expenditure on pensions of retired civil servants who, in contrast to employees, do not pay their own contributions. Since the late 1990s, various cost-containing measures have been introduced in order to control the growth of this expenditure (among others, creation of pension funds and reserves, gradual increase of the age of regular retirement as well as the minimum age of early retirement, reduction of maximum pension rates).

The emerging need to hire significant numbers of qualified replacements exists primarily at the state and municipal levels and has been evident for some time but has not been high on the agenda (Lodge and Hood 2012). Due to well-known demographic changes, the age cohorts entering the labor market will be smaller and, therefore, will increase difficulties for public employers. The employment opportunities they have to offer are not overtly attractive compared with private industry, especially not for highly educated applicants (such as IT experts).

The more recent introduction of debt brakes (*Schuldenbremsen*) has been a highly contentious political issue from the start. Finally, they acquired political majorities at the national (enshrined in the Basic Law, Article 109) as well as at the EU level (in the fiscal compact as part of the reinforced 'new economic governance regime'). Debt brakes determine extremely narrow limits for new structural debts; they are supposed not only to contribute to more fiscal consolidation and discipline, but even to reinstall the principle of balanced budgets. These strict budgetary constraints define permanent limits for future public expenditure at all three levels of government. Therefore, the institutionalization of these restrictions will have major consequences not only for the overall number of employees as well as for their working conditions, but also for the consumers of goods and services. Amazingly enough, hardly anybody thinks of the opposite option, not to focus on short-term stricter limits of public expenditure but on an increase of revenues, especially in times of low interest rates.

The broader question reaches far beyond employment relations and is of a political nature for civil society. It has to be debated and answered not only by public employees and their unions and interest representation but, first of all, by the citizens who are not only voters but also consumers of publicly provided goods and services: what kind of a public sector do we want in a quantitative as well as a qualitative sense? Are we willing to accept the further deterioration? Last but not least, how much taxation are citizens willing to pay for the delivery of high-quality services in the consolidated social welfare state of an advanced economy?

References

Altis, A. and Koufen, S. (2011) 'Entwicklung der Beschäftigung im öffentlichen Dienst', *Wirtschaft und Statistik*, November: 1111–1116.

Altvater, L., Baden, E., Kröll, M., Lemcke, M. and Peiseler, M. (2011) *BPersVG—Bundespersonalvertretungsgesetz mit Wahlordnung und ergänzenden Vorschriften. Kommentar für die Praxis.* 7th ed., Frankfurt am Main: Bund-Verlag.

Bach, S. and Bordogna, L. (eds.) (2013a) 'Special Issue: Reframing Public Service Employment Relations', *European Journal of Industrial Relations*, 19(4): 277–389.

Bach, S. and Bordogna, L. (2013b) 'Reframing Public Service Employment Relations: The Impact of the Economic Crisis and the New EU Economic Governance', *European Journal of Industrial Relations*, 19(4): 279–294.

Bach, S. and Kessler, I. (2007) 'HRM and the New Public Management', in Boxall, P., Purcell, J. and Wright, M. (eds.) *The Oxford Handbook of Human Resource Management*, Oxford: Oxford University Press, 469–488.

Bogumil, J. (2014) '20 Jahre Neues Steuerungsmodell—Eine Bilanz', in Wiechmann, E. and Bogumil, J. (eds.) *Arbeitsbeziehungen und Demokratie im Wandel. Festschrift für Leo Kißler*, Baden-Baden: Nomos, 41–58.

Bordogna, L. (2008) 'Moral Hazard, Transaction Costs and the Reform of Public Service Employment Relations', *European Journal of Industrial Relations*, 14(4): 381–400.

Briken, K., Gottschall, K., Hils, S. and Kittel, B. (2014) 'Wandel von Beschäftigung und Arbeitsbeziehungen im öffentlichen Dienst in Deutschland—zur Erosion einer sozialstaatlichen Vorbildrolle', *Zeitschrift für Sozialreform*, 60(2): 123–148.

Bull, H. P. (2006) *Vom Staatsdiener zum öffentlichen Dienstleister: Zur Zukunft des öffentlichen Dienstrechts*, Berlin: edition sigma.

Burke, R. J., Noblet, A. J. and Cooper, C. L. (eds.) (2013) *Human Resource Management in the Public Sector*, Cheltenham: Edward Elgar.

Casale, G. and Tenkorang, J. (2008) *Public Service Labour Relations: A Comparative Overview*, Geneva: ILO.

DBB und Tarifunion (2014) *Daten, Zahlen, Fakten*, Berlin: DBB.

Della Rocca, G. (2013) 'Employment Relations in the Public Sector. Between Hierarchy and Contract', in Arrowsmith, J. and Pulignano, V. (eds.) *The Transformation of Employment Relations in Europe. Institutions and Outcomes in the Age of Globalization*, New York-London: Routledge, 51–68.

Demmke, C. and Moilanen, T. (2010) *Civil Services in the EU of 27: Reform Outcomes and the Future of the Civil Service*, Frankfurt-Bern: Peter Lang.

Deutscher Städtetag (2014) *Finanzbeziehungen neu regeln, Städte stärken: Schlaglichter aus dem Gemeindefinanzbericht 2014 des Deutschen Städtetages*, Berlin: Deutscher Städtetag.

Dewan, S. (2012) 'Public Sector Employment in OECD Countries Post-economic Crisis', in Mitchell, D. J. B. (ed.) *Public Jobs and Political Agendas. The Public Sector in an Era of Economic Stress*, Urbana-Champaign: LERA, 59–77.

DGB-Bundesvorstand (2014a) *Personalkostenreport Öffentlicher Dienst 2014*, Berlin: DGB.

DGB-Bundesvorstand (2014b) *Besoldungsreport 2014: Entwicklung der Einkommen der Beamtinnen und Beamten und Bewertung der Besoldungspolitik von Bund und Ländern*, Berlin: DGB.

Ellguth, P. and Kohaut, S (2011) 'Der Staat als Arbeitgeber: Wie unterscheiden sich die Arbeitsbedingungen zwischen öffentlichem Sektor und der Privatwirtschaft?' *Industrielle Beziehungen: The German Journal of Industrial Relations*, 18(1): 11–38.

European Commission/Directorate-General for Employment, Social Affairs and Inclusion (2011) *Industrial relations in Europe 2010*, Luxembourg: European Commission.

European Commission/Directorate-General for Employment, Social Affairs and Inclusion (2013) *Industrial Relations in Europe 2012*, Luxembourg: European Commission.

Federal Ministry of the Interior (2009) *The Federal Public Service*. http://www.bmi. bund.de/SharedDocs/Downloads/DE/Broschueren/2009/oed_en.pdf?__ blob=publicationFile

Flecker, J., Schultheis, F. and Vogel, B. (Hg.) (2014) *Im Dienste öffentlicher Güter. Metamorphosen der Arbeit aus der Sicht der Beschäftigten*, Berlin: edition sigma.

Glassner, V. (2010) *The Public Sector in the Crisis*, ETUI Working Paper 2010.07. Brussels: ETUI.

Hebdon, R. and Kirkpatrick, I. (2005) 'Changes in the Organization of Public Services and Their Effects on Employment Relations', in Ackroyd, S., Batt, R., Thompson, P. and Tolbert, P. S. (eds.) *The Oxford Handbook of Work and Organization*, Oxford: Oxford University Press, 531–553.

Karamessini, M. and Rubery, J. (2013) 'Economic Crisis and Austerity: Challenges to Gender Equality', in Karamessini, M. and Rubery, J. (eds.) *Women and Austerity: The Economic Crisis and the Future of Gender Inequality*, Abingdon: Routledge, 314–351.

Keller, B. (1993) *Arbeitspolitik des öffentlichen Sektors*, Baden-Baden: Nomos.

Keller, B. (2005) 'Union Formation through Merger: The Case of Ver.di in Germany', *British Journal of Industrial Relations*, 43(2): 209–232.

Keller, B. (2010a) *Arbeitspolitik im öffentlichen Dienst: Ein Überblick über Arbeitsbeziehungen und Arbeitsmärkte*, Berlin: edition sigma.

Keller, B. (2010b) 'Arbeitgeberverbände des öffentlichen Sektors', in Schroeder, W. and Weßels, B. (Hg.), *Handbuch Arbeitgeber- und Wirtschaftsverbände in Deutschland*, Wiesbaden: VS Verlag, 105–125.

Keller, B. (2011) 'After the End of Stability: Recent Trends in the Public Sector of Germany', *The International Journal of Human Resource Management*, 22(11): 2331–2348.

Keller, B. (2013a) 'Germany: The Public Sector in the Financial and Debt Crisis', *European Journal of Industrial Relations*, 18(4): 359–374.

Keller, B. (2013b) 'The Public Sector in the United States and Germany: Comparative Aspects in an Employment Relations Perspective', *Comparative Labor Law and Policy Journal*, 34(2): 415–441.

Keller, B. (2014) 'The Continuation of Early Austerity Measures: The Exceptional Case of Germany', *Transfer: European Review of Labour and Research*, 20(4): 387–402.

Keller, B. and Henneberger, F (1992) 'Der öffentliche Dienst in den neuen Bundesländern: Beschäftigung, Interessenverbände und Tarifpolitik im Übergang', in Eichener, V., Kleinfeld, R., Pollack, D., Schmid, J., Schubert, K. and Voelzkow, H. (Hg.), *Organisierte Interessen in Ostdeutschland*, Marburg: Metropolis, 175–194.

Keller, B. and Kirsch, A. (2015) 'Employment Relations in Germany', in Bamber, G. J., Lansbury, R. D., Wailes, N. and Wright, Ch. F. (eds.) *International and Comparative Employment Relations: Globalization and Change*. 6th ed., Sydney-London: Sage, 179–207.

Keller, B. and Schnell, R. (2003) 'On the Empirical Analysis of Staff Councils—Structural Data and Problems of Interest Representation', *WSI-Mitteilungen* 56 (Special Issue "Industrial Relations in Germany—An Empirical Survey"): 14–23.

Keller, B. and Schnell, R. (2005) 'Sozialstruktur und Problemfelder der Interessenvertretung im öffentlichen Dienst: Eine empirische Untersuchung von Personalräten in West—und Ostdeutschland', *Berliner Journal für Soziologie*, 15(1): 87–102.

Keller, B. and Seifert, H. (2014) 'Atypische Beschäftigungsverhältnisse im öffentlichen Dienst', *WSI-Mitteilungen*, 67(8): 628–638.

Kroos, D. and Gottschall, K. (2012) 'Dualization and Gender in Social Services: The Role of the State in Germany and France', in Emmenegger, P., Häusermann, S., Palier, B. and Seeleib-Kaiser, M. (eds.) *The Age of Dualization: The Changing Face of Inequality in Deindustrializing Societies*, Oxford: Oxford University Press, 101–123.

Kuhlmann, S., Bogumil, J. and Grohs, S. (2008) 'Evaluating Administrative Modernization in German Local Governments: Success of Failure or the "New Steering Model"?' *Public Administration Review*, 68(5): 851–886.

Leisink, P. and Bach, S. (eds.) (2014) 'Special Issue: Austerity and Public Sector Restructuring: Local Government in Focus', *Transfer: European Review of Labour and Research*, 20(3): 323–469.

Lodge, M. and Hood, Chr. (2012) 'Into an Age of Multiple Austerities? Public Management and Public Service Bargaining Across OECD Countries', *Governance: An International Journal of Policy, Administration, and Institutions*, 25(1): 79–101.

Matiaske, W. and Holtmann, D. (Hg.) (2007) *Leistungsvergütung im öffentlichen Dienst*, München-Mering: Hampp.

Möller, J. (2010) 'The German Labor Market Response in the World Recession: De-Mystifying a Miracle', *Zeitschrift für ArbeitsmarktForschung*, 42(4): 325–336.

Morgan, P., Allington, N. and Heery, E. (2000) 'Employment Insecurity in the Public Services', in Heery, E. and Salmon, J. (eds.) *The Insecure Workforce*, London-New York: Routledge, 78–111.

Naschold, Fr. and Bogumil, J. (2000) *Modernisierung des Staates: New Public Management in deutscher und internationaler Perspektive*. 2. völlig überarb. Aufl, Opladen: Leske & Budrich.

OECD (2005) *Performance-related Pay Policies for Government Employees*, Paris: OECD.

OECD (2011) *Government at a Glance*, Paris: OECD.

OECD (2012) *Public Sector Compensation in Times of Austerity*, Paris: OECD.

OECD (2013) *Government at a Glance*, Paris: OECD.

Pollitt, C. and Bouckaert, G. (2011) *Public Management Reform: A Comparative Analysis*. 2nd ed., Oxford: Oxford University Press.

Rietzler, K. (2014) *Anhaltender Verfall der Infrastruktur—Die Lösung muss bei den Kommunen ansetzen*. IMK Report 94, Düsseldorf: HBS.

Rubery, J. (2013) 'Public Sector Adjustment and the Threat to Gender Equality', in Vaughan-Whitehead, D. (ed.) *Public Sector Adjustments in Europe: Scope, Effects and Policy Issues*, Cheltenham: Edward Elgar, 43–84.

Schmidt, W. and Müller, A. (2013) *Leistungsorientierte Bezahlung in den Kommunen: Befunde einer bundesweiten Untersuchung*, Berlin: edition sigma.

Schneider, K. (2014) 'Einkommenspolitik im öffentlichen Dienst', *Der Personalrat*, 31(9): 1–5.

Statistisches Bundesamt (2008) 'Atypische Beschäftigung auf dem deutschen Arbeitsmarkt'. Begleitmaterial zum Pressegespräch am 9.September 2009 in Frankfurt am Main. Wiesbaden.

Tepe, M. and Kroos, D. (2010) 'Lukrativer Staatsdienst? Lohndifferenzen zwischen öffentlichem Dienst und Privatwirtschaft', *WSI-Mitteilungen*, 63(1): 3–10.

Traxler, F. (1998) 'Collective Bargaining in the OECD: Developments, Preconditions and Effects', *European Journal of Industrial Relations*, 4(2): 207–226.

Traxler, F., Blaschke, S. and Kittel, B. (2001) *National Labor Relations in Internationlized Markets: A Comparative Analysis of Institutions, Change and Performance*, Oxford: Oxford University Press.

Vaughan-Whitehead, D. (ed.) (2013) *Public Sector Shock: The Impact of Policy Retrenchment in Europe*, Cheltenham: Edward Elgar.

Vesper, S. (2012) *Finanzpolitische Entwicklungstendenzen und Perspektiven des Öffentlichen Dienstes in Deutschland: Gutachten im Auftrag des Instituts für Makroökonomie und Konjunkturforschung (IMK) in der Hans-Böckler-Stiftung*, Berlin: HBS.

Walton, R. E. and McKersie, R. B. (1991) *A Behavioral Theory of Labor Negotiations: An Analysis of a Social Interaction System*. 2nd ed., Ithaca-New York: ILR Press.

Warner, M. E. (2012) 'Local Government Restructuring in a Time of Fiscal Stress', in Mitchell, D. J. B. (ed.) *Public Jobs and Political Agendas. The Public Sector in an Era of Economic Stress*, Urbana-Champaign: LERA, 41–58.

Warsewa, G., Osterland, M. and Wahser, R. (1996) *Zwischen Sparzwang und sozialer Verantwortung: Normalarbeit und abweichender Beschäftigung in der kommunalen Personalpolitik der 80er Jahre*, Weinheim: Deutscher Studienverlag.

9 Denmark and Sweden: The Consequences of Reform and Economic Crisis for Public Service Employment Relations

Mikkel Mailand and Nana Wesley Hansen

Introduction

Denmark and Sweden have some of the largest public sectors in Europe. They are also characterized by predominantly voluntaristic labor market models where collective bargaining and employee involvement play a relatively strong role in public sector employment relations (ER).

In this chapter, we will analyze similarities and differences between the two countries regarding their public sectors and their public sector ER. The analysis focuses on three themes: main public services reforms and New Public Management (NPM), changes in the ER and job levels and the relationship between parliamentary politics and ER. Finally, the multiple austerity typology proposed by Lodge and Hood (2012) will be applied to the two Scandinavian cases, including three expressions of public service bargains: a) a directing state (or back-to-the-future state) associated with a new era of state intervention, critical of short-termism and NPM-style reforms; b) a hollow state in which neoliberal or NPM policies of marketization and privatization are accelerated; c) a local communitarian (third way) state involving the advancement of social enterprises, faith groups and charities into the provision of public services; and d) a 'coping' (or barely coping) state, which implies a postponement of long-term reform and short-term reactive responses.

It is argued that although job levels remain high, and the public sector ER systems are still basically voluntaristic, changes have been seen in ER models. These changes have been more profound in Sweden than in Denmark, but they took place before the 2008 crisis. In Sweden, an economic crisis in the 1990s was a much more important driver than the post-2008 crisis. The 1990s crisis contributed to an earlier implementation of NPM and to a higher degree of decentralization of public sector wage setting than in Denmark. It is furthermore argued that post-2008 austerity policies have been relatively mild in the two countries and cannot alone explain recent changes. These changes—which have not fundamentally changed the ER systems in Denmark—include attempts to strengthen the management prerogative and some degree of recentralization. In Sweden, the changes similarly include recentralization, but contrary to Denmark, Sweden has continued the decentralization of wage formation. Thus, in applying the Lodge and Hood typology of multiple austerities to the two Scandinavian countries, both involve relatively limited austerity measures. However, recent developments in both countries increasingly reflect a mix of the 'hollow state' scenario with developments that to some extent reflect 'the redirecting state'.

Following the introduction, the second section of this chapter presents the organizational structures and employment levels of Sweden's and Denmark's public sectors. Subsequently, the third section presents public sector ER and pay determination, whereas the fourth section describes the structure and coverage of public sector social partners. The fifth section then presents the history of the last 30 years of public sector reforms in the two countries and their relations to ER, after which section six analyzes the impact of the economic crisis for ER. Finally, the chapter systematically compares the two countries regarding the three themes mentioned above and afterwards applies the Lodge and Hood typology.

Organizational Structure and Employment

Some 31% of the *Danish* workforce is employed in the public sector. This comparatively high share has remained relatively stable over the past 20 years despite increasing outsourcing and despite the crisis. The number of employees in the three main areas of the public sector is 430.000 in the municipalities, 121.000 in the regions and 173.000 in the state area (Statistics Denmark 2014). As many as 38% are working part time—and the large majority of these people are women. Moreover, 10% are on temporary contracts (Mailand 2015b).

Responsibilities for the three main areas of public services were changed by the so-called Structural Reform of 2007, under which 273 municipalities were amalgamated into 98 and 14 counties were eliminated, having been replaced by 5 regions with a narrow range of responsibilities. The reform's aim was to create economies of scale and to improve welfare services by reshuffling the division of responsibilities among the three main areas. This move provided the municipalities with responsibility for more policy areas. Another dimension of the municipality's importance is its relative autonomy ('*Det kommunale selvstyre*'), which includes the right to set local authority taxes. These revenues make up more than 50% of their municipality earnings (Mailand 2014a).

Employment in the public sector was reduced in the early 1990s (Andersen *et al.* 1999), but has since increased over a longer period. The public sector's share of employment has remained nearly constant before and after the recent economic crisis. Nevertheless, while employment in the municipalities declined by 2.7% from 2009–14 (Q1), employment in the state sector increased 2.5% and in the regions no less than 5.4% (Momentum, May 14, 2014), which is also illustrated in Table 9.1. In fact, the table illustrates how, despite the decline in employment from the peak

Table 9.1 Employment in the Employment in the Public Sector in Denmark by Sub-sectors 2002–2014

	Central government (state sector)	Regional government	Local government (municipal sector)
2002*	159.000	159.000	409.000
2005*	151.000	164.000	408.000
2008	166.000	113.000	433.000
2009	171.000	116.000	444.000
2010	174.000	119.000	454.000
2011	176.000	117.000	448.000
2012	175.000	116.000	439.000
2013	175.000	119.000	434.000
2014	174.000	122.000	433.000

Source: Statistics Denmark, OFBESK2 and OBESK3, 1Q-figures, full-time equivalents * = The dramatic changes in some of the figures between 2005 and 2008 are not only a result of the Structural Reform, but also due to change in calculation methods. Figures before 2002 not available.

in 2010/2011 to 2014, the total number of public sector employees was slightly higher in 2014 than in 2008. Thus, the crisis has had no effect on the overall number of employees.

In *Sweden*, about 30% of all employees are employed in the public sector (SCB 2014), which similarly comprises a three-tier structure. Prior to NPM ideas taking hold, the central government developed a clear division of departments and agencies secured by the constitution. Swedish local government also holds a high degree of autonomy (self-government) secured by the national constitution. In addition, local government comprises 290 municipalities and 20 county councils (including four regions), which all have the right to levy taxes.

On average, 17% were temporarily employed in 2014 (SCB 2015). As such, part-time work is most widespread among women. Although the numbers have been declining, 30% of employed women were working part time in 2013 (Bernhardtz 2015). Similar to Denmark, Sweden's public sector is dominated by female employees except for the police and the defense subsector. Meanwhile, from 1995 to 2010, the number of employees rose in the private sector by 17%, while a decline was seen in the public sector of about 9% among state employees and 5% among regional and municipal employees. This change was mainly due to the continuous privatization efforts of specific areas in public enterprise going back further than the 2008 financial crisis. As a result, the declining number of public sector employees reveals a redistribution of jobs from the public sector to the private sector (Medlingsinstitutet 2010).

As Table 9.2 demonstrates, the number of public employees has in fact risen within the last couple of years within the central welfare areas of the Swedish public sector. In a situation similar to Denmark's, the total number of public sector employees in Sweden was a bit higher in 2013 than in 2009. Hence, the post-2008 crisis has had no impact on the overall number of employees.

Table 9.2 Employment in the Public Sector in Sweden by Sub-sectors, 1995–2014

	Central government	Share of total employment	Local Government	Share of total employment
1995	252,000	6,1	1,096,000	26,6
2000	236,000	5,5	1,057,000	24,6
2005	239,000	5,5	1,103,000	25.4
2008	229,000	5.0	1,099,000	24.1
2009	228,000	5.1	1,074,000	24.1
2010	233,000	5.2	1,063,000	23.6
2011	234,000	5.1	1,068,000	23.2
2012	238,000	5.1	1,073,000	23.2
2013	243,000	5.2	1,085,000	23.2
2014	246,000	5.2	1,095,000	23.1

Source: *Medlingsinstitutet (2014)*

Public Sector Employment Relations and Pay Determination

Overview of the Public Sector Employment Relations System

Whereas the formation of the ER system in the private sector in *Denmark* is normally dated to 1899 and the so-called September Compromise, the ER system in the public sector has a much shorter history. Some bargaining took place in the public sector since the Law on Civil Servants came into force in 1919. However, it was as late as 1969 that collective bargaining on wages and working conditions were formally recognized and the government became obliged to bargain with trade unions. The right and duty to negotiate covered both state employees and the increasing number of regional and municipal employees, but civil servants were still not allowed the right to strike (Due and Madsen 2009). In sum, the Danish public sector ER model is characterized by relatively limited legislation, bipartite collective agreements at all levels with high coverage rates, (ad hoc) tripartite social dialogue, an extensive system for employee involvement and relatively strong trade unions.

Swedish ER is also based on voluntarism and collective bargaining. The ER system was established in 1938 by the Saltsjöbaden Agreement between the Swedish Trade Union Confederation (LO) and the Swedish Employers' Confederation. Civil servants gained the right to participate in collective bargaining and conflict in 1965 (Elvander 2002). At the same time, a new government body was formed with responsibility for the bargaining process, but in these cases, agreements still had to be approved at the political level (SOU 2002). As with the Danish ER model, the Swedish public sector ER model is characterized by limited legislation, bipartite collective agreements at all levels with high coverage rates, strong trade unions, an extensive system for employee involvement and (ad hoc) tripartite social dialogue, (although this activity went through a crisis period in the 1990s). However, even though labor market legislation is limited, it plays a larger role in Sweden than in Denmark. Two examples of this are the more encompassing Swedish Employment Protection Act and the Swedish Employee Involvement Act. Similar measures in Denmark are based on a bipartite agreement.

The Collective Bargaining Structure and Pay Determination

Denmark

Collective agreements cover wages and all concerns about working conditions and employment conditions and work alongside a well-developed co-determination system. Social partners establish general wage scales and terms and conditions at an overall level (state, region or municipality), which are integrated into individual agreements for different occupations. However, wage reforms since the 1990s have introduced local-level wage-bargaining, allowing for individual or group supplements at the administrative unit/workplace. The wage sum used for local bargaining has always been relatively low and stands at only around 10% (Hansen 2013).

The importance of collective bargaining in the Danish public sector is reflected in the fact that it covers 98% of employees in the state sector (Due and Madsen 2009: 360). No statistics exist for the regional and municipal sectors, but the collective bargaining coverage is estimated to be at least as high as in the state sector. The importance of collective bargaining is also reflected in the limited and declining number of civil servants with special statutory employment protection and special pension rights. This development has mainly taken place due to employers' wishes to reduce 'outdated' civil servants' positions and mainstream public employees on (cheaper) contracts that are exclusively collectively agreed upon. Moreover, civil servants are now generally covered by collective bargaining, not unilateral regulation (Due and Madsen 2009).

Nevertheless, it is not so that collective bargaining is the only important type of regulation of pay and conditions. Legislation plays a role, most importantly when it comes to employment conditions (terms of notice etc.), holiday regulation, leave of absence due to childbirth and working- environment issues. Moreover, in the higher parts of the job hierarchy, individual agreements often supplement collective agreements.

Regarding pay determination, attention should also be paid to the so-called 'regulation mechanism', which ties public-sector wages to wage development in the private sector, although with a certain delay. The underlying consensus is that the private sector—because it is exposed to competition—should be wage leading, while public sector wages should not develop into a secondary labor market regarding pay. The regulation mechanism is part of the ER system because it has to be agreed upon during collective bargaining rounds. If no agreements can be reached, the mechanism will terminate, but since its introduction in 1983, social partners have been able to renew agreements on it during all bargaining rounds.

Concerning the structure of collective bargaining, all three main bargaining areas—state, regions, and municipalities—have a two-tier structure, where the first (highest) tiers can be subdivided into two (see Table 9.3). The first tier includes 'cartel bargaining', which normally takes place every second or third year. During these bargaining rounds, the state, regional and municipal employers respectively bargain with cartels (coalitions) made up of trade union representatives. The first tier also includes organizational bargaining (individual unions), which takes place more or less simultaneously with the sector-level bargain. Here, the individual trade unions bargain themselves on all occupation-specific aspects of wages, pensions and working conditions within a decided economic framework that is agreed upon during cartel bargaining. In times of tight budgets, there can be very little to bargain with at this level. The local level is the second bargaining level. As a general rule, it is a trade union-related shop steward who bargains. Bargaining issues include wages, working time, training and policies for senior employees.

Decentralization has, as described, taken place since the 1990s, but it has never been taken as far as in the private sector. Employers still push for decentralization in the co-determination system, whereas efforts to further decentralize wage formation have weakened somewhat. Employers now openly discuss how using individual wages is not the right solution for all employee groups.

Regarding conflict, if Danish social partners fail to strike an agreement during bargaining rounds, and after attempts by the national arbitrator have failed, it is possible for both trade unions and public employers to initiate an industrial conflict: a strike or a lockout. This possibility

Table 9.3 Bargaining Levels and Actors in the Danish Public Sector ER Model

	The bargaining process	*The actors*
Sector level	Cartel bargaining (bi/tri-annual) Organizational bargaining (bi-/triannual)	Ministry of Finance, Local Government Denmark (LGDK), Danish Regions Trade union bargaining cartels (coalitions) Ministry of Finance, LGDK, Danish Regions Individual trade unions
Local level	Local-level bargaining (continuous)	Institutions within the government Regions/institutions within regions Municipalities/institutions within municipality Local branch union officials/shop stewards Single employees (re: individual bargaining, mostly for managers)

is contrary to the situation in several other European countries, where it is either illegal for both social partners or illegal for only employers to do so. Although not necessarily fruitless, since they can be efficient politically, strikes are, in general, less efficient in the public than in the private sector because it is impossible to make public institutions bankrupt—they just save money during the strike. Together with the double role of the Ministry of Finance as both negotiator and legislator, this reality implies that the power balance between public employers and employees is more unequal than in the private sector.

Sweden

Collective bargaining plays a pivotal role, covering 90% of the Swedish labor market and 100% of the public sector (Medlingsinstitutet 2014). Similar to Denmark, the Swedish wage-bargaining model is a two-tier system where company bargaining is framed within sector agreements (Stokke 2008). Sweden had experienced wide public sector disputes during the so-called 'great conflict' in 1980 (Stokke and Seip 2008). Conflicts went on during the 1980s and ended with a major change in Swedish wage formation, with large groups in the public sector favoring decentralized wage formations over centralized ones. Indeed, differences do persist regarding how to view the challenges of decentralization. The organizations represented by the Swedish Confederation of Professional Associations (Saco) are among the strongest advocates for bringing more decentralization, while the large Swedish Municipal Workers' Union—organizing more than half a million employees within both the public and private sectors—and the Swedish Association of Health Professionals are critical concerning wage development among their members.

Another major change took place in the ER system in the 1990s. This included a strengthening of the norm-setting mechanism of the industry, which ties public and private sector negotiations (Medlingsinstitutet 2010; Johansson Heed 2014). Today, wage formation in Sweden is adjusted to the internationally exposed industrial sector. Unlike Denmark, there is no formal regulation mechanism in Sweden that secures wage regulations in case of non-adherence to this principle, but the norm-setting mechanism is in practice very strong. One of the tasks undertaken by the Swedish National Mediation Office (*Medlingsinstitutet*) is to secure an efficient wage formation along with an adherence to this norm-setting mechanism. Since 2000, the National Mediation Office has also been the governmental body responsible for public statistics on wages and salaries.

Within the Swedish two-tier bargaining system, the state employer and the representative body of all Swedish local authorities and regions bargain with central trade union negotiation bodies. This process constitutes coalition bargaining (and in some cases, 'cartel bargaining') at sector levels every second or third year. Issues concerning working time, holidays, wages during maternity and sick leave and pensions are mainly bargained across sectors. Moreover, bargaining takes place within both coalitions and individual trade unions on framework agreements on wages (Ibsen *et al.* 2011; Mailand 2011). The framework agreements guarantee that most of the wage formations are negotiated at the local level. At the second tier, local bargaining takes place every year over wages. Meanwhile, decentralization began in 1996 and has developed gradually. Comparing wage agreements in the public and private sectors, wage formation is more decentralized in the public sector in Sweden, with some variations (Granqvist and Regnér 2004; Mailand 2011). Decentralization of wage formation is the most extensive in the central government sector and among the groups with tertiary education (Mailand 2011; Medlingsinstitutet 2014).

Framework agreements vary regarding the degree to which numbered wage shares are stipulated or not stipulated and as to whether bargaining is designated to take place between local trade union representatives and public institutions or between individual employees and managers (Granqvist and Regnér 2009). Some framework agreements assure minimum wage increases and/or individual guarantees, while others are void of such stipulations. In 2001, the first numberless agreement was entered into by Saco. This type of contract is a framework agreement with no set minimum on wage development. As such, it is more widespread within the public sector than within the private sector and more common within the central government as opposed to the local government.

Table 9.4 Bargaining Levels and Actors in the Swedish Public Sector ER Model

	The bargaining process	*The actors*
Sector-level	Cartel bargaining (bi-/triannual) Organizational bargaining (bi-/triannual)	The Swedish Agency for Government Employers (SAGE) Swedish Association of Local Authorities and Regions (SALAR) Trade union bargaining cartels (coalitions) Individual Trade Unions
Local level	Local-level bargaining (continuous/yearly bargaining)	Institutions within the Government, Regions/institutions within regions, Municipalities/institutions within municipality Local branch union officials/shop stewards Single employees (re: individual bargaining)

Regarding conflict, a strike does not terminate or suspend an individual work contract. Thus, legal and industrial action is more flexible in Sweden than in Denmark (Stokke Seip 2008; Ibsen *et al.* 2011). In order to protect essential services, conflict rights among public employees are somewhat restricted. During conflicts, employees who exercise authority are not permitted to engage in other types of industrial action other than strikes or overtime bans. Consequently, in Sweden, only once—in 1971—has a strike been stopped by law.

As in Denmark, the mediation institution in Sweden is financed through the state budget and is regulated by law. The law enables parties to agree on their own negotiation procedures, and as mentioned, Sweden holds little tradition for government intervention in conflicts. Previous research has accordingly pointed out that the main divergence in the Nordic bargaining models concerning public sector disputes seems to be the extent to which a principle of self-regulation has been created and maintained, and here, Sweden stands out as the country with the strongest self-governing tradition (Stokke and Seip 2008).

The Social Partners in the Public Sector

Characteristics of Public Employers

In *Denmark*, the employer in the state sector is the Ministry of Finance (de facto, the Agency of Modernization, until 2011 the Personnel Agency). Hence, the state employer is not a separate unit. This situation emphasizes the political character of employers in the state sector and might have facilitated the public sector ER having become a more important part of the budget policy in recent years. During the reconstruction of the Agency of Modernization in 2011, nearly all managers were replaced as part of a merger between this and another department. In some subsectors, trade unions have since then experienced a tougher management approach, and they have understood the replacement of managers as a part of this development, whereas in other subsectors, they have experienced a more cooperative approach (Mailand 2014b). This issue will be discussed further below.

As for the municipalities, their employer is LGDK. The large number of responsibilities, the relative autonomy of the municipalities and the high number of municipal employees means that LGDK is a relatively strong organization. This is true even though it may have lost power during recent decades due to the centralization of political power in the Ministry of Finance. At the local level, individual municipalities and public institutions themselves are the employers. In the regional area, the employer is Danish Regions (with the bargaining unit being the Regional Pay Council). At the local level, bargaining takes place between the individual regions and the unions, but public institutions (de facto, the hospitals) might be the most important employer units because of their size.

An important feature of the public employers is a hierarchy. Although they are formally independent of each other, the Ministry of Finance and the state bargaining areas are de facto leading the other two. Another characteristic of the state employer's powerful position is the aforementioned double role of the Minister of Finance. One consequence is that if the government fails to get a bargaining demand through during a collective bargaining round, the Minister of Finance often has opportunities to push it through in the political arena. Moreover, when all other attempts to gain agreement during a collective bargaining round have failed, it is possible for the government—if it has support from a majority in Parliament—to intervene via legislation.

In *Sweden*, the main employer is SAGE, operating on behalf of the central government. In 1994, this institution gained a semi-autonomous status by separating it from the rest of the state apparatus. Thus, the previously described double role of the Ministry of Finance is less significant in the Swedish public sector bargaining system. SAGE members include 250 agencies in the central government sector, and the organization is funded by membership fees in proportion to the payroll expenditures of these member agencies. Hence, SAGE receives no direct government funding. Furthermore, the head of SAGE is elected among its members.

At the local level, SALAR is the main employers' organization. All of Sweden's municipalities, county councils and regions are members of SALAR; together, these have more than one million employees. The hierarchical relationship between municipalities, county councils and regions is different in Sweden than in Denmark. This difference is probably due to both local government types having independent funds collected through taxes. In addition to SALAR, a number of smaller employers' organizations bargain within the local government.

Public Sector Trade Unions: Structure and Membership

Whereas the employer structure in *Denmark* as described is generally straightforward, it is more complex on the trade union side. Of the three confederations—the Danish Confederation of Trade Unions (LO), the Confederation of Professionals in Denmark and the Danish Confederation of Professional Associations (*Akademikerne*)—only the latter plays a direct role in collective bargaining.

Put simply, one or two bargaining cartels exist in each of the three main bargaining areas. The unions in the state and regional areas are predominantly professional unions, organizing one or a few occupations. The professional unions are also important in the municipal sector, but so are the general unions. The two largest of these are 3F and FOA. 3F is cross sectoral and covers many unskilled and semi-skilled workers, whereas FOA is focused on the social policy area and health. In addition, the average education level and income level is highest in the state area and lowest in the municipal area.

There has been a decline in trade union organizational density between 1996 and 2011, but less so in the public than in the private sector. For the subsectors where statistics exist for the whole period from 1996 to 2011, the decline has been from 91 to 89% (public administration), 86 to 80% (education) and 92 to 83% (health) (Statistics Denmark, 'tailor-made' figures).

Sweden also has three peak-level confederations including the Swedish LO, the Swedish Confederation of Professional Employees and Saco. In relation to collective bargaining, public employee trade unions are similarly organized into various negotiating bodies. Considering the educational tier system, Saco-S is the main negotiating body on behalf of professional government employees. The Public Employees' Negotiation Council (OFR) is the largest negotiation body in public sector, as it represents fourteen trade unions, including one Saco member and the union of managers (*Ledarna*). The OFR includes unions that organize teachers, health professionals, police and employees within defense. LO includes amongst other the aforementioned large Swedish Municipal Workers' Union (*Kommunal*) and SEKO who organize about 18,000 public sector employees working within traffic, prisons and defense. The number of unions in local government in Sweden is lower compared to Denmark, which simplifies collective bargaining somewhat. However, there are a number of profession- specific trade unions representing doctors, teachers, nurses etc.

In Sweden, union density rose in the 1980s and peaked in 1986, with 86% being unionized, but these numbers have since been declining. A strong decline was seen in the years 2007–2008 owing to changes in legislation concerning unemployment insurance funds. The legislation forced employees to weigh their contributions to these against their contributions to their trade union membership. Nonetheless, union density has since stabilized at 70% in 2011–2014 (Bengtsson Berglund 2010; Medlingsinstitutet 2014; Kjellberg 2015). In 2008, union density for the public sector was higher than in any other sector at 84%, but as Kjellberg (2015) records, this figure has declined slowly to 82% in 2014.

Reforms of Public Sector Employment

Regarding *Denmark*, it is important to note that most of the reforms presented below have been bargained or at least consulted over with the trade unions. Some are the social partners' own initiatives agreed upon in the collective bargaining arena, while others have political origins. The NPM reforms have included, inter alia, privatization, contracting out, consumer choice, competitive tendering, performance-related management and decentralization (of wage setting and other issues) (Greve 2006; Ibsen *et al.* 2011). The NPM reforms—or reforms with NPM elements—have in recent years been accompanied by other reform trends that, nevertheless, only rolled back NPM to a limited extent (Greve 2012).

The basic features of the public sector industrial relations system remained unchanged; rather, this system shaped the type of NPM that was introduced. Some researchers find it more accurate to talk about 'modernization' rather than 'marketization', meaning that the reform path taken in Denmark has mixed marketization with other types of reforms, and hence, NPM has been described as moderate. The path has also been moderate in the sense that social partners have by and large been dedicated to the modernization agenda, initiated in the early 1980s through the following decades (e.g, Ejersbo and Greve 2005; Ibsen *et al.* 2011; Hansen and Mailand 2013).

The development of NPM in Denmark has gone through several phases. Firstly, in the 1980s, the Conservative-led government initiated the first 'modernization program', which included NPM. However, privatization and contracting out were not achieved to any large extent, but consumer choice was introduced, and local wage determination in various forms was tailored from 1987 (Ibsen *et al.* 2011).

In the 1990s, a center-left government continued many of the NPM-oriented reforms, especially regarding management by contract and large-scale privatizations of public utilities. Regarding wages, the trials from the 1980s were made permanent and formalized when social partners in 1998 agreed to decentralize part of wage determination within the framework of the new wage system '*Ny Løn*' and allow deviations from central working time provisions (Ibsen *et al.* 2011). It was also in the 1990s that the important system of occupational pensions was established, covering private as well as public sector employees and linked to the collective agreements (Due and Madsen 2005).

The development of this new form of pension was not a NPM reform in a strict sense, but can be seen as a special form of privatization of a public service involving social partners (Trampusch 2006). This development marked the beginning of the gradual development of a comprehensive, bipartite occupational pension system into which contributions or 'bonuses' equal to up to 19% of public sector employee wages are now paid. In addition, rights to further training and tools to include employees with reduced capacity to work were introduced in the public sector collective agreements during this period.

In the 2000s, the Liberal-Conservative government strengthened NPM with free customer choice in welfare services and extended compulsory competitive tendering while strong central controls through performance and quality management prevailed (Ibsen *et al.* 2011). However, the government also introduced a number of reforms that were not NPM reforms in a strict sense, although they included some NPM elements: a) the Welfare Reform from 2006, whose aim was to redesign the public sector and its financing in order to meet the challenge of an aging population and b) the Quality Reform from 2007 that aimed to improve service levels and job satisfaction for public employees; this reform promised to end detailed control systems and enhance the focus on skills development and local innovation.

Social partners in the public sector followed up this reform by allocating financial resources when they made a tripartite agreement to support it in 2007 (Mailand 2008). NPM dimensions of the aforementioned Structural Reform, which was implemented from 2007, included central control of performance and the mandate that quality and budgets should also be increased (Ibsen *et al.* 2011). Regarding the ER system, the Welfare Reform and the Quality Reform had consequences for the retirement age and further training, whereas the Structural Reform has led to larger workplaces and larger areas to be covered by collective bargaining and co-determination. Moreover, it has contributed to a decline in municipal employment.

In the 2010s, a new center left government continued the work on reforms with NPM features. One area where this can be seen is in the subcontracting of public services, which is possible in the majority of public service areas and is used to a large extent. LGDK agreed in 2007 that 25% of municipal public services (of the services it is legally possible to subcontract) should be 'exposed to competition', meaning that they should be contracted out, but that it would also be possible for the municipality itself to put in a bid. A non-binding target was set in 2011 aimed at increasing the share to 32%. In 2011, 25% of all municipal public services legally capable of subcontracting were exposed to competition. In the municipal sector, the de facto volume of services subcontracted to private providers reached 25% in 2011 (Økonomi- og indenrigsministeriet 2013). It is notable that the level of outsourcing (measured as the percentage of spending on services exposed to competition) remained the same before and after the crisis. Exposure to competition has increased substantially, but this development occurred before the crisis and was a reaction to the political demand to increase exposure in connection with the Structural Reform (Mailand 2014a). There is no doubt that subcontracting has had consequences for wages and working conditions, but the issue is under-researched in Denmark. The studies that have been conducted point mainly in the direction of a negative impact from outsourcing on wages and working conditions (Mori 2014; Petersen *et al.* 2014).

To some extent, the present decade has also seen a slowing down in the deepening of existing NPM initiatives and in the introduction of new ones. In the ER system, this is reflected in the low and stagnating share of wages negotiated at the local level. This wage-related development is partly crisis connected, but the slowing down of NPM is in some cases also a reaction to NPM itself. The so-called 'trust reform' launched by the center left government illustrates this. The reform aims at reducing control over public sector employees and managers and reducing the time they spend on reporting in order to allow them more time for the core tasks of delivering quality welfare services (Mailand 2012). Social partners in the public sector have also picked up on this agenda and have signed both tripartite and bipartite agreements on the issue. Furthermore, at least in some parts of the public sector, user involvement is now an important tool (Hansen and Mailand

2015). In addition, there is currently a lack of willingness at the national level to allocate financial resources for decentralized wage increases, and in the Ministry of Finance, it is now openly admitted that individual wage setting is not fitting in all subsectors.

Some observers see the reform trend from the 2000s onwards as a departure from NPM and into New Public Governance and other trends, with an emphasis on networks, partnerships, user involvement and digitalization rather than NPM focusing on marketization in various forms (e.g. Greve 2012). Such changes are occurring, but NPM certainly still plays a role in public sector employment. In reality, a whole new reform paradigm has been added to NPM rather than replacing it. This is reflected in the center-left government's grand-scale economic plan from 2012, '*Danmark i arbejde*', in which the chapter on the public sector calls simultaneously for an increasing use of governance by goal and measurement and for a trust reform (Regeringen 2012). The same development was illustrated during the 2015 collective bargaining round, where the Ministry of Finance was criticized. The criticism was for, on one hand, negotiating a large-scale project on increasing trust and cooperation with trade unions, and at the same time, developing a new 'employer policy' where performance-related management was planned to play an important role. The challenge here is to make NPM and post-NPM features work together in a fruitful way. That goal is something the Ministry of Finance thinks is possible, but is one that some trade unions and other interests doubt will succeed.

Like Denmark, *Sweden* has been described as a modernizer rather than a marketizer, indicating that NPM has been implemented through negotiations, including several actors, and only moderately (Hansen 2011; Pollit and Bouckaert 2011; Weisel and Modell 2014). Furthermore, Sweden has similarly maintained the basic features of the public sector ER system, although the decentralization of the wage system, as described above, has been much wider and more profound (Ibsen *et al*. 2011). However, Sweden has marketized more within certain areas of the public services and earlier than Denmark (Green-Pedersen 2002). Also, the political promotion of NPM has been somewhat different, with the Social Democrats being the initiators in Sweden. The early NPM initiatives were taken under a Social Democratic-led government in 1982 (Green-Pedersen 2002). The initial focus was not on marketizing reforms, but rather, on further decentralization, the introduction of management by objective and more service-oriented welfare in terms of—amongst others—free choice (Green-Pedersen 2002; Hansen 2011). Not until the late 1980s did this change, with the Social Democrats being forced to admit to more market-oriented reforms. This followed a growing concern about productivity initiating a productivity investigation in 1989 focusing on both the private and public sectors (Thörnqvist 2007).

Furthermore, in the early 1990s, Sweden was hit by a severe financial crisis. The emergency was caused by low national regulatory restrictions on borrowing and lending that catalyzed another wave of public sector reforms. This crisis was severe, so that while unemployment was low in Sweden in 1990, with 1.6% of the workforce being unemployed, unemployment rose to over 10% following the crisis (Kjellberg 2011; Murhem 2012). In 1991, the Social Democratic government was replaced by a Conservative-led coalition government, and in autumn 1992, the crisis reached its climax, with Sweden leaving the European Exchange Rate mechanism and letting the krona float. Emergency cutbacks were negotiated with the Social Democrats during the crisis. In addition to a general tightening of public spending, measures also included a reform of the unemployment insurance system, a liberalization of temporary employment and a major tax reform in 1991 that reduced marginal tax rates (Fölster and Kreicksberg 2014).

In terms of NPM, Sweden also underwent a series of financial management reforms in the early 1990s. This included results-oriented budgeting, accruals accounting and a tightening of budget control within municipalities (Hansen 2011). In the 1990s, more market-oriented reforms were also further promoted in the postal, telecommunications, rail and utilities sectors and within the healthcare sector as well. The latter sector was dealt with through a mix of splitting providers and purchasers and introducing free choice for patients (Green-Pedersen 2002). Then in 1994, a Social Democratic government took over once again. However, the NPM inspiration continued much in the same form. A fiscal rule requiring a spending surplus was introduced in 1997 in order to further control public spending. This also introduced a target for government spending equal to 2% of the GDP on average over the course of the business cycle, which was later lowered to 1% of the GDP. Additionally, internal budgeting procedures were revised and urged individual ministries to act restrained and adhere to budgeting (Fölster and Kreicksberg 2014). Not NPM related, the Swedish Parliament simultaneously passed a new law on the old-age pension system in 1998, thoroughly revising the system.

In 2006, the center-right coalition 'Alliance for Sweden' won the election. In order to reduce public spending, the new government (amongst others) reduced access to and coverage of unemployment insurance by increasing membership fees, which caused many low-income workers to exit the system (Kjellberg 2011; Schnyder 2012). Another tax reform was also introduced in 2006 that included high-income tax reductions and advanced a form of earned income tax credits for low-income groups but excluded unemployment benefit recipients in order to promote incentive to work (Holmlund 2011). Moreover, as with the Danish NPM trajectory, Sweden also continued focusing on financial performance and management via objectives (Hansen 2011). As in Denmark, the focus on managerial performance has been interpreted as being closely related to an increase in power of the Ministry of Finance over the budget process and the ambition of the Ministry to control all policy in a similar way, rather than using sector-specific control principles (Hall 2013). Some of these initiatives as described above—especially the measures taken in light of the Swedish crisis in the early 1990s—together with a more restrained banking sector, seem to have protected the Swedish economy from the subsequent global financial crisis in 2008 (Holmlund 2011).

The Consequences of the Crisis for Public Sector Employment Relations

Austerity Measures and Crisis-Related Policies

It is difficult to differentiate 'austerity measures' from other crisis-related policies, and both assets of the measures are discussed. In *Denmark*, the Liberal-Conservative government responded initially to the economic crisis by introducing stimulus packages and bank packages. These packages were followed by budget cuts and welfare reforms that combined austerity measures with measures to increase labor supply in the long term. With the first of these reforms, the government included a tax reform and a gradual liquidation of the mostly tax-financed early retirement scheme for employees and self-employed aged 60–64. The government's main policy response to the crisis was the 2010 Recovery Plan (including an unemployment benefit reform). The plan was implemented, inter alia, via the 2010 and 2011 budgets and was the first real austerity measure. It included postponing the tax reductions, a 0.5% spending cut for all ministry budgets, a ceiling on tax reductions for unemployment insurance contributions and an unemployment benefit reform reducing the maximum unemployment benefit period from four to two years. In 2011, municipal budget cuts—as a result of the Recovery Plan—totaled €0.6bn. Partly as a result of this plan, 20% of municipalities experienced cuts in their budget of 4% or more between 2009 and 2011 (KL 2011).

The center-left government that came into office in September 2011 continued the tight budget policy, but also introduced a stimulus package ('Kickstart') for 2012–2013. The aim here was to stimulate the economy by investing €2.3bn in public infrastructure and other public spending measures in 2012 and 2013. As such, the package was part of the 2012 and 2013 budgets. The purpose of improving public finances and increasing labor demand is found in several of the government initiatives included in its '2020 Plan' (Regeringen 2012).

Exclusively related to the public sector was the aforementioned 2020 Plan's section on 'Modernizing the public sector', where the government both calls for greater use to be made of performance measurement, management by results and evaluations and trust. Furthermore, the government calls for initiatives to streamline work processes and eliminate unnecessary tasks, increase working hours in general (part-time work is very widespread in the public sector) and particularly in education (see below for how this aim was fulfilled). Also directly related to the public sector is the 'Growth

Plan DK—Strong companies, more jobs' (Regeringen 2013). In the plan, the government states that it will 'set free' €1.6bn in the public sector for 'new initiatives' and 'targeted improvements in the public sector'. Furthermore, the government will aim for 'balanced growth' in the public sector of between 0.4 and 1.0% per year until 2020. Certain public sector trade unions see the sum of these formulations and calculations as de facto austerity, leading them to refuse to cooperate with the government (also because of the 2013 bargaining round described below), whereas other unions do not see any dramatic measures here and are willing to cooperate. No matter which of these interpretations is correct, it is clear that the public sector collective bargaining system will increasingly be leveraged to make the public sector more efficient (Mailand 2014b).

Sweden was also initially hit hard by the more recent post-2008 crisis, but compared to the situation in the early 1990s, the consequences of the post-2008 recession were not as severe. Unemployment increased from 5.8% in May 2008 to 8.9% in May 2009 (Statistics Sweden). However, already during 2010, employment began rising. In the beginning of the post-2008 crisis, the Swedish crown was significantly weakened to the benefit of general Swedish competitiveness, but from the spring of 2009, it began regaining its strength (Holmlund 2011). The Swedish government continued using a relatively tight fiscal policy in the aftermath of the crisis with the aim to maintaining a public finance surplus yet also incorporating some stimulus initiatives. These initiatives were mainly targeted at preventing exclusion from the labor market, investing in education and promoting growth. During 2010, the GDP rose by about 5.5% in Sweden, which was more than any other European country at that time (Medlingsinstitutet 2010).

In the autumn of 2011, tripartite negotiations took place over a jobs pact to reduce youth unemployment. The jobs pact included the reduction of working hours and wages for young people under 25, improvement of the possibility of combining employment and education and a reduction of high and differentiated unemployment insurance fund payments (SVT Nyheter, November 27, 2012, *Facken i LO ställer sig bakom regeringens jobbpakt*).

The financial budget for 2013 suggested a slightly more expansionist policy, including tax reforms, continued initiatives to reduce youth unemployment and various public investments in infrastructure and education and research (Ministry of Finance, press release, October 12, 2010; the budget for 2011, September 20, 2011; the budget for 2012, September 20, 2012; the budget for 2013). However, economic development has still remained low, with no major changes in unemployment but with some economic stabilization and some job growth (Budget Statement 2014). Furthermore, Sweden has had a deficit in public finances, and accordingly, new budgeting measures are being proposed in hopes of securing the stated surplus financing target. However, reforms continue to be mainly targeted at securing more jobs and less on austerity.

*Consequences of the Crisis and Responses From Employers
and Trade Unions*

The impact of the crisis has already been touched upon in several of the sections above. Regarding *Denmark*, section two explained that although the municipal sector has experienced rounds of layoffs, overall employment in the public sector shows a minor increase from 2009 to 2013. Moreover, job reductions that have taken place in the municipal sector represent as much an expression of the implementation of pre-crisis changes (the Structural Reform) and demographic trends (fewer children being born) as a manifestation of the direct impact of the crisis (Hansen and Mailand 2013).

Regarding employer and trade union reactions, there have been no formal pay reductions or pay freezes, but the development in real wages has in some years been negative. Similar to developments in 2008–09, when economic conditions deteriorated quickly, the 'regulation mechanism' has worked as a hidden austerity measure in that it led to an automatic downward regulation of wages in the public sector. Moreover, employers have strengthened the management prerogative, likely under the influence of the crisis, but there were no radical changes in wages, working conditions, employee rights or any other basic qualitative features of the public sector employment regulation system. Trade union membership is declining, but only marginally and less so in the public than in the private sector. Membership-related protests, including a one-day large-scale protest in June 2010, was organized by the largest Danish trade union confederation (LO) and a number of their member-organizations against the Conservative-Liberal government's austerity measures. But in general, protests have been few in number and there have been no calls for general strikes (Mailand 2013a). The crisis and austerity policies have not so far led to important qualitative changes in public sector ER.

The strengthening of the management prerogative could, however, be part of more substantial changes, where the crisis might have been the trigger but not the only driver. Since 2011, there has been increasing pressure on LGDK from the Ministry of Finance to adopt a 'tougher' stance, and now the employers—and not the trade unions—are turning up to the negotiation tables with the most far-reaching demands. This situation was most clearly illustrated by the collective bargaining round in 2013, where the Ministry of Finance and LGDKs successfully used a lockout followed by legal intervention in order to move teachers' working time issues from collective bargaining to a unilateral regulation.

Again, the crisis (weakening trade unions and increasing budget pressure) signified only one element in the creation of a rare 'window of opportunity' that the government would not let pass. Other elements included the political situation (very limited opposition in Parliament, a Social-Democratic government and the inclusion of the new working time regulation in a high-profile educational reform) as well as historical factors (government defeat on similar issues in previous bargaining rounds and widespread LGDK dissatisfaction with the trade unions' role in working time regulation) (Mailand 2015a). Some public sector trade unions saw this process as violating the self-governing principle in the Danish ER model (Mailand 2014a, 2014b). The 2015 bargaining round was not so marked by this 'tougher' employer approach, but it is too early to consider it only a temporary phenomenon.

In *Sweden*, the prelude to the bargaining rounds in 2010, 2012 and 2013 included debates between employers and trade unions over the necessity of wage restraints (Medlingsinstitutet 2010). The public sector bargaining round in 2010 followed the norm of wage restraint set by the industry that secured real wages but resulted in a slowing down of wage development as well as a further strengthening of the decentralized parts of the wage system. Thus, individual guarantees of wage increases, if no agreement could be reached in cases of individual wage bargaining, was removed from some state, regional and municipal employees. Nevertheless, some of these agreements still maintain individual guarantees (Medlingsinstitutet 2010).

In 2012, a new round of collective bargaining measures ensued with wage restraint as the continued norm set by the industry. A 2.6% wage increase within a one-year agreement was reached on behalf of 100.000 white-collar state employees. Also, a three-year agreement with a 3.6% wage increase but without individual guarantees was reached on behalf of, among others, police and officers. In 2012, wage negotiations in the central government implemented more of the numberless agreements. Some groups continued to resist, since they preferred number-fixed wage increases (Johansson and Heed 2014). However, for state-employed professionals and employees holding a master's degree and/or a Ph.D., the agreement reached was without specific wage percentages, and moreover, with no end date.

Tough negotiations also took place with the main teachers' unions attempting to achieve wage rises above the norm. Based on a recognition of the teachers' real wages having fallen behind other comparable groups, a new agreement was reached for four years until March 2016, giving the teachers a wage rise of 4.2%. This figure was the highest for any sector during the 2012 round of negotiations (Johansson and Eriksson 2012).

On the agenda for the bargaining round of 2013 was a concern over the increasing use of fixed-term contracts among municipal workers, continued wage restraint and wage decentralization. The possibility of prolonging the collective agreement period was also an issue. The industry set the norm with a 6.8% increase in labor costs over three years, securing a real-wage increase (Medlingsinstitutet 2014). In addition, more numberless agreements with no end date were concluded. Thus, in 2015, about 800.000 employees were covered by numberless framework agreements without a set minimum wage development. During 2014, wages further increased at a moderate pace, but due to low inflation, real wages grew 3%. This outcome has been beneficial for real wages and growth in the Swedish economy, but international competitiveness remains challenged (Medlingsinstitutet 2014).

In sum, the Swedish government has not implemented austerity measures that directly target wages and working conditions, but instead, economic challenges connected to the 2008 financial crisis have been handled by social partners within the Swedish collective bargaining system. Moreover, wage restraint and decentralization have been some of the main trends (Johansson and Heed 2014).

Comparative Discussion and Conclusions

Public Services Reforms and New Public Management

A number of similarities between the two countries can be highlighted regarding NPM. Both countries have introduced NPM reforms in a moderate form, often labeled 'modernization'. This form of NPM that combines marketization with other measures does not exclude trade unions and leaves public services as a distinct employer. A difference between the two countries can be seen in the *timing* of the reforms' introduction. Sweden has marketized more within certain areas of public services and earlier than Denmark (Green-Pedersen 2002). However, it is difficult to compare the *degree* of marketization between the two countries due to differences in registration methods. Denmark seems to have moved ahead in some public service areas, especially within cleaning and waste collection, whereas Sweden continues to be a forerunner within areas such as childcare (Houlberg and Petersen 2012).

Although clearly not solely driven by economic business cycles, the economic crisis of the 1990s in Sweden accentuated the need for reform by promoting more NPM with an emphasis on marketization and financial reform. In Denmark, where the economic conditions from the mid-1990s were better, NPM policies were introduced more gradually. Denmark was hit harder by the economic crisis starting in 2008. This could potentially be an explanation for the closing in on Sweden regarding marketization in some subsectors. However, the increase in the rate of public service exposure to competition increased before the crisis and not after. Furthermore, the present decade has in general not seen a growth in NPM initiatives, but rather, NPM as the dominant trend has been challenged.

Changes in Employment Relations and Employment Trends

To some extent, changes in the Danish and Swedish public sector ER systems resemble the NPM policy trajectory. The most important changes took place in the 1990s, not in the post-crisis period, and the changes were deeper in Sweden than in Denmark. In both countries, wage decentralization took off in the 1990s, but much more radically so in Sweden than in Denmark. Moreover, in Denmark, a development took place in the 1990s that extended collective agreements to include rights to training, extensive occupation pensions and other social benefits. In Sweden, other and more numerous changes took place in public sector ER. These included, inter alia, connecting public sector wage development to the private sector being exposed to competition and the establishment of SAGE. A reduction in the public sector employment level was seen in Sweden in the mid-1990s, which was followed by near stagnation. In Denmark, public sector employment continued to grow slowly but steadily during the 1990s and until 2010, when stagnation occurred.

The post-2008 economic crisis has impacted ER, although only to a limited extent, and less so in Sweden than in Demark. Job growth has stopped in the public sector in Denmark, and wage growth has been reduced in both countries. In Denmark, the impact on wages has been formal and happened automatically though the 'regulation mechanism', which limits wage growth in the public sector when private sector wage growth is reduced. In Sweden, there is no such formal and automatic mechanism, but a consensus on letting the manufacturing industry act as the lead bargaining sector has led to very limited wage growth after 2008. In neither country, however, have fundamental changes in ER systems been seen post-2008. In Denmark, public employers have attempted to strengthen the management prerogative during recent collective bargaining rounds, which has led to incremental adjustments. The only subsector where fundamental changes have taken place is in education, where the 2013 collective bargaining round removed decisions on the use of working time from the collective bargaining arena and transformed it into a management prerogative. This was done in a process that included a large-scale lockout and a parliamentarian intervention. The processes simultaneously used—and further deepened—the power imbalance between employers and trade unions. In Sweden, public employers have continued to emphasize decentralization of wages, especially promoting the so-called numberless agreements with no minimum wage development stipulated. In particular, professionals in the state sector with tertiary education have entered into such agreements, but other welfare groups continue to be more reluctant. However, there is no direct challenge to decentralization as such. Another development is the new type of framework agreements with no end date. Furthermore, there appears to be no change in the role of the state employer, as seen in Denmark.

The Relationship Between Parliamentary Politics and Employment Relations

The third theme addresses the autonomy of the public sector ER system in relation to parliamentary democracy. Social partners are granted a greater role in the Nordic ER models than anywhere else, and this is also the case for the public sector part of the ER model. However, in the public sector, the social partners' autonomy is weaker due to their closeness to the political system. A number of work and employment relations issues have been laid down in legislation and further depend on economic agreements for the public sector. The state employer is also—to a major or minor degree— embedded in the government. This is a structural feature of the public sector that implies challenges for the public sector employers, but also provides them with power resources (Mailand 2014).

However, there are some differences in this autonomy between the two countries. As mentioned above, SAGE acts independently from direct government involvement. Looking at their personnel policy, it is of course heavily influenced by political administrative changes to public sector management, but how it is to be implemented in the state departments and agencies is solely a matter for SAGE in the collective bargaining rounds. Furthermore, it is the job of the rather strong Medlingsinstitut to assure that the industrial norm for wage development is being upheld and to monitor developments and mediate conflict; there is no tradition of government intervention. Thus, it is unlikely that a lockout such as the Danish teachers' conflict in 2013 could occur in Sweden, due to the stronger autonomy of the Swedish ER system. Yet, on occasion, collective bargaining issues do enter the political arena in Sweden. Recently, a political discussion concerning wages and motivation among teachers at the municipal and regional levels impacted the collective bargaining round in 2013 and led to an agreement of wage increases above the industry norm. This did not directly involve SAGE and is yet another reflection of the difference between the two public sector ER models.

Another type of autonomy is relevant to include here. Both Denmark and Sweden have large local community subsectors, and their municipalities have relatively extensive autonomy, including the right to collect taxes. Even so, in recent years, a recentralization has to some extent taken place, but of a partly different nature than the wage recentralization noted by Bach and Bordogna (2013). The Ministry of Finance has in both countries developed into a type of 'super-ministry', controlling spending and to some extent also controlling policy initiatives in other ministries as well as in the municipalities and regions. In Denmark, a degree of recentralization can also be seen in the ER system, where the long established hierarchy—with the Ministry of Finance at the top—has been strengthened. Thus, the room of maneuver for other municipal and regional employers has been diminished. Moreover, the employers' previously strong commitment to decentralize wages further seems somewhat weaker in recent years. In Sweden, public employers continue to act more independently of one another, although within the norm set by the industry. Consequently, the autonomy within Swedish public sector ER remains more intact even though employers do look to each other to maintain similarities in rule setting. Moreover, the Swedish system relies heavily on broad framework agreements, whereas the Danish system continues to bargain wages and many other issues with the individual organizations, resulting in greater rule complexities.

Applying the Lodge and Hood Typology

Applying the Lodge and Hood typology on multiple austerities to the two Scandinavian countries is challenged by relatively mild and limited austerity measures used in Denmark and Sweden. However, it could be said that the recent Danish development shows mixed results where the NPM track—in Lodge and Hood's typology, close to the 'hollow-state' scenario—has been added to developments that to some extent reflect 'the redirecting state'. The strengthening of the hierarchy in public sector ER (mirrored in the development of the Ministry of Finance into a 'super-ministry' in administration generally), public employers' attempts to strengthen the management prerogative and the weakening of the same employers' commitment to decentralized wage formation show this development, which still does not change the ER model fundamentally. Changes have taken place, but mainly in the form of incremental adjustments (Starke 2006) and some 'redirecting state' type initiatives, adding to NPM. Moreover, part of this development—and especially the 2013 lockout—shows a strengthening of the parliamentarian side of the public sector ER model at the expense of the self-governing side. It remains to be seen if the more active and dominant public employers represent more fundamental change.

Much the same can be said for Sweden. Thus, in Sweden—where the recent crisis has had even less impact and NPM was developed at an earlier stage—recent changes have been even more limited than in Denmark. There is a continued NPM trajectory, but the post-2008 crises have not accentuated further marketization on any grand scale. Looking at the continued emphasis on employment, the norm-setting mechanism and (among public employers) further decentralization of the wage formation, we find indications of a tendency towards a 'directing state'. However, elements relating to the 'local communitarian state' can also be identified in the continued reluctance to centralize and control the public sector bargaining model and commitment to strengthen local-level bargaining. In addition, looking more broadly at public sector reform initiatives, it appears that Sweden is, like Denmark, experiencing a diversification of administrative forms developing in the public sector, including post-NPM elements (Hansen 2011; Weisel and Modell 2014).

In the above comparison of the Danish and Swedish ER models, the tension between political intervention and voluntarism of social partners has been touched upon several times. In relation to the application of the Lodge and Hood typology, this tension poises yet another challenge. Thus, the Lodge and Hood typology of multiple austerities builds on an analysis of the public sector bargains attained between public servants and the political system. On the other hand, the development of the Nordic public sector ER models is not driven by bargains among politicians and bureaucrats. The voluntarism of the Nordic labor market models still leaves much of the initiative with the social partners.

Acknowledgement

Thanks to Professor of Sociology Anders Kjellberg of Lund University for commenting on a draft version of the Swedish sections. Any errors are the sole responsibility of the authors.

References

Andersen, S. K., Due, J. and Madsen, J. S. (1999) 'Negotiating the Restructuring of Public Services Employment', in Bach, S. (ed.) *Public Services Employment Relations in Europe: Transformation, Modernization or Inertia?* London: Routledge, 198–232.

Bach, S. and Bordogna, L. (2013) 'Reframing Public Service Employment Relations: The Impact of Economic Crisis and the New EU Economic Governance', *European Journal of Industrial Relations*, 19(4): 279–294.

Bengtsson, M. and Berglund, T. (2010) 'Negotiating Alone or Through the Union? Swedish Employees' Attitudes in 1997 and 2006', *Industrial and Economic Democracy*, 32(2): 223–242.

Bernhardtz, L. (2015) 'Gapet mellan kvinnors och mäns arbetstid består', *Statistiknyhet från SCB* Nr 2014: 55. Statistiska Centralbyrån. statistik/Artiklar/ Gapet-mellan-kvinnors-och-mans-arbetstid-bestar/

Due, J. and Madsen, J. S. (2009) *Forligsmagere og Forumshoppere—analyse af OK08 i den offentlige sektor*, Copenhagen: Jurist og Økonomforbundets Forlag.

Ejersbo, N. and Greve, C. (2005) *Moderniseringen af den offentlige sektor*, Copenhagen: Børsens Forlag.

Fölster, S. and Kreicksberg, J. (2014) *Twenty Five Years of Swedish Reforms*, Paper. Stockholm: Reforminstituttet.

Granqvist, L. and Regnér, H. (2009) *Lokal lönbildning i praktiken*, Stockholm: Swedish Confederation of Professional Associations (Saco).

Green-Pedersen, C. (2002) 'New Public Management Reforms of the Danish and Swedish Welfare States: The Role of Different Social Democratic Responses', *Governance: An International Journal of Policy, Administration, and Institutions*, 15(2): 271–294.

Greve, C. (2006) 'Public Management Reform in Denmark', *Public Management Review* 8(1): 161–169.

Greve, C. (2012) *Reform analyse—Hvordan den offentlige sektor grundlæggende blev forandret i 00'erne*, København: Jurist- og Økonomforbundets Forlag.

Hall, P. (2013) 'NPM in Sweden: The Risky Balance between Bureaucracy and Politics', in Sandberg, Å. (ed.) *Nordic Lights. Work, Management and Welfare in Scandinavia*, Stockholm: Studieförbundet Näringsliv och samhälle (SNS Forlag), 406–419.

Hansen, H. F. (2011) 'NPM in Scandinavia', in Christensen, T. and Lægreid, P. (eds.) *The Ashgate Hansen, Research Companion to New Public Management*, Farnham: Ashgate, 113–129.

Hansen, N. W. (2013) 'Lokal løn i det offentlige'. *Fakta*. FAOS, Sociologisk Institut, University of Copenhagen.

Hansen, N. W. and Mailand, M. (2013) 'Public Service Employment Relations in an Era of Austerity: The Case of Denmark', *European Journal of Industrial Relations*, 19(4): 375–389.

Hansen, N. W. and Mailand, M. (2015) 'New Challenges for Public Services Social Dialogue—National Report Denmark'. *Forskningsnotat nr. 142*. FAOS, Sociologisk Institut, University of Copenhagen.

Holmlund, B. (2011) *Svensk arbetsmarknad under två kriser*, Working Paper 2011:12, Uppsala Center for Labor Studies. Department of Economics.

Houlberg, K. and Petersen, O. H. (2012) 'Indikatorer for kommunernes køb af eksterne ydelser i Danmark og Sverige'. *AKF Notat*. København: AKF, Anvendt KommunalForskning.

Ibsen, C. L., Larsen, T. P. and Madsen, J. S. (2011) 'Challenging Scandinavian Employment Relations—The Effects of New Public Management Reforms', *International Journal of Human Resource Management*, 22(11): 2295–2310.

Johansson, E. and Eriksson, H. (2012) 'Teachers Win New Pay Deal after Tough Negotiations', *EIROnline*, Eurofond, s/se1209019i.htm

Kjellberg, A. (2011) 'The Decline in Swedish Union Density Since 2007', *Nordic Journal of Working Life Studies*, 1(1): 67–93.

Kjellberg, A. (2015) *Kollektivavtalens täckningsgrad samt organisationsgraden hos arbetsgivarförbund och fackförbund*, Lund University: Studies in Social Policy, Industrial Relations, Working Life and Mobility. Research Reports 2013:1 (Appendix 3 in English). Updated 2015.

KL (2011) *Massive besparelser i kommunerne*. /momentum2011–3–1-id83287/. (Accessed 14 March 2011).

Lodge, M. and Hood, C. (2012) 'Into an Agee of Multiple Austerities? Public Management and Public Sector Bargains across OECD Countries', *Governance: An International Journal of Policy, Administration and Institutions*, 25(1): 79–101.

Mailand, M. (2008) *Regulering af arbejde og velfærd—mod nye arbejdsdelinger mellem staten og arbejdsmarkedets parter*, København: Jurist- og Økonomforbundet Forlag.

Mailand, M. (2011) 'Lokal løndannelse i den offentlige sektor i Sverige'. Fakta. København: FAOS.

Mailand, M. (2014a) ' "Austerity Measures and Municipalities": The Case of Denmark', *Transfer*, 30(3): 417–430.

Mailand, M. (2014b) 'Overenskomstforhandlinger under pres—OK2013 i den offentlige sektor', FAOS, Sociologisk Institut, Københavns Universitet.

Mailand, M. (2015a) Active Employers and Teachers Working Time Regulation—Public Sector Industrial Conflicts in Denmark and Norway. Unpublished paper.

Mailand, M. (2015b) 'Dagpengereformer, flexicurity og atypisk ansatte—Delrapport 2 i projektet "Dagpengereformer og flexicurity".' FAOS, Sociologisk Institut, Københavns Universitet. Upubliceret paper.

Medlingsinstitutet (2008, 2010, 2014) 'Avtalsrörelsen och lönebildningen'. *Medlingsinstitutets årsrapport*, Stockholm: Medlingsinstitutet.

Mori, A. (2014) *Outsourcing in Public Sector Organisations. Impacts on Labour and Employment Relations in a Comparative Perspective*. Paper Presented at IREC Conference, September 12–14, Dublin.

Murhem, S. (2012) 'Security and Change: The Swedish Model and Employment Protection 1995–2010', *Economic and Industrial Democracy*, 34(4): 621–636.

Økonomi- og indenrigsministeriet (2013) *Kommunale nøgletal*. www.noegletal.dk

Petersen, O. H., Hjelmer, U., Vrangbæk og, K., & Larsen, P. T. (2014) 'Effekter ved udlicitering af offentlige opgaver'. Delrapport 1. Forskningsprojektet 'Dokumentation af effekter ved konkurrenceudsættelse af offentlige opgave.' Copenhagen, KORA.

Regeringen (2012) *Danmark i arbejde. Udfordringer for dansk økonomi frem mod 2020*, Copenhagen: Regeringen.

Regeringen (2013) *Vækstplan DK—stærke virksomheder, flere job*, Copenhagen: Regeringen.

SCB (2015) 'Tidsbegränsade anställningar—en vanlig ingång till arbete', *Statistiknyhet från SCB* 2015–02–24 09:30, Nr 2015:286. Statistiska Centralbyrån.

Schnyder, G. (2012) 'Like a Phoenix from the Ashes? Reassessing the Transformation of the Swedish Political Economy Since the 1970s', *Journal of European Public Policy*, 19(8): 1126–1145.

Thörnqvist, C. (2007) 'Changing Industrial Relations in the Swedish Public Sector: New Tensions within the Old Framework of Corporatism', *International Journal of Public Sector Management*, 20(1): 16–33.

Trampusch, C. (2006) 'Industrial Relations and Welfare States: The Different Dynamics of Retrenchment in Germany and the Netherlands', *Journal of European Social Policy*, 16: 121.

Weisel, F. and Modell, S. (2014) 'From New Public Management to New Public Governance? Hybridization and Implications for Public Sector Consumerism', *Financial Accountability & Management*, 30(2): 175–205.

10 Hungary: State-Led Responses to the Crisis and Protracted Austerity

Imre Szabó

Introduction: Three Dimensions and Three Critical Junctures

This chapter focuses on three dimensions of Hungarian public sector employment: activities, legal statuses and organization of delivery. By exploring activities, we can find out what public sector workers actually do, what kind of duties they perform and how the services that the state delivers via its own employees have changed over time. A focus on legal status is justified by the country context. In Hungary, instead of collective bargaining, unilateral legislation determines the most important elements of employment conditions (including wages). Finally, by looking at the organization of public service delivery, we can also tell how much autonomy local governments or establishment-level managers have vis-à-vis the central government in terms of their relationship with employees. Tracking developments along these three dimensions over time provides the structure of the chapter. Three critical junctures will be identified over the period 1990–2015: the early years of the post-communist transition in the 1990s, the turn to austerity in 2006 and the changes that the conservative Orbán government enacted after 2010. In all three of these critical periods, significant changes are observed in all three dimensions.

In the initial years of the post-socialist transition, the employer function of the state had to be redefined in the context of moving away from a state-controlled into a mixed-market economy. Within the region, Hungary reached market economy levels of private ownership relatively quickly (EBRD 2000: 170), which by definition reduced the role of the state as an employer. Apart from public transportation and the post, the state as an employer was essentially reduced to activities of public administration, defense and compulsory social security, as well as education, health and social care.

Following the continental European tradition, the legal status of employees in these activities was separated from those working in the private sector (Edelényi and Neumann 2014a: 147–148). Rather than following the Labour Code, public sector employment relations came to be regulated by laws that also distinguished between specific employee categories within the public sector itself. A difference from Germany that makes the Hungarian case somewhat purer analytically is that legal statuses were tied to activities. In Hungary, civil servants can only be found in public administration, whereas in Germany, employees in other activities, for example, teachers, can obtain this legal status (Bosch *et al.* 2012). Apart from the internal fragmentation of legal statutes, all public sector employees enjoyed a higher level of employment security than private sector employees, but this security has been eroding since the early 2000s and especially after 2006 (Nacsa 2014).

The transition also affected the levels where public sector activities were organized. While Hungary remained a centralized, unitary state, the responsibility to provide public services (including basic health and primary education) was delegated to individual settlements. In 2010, Hungary had 3,177 municipal governments at the settlement level, all having a wide range of competences independently of population size and financial capabilities. The decentralization of public service provision in the early 1990s also set the baseline for greater managerial autonomy and embryonic New Public Management (NPM) reforms in later years, as some local governments were experimenting with outsourcing and new managerial practices.

NPM ideas were more explicitly encouraged in the period after 2006, when the central government took a turn from excessive public sector spending towards austerity and neoliberal reforms. Healthcare was the most affected area, with organizational change and the related loss of special legal status for a large proportion of employees (Kahancová and Szabó 2015). In other parts of the public sector, changes were less radical, as employees were not deprived of their status. At the same time, their wages were cut and their legal status weakened from within through the introduction of flexible employment standards and performance-related pay elements (Berki 2014: 128).

From 2010 onwards, a conservative government backed by a parliamentary supermajority reversed many previous structural reforms in public services, but also imposed new ones as part of a broader statist agenda (Szabó 2013). In the framework outlined by Lodge and Hood (2012), developments in Hungary after 2010 could be best categorized as part of a directing state response. In terms of activities, the post-2010 period is marked by the significant expansion of public works programs as a new state activity relying on low skilled manual labor, employing 19% of all public sector workers in 2014 (author's calculation based on KSH Stadat Tables 2.1.34 and 2.1.4). The legal status of participants in public works programs is separated from the regular labor code, but also from the existing statutes of civil servants and public service employees. In 2010, a new legal category of government officials was created, giving the government almost unlimited power over employees in the central public administration. Finally, when it comes to the dimension of organization, education and healthcare were rapidly and almost completely recentralized—the central government took back owner-ship of schools and hospitals from municipalities. As a result, managerial autonomy was further constrained at lower levels of decision-making.

What also seems to be a substantive difference after 2010 is the unprec-edented curtailment of strike rights and the creation of corporatist interest representation bodies with compulsory membership. Furthermore, while previous governments preferred legislation and negotiations that encom-passed the entire public sector, the Orbán government focuses more selec-tively on specific activities, for example, by setting up separate pay scales in healthcare and education.

It also has to be noted that the state's turn towards more directionism after 2010 has been accompanied by handing over establishments and also providing more favorable financial conditions to churches (Fazekas and Neumann 2014: 14). In sum, the concept of directionism in the Hungarian case has to be modified to be able to account for the fact that directionism does not necessarily imply better deals for employees and also that it can be blended with a large dose of communitarianism (Lodge and Hood 2012).

Despite significant differences between these periods, what connects them is an overwhelmingly unilateral and statutory management of public sector human resources. The most crucial decisions affecting employment conditions have always been taken unilaterally by governments (or before 2010, municipalities), and legislation has always dominated over collec-tive bargaining. In this respect, the changes that have been taking place since 2010 are changes in degree rather changes in kind. Recentralization has only further weakened collective bargaining in public services by mak-ing the local level obsolete. Correspondingly, there is even more power on the side of the central government to set wages and employment condi-tions unilaterally.

What also connects the pre- and post-2010 periods is austerity: Hungar-ian public finances were under severe pressure from 2006 on, so the 2008 crisis only intensified an already quite pronounced austerity course further. In 2004, during the country's entry into the European Union, Hungary was put under the excessive deficit procedure, starting the longest procedure of that kind in the EU's history. Recentralization after 2010 has been combined with continuing austerity: between 2009 and 2012, spending on the com-pensation of government employees fell from 11.3 to 9.98% of the GDP (OECD Government at a Glance indicators 2015). While decentralization and more managerial autonomy in the years before 2010 brought some divergence based on regional economic development and the preferences of local governments, after 2010, austerity was experienced uniformly in the public sector.

This chapter combines perspectives from labor sociology and labor eco-nomics, law and political science to give a broad overview of the structures, actors and processes of Hungarian public sector employment relations. The research mostly relied on secondary sources authored by Hungarian labor relations experts, but it was complemented by primary sources: national legal documents, press releases and European Industrial Relations Observatory reports, Statistics was obtained from the Hungarian Statistical Office and administrative surveys.

Organization Structure and Employment

After successive rounds of privatization in the 1990s, the employment structure of the Hungarian economy by and large came to resemble the patterns of established market economies. Privatization of socialist enterprises was completed by the early 2000s, with a few exceptions that remain in state hands to this day (most importantly, the passenger section of the national railways and the postal service). State activities became confined to public administration, defense and public services (education, health and social care). Compared to the freefall of employment in state-owned enterprises, employment increased considerably in these areas during the early transition years, as some administrative and welfare functions formerly carried out by the communist party apparatus and socialist enterprises were transferred to the general government (Köllő 2014a: 45–46). Between 1986 and 1994, the number of employees in the public sector increased from 665 to 800,000 (Köllő 2014a: 46, János Köllő's estimates based on wage survey data). The first significant employment cuts in the 'newly defined' public sector occurred in 1995 as part of a fiscal consolidation package (Köllő 2014a: 45). Employment fell from 800,000 to 740,000 and then consolidated in the late 1990s and early 2000s.

Table 10.1 displays developments in different NACE (Statistical Classification of Economic Activities in the European Community) categories in the Hungarian public sector since 2000—data presented in the previous paragraph for the period before 2000 came from a different source; therefore, they are not directly comparable. Relative stability characterized the early 2000s, with moderate gains in public administration, defense and compulsory social security and stagnation in the other two main public sector activities (education and health and social care). Employment levels started decreasing moderately after 2003 and radically after 2006, resulting in a reduction of the workforce by almost one in eight (97,000) from 2003 to 2008. Trends are more ambiguous after 2008. While large-scale labor shedding definitely stopped around 2008, it has to be noted that the subsequent increase displayed in Table 10.1 results from the rapid expansion of public works programs, which fit uneasily in the regular employment landscape of the public sector. After some initial hesitation—reflected in the stagnation between 2010 and 2012, the Orbán government fully embraced the idea of employment creation via public works programs, which pushed public sector headcounts to unprecedented levels. In 2014, state employment stood at 854,100, a figure larger than in the previous peak year, 2003. Nevertheless, if public works employment is subtracted, the 2014 number drops to 694,000, which is almost the same as the 2008 figure (691,000). The institutional setting of these programs will be discussed at length in later sections.

Table 10.1 Public Sector Employment in Hungary, 2000–2014

	2000	2002	2004	2006	2008	2010	2012	2014
Public sector total	791.5	800.4	816.5	788.3	722.0	772.6	751.3	854.1
Public sector, excluding public works					691.5	685.6	660.6	694.7
Public administration and defense, comp. soc. security	300.9	309.8	318.3	312.5	262.6	261.7	259.5	276.0
Education	232.9	233.6	238.0	234.1	237.6	245.6	233.1	227.4
Human health and social work	194.1	197.5	200.0	186.1	170.7	211.8	212.6	302.0
Participants in public works programs					30.5	87	90.7	159.4

Source: KSH, for public works programs "KSH jelenti" reports (2009: 37, 2010: 5, 2012: 63–64, 2013: 111, 2014: 99)

Corresponding to OECD patterns, the public sector labor force in Hungary is feminized, and the proportion of women has remained stable throughout the crisis years. In some sectors, e.g., healthcare, feminization has even increased—from 78 to 80%—between 2008 and 2014. In education, it stood at 77–78% throughout the entire period. The gender composition of public administration and defense is closer to the national average, with a 50–52% female share—in the overall economy, it is 46%. However, once we exclude defense, the proportion jumps to similar levels as in health and education (KSH Dissemination Database).

Hungarian public sector employees typically have full-time, permanent contracts. In 2008, the share of part-time workers—with at least 60 hours per month—was around 7% in the public sector, declining to 5% to 2014 (own calculation based on KSH Dissemination Database). Part-time work is also constrained on the supply side by the very low wages in the sector. In terms of contract type, legislation allows only a limited use of fixed-term contracts, mostly at the beginning of the career. Public works programs are an exception because they exclusively comprise fixed-term contracts (Busch and Bördős 2015: 78).

Public Sector Employment Relations and Pay Determination

Legal Regulation

Detailed statutory legislation regulates all major aspects of Hungarian public sector employment. Laws prescribe not only in-depth rights and obligations for employees and employers, but also outline the main features of wage formation. This reliance on statutory arrangements has traditionally left little room for collective bargaining, especially at the level of specific activities, where unions are mostly organized. The statutory nature of regulation has allowed successive governments to act unilaterally and impose any type of change by the force of law. Until the government change in 2010, this unilateral-statutory system was complemented by quasi-collective negotiations at the central and actual collective bargaining at the establishment level (Berki *et al.* 2012: 12). The scope and content of these negotiations had been limited. The outcomes of consultations in encompassing forums between the government and the main trade union confederation were memoranda of understanding rather than legally binding contracts (Berki 2014: 127). Probably this is the reason why authors call this system quasi-bargaining (Berki *et al.* 2012: 12). Moreover, over the years 2006–2010, these agreements were all concessionary, with the goal of mitigating the effects of wage and employment cuts that would have been legislated anyway. At the local (establishment) level, the laws leave room for bargaining partners to deviate upwards from the legally stipulated wages and working conditions. Local bargaining was, however, mostly restricted to non-core pay elements, and its foundations were shaken by the recentralization of public services after 2010.

The two main features characterizing the legal environment of the Hungarian public sector are separation from the private sector and internal fragmentation. The legal separation from the private sector has its roots in the continental European tradition, which Hungary opted to follow in other legal subfields as well during early transition lawmaking (Kollonay-Lehoczky 2009: 302–303). In the continental, 'sovereign' tradition, the state separates the employment regulation of the public from the private sector in a bid to secure higher levels of employee loyalty in the former than in the latter. It does so on the one hand by restrictive measures, for example, by the prohibition of strikes, collective bargaining or union presence in general, but also by rewarding loyalty with a protected employment statute and predictable career paths (Bordogna 2008: 15–16). Following this model, when the first democratically elected parliament of Hungary adopted a new Labor Code in 1992 (Act XXII/1992, in force until 2012), it also passed separate legislation for the public sector.

In fact, two distinct public sector acts were adopted: one applying to *civil servants* (Act XXIII/1992) and the other for *public services employees*—education, health and social care, cultural services (1992/XXXIII). The second category is often also translated into English as 'public servant'. Following Berki *et al.* 2012, this chapter will use the term public service employee, with an emphasis on the fact that this is a subcategory of public sector employees, but distinct from civil servants. In 2010, a third category, 'government official' was added that covers employees in the central government. Government officials' legal status is similar to civil servants, but they enjoy even less professional and individual autonomy from the employer (Berki *et al.* 2012: 3).

The legal distinction between civil servant and government officials on the one hand and public service employees on the other has its roots in the different access to executive power (Berki *et al.* 2012: 2). While civil servants and government officials are fulfilling executive functions of the state, public service employees are delivering services that fall outside the executive core of the state. Therefore, legal arrangements for civil servants and government officials resemble more closely the 'sovereign ideal type', whereas public service employment is more flexibly regulated, in conjunction with the Labor Code. Different legal statutes are clearly linked to different activities, with civil servants and government officials almost exclusively concentrated in public administration (judges, police and the military have their own statutes). Education, health and social care employees never obtain civil servant status. Table 10.2 demonstrates that almost all teachers are public service employees, while in health and social care, public works contracts are also relatively common. As of 2014, only 53% of employees in health and social care had a public service employee status.

Table 10.2 Legal Status of Employees in Different Public Sector Activities in Hungary, 2008 and 2014

		Total	Civil servant	Public service employee	Government official	Other statuses, including judges, military and law enforcement personnel and public works employees
2008	Public administration and defense, compulsory social security	262.6	102.8	32.9	...	126.9
	Education	237.6	...	236.1	...	1.5
	Health and social work	170.7	2.5	164.1	...	4.1
	Total public	722.0	105.7	479.3	...	137.0
2014	Public administration and defense, compulsory social security	276.0	34.2	27.8	76.6	137.4
	Education	227.4	...	223.9	...	3.6
	Health and social work	302.0	...	160.5	...	141.5
	Total public	854.1	34.5	455.2	77.8	286.7

Source: KSH Stadat Table 2.1.34

Original legislation set dismissal rules quite restrictively for both categories, but these were relaxed in subsequent years (Nacsa 2014). The immediate employer—for instance, the manager at a specific public sector establishment—could terminate a contract only under strictly defined circumstances. The employer was also obliged to provide detailed justification for the dismissal decision. However, after 1992, the law allowed for dismissals necessitated by the decision of a higher-level authority. Up until 2007, strict reinstatement rules were in place: in case of an unlawful dismissal, employees had to be reinstated exactly in their original position (Nacsa 2014: 118).

While the level of employment protection had been similar in the categories of public sector employees and civil servants (still slightly higher for civil servants), significant differences could be observed between them in pay determination and bargaining rights. The logic of wage setting is similar for the two groups in that their respective acts contain salary scales, which set different salaries for employees with different education levels and ensure automatic pay increments based on seniority. This is done by assigning different multipliers to the 'base salary' (Berki 2014: 124). The sum of the base salary is laid down in the act on the yearly budget. Despite the similarity of the two systems, early transition pay legislation gave civil servants a significant advantage, which persists to this day (Berki 2014: 125). It has to be noted, however, that this difference in remuneration between the two categories was not a result of direct action from civil servants or from their trade unions. Rather, it can be explained by the attitude of subsequent legislatures that treated more preferably those employees who were carrying out the core, executive functions of the state.

Participants in public works programs occupy a precarious legal position compared to civil servants and government officials, despite their rapidly growing number after 2011. Public works programs are also part of the system of unemployment benefits and social assistance that was comprehensively reshuffled in 2011 around the idea of workfare. The maximum duration of unemployment benefits was reduced from 270 to 90 days and as a main rule, social assistance schemes that are available for the long-term unemployed were made conditional on (previous) involvement in public works programs. In this system, registering as a job seeker in most cases automatically entails application for public works. Any registered job seeker can be called upon to participate, and local job centers select suitable candidates for specific tasks. If the job seeker rejects the public works offer, s/he is automatically excluded from the unemployment registry and loses eligibility for social assistance as well.

In general, the main target group of public works include the long-term unemployed and young people who had never had a job in the formal economy. From January 2013 to April 2015, 16.7% of all participants were under 25, much higher than the 6.4% overall employment rate of this age group (calculations based on Government of Hungary, 2015, KSH Stadat

Table 2.1.4). It also has to be noted that after 2011, the distinction between short- and long-term unemployment became rather fuzzy due to the drastic reduction in the duration of the unemployment benefit. Public works programs are coordinated and financed by the central government, but usually organized by municipalities and in some cases NGOs (including churches) and state-owned enterprises, although as of 2015, the main employer for these schemes remains the local government (Bördős 2015: 73). Typically, over 80% of tasks require unskilled manual labor and little capital investment (cleaning, maintenance).

The regulation of public works programs only allows for fixed-term employment contracts, typically less than four months in 2011, extending to around six months in 2012 (Cseres-Gergely and Molnar 2015: 91). The gradual increase in the duration of public works is part of a process in which this policy instrument is becoming a stable source of social assistance for the long-term unemployed, and the original purpose of activation is by and large abandoned (Koltai 2015: 108–109). At the same time, the activation dimension has not entirely disappeared, as the introduction of winter schemes testify. These winter schemes include compulsory training—both the improvement of basic skills and certified vocational courses (Busch 2015). Participants in public works programs are only entitled to compensation that is lower than the minimum wage (Bördős 2015). There have been attempts to organize public works employees into a separate trade union, but so far, there is very limited union presence and no collective bargaining in public works programs.

Collective Bargaining Structure

While forums for consultation between the government and public sector unions have been in existence since 1991, their relevance has always been questionable. At best, they can be called institutions for quasi-bargaining, because the participating actors could not conclude legally binding and enforceable collective agreements. As will be discussed later, collective bargaining is also hindered by power asymmetries of the bargaining partners. The central government is the strongest actor, while trade unions are weak and fragmented, especially at the confederation level. Local governments who had the formal employer function in public services (both in education and healthcare) until 2010, did not even form an effective employers' association. The reliance on central government decisions also means exposure to the political business cycle. Governments until 2006 and after 2010 granted wage increases close to elections, while they imposed austerity at other times.

With these caveats in mind, the following section examines the pre-crisis system of wage setting in the Hungarian public sector. While the majority of its elements were in place before, the system took its final shape in 2002, when an incoming left liberal coalition pledged to public sector unions to restore a more inclusive and encompassing system of interest reconciliation. The previous conservative government (1998–2002) had a more unilateral approach to public sector human resource management and it also preferred dealing with unions representing different activities (public administration, health and social care, education) separately (Berki 2014: 127). Apart from the non-binding nature of the agreements mentioned beforehand, the most important feature of the system between 2002 and 2010 (and before 1998) was its inclusiveness. It covered both legal categories (public service employee and civil servant), all activities and it also had links to the private sector. While in the literature, this system is referred to as 'centralized quasi bargaining' (Berki *et al.* 2012), this author prefers the term 'encompassing quasi-bargaining' to emphasize the lack of confederational authority on the level of the trade union side and the lack of coordination on the local government side.

Figure 10.1 displays the relationship between the parts of the bargaining system in the Hungarian public sector until 2010. It is essential to clarify the links between the parts because despite changes after 2010, the institutions before 2010 still serve as a reference point. The setting of the minimum wage falls outside the scope of public sector bargaining, but it provides an important benchmark for it. The main function of

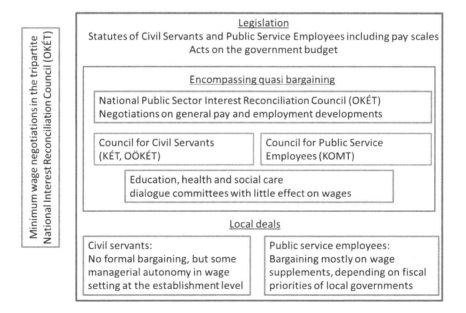

Figure 10.1 Wage Setting in the Hungarian Public Sector, 2010

the tripartite National Interest Reconciliation Council (OÉT, disbanded in 2011)[1] was to set the yearly rate of the minimum wage, which had implications for the public sector for two reasons. First, the lowest grades of the public sector pay scale fall from time to time below the minimum wage, and therefore need to be topped up—this was the automatic link (Berki 2014). A second effect was that minimum wage increases led to serious wage compression between the private and the public sectors and within the public sector as well. When an increase in the minimum wage was not accompanied by an upgrade of the public sector pay scale—which happened quite often—the wages of higher qualified public sector employees converged downwards in terms of pay relativities.

Apart from the relevance of the minimum wage, Figure 10.1 highlights the primacy of legislation in public sector wage setting. It also details the elements of encompassing quasi bargaining. Before 2010, the most important discussions on wage developments and employment levels were taking place in the encompassing forum OKÉT, which covered all public sector employees. Unlike OÉT, OKÉT is still operating, but its importance has declined since 2010 (Berki 2014: 128). Negotiations on issues specific to civil servants or public service employees were conducted in separate councils (KÉT, OÖKÉT, KOMT). All of the mentioned bodies had a tripartite structure, with associations of local governments also represented, but in practice, the talks were conducted between the central government and public sector unions (Berki 2014: 126). Finally, the encompassing forums were complemented by subsectoral dialogue committees under the guidance of respective ministries, but their effect on wage setting was insignificant.

Figure 10.1 also details information on the role of the local/establishment level in wage setting. As mentioned above, collective agreements with contractual obligations for employers were mostly concluded at the establishment level and only in public services. Typically, these single-employer agreements settled issues other than core pay, depending on the fiscal capacities and priorities of local governments. According to 2008 surveys quoted in Rindt (2011) and Tarnóczyné and Neumann (2011), local collective agreement coverage stood at 67.6% in public healthcare and 40% in education. The same surveys also conclude that local agreements were relevant in providing wage supplements and non-pay-related benefits. Their generosity is very difficult to judge, but given the low basic wages, any supplement provided in collective agreements could be important for employees. While the civil service statute does not allow for establishment level collective bargaining, some non-core pay elements such as fringe benefits are stipulated by legislation, meaning that every employee receives them (Berki *et al.* 2012: 11). Again, in this case too, although not having collective bargaining rights, civil servants might actually come out more favorably in comparison to public service employees.

State Policy and Reforms of Public Sector Employment
Regulation Until 2006

It is difficult to talk about NPM-type reforms in Hungary before the 2000s. While there were a lot of legislative amendments in the 1990s, their purpose was to set up the basic rules of employment in the public sector in relation to a newly emerging private sector. As will be discussed later, the most important measure in the early 1990s that can be seen through the lens of NPM was decentralization of public service provision to the local settlement level. Nevertheless, this move was not couched in NPM rhetoric, but rather, it was posited as a backlash against a highly centralized system before 1989. Debates about the public sector in the early 2000s focused on the pay disadvantage compared to the private sector (Köllő 2014a: 47). This pay disadvantage coupled with a more favorable fiscal situation and cutthroat competition between political parties resulted in large centrally administered pay hikes for public sector employees between 2001 and 2003. Civil servants were awarded a large pay increase in 2001, and public service employees followed suit with a 50% rise in 2002 (Köllő 2014a: 47). The pay increases caused some tensions on the employer side, as the central government did not allocate the full sum that was needed by local governments to cover the pay hike.

NPM-type reforms of public sector employment relations were first put on the agenda of consultative forums between 2003 and 2006. The first significant measures in the NPM direction included the introduction of performance assessment system and performance-related bonuses in the civil service (Berki 2014: 127). In the early 2000s, organizational reforms in certain public sector activities—mostly in healthcare—were implemented that had direct relevance for workplace-level employment relations. For example, the 2001/CVII Act on the Provision of Publicly Funded Health Care Services and on the Forms of Practising Medicine 'widened the range of organizational options open to institutional and individual providers of health services, including the possibility of corporatization of hospitals and self-employment of medical doctors and pharmacist' (Gaál and Riesberg 2004: 138).

Characteristics of Public Employers

Hungary has a centralized and unitary state, but until 2010, settlement-level municipalities enjoyed a relatively high degree of autonomy as administrative units and as public service providers. Regions (on the NUTS (Nomenclature of Territorial Units for Statistics) 2 level) fulfill only statistical and administrative functions, mostly related to the allocation of EU structural funds. The more relevant territorial administrative units of Hungary are counties—there are 19 counties and the capital, Budapest—corresponding to the NUTS 3 level. At the same time, counties have limited competences and a limited role as employer, constrained on one side by the power of the central government and on the other (at least until 2010) by the autonomy of the around 3,100 individual settlements (KSH).

Until 2010, the employer side of the public sector was characterized by a high degree of fragmentation. As already mentioned, this fragmentation was due to the decentralization of public service provision in the early 1990s to the level of local settlements. Act 1990/LXV on Local Governments delegated the responsibility of providing a wide range of public services—including basic healthcare and primary education—to municipalities (Edelényi and Neumann 2014b: 167). The same legislation adapted the principle of 'one settlement, one local administration', granting administrative powers to these settlements irrespective of size. Moreover, decentralization was associated with an ill-defined distribution of financial responsibilities, with local governments predominantly financing activities from earmarked central funds (Edelényi and Neumann 2014b). Despite fulfilling ownership and employer functions at the local level, municipalities were reluctant to effectively coordinate as employers at a larger scale. For example, in the public sector and public service interest reconciliation bodies (OKÉT and KOMT), they have been represented by seven very loosely organized associations, which could serve as information-sharing platforms rather than the place for coordination (Márkus and M. Tóth 2010: 48). It has to be noted, however, that the problems arising from decentralization were limited to public service employees, while in the case of civil servants, there was a more efficient division of labor between the central and the local levels.

Responsibility for provision of public services coupled with autonomy and insufficient finances gave incentives for local governments to experiment with organizational reforms. Municipalities had been outsourcing auxiliary activities (cleaning, maintenance and some daycare activities) from the early 1990s on (Edelényi and Neumann 2014b: 172). The first instance of corporatizing an entire hospital and involving private capital in its operation happened in 1995 (Állami Számvevőszék 2009: 27). Even though private investors withdrew later on, the organizational change—running the hospital in a company form rather than as a public sector institution—was not reversed. In education and social services, the role of churches started to increase in the 1990s as part of the restitution process—many church-run establishments that were closed down by the communist regime in the 1940s and 1950s were re-opened after 1990. Besides, church-run institutions usually faced less financial and regulatory constraints than their municipality-run counterparts. Employment relations in church-run institutions are regulated by the labor code; employees do not have any special legal status.

Until the early 2000s, managers in the public sector had almost always been recruited internally for three main reasons. First, in the early transition years, it would have been difficult to find anyone with significant managerial experience in the private sector because until 1989, the entire economy—or at least all the major companies—was state owned. Second, even when the private sector expanded, there was little that could have attracted managers from there. Even if there was a political will to do so, large pay differentials favoring the private sector prevented external managerial recruitment (Köllő 2014b: 88). Finally, in public services, the professional specificities of each activity (healthcare, education etc.) require that mid-level managers (hospital managers or school principals) be internally selected. Internal and professional recruitment, however, did not equal independence from political, let alone fiscal, pressures.

Even in a decentralized system, these mid-level managers were appointed by political bodies representing the interests of the owners (usually municipal or regional councils). Before 2010, school principals and hospital directors were elected and appointed by local councils. Employees—and in the case of schools—parents and pupils' representatives had consultative rights, but the final decision was made by local government. The only change in the post-2010 system is that now administrative bodies representing the central government as the owner appoint heads of schools and hospitals.

Trade Unions

The structure of employee representation in the public sector reflects the political and professional fragmentation of the labor movement as a whole in Hungary. The main public sector confederation, the Forum for the Co-operation of Trade Unions (SZEF) connects the majority of trade unions in the sector, but confederation authority over affiliated members is limited, making it difficult for SZEF to act as an effective peak association. In addition, while SZEF is the dominant confederation in the public sector, its representational monopoly has been challenged right from its formation at the beginning of democratic regime change. In 2015, SZEF had 13 affiliated unions (Szakszervezetek Együttműködési Fóruma 2015).

The Hungarian labor movement split along multiple dividing lines in the early transition years, leading to an internationally unmatched degree of fragmentation that continues to hinder effective employee representation. As of 2015, there are five national-level trade union confederations in Hungary (SZEF, MSZSZ, LIGA, ÉSZT and Munkástanácsok), all of them active in the public sector. The reformed successor of the communist-era umbrella organization, MSZOSZ (since 2015, MSZSZ) is the largest confederation in the private sector, and it still has a noticeable presence in the public sector. However, in 1989, most trade unions active in the public sector decided not to join MSZOSZ, but formed SZEF. Despite this separation, SZEF was still regarded as a 'successor organization' by public sector unions newly emerging around the regime change. They joined the confederation associated with the democratic opposition, LIGA (created already in 1988, two years before SZEF), or ÉSZT, a small confederation mostly drawing its members from higher education institutions (Tóth 2001: 41). To give an example, most union members in public education are organized either by the reformed successor union Union of Teachers or by the much smaller but rather active and vocal Democratic Union of Teachers. Relations between the two unions remain strained, ranging from open hostility to lack of coordination in bargaining.

According to administrative data provided by the unions and validated by the government, in 2008, 113,122 out of 523,518 public service employees (21.6%) were trade union members, most of them (73.3%) represented by SZEF-affiliated unions (NMORMB 2008, the same figures are unavailable for civil servants due to the lack of similar representativeness surveys, as civil servants lack collective bargaining rights). Overall union density among public service employees dropped to 19.7% by 2011 and to 15.9% by 2014. SZEF's share within total union membership dropped to 55.4% by 2011 and to 50.6% in 2014 (ORMB 2011, 2014). The sharp decline between 2008 and 2011 can be attributed to a single event: the largest healthcare union, EDDSZ, defected from SZEF to LIGA in 2009 due to a lengthy and politicized conflict between the leadership of SZEF and EDDSZ (MSZ-EDDSZ 2009, EDDSZ later on left LIGA too, due to similar issues).

Apart from political divisions, public sector unions are organized on the basis of activities and professions. Most trade unions represent a mixture of these two principles, meaning they have one dominant profession but they are also open to other grades within the given activity area. For example, EDDSZ counts most of its members among nurses, but it also aims at covering all other health and social care grades, from doctors to manual workers in hospital maintenance. One of the few strictly professional/craft unions is the Federation of Hungarian Physicians, the interest representation branch of the Hungarian Medical Chamber. As mentioned earlier, these unions, organized along different public sector activities, did not have an equivalent partner on the employer side, which puts them in a situation of an institutional vacuum when it comes to collective bargaining.

Despite data limitations, it is evident that public sector unions have been continuously losing members since the transition started. Table 10.3 indicates trends between 2001 and 2009 for the most important public sector activities compared to the whole economy. Throughout the entire period, union density remained higher in the public than in the private sector, but the pace of membership loss was similar in the two domains. In 2001, roughly every third public sector employee was a union member; by 2009, this ratio dropped to one in five. While this number still compared favorably to the national average—only one in ten employees having a union card in 2009 there—it suggests that public sector unions also have serious difficulties keeping members, let alone recruiting new ones.

At the same time, Table 10.3 suggests some internal differences within the public sector according to different legal categories—at least until 2009. Albeit starting from a lower position, unions in public administration and defense managed to hold on to their positions more effectively than their partners in public services—the 6.9 percentage point loss in administration

Table 10.3 Trade Union Membership by Public Sector Activities and in the Overall Economy in Hungary 2001–2009

	2001	*2004*	*2009*
Economy total	19.7	16.9	12
Public administration and defense;	29.3	26	22.4
Education	39.4	29.3	23.9
Human health and social work	33.8	26.3	20

Source: Busch *et al.* 2010: 296

and defense (from 29.3 to 22.4) compares favorably to a 15.5 percentage points decline in education and 13.8 decline in healthcare. This also means that by 2009, density figures in the three main public sector activities had converged.

The same level of union density in public administration, defense and social security as in healthcare and education might seem surprising, given the fact that workplace-level collective bargaining is not allowed for civil servants (and members of the armed forces), who are mainly employed in public administration, defense and compulsory social security. However, if we take into account that establishment-level collective bargaining is only part of the functions that Hungarian public sector trade unions have, this becomes less of a puzzle. Trade unions of civil servants are still represented in the encompassing consultative, quasi-bargaining forums, and at the workplace, they can still provide valuable services to their members—in most cases, welfare benefits and representation in individual legal disputes with the employer. Finally, the Hungarian case is not unique in this respect, as in Germany too, civil servants are unionized despite not having the right to bargain collectively on wages (see Chapter 8).

Public sector institutions for workplace representation correspond to the legal status of employees. Similarly to the private sector, a dual-channel workplace representation exists for public service employees, who can rely on works councils—officially called councils of public service employees— to exercise their information and consultation rights. Civil servants have no similar institutions (Berki *et al.* 2012: 4). Public service employees are allowed to strike, but this right is constrained by strict minimum service requirements. For instance, Hungarian laws oblige schools to provide supervision for pupils even if instruction is suspended due to a strike (Művelődési és Közoktatási Minisztérium1994) Civil servants' right to strike is limited, while law enforcement and military professionals are entirely prohibited from taking industrial action (Berki *et al.* 2012: 5) Due to these limitations and as a result of the limited organizational capacity of trade unions, strikes are rare events in the Hungarian public sector. Nevertheless, compared to the private sector, until 2010 the public sector was still relatively vocal, reacting to government measures with short-term but very large strikes or strike threats. In the period 2006–2010, setting up a Unified Public Service Strike Committee was a tool strong enough to force the government to negotiate, even if the basic policy course could not be altered (Berki *et al.* 2012: 12).

The Consequences of the Crisis for Public Sector Employment Relations

Background: Hungary, a Case of Protracted Austerity

The specificity of the Hungarian case comes from the more protracted nature of the crisis and the magnitude of the political changes it triggered (Szabó 2013). Reacting to fiscal imbalances, the then-ruling government introduced severe cuts in the public sector as early as 2006. The period following 2006 can be divided into three stages corresponding to crisis waves and government alternations: from 2006 to 2009, a left liberal government imposed austerity and an NPM-inspired comprehensive reform agenda on the public sector. The onset of the financial crisis in 2009 led to the resignation of Ferenc Gyurcsány, prime minister since 2005. The succeeding technocratic government of Gordon Bajnai presided over a further and even more drastic cut of public expenditure. The new government also pushed ahead with structural reforms in some areas, but due to its caretaking mandate, it could not influence longer-term developments.

The 2010 elections brought into power a conservative government with a parliamentary supermajority, enabling radical changes in the institutional framework of bargaining (Szabó 2013). The new administration did not ease the fiscal pressures on the public sector, but it led to a systemic turnaround in the way public administration and services are managed. Reasserting authority as a sovereign employer, the central government has taken back control of healthcare and education provision from municipalities. While recentralization went against the basic principles of NPM in terms of reducing managerial autonomy at lower levels and precluding market-based solutions, most human resource principles of NPM—such as the flexibilization of employment through the relaxation of firing rules and through the introduction of posting, transfer, secondment and redeployment—were preserved or even strengthened in the post-2010 period (Berki *et al.* 2012: 8). This contradictory agenda of the Orbán government is infused with illiberal and communitarian elements, manifested in the government-sponsored expansion of church-run public services in the creation of compulsory interest representation organizations for public sector employees and by forcing the reverse army of labor into public works programs (Berki *et al.* 2012: 32; Berki 2014). Moreover, these measures were introduced unilaterally without consulting trade unions, whose protest capacities were very weak to start with but were further undermined by anti-strike legislation in 2010.

In essence, the new strike law stipulates that minimum service levels must be maintained during a strike and industrial action can only be started with the prior consent of a labor court. The new terms make it almost impossible or at the very least seriously slow down the process of calling public service strikes (Rindt 2012; Szabó 2013: 210).

Type and Sequence of Austerity and Public Sector Reform Measures

Table 10.4 gives an overview of the measures that have been implemented since 2006. Some of them, especially those with more significant cost reduction elements featured in the country's subsequent convergence programs, submitted to the European Commission. The first wave of significant deficit reduction measures was initiated after the 2006 elections and included a wage freeze in the public sector but also a general payroll tax increase, further impinging on public sector workers. Public sector unions responded by a strike threat. Talks at the public sector interest reconciliation council resulted in an agreement that compensated for the wage freeze by bringing forward the payment of the 13th month salary in monthly installments (Berki *et al.* 2012: 12).

Parallel to cutting back spending on wages, the Gyurcsány government also embarked on a mission of reforming human resource management practices in the public sector. This time, reforms were more explicitly framed in an NPM rhetoric, with new top-level managers in central administration

Table 10.4 Austerity Measures and Public Sector Reform in Hungary, 2006–2014

Year	Measure	Consequences
2006	Fiscal consolidation package	Wage freeze in the public sector and general tax increase
2007	Amendment of public sector employee statutes	Relaxing employment protection
2006–2008	Healthcare reform	Restructuring the healthcare system, resulting in significant layoffs
2009	Emergency financial legislation	Basic pay frozen, abolition of 13th month salary
2010	Act on government officials, amendment of civil servant statute	Dismissal protection relaxed, introduction of posting, secondment, transfer
from 2011 on	Public service recentralization	Transfer of responsibility for service provision from the local to the central level, decreasing managerial autonomy, accompanied by new wage systems in healthcare and education
2011	Act on employment in public works programs	Providing the legal background for the expansion of public works participation

and healthcare recruited on the basis that they had experience in the private sector. A governmental committee on 'state reform' was set up with a mandate to design plans for the comprehensive restructuring of the public sector. In 2006, the Act on the Status of Public Service Employees and the Act on the Status of Civil Servants were amended. The stated goal was to achieve flexibility and cost containment through a relaxation of hiring and firing rules. Downsizing related to budgetary reasons was made easier, the amount of severance pay has been decreased substantially and employees were obliged to accept any position offered to them in case of a restructuring, even if the new job did not suit their qualifications. Severance payment rules were tightened. Likewise, a compulsory probationary time was introduced and the period of notice was shortened (Berki and Neumann 2006). The principle of full reinstatement was also discarded in a bid to alleviate the consequences of unlawful dismissals for employers (Nacsa 2014: 118). The employment laws in the public sector were further amended. For example, in 2008, the right of the employer to give supplements rewarding outstanding employee results at performance assessments was introduced.

Among the public sector activities, healthcare was the main target of NPM-inspired reforms in the period between 2006 and 2008. That extended to all parts of this very complex system, from the regulation of pharmacies to the attempted partial privatization of the health insurance system. Human resource management practices were mostly affected by the reform of the provider side. The rationalization of the hospital system led to mass redundancies. Organizational reforms—most importantly, the change in the status of hospitals from budgetary institutions into corporations—deprived many hospital employees of their public service employee status (Kahancová and Szabó 2015). In 2004, 94.1% of the workforce in in-patient care was directly employed by the state (mostly by local governments). In 2011, their share dropped to 72% as a result of several municipalities turning their hospitals from budgetary institutions into non-profit corporations (KSH Dissemination Database). The process extended mostly to general hospitals in the country, while specialized institutions and university hospitals that were mostly run by the central government to begin with were not affected.

It is worth noting that during the period of downsizing after 2006, the government took some pacifying measures to cushion the social effects of restructuring. Probably the most extensive among these was the early retirement scheme called 'Premium Years', which allowed public employees who faced redundancy to continue working part time, for a maximum of 12 hours per week, in a job that matched their educational attainment and work experience. The program targeted senior employees reaching retirement age within three years who had worked in the public sector for at least 25 years. The program started in 2004, but it took full effect in 2006–2007 as a palliative measure to deal with public sector layoffs (Fiedler and Neumann 2005).

The financial collapse of 2008 hit a public sector that was just about to recover from the effects of the 2006 austerity round. In 2009, the incoming technocratic government unilaterally scrapped the 13th month salary and froze wages once again. In the wake of these measures, the public sector strike committee renewed its activities and negotiations started at OKÉT. The only achievement of the committee was a minor wage supplement that was distributed among low-income earners in the public sector (Berki *et al.* 2012: 13). It also has to be noted that in terms of net wages, the effects were less severe due to a tax reform favoring medium-income earners.

The 2010 elections brought into power the conservative FIDESZ party of Viktor Orbán with a two-thirds parliamentary majority. One of its first major legislative moves was to establish a new employee category of government officials exclusively employed by the central government and only in public administration, defense and compulsory social security. As Table 10.2 indicates, they numbered 77,800 in 2014 (9.1% of all general government employees, including the participants of public works programs), while the number of 'regular' civil servants in the same year was only 34,200 (4%). The purpose of the new legislation was to reassert sovereign authority over employees who perform the basic administrative functions of the state. It decreased these employees' independence and remuneration (Berki *et al.* 2012: 3). It also introduced the possibility of dismissal without cause as well as the institutions of posting, secondment, temporary transfer and transfer (Berki *et al.* 2012: 8; Nacsa 2014: 120). Even though the original legislation was struck down by the constitutional court, its main elements were still introduced with only minor modifications.

The Orbán government also used its legislative power to recentralize public service provision. In fact, one of the motivating factors of recentralization was to gain more direct control over expenditure at the local level, breaking the previous cycle of overspending and bailout by the central level. The recentralization had ambiguous effects on employee wages and working conditions: it basically annulled local collective agreements and erased the possibility of local bargaining altogether. Wage supplements provided in establishment-level agreements disappeared for many public sector workers (especially teachers) from one year to the other. Recentralization was also accompanied by the removal of healthcare and education workers from the public service employee pay scale. In both cases, new pay scales were created that take the minimum wage as their basis, but the career advancement paths are less straightforward than in the old system (Berki 2014: 131). In education, working hours were lengthened, and the fulfillment of strict assessment procedures was introduced as the requirement of entering higher pay grades. The new wage system meant an overall modest real increase with significant disparities based on seniority and qualifications, with older and more qualified employees ending up worse off. Parallel to the recentralization process, many schools and social service institutions were handed over to churches, in accordance with the Conservative government's agenda. The effect of a transfer to church management on employment conditions is unclear, but it does not necessarily lead to deterioration (Edelényi and Neumann 2014b). Finally, the public works program was expanded and by 2011, public works came to be the only source of subsistence for a large segment of the long-term unemployed in Hungary. Although counted in public sector employment statistics, the legal status of public work participants is clearly demarcated from and inferior to 'standard' public sector employees.

Responses of Employers and Trade Unions

Compared the magnitude of changes implemented since 2006 and especially after 2010, employer and trade union resistance has been minimal. Local governments gave up their employer rights without much protest. The autonomy of establishment-level managers has shrunk even further in the wake of recentralization. For example, school principals after 2013 have been appointed by a central authority closely linked to the Ministry of Human Capacities (the name of a new super-ministry encompassing education and health ministries) and lost their limited—pre-2013 decision-making authority.

In the period from 2006–2010, trade unions could moderate austerity to some extent by setting up strike committees. After the 2010 government change, some of the traditional channels of negotiations (see Figure 10.1) were disbanded altogether (such as OKÉT or KÉT) or sidelined (KOMT). If anything, the government prefers negotiating with individual unions at the level of different activities, and as we have seen, wage setting has gravitated there also. Apart from the traditional problems of fragmentation and membership loss, trade unions were further weakened by new restrictions on strikes (Rindt 2010) and membership decline has accelerated; net density in public services declined from 21.5% to 16% between 2008 and 2014.

New actors of professional and interest representation have also emerged that may pose a longer-term challenge to trade unions. The Orbán government restored compulsory membership in medical chambers and chambers of qualified healthcare professionals and brought to life new compulsory, chamber-like representation bodies for other public sector employees too. The exact role of these new organizations is unclear as of 2015. They are not entitled to bargain collectively, but in terms of professional representation, they already provide competition for trade unions. In addition, there are some independently emerging new actors, such as the Hungarian Association of Resident Physicians, which was capable of forcing the government to initiate a wage increase in healthcare (Szabó 2014: 193). Confederation mergers are also discussed but an integration of the largest private and the largest public sector confederation (MSZOSZ and SZEF) failed.

Consequences of Public Service Reforms and Austerity

There has been continuity between different government periods, and from a purely fiscal perspective, the reforms proved to be extremely successful, even by international standards. Expenditures on public employment were put under control: OECD Government at a Glance data indicates that spending on compensation of government employees fell from 11.5% of the GDP in 2007 to 10.2 % in 2013. Taking into account the declining GDP levels after 2008, this becomes an extraordinary magnitude. The OECD average increased slightly in the same period (from 10.1 to 10.6%). Only Portugal and the United Kingdom had downwards trajectories comparable to Hungary (–0.7 and –0.9 percentage point decrease, respectively). Partly as a result of these savings, Hungary was released from the EU's excessive deficit procedure in 2013, nine years after it started (Council of the European Union 2013: 3).

Rhetorically, citizens were always assured that any measures would not impinge on service quality. For example, the radical phase of healthcare reforms between 2006 and 2008 included the strengthening of patient choice and advocacy. Nevertheless, the reforms were otherwise so much about downsizing and the introduction of co-payments that the silver lining of patient empowerment was not sufficient to rally popular support.

It is difficult to establish correlational, let alone causal links between organizational reforms and wage developments on the one hand and changes in service quality on the other. It is difficult to pin down measures that capture the notion of quality appropriately, but staffing remains integral to quality in the service sector. In healthcare, emigration-related labor shortages have become especially severe during the reform years. For example, while the yearly number of physicians who intended to emigrate and therefore applied for overseas recognition of their qualifications declined slightly between 2005 and 2007, it increased from 695 to 1,108 between 2007 and 2012 (Szabó 2014: 195). What makes this figure even more striking is that in the period from 2006–2010, on average, 650 Hungarian medical students graduated annually (Teperics 2013). By intensifying already existing labor shortages and further lengthening waiting lists, the emigration of health workers is the biggest austerity-related challenge that affects consumers of public services.

Conclusions

This chapter has described and analyzed the structure of public sector employment and the major reforms that shaped public sector employment relations in Hungary after 1990. The chapter has identified a period of protracted austerity that started in 2006. It also highlighted the importance of the political changes that took place in 2010 as a result of the

2008 crisis. In a longer-term perspective, the crisis brought more of the same: Hungarian public sector management has always been dominated by government unilateralism, and the crisis strengthened this feature even further. By recentralizing public service provision, the Orbán government removed an inconsistent element from this top-down system, but at the same time, eliminated a last major source of systemic flexibility. Similarly, the Orbán government's reluctance to use traditional bargaining channels and its policy of negotiating with unions only on an ad hoc basis is certainly an extreme case of unilateralism. Besides, the creation of compulsory chambers of representation for employees contradicts democratic practices of most European countries. These elements, however, except the creation of compulsory associations, are consistent with the path that has been set by previous governments, who also typically relied on legislation.

Focusing on the sequence of public sector reforms in Hungary after 2006 provides an opportunity to study the effects of a drawn-out fiscal crisis on public sector employment relations. From a comparative perspective, the Hungarian state's turn to austerity in 2006 is a noteworthy event because in the majority of European countries, 2006 was still a 'boom year'. Moreover, the global financial crisis entered its 'Eurocrisis' phase only in 2009, meaning that the peripheral countries of the Eurozone had more financial leeway until that time (De Grauwe 2010). This stands in sharp contrast with Hungary, where the first large-scale austerity measures were implemented three years earlier. Therefore, in Hungary, large-scale public sector cuts can be analyzed as a long-term experience.

The protracted nature of the fiscal crisis also allows for the disaggregation of the crisis period into shorter phases, taking into account political changes. It can be argued that different types of austerities were associated with each crisis phase. The 2006–2010 period was characterized by a hollowing out response. Developments after 2010 have partly pushed Hungary towards the directing state type, but also strong communal elements could be documented. The Hungarian case provides an instance of how Lodge and Hood's (2012) framework of multiple austerities can be extended to cover not only cross-country differences, but also temporal differences within one country over a long period of budget cuts. In conclusion, it has to be noted, however, that the directing state response can be compatible with ongoing austerity and the further erosion of public sector employee status.

Acknowledgments

János Köllő's help in providing public sector employment data for the period before 2000 is gratefully acknowledged.

Note

1. A list of acronyms can be found at the end of this chapter.

References

Állami Számvevőszék (2009) 'Jelentés az egyes kórházi tevékenységek kiszervezésének ellenőrzéséről [State Audit Office: Report on the Monitoring of Outsourced Hospital Activities]', http://www.asz.hu/jelentes/0921/jelentes-az-egyes-korhazi-tevekenysegek-kiszervezesenek-ellenorzeserol/0921j000.pdf

Berki, E. (2014) 'The Specifics of Setting Salaries and Interest Reconciliation in the Public Sector', in Fazekas, K. and Neumann, L. (eds.) *The Hungarian Labour Market 2014*. Hungarian Academy of Sciences, Institute of Economics, 124–135.

Berki, E. and Neumann, L. (2006) *Reform in Public Sector Threatens Job Security*, Dublin: European Industrial Relations Observatory. http://eurofound.europa.eu/observatories/eurwork/articles/reform-in-public-sector-threatens-job-security

Berki, E., Neumann, L., Edelényi, M. and Varadovics, K. (2012) Public Sector Pay and Procurement in Hungary. Report. European Commission Project Coordinated by EWERC, University of Manchester, Public Sector Pay and Social Dialogue during the Fiscal Crisis, VS/2011/0141. http://www.research.mbs.ac.uk/ewerc/Portals/0/docs/Hungary-national%20report.pdf

Bordogna, L. (2008) *Industrial Relations in the Public Sector Dublin: European Industrial Relations Observatory*. http://eurofound.europa.eu/observatories/eurwork/comparative-information/industrial-relations-in-the-public-sector

Bördős, K. (2015) 'A közfoglalkoztatás intézményi környezete—történeti áttekintés [The Institutional Background of Public Works Programs—Historical Overview]', in Fazekas, K. and Varga, J. (eds.) *Munkaerőpiaci tükör 2014*. MTA Közgazdaság- és Regionális Tudományi Kutatóközpont Közgazdaság-tudományi Intézet, 66–76.

Bosch, G., Mesaros, L., Schilling, G. and Weinkopf, C. (2012) 'The Public Sector Pay System and Public Procurement in Germany,' European Commission Project Coordinated by EWERC, University of Manchester 'Public sector pay and social dialogue during the fiscal crisis' VS/2011/0141. http://www.research.mbs.ac.uk/ewerc/Portals/0/docs/Germany-national%20report.pdf

Busch, I. (2015) 'A téli közfoglalkoztatás [Public Works Programs during Winter],' in Fazekas, K. and Varga, J. (eds.) *Munkaerőpiaci tükör 2014*. MTA Közgazdaság- és Regionális Tudományi Kutatóközpont Közgazdaság-tudományi Intézet, 139–143.

Busch, I. and Bördős, K (2015) 'Adatgyűjtések a közfoglalkozatásról [Data Collection on Public Works Programs]', in Fazekas, K. and Varga, J. (eds.) *Munkaerőpiaci tükör 2014*. MTA Közgazdaság- és Regionális Tudományi Kutatóközpont Közgazdaság-tudományi Intézet, 76–85

Busch, I., Fazekas, K., Köllő, J. and Lakatos, J. (2010) *Statistical Data to the Hungarian Labour Market—Review and Analysis*. Hungarian Academy of Sciences. http://econ.core.hu/file/download/mt2010_eng/stat.pdf.

Council of the European Union (2013) Council Closes Excessive Deficit Procedures for Italy, Latvia, Lithuania, Hungary and Romania. *Press Office of the European Council.* http://www.consilium.europa.eu/uedocs/cms_data/docs/pressdata/en/ecofin/137561.pdf

Cseres-Gergely, Zs. and Molnar, Gy. (2015) 'A közfoglalkoztatás a munkaügyi rendszerben, 2011–2013—alapvető tények [Public Works Programs in the System of Employment—Basic Facts 2011–2013]', in Fazekas, K. and Varga, J. (eds.) *Munkaerőpiaci tükör 2014*. MTA Közgazdaság- és Regionális Tudományi Kutatóközpont Közgazdaság-tudományi Intézet, 85–100.

De Grauwe, P. (2010) 'The Financial Crisis and the Future of the Eurozone', *European Economic Studies Department, College of Europe.* (No. 21).

EBRD—European Bank for Reconstruction and Development (2000) Transition Report 2000 Employment, Skills and Transition. Economic Transition in Central and Eastern Europe, the Baltic States and the CIS. http://www.ebrd.com/downloads/research/transition/TR00.pdf

Edelényi, M. and Neumann, L. (2014a) 'Crisis Driven Changes in Wage Setting Systems in the EU', in Fazekas, K. and Neumann, L. (eds.) *The Hungarian Labour Market 2014.* Hungarian Academy of Sciences, Institute of Economics, 146–157.

Edelényi, M. and Neumann, L. (2014b) 'Privatisation of Municipal Services, Outsourcing and In-sourcing Efforts and their Employment Impacts in the European Union Countries and Hungary', in Fazekas, K. and Neumann, L. (eds.) *The Hungarian Labour Market 2014.* Hungarian Academy of Sciences, Institute of Economics, 158–177.

Fazekas, K. and Neumann, L. (eds.) (2014) *The Hungarian Labour Market 2014.* Hungarian Academy of Sciences, Institute of Economics.

Fiedler, Á. and Neumann, László (2005) Pre-pension Programme Extended to Private Sector. EIRO Report. http://eurofound.europa.eu/observatories/eurwork/articles/pre-pension-programme-extended-to-private-sector

Gaál, P. and Riesberg, A. (2004) Health Care Systems in Transition: Hungary. *World Health Organization.* http://www.euro.who.int/__data/assets/pdf_file/0008/80783/E84926.pdf

Government of Hungary (2015) 'A közfoglalkoztatás főbb statisztikai adatainak idősora [Time Series of the Main Statistical Data of Public Works Programs]'. http://kozfoglalkoztatas.kormany.hu/a-kozfoglalkoztatas-fobb-statisztikai-adatainak-idosora-2013-tol-havonta.

Kahancová, M. and Szabó, I. G. (2015) 'Hospital Bargaining in the Wake of Management Reforms: Hungary and Slovakia Compared', *European Journal of Industrial Relations,* 0959680115580689.

Köllő, J. (2014a) 'What Do We Know about Public Sector Employment', in Fazekas, K. and Neumann, L. (eds.) *The Hungarian Labour Market 2014.* Hungarian Academy of Sciences, Institute of Economics, 43–54.

Köllő, J. (2014b) 'Pay Level and Selection to the Public Sector', in Fazekas, K. and Neumann, L. (eds.) *The Hungarian Labour Market 2014.* Hungarian Academy of Sciences, Institute of Economics, 79–90.

Kollonay-Lehoczky, Csilla 2009: Country Study on Hungary, in *The Evolution of Labour Law in the EU-12. (1995–2005).* Volume 3. European Commission. Directorate-General for Employment, Social Affairs and Equal Opportunities, 295–361. ec.europa.eu/social/BlobServlet?docId=2347&langId=en

Koltai, J. (2015) 'A közfoglalkoztatást szervezők és a közfoglalkoztatottak értékei [Values Held by the Participants and Organizers of Public Works Programs]', in Fazekas, K. and Varga, J. (eds.) *Munkaerőpiaci tükör 2014.* MTA Közgazdaság- és Regionális Tudományi Kutatóközpont Közgazdaságtudományi Intézet, 100–111.

KSH—Hungarian Central Statistical Office. STADAT Tables, Dissemination Database. http://statinfo.ksh.hu/Statinfo/themeSelector.jsp?&lang=en; http://www.ksh.hu/stadat_annual_2_1

KSH Jelenti Reports 2009–2010,2012–2013,2014. http://konyvtar.eski.hu/tmpimg/700996508_0.pdf; http://www.ksh.hu/docs/hun/xftp/gyor/jel/jel1212.pdf; http://www.ksh.hu/docs/hun/xftp/gyor/jel1/jel11012.pdf; http://www.ksh.hu/docs/hun/xftp/gyor/jel/jel20912.pdf; http://www.ksh.hu/docs/hun/xftp/gyor/jel/jel1412.pdf

Lodge, M. and Hood, C. (2012) 'Into an Age of Multiple Austerities? Public Management and Public Service Bargains Across OECD Countries', *Governance: An International Journal of Policy, Administration, and Institutions*, 25(1): 79–101.

Márkus, E. and M. Tóth, L. (2010) 'Institutions and Forums of Social Dialogue', *Prime Minister's Office, Budapest.* http://lex.jak.ppke.hu/~holmes/egyeb/jogalkotas/TPIF_2010.pdf

MSZ-EDDSZ (2009) 'Az EDDSZ meghozta döntését: csatlakozni szeretne a LIGA Szakszervezetekhez' Press Release by President Agnes Cser. http://www.liganet.hu/page/88/art/5449/akt/1/html/az-eddsz-meghozta-donteset-csatlakozni-szeretne-a-liga-szakszervezetekhez.html

Művelődési és Közoktatási Minisztérium (1994) 'Rendelet a nevelési-oktatási intézmények működéséről 11/1994. (VI. 8.)', Ministerial Decree Regulating the Operation of Education Institutions, Ministry of Education and Culture.

Nacsa, B. (2014) 'Trends in Labour Law—The Dismantling of Job Security in the Public Sector', in Fazekas, K. and Neumann, L. (eds.) *The Hungarian Labour Market 2014.* Hungarian Academy of Sciences, Institute of Economics, 114–123.

NMORMB (2008, 2011, 2014) 'Nemzetgazdasági Minisztérium Országos Reprezentativitást Megállapító Bizottság. Országos szakszervezeti konföderációk közalkalmazotti jogviszonyban álló tagjainak összesítése. [Ministry for National Economy, Committee on Trade Union Representativeness. Aggregate Membership of National Trade Union Confederations among Public Service Employees]'. January 2008, January 2011, January 2014 http://mkir.gov.hu/doksik/letszam/ormb_2008_1.pdf http://mkir.gov.hu/tag2011/dokumentumok/ormb_2011_1mell.pdf http://mkir.gov.hu/tag2014/dokumentumok/2014_tablazat_1.pdf

OECD (2015). *Government at a Glance.* http://www.oecd.org/gov/govataglance.htm

Rindt, Zs. (2011) *Hungary: Industrial Relations in the Health Care Sector (in Particular the Situation of Nurses and Care Workers)*, Dublin: European Industrial Relations Observatory. http://eurofound.europa.eu/observatories/eurwork/comparative-information/national-contributions/hungary/hungary-industrial-relations-in-the-health-care-sector-in-particular-the-situation-of-nurses-and

Rindt, Zs. (2012) *Amended Strike Law One Year On*, Dublin: European Industrial Relations Observatory. http://www.eurofound.europa.eu/eiro/2012/02/articles/hu1202051i.htm

Szabó, I. (2013) 'Between Polarization and Statism–Effects of the Crisis on Collective Bargaining Processes and Outcomes in Hungary', *Transfer: European Review of Labour and Research*, 19(2): 205–215.

Szabó, I. (2014) 'Labour Mobility and Employee Bargaining Power in Healthcare–Regional Overview', in Fazekas, K. and Neumann, L. (eds.) *The Hungarian Labour Market 2014*, Hungarian Academy of Sciences, Institute of Economics, 193–197.

Szakszervezetek Együttműkdési Fóruma (2015) Online Introduction to the Activities of SZEF. http://www.szef.hu/bemutatkozunk/tagszakszervezetek

Tarnóczyné, J. Gy. and Neumann, L. (2011) *Representativeness of the European Social Partner Organisations: Education Sector—Hungary*, Dublin: European Industrial Relations Observatory. http://eurofound.europa.eu/observatories/eurwork/compara tive-information/national-contributions/hungary/representativeness-of-the-european-social-partner-organisations-education-sector-hungary

Teperics, K. (2013) *A Debreceni Egyetem Területi Kapcsolatai*. Online Lecture Slides. http://www.mandula.pte.hu/files/tiny_mce/File/2013/PPT/3/TepericsKaroly.pdf

Tóth, A. (2001) 'The Failure of Social-democratic Unionism in Hungary', in Stephen Crowley, S. and David Ost, D. (eds.) *Workers After Workers States. Labor and Politics in Postcommunist Eastern Europe*, Lanham: Rowman & Littlefield Publishers, 37–58.

List of acronyms:

EDDSZ—Democratic Union of Health Care Workers
KÉT—Interest Reconciliation Council for Civil Servants
KOMT—Interest Reconciliation Council for Public Service Employees
LIGA—Democratic League of Independent Trade Unions
MSZOSZ—National Confederation of Hungarian Trade Unions
MSZSZ—Hungarian Trade Union Confederation
OÉT—National Interest Reconciliation Council
OKÉT—National Interest Reconciliation Council for the Public Sector
OÖKÉT—Interest Reconciliation Council for Civil Servants in Local Governments
SZEF—Forum for the Co-operation of Trade Unions

11 Czechia and Slovakia: Facing Austerity Through Collective Action

Economic Crisis and Public Service Employment Relations

Marta Kahancová and Monika Martišková

Introduction

Czechia and Slovakia share similar historical legacies in their public sector developments. Embarking on a transition from state socialism to market capitalism and democracy in 1989, both countries underwent wide-ranging economic, political and societal changes. Facing challenges of democratization, transparency and effectiveness, the public sector in both countries underwent important structural and institutional changes during the 1990s and 2000s. During the 1990s, public sector reforms in both countries focused predominantly on incremental changes to legislative structures and capacity building in central and local governments (Nemec 2010). While Czechia selectively introduced reforms towards public sector marketization in the early transition years and remained reluctant to continue with major reforms on other areas, Slovakia started reforming its public sector later but continued in efforts to introduce New Public Management (NPM) principles into some arenas of public sector governance also over the 2000s. Besides domestic political and economic targets, the most important external factors affecting public sector developments over the 2000s were the EU accession of both countries in 2004 and the outburst of the economic crisis in 2008.

This chapter examines the formation of public sector employment relations in Czechia and Slovakia. While the focus is on the effects of crisis-driven austerity measures on employment relations, post-crisis developments are analyzed in the context of public sector reform during 1990s and 2000s. Attention is devoted to the implementation of NPM reforms before and after the crisis and their effects on employment relations in the post-crisis years. In particular, we address the impact of the crisis on the longevity of previous reforms of public service employment relations and the consequences for parties and institutions of public service employment relations in Czechia and Slovakia. We also analyze the responses of employers and trade unions to public sector reforms and to the formation of public services since the transition years. Evidence has been collected through original empirical research and ten interviews with social partners in 2014 and 2015, earlier research by the authors and mostly local literature available on public sector reforms and employment relations.

The scope of public services covered in this chapter includes the central government, local government, public healthcare and public education. *Central government* refers to centralized state administration at the level of ministries and similar high-level state offices, statistically differentiated through the assigned NACE codes (group 8) and through distinct legal regulation for civil service. Second, the *local government* subsector covers the territorial structure and governance, i.e., regions, higher territorial self-governing units (counties) and municipalities. Third, *education* refers to public services offered predominantly through schools in primary and secondary education (up to level 3 in the International Standard Classification of Education). Fourth, *healthcare* refers to services in public health (Group 86, Section Q in NACE Rev.2 categorization), excluding social services. While Section Q covers also private providers and their employees, it is included in the analysis because in Czechia and Slovakia private healthcare providers are subject to the same regulations as public service providers, and a large share of their funding occurs through the public health insurance system. More specifically, we focus on reforms and working conditions in the hospital subsector (Group 86.1 of NACE Rev.2), which was exposed to wide-ranging transformations with consequences for employment relations.

Employment relations refer to the changing relationship between employers and the workforce in the course of public service reforms, including those inspired by NPM principles. NPM reforms are understood as 'deliberate changes to the structures and processes of public sector organizations with the objective of getting them [. . .] to run better' (Pollit and Bouckaert 2011: 8). NPM reforms also target more individualistic and flexible human resource management through performance pay, short-term contracts, managerial autonomy in pay setting and deregulation in hiring and firing (Hannigan 1998: 308). To facilitate institutional background for these changes, NPM also entails collective bargaining decentralization (Hood 1995; Bordogna 2008; Galetto *et al.* 2014).

While in some countries, the crisis-induced pressures on employment relations in the public sector materialized both through domestic austerity measures and prerogatives of supranational actors, including the EU and IMF, we argue that in Czechia and Slovakia, public sector employment relations remained largely sheltered from external pressures. The regulatory power and discretion over reform decisions remained in the hands of the state and domestic actors. Therefore, the character and extent of reforms varied across both countries and across the studied subsectors despite a common historical legacy. While the crisis did not cause major changes to reform efforts and employment relations, austerity measures escalated wage cuts, wage freezes and conflicts in wage bargaining. The interaction of the state with other domestic actors in post-crisis adaptation saw the involvement of trade unions and civil society organizations in shaping reform trajectories in both Czechia and Slovakia. In sum, the effect of the crisis played out mostly on wage moderation and employment, while the impact on other working conditions remained marginal. Social dialogue in public services remained sheltered from the crisis effects and continued to evolve within its previously established institutional domain.

The chapter is divided into five sections. The first section presents the major trends in reform trajectories in Czechia and Slovakia since the early 1990s until the post-crisis years. The second section reviews trends in public sector organization and workforce. The third section discusses the distinctive features of public sector stakeholders and employment relations in Czechia and Slovakia to assist the understanding of crisis effects on employment relations. The fourth section addresses the crisis effects on employment relations and responses of employers and trade unions. The concluding section summarizes our findings.

Public Sector Reforms in Czechia and Slovakia

The formation of the public sector in Czechia and Slovakia evolved hand in hand with economic and political transitions after the fall of state socialism in 1989. While the central and local governments were subject to reforms already in the 1990s as part of the countries' transition to capitalism, reforms in healthcare and education were delayed to the 2000s and post-crisis years. The extent to which NPM principles penetrated the reform processes also varied across each country and public sector domain.

The post-1989 reform efforts can be divided into four main periods. First, the reform period from 1990–1998 laid down the foundations of a new public sector by wide-ranging *decentralization* efforts. In the initial years after the fall of state socialism, political principles dominated over the selection of public servants. The effort to decrease centralization and politicization was translated into a gradual development of legislative structures and capacities for depoliticization and decentralization of public service in the central and local governments (Staroňová and Láštic 2011). Developments in Czechia and Slovakia were similar in their attempts to depoliticize local level government units, decentralize education and create new structures in the central and local governments, such as labor offices. However, Czechia remained more conservative in its reform efforts than Slovakia in this period and focused predominantly on legislative changes to meet the basic prerogatives of public sector governance in democratic societies (Nemec 2010). Slovakia embarked on a more extensive transformation of governance structures than Czechia. Public administration underwent decentralization with a delegation of power and responsibility to newly established self-governing municipalities (Jacko and Malíková 2013). The central state administration underwent reorganization in 1996, and Slovakia's administrative structure was adjusted through the creation of 79 new districts

(*okresy*) and 8 regions (*kraje*), each with its own authorities and civil servants on behalf of the central government (Jacko and Malíková 2013).[2]
Besides government structures, reforms also aimed at deregulating education in both countries. In Czechia, schools were granted great autonomy
in shaping their curricula and personnel management, with the exception
of hiring and firing school principals (Čerych *et al.* 2000). The state's role
in education reform remained limited, providing only operational measures
without providing a long-term vision (Greger and Walterová 2007). In Slovakia, new legislation on state administration in education and school self-
governing bodies institutionalized school councils and district councils as
self-governing entities in education already in 1990, thereby improving par-
ticipatory democracy in the public sector (Kahancová and Sedláková 2015).
Despite these first successes in transformation, this period was accompanied
by a lack of financial resources and expert knowledge in both countries.
Budget cuts in education decreased teachers' real income and degraded their
legitimacy in society (Greger and Walterová 2007). Despite generally similar
trends in both countries, divergence occurred in reform processes in healthcare. Over the 1990s, Czechia embarked on a wide-scale privatization of
public hospitals, while Slovakia did not yet launch significant healthcare
reforms. Rapid hospital privatization in Czechia was accompanied by a
decentralization of the remaining public hospitals and transfer of their ownership and management onto the counties and municipalities that emerged
from public administration reforms.

After the early transition years, the second reform phase is closely related
to Czechia's and Slovakia's EU accession. Between 1998 and 2002, the pre-
accession requirements accelerated reforms to increase transparency and
effectiveness in public sector governance. These included professionalization of the civil service and its alignment with the concept of the European
Administrative Space, elaborated jointly by the EU and OECD (Staroňová
and Staňová 2013). This period is best characterized as *depoliticization*
and *modernization* of public sector governance (c.f. Staroňová and Láštic
2011; Jacko and Malíková 2013). Czechia and Slovakia further decentralized public administration to local-level governments by introducing higher-
level territorial units (counties). In Czechia, 14 self-governed territorial units
were introduced in 2000. In Slovakia, governance of public administration
underwent decentralization and delegation of power to eight newly created
higher territorial self-governing units in 2002.

Both countries gradually implemented a dual system of public administration where some public sector competences shifted to the local government
and some remained controlled by the central government. However, this division of competences was not exclusive, and many activities performed by
local government units are continuously subject to management and financing
by central government. Dualism in financing, management and competences
raised complexity in how public organizations operate, blurred transparency
and slowed down efforts of modernization and efficiency seeking.

In healthcare, the pre-accession period resembled a continuation of NPM-style reforms in Czechia and a lack of political will to launch healthcare reforms in Slovakia. The 2003 healthcare decentralization reform in Czechia aimed at transferring competences from the central level government to the local government. As a result, self-governing territorial units and similar local government bodies became regional healthcare providers. Hospitals that did not undergo privatization faced corporatization or transformation aiming at hospital behavior similar to private corporations while remaining in public ownership. Slovakia mimicked the same reform effort a few years later. In education, the absence of a long-term strategy in earlier years resulted in increased efforts of the Czech government to adopt a different approach with elements of NPM principles. In 2002, the responsibility for school management and administration was transferred to the self-government units for secondary and special schools or municipalities for elementary schools. However, the Ministry of Education, Sport and Youth is still responsible for budget allocations in education. This reinforces the financial dependence of schools on the central government despite their considerable operational autonomy, including autonomy in employment relations.

The third reform period covers the years from 2004–2009, starting with Czechia's and Slovakia's EU accessions in 2004 and followed by rapid economic growth until the outburst of the crisis in 2008. From a public sector reform perspective, this period resembles a *post-accession crisis* and even some return to *politicization*. The Post-accession crisis demonstrated itself in many Central and Eastern European (CEE) countries where reforms slowed down after EU accession (Nemec 2010). Politicization refers to 'any type of intrusion into the civil service system that enforces anything else than merit' (Staroňová and Gajduschek 2013: 2). During the 2000s, Czechia remained reluctant to go beyond marginal management reforms in the central and local governments, with minor administrative changes (Nemec 2010). Education did not face relevant reforms, but the Czech healthcare was subject to failed efforts to transform health insurance companies into private-sector-like corporations and to change healthcare financing. The reason for the failure was the high complexity of proposed changes without stakeholder and government support (Darmopilová and Špalek 2008).

The post-accession reform crisis in Czechia contrasts with intensive reforms in Slovakia. The Slovak right-wing government coalition launched wide-ranging healthcare reforms and to a smaller extent, reforms in education. Healthcare experienced hospital corporatization, management decentralization, reorganization of service provision and the first state bailout of public hospital debt (Kahancová and Szabó 2015). In contrast to earlier reforms in Czechia, Slovak healthcare reforms did not see hospital privatization as a feasible option and preferred corporatization under public ownership. In education, the school self-governance system was further reinforced by legislative changes in 2003. The new legislation stipulates greater involvement of stakeholders in school management through student councils (Kahancová and Sedláková 2015). After a government change in Slovakia in 2006, reform efforts to introduce principles of NPM in some areas of public services slowed down and were accompanied by a return to a dominant role for the state and the politicization of public services. Except for employment relations, politicization demonstrated itself by strengthening the state's fiscal control over local government and by reintroduced the subordination of the Healthcare Surveillance Authority to the Ministry of Healthcare (Jacko and Malíková 2013; Kahancová and Sedláková 2015).

The fourth reform period corresponds with the post-crisis years until the present (2009–2015). The economic crisis demonstrated itself to greater extent in product and labor markets than in financial markets in both countries (Dvořáková and Stroleny 2012; Kahancová 2013). In an effort to avoid relevant employment cuts, public budgets faced increasing constraints and governments were forced to adopt austerity measures in employment and pension policy besides direct measures to improve the performance of public sector employment. Efficiency of public institutions became a priority and replaced earlier priorities of democracy making and citizen participation in public administration. Consequently, the reforms adopted after 2009 followed an efficiency principle rather than a democracy principle. This contrasts with some other CEE countries, where the efficiency principle governed public sector reforms already since the early 1990s (Nemec 2010). To sum up, the post-crisis reform trajectory in both Czechia and Slovakia brought a renewed stage of modernization for some subsectors but austerity and lack of reforms in other subsectors. In the central and local governments, the milestone for Czechia has been the adoption of distinct legislation on employment conditions in civil service in 2014, which also paves the way to more social dialogue and bargaining in the public sector. With modernization and extensive reorganization of state offices, Slovakia saw a revived reform effort only after 2012. Broader NPM-style reforms in healthcare were put on halt in Slovakia because of austerity, political interests and stakeholder resistance. In Czechia, the 2% of hospitals that were still in public hands by 2010 experienced similar challenges to the Slovak hospitals (Veverková 2011). Education did not undergo any major reforms in direct response to the crisis in either of the two countries.

In sum, both Czechia and Slovakia experienced transformations of their public sectors in the past 25 years. Some of these reforms were initiated by internal drivers of broader societal transformation towards democracy, while others were implemented in response to external influences. In the light of these reform trajectories, in the remainder of this chapter, we take a closer look at the formation of workforce trends and employment relations in order to assess the impact of the economic crisis and post-crisis austerity measures on the institutions, processes and outcomes of employment relations in the public sector.

Organization Structure and Employment

Reform trajectories occurred alongside remarkable stability and growth in public sector employment in both countries (Glassner 2010; Eurofound 2015). Since 1999, employment levels underwent only minor changes (see Table 11.1). In a comparative perspective, Czechia experienced slightly more turbulence in employment trends, while Slovakia shows remarkable stability during the whole period of 1999–2013, according to Eurostat data. The average share of public sector employment on total employment between 2008–2011 belonged to the lowest in the EU, reaching 19.1% in Czechia and 21.1% in Slovakia against the EU average of 24.4% (European Commission 2012: 94, Eurostat). Stagnation in employment is noted in both countries in the mid-2000s before the crisis, followed by a continuous rise in employment levels until 2010. Both countries resorted to reductions in workforce size in public administration (including central and local governments) only in 2011, before resuming employment growth in 2013 (ILO 2014). In other subsectors, including health and education, employment growth resumed even earlier after the crisis. This trend suggests that the crisis impact on public sector employment remained limited. Lacking exposure to international market pressures, a delay in austerity measures on the government side and the generally low share of public sector employment on total employment help explain this limited impact (European Commission 2012; Hancké 2014).

While overall employment trends show stability, the reform efforts presented in the previous section increased the complexity of employment structures in public sector organizations. The division of competences between the central government and the local government, the privatization or corporatization of selected hospitals and the emergence of self-governance in education influenced the employees' statuses. While competences, job security, recruitment procedures and rights to strike were increasingly differentiated among civil servants, public servants and regular employees according to the Labour Code, each level of state administration and local government incorporated all three kinds of employees. A similar trend is observed in healthcare and education, with public servants and regular employees dominating the employment structure. This complex structure increased the diversity of working conditions and created a challenge for efficient and transparent pay regulation. As a result, pay regulation became increasingly decentralized in Slovakia and increasingly centralized in the government's hands in Czechia.

The share of temporary employment on total public sector employment remains below 10% in both countries and across all studied subsectors. The only exception is the increase of temporary employment in public administration in Slovakia after 2010. This trend coincides with growing overall employment in this subsector in the post-crisis period (see Table 11.1), suggesting that the modest post-crisis employment growth occurred increasingly through temporary contracts (see Table 11.2).

Table 11.1 Public Sector Employment Trends in Czechia and Slovakia (1994–2014)*

	Czechia					Slovakia				
	Public administration and defense; compulsory social security	Education	Health and social work	Total public sector Eurostat	Total public sector CSO	Public administration and defense; compulsory social security	Education	Health and social work	Total public sector Eurostat	Total public sector SSO
1994										1,350.4
1995										1,250.2
1996										1,237.8
1997										1,140.5
1998										1,072.6
1999	291.9	274.9	262.2	829.0		149.8	165.0	155.2	470.0	1,030.9
2000	304.8	289.4	280.9	875.1		159.9	161.4	146.2	467.5	1,006.9
2001	306.0	296.5	291.1	893.6		159.5	170.5	145.6	475.6	958.2
2002	295.2	304.4	287.5	887.1		147.9	163.4	137.9	449.2	864.1
2003	304.7	283.5	290.8	879.0		163.4	160.3	145.9	469.6	820.8
2004	304.6	273.7	308.3	886.6	989.8	154.2	158.4	150.1	462.7	797.5
2005	329.7	289.6	323.3	942.6	1,000.6	155.0	161.9	148.7	465.6	724.6
2006	321.8	279.0	323.7	924.5	989.3	161.2	165.6	153.6	480.4	667.9
2007	322.9	282.7	330.7	936.3	965.6	159.1	162.5	153.6	475.2	643.8
2008	312.3	276.0	315.7	904.0	966.1	166.4	163.0	149.9	479.3	639.6
2009	316.7	286.3	320.8	923.8	957.1	177.6	161.2	148.2	487.0	618.1
2010	325.3	287.1	333.5	945.9	935.1	187.7	163.1	156.0	506.8	607.6
2011	311.5	288.7	317.3	917.5	921.4	189.3	159.3	156.1	504.7	611.9
2012	302.8	310.2	326.2	939.2		184.1	156.0	159.6	499.7	633.8
2013	311.7	314.1	329.6	955.4		200.1	162.1	163.5	525.7	633.3
2014										635.3

*In thousands of employees, age range 15–64.
Education and Health and Social Work include also private service providers.

Source: Eurostat, Czech statistical office (CSO), Slovak statistical office (SSO).

Differences between Eurostat and SSO data derive from a different methodological approach.

Table 11.2 Share of Female and Temporary Employment in the Public Sector (2008–2013) in Czechia and Slovakia

		2008	2009	2010	2011	2012	2013
% female employment, 15–64 years of age							
Public administration and defense; compulsory social security	Czechia	47,5	48,0	47,6	47,7	46,9	47,1
	Slovakia	51,0	48,9	48,6	51,5	51,4	51,9
Education	Czechia	76,3	78,0	76,6	76,9	78,2	77,5
	Slovakia	78,8	79,1	81,2	80,5	79,9	78,9
Human health and social work activities	Czechia	81,8	81,6	80,1	81,8	80,1	80,2
	Slovakia	82,1	83,7	84,3	83,3	83,1	84,0
% temporary employment, 15–64 years of age							
Public administration and defense; compulsory social security	Czechia	9,4	9,2	9,9	9,5	8,1	9,2
	Slovakia	4,9	9,0	11,9	16,4	14,3	15,1
Education	Czechia	10,3	10,2	8,8	8,5	8,8	9,5
	Slovakia	2,7	3,5	4,2	3,8	3,5	2,5
Human health and social work activities	Czechia	7,6	7,2	6,2	6,3	6,9	7,0
	Slovakia	3,2	2,4	3,0	2,7	2,3	1,6

Source: Eurostat.

Possible factors explaining this trend include the government's search for austerity measures through containing hiring and firing costs in case of expected reforms (c.f. European Commission 2012: 97). Alternatively, the rise of temporary employment can be explained through the government's search for numerical flexibility during periods of wage cuts or wage freezes, or in case of a rigid regulatory framework of public sector employment relationships (European Commission 2012: 97). Below, we show that the Czech government resorted to post-crisis wage cuts, while Slovakia reached a compromise of wage freezes and employment growth. In addition, both countries launched reforms that affected working conditions in the public sector—through the new regulation of the civil service in Czechia (2014) and the reorganization of the public administration in Slovakia (2012).

Besides temporary employment, other forms of non-standard employment remain marginal. However, employee exposure to precariousness is increasingly relevant because of several factors. First, public servants generally perceive their wages to be too low to provide a decent living standard (e.g. in education and healthcare). Second, trade unions increasingly view work organization as a source of precariousness due to high workloads in the post-crisis years and involuntary changes to work organization among nurses in the healthcare sector to contain labor costs after legislatively stipulated wage increases in Slovakia (c. f. Kahancová and Martišková 2015). In addition, the Labour Code in both countries incorporated several forms of flexible work, e.g., job sharing, in the post-crisis period. However, their use in the public sector remains marginal or even nonexistent (Mandl, I. *et al.* 2015). This is partly explained by the existence of distinct legislation that excludes the use of some non-standard employment forms, including job sharing, among public servants.

Public Sector Employment Relations and Pay Determination

Employment relations evolved in close interaction with the reform efforts discussed above. Legislative and institutional developments shaped the actors, structures and processes in public sector social dialogue. The years following the fall of state socialism in 1989 saw a gradual formation of employment relations in newly emerging democracies. While the Labour Code played a dominant role in determining public sector employment terms in Czechia until 2014, Slovakia adopted distinct legislation on civil service and public service, including remuneration rules, already in 2002.

Historical Context of Employment Regulation

The relevant historical context of employment regulation includes the 1990s decentralization period, the structural adjustments period in early 2000s due to EU membership followed by a divergence between Czechia and Slovakia in their post-enlargement reform efforts, the immediate aftermath of the economic crisis (2009–2011) aiming at quick austerity measures and finally, the years after 2012 with reform efforts seeking to align employment regulation with a long-term strategy to increase public sector efficiency.

In the 1990s, the Labour Code played the dominant role for governing public sector employment conditions and relations in both countries. While distinct employment regulation for public sector employees did not yet exist, the character of employment conditions, remuneration and social rights developed through a series of regulatory government decrees (Staroňová and Láštic 2011). This trend informed a gradual shift of policy makers' attention to the formation of distinct legislation for public sector employment relations and conditions.

Upon pressure of EU accession, both countries were pushed to adjust their public sector employment regulation. A distinctive feature of these developments was a split between *civil (or state) service* and *public service*, which broadly but not exclusively corresponds to distinct working conditions in state administration (higher-level civil servants in the central government and specialized institutions) on the one hand and regular employees in territorial administration (local government), healthcare and education on the other hand. Czechia adopted a conception of public administration reform in 1999 and drafted specific legislation on employment conditions and pay in the civil service (Act No. 218/2002 Coll., *Služební zákon*). However, this act was not enforced due to a lack of political capacity and frequent government changes. Consequently, Czechia lacked a distinct legal regulation of employment conditions in the civil service until 2014. Employment relations were governed by the Labour Code and government decrees with remuneration tariffs. In contrast, employment relations in the Czech public service saw a much earlier introduction of distinct legislation: the Public Service Act (Act No. 312/2002 Coll.), approved in 2002 and enforced in 2003, regulates employment terms in self-governing territorial units. Distinct legal regulation emerged also in public education after 2002 when the government approved a long-term plan for the development of the education system (the White Book). Subsequently, new educational acts were adopted to regulate the duties, requirements and remuneration of employees in education (i.e., Act No. 573/2004 Coll. on Pedagogical Staff) (Greger and Walterová 2007). Healthcare underwent massive privatization already in the 1990s, and thus the relevance of regulations for public and civil services remained marginal for healthcare workers. Instead, the role of the general Labour Code has increased, granting more room for enterprise-level collective bargaining over wages and working conditions.

Slovakia saw more political will than Czechia to replace government decrees from the 1990s by new legislation in civil and public services. Between 1998 and 2002, the distinctive character of public sector employment relations has crystallized and resulted in the adoption of the Act on the Civil Service (Act No. 312/2001 Coll.) and the Act on the Public Service (Act No. 313/2001 Coll.). Together with an ethical code of conduct for public servants and the creation of the Office for the Civil Service (*Úrad pre štátnu službu*), this regulatory package, supported by Labour Code regulations, became the cornerstone for public sector employment relations in Slovakia. It sought to establish a merit-based public service liberated from dependence on political power (Staroňová and Láštic 2011). Subject to further amendments after 2003, the Act on the Civil Service and the Act on the Public Service continue to shape individual and collective employment relations, remuneration and working conditions.

In some public sector domains, i.e., Slovak healthcare, reforms in the post-enlargement years significantly influenced employment relations. Hospital corporatization, adopted in the mid-2000s along NPM principles, fueled a gap in working conditions and bargaining structures between larger hospitals operated by the central government and smaller public hospitals with management delegated to the local government. Moreover, hospital employment was excluded from public service legislation and developed its own employment relations system after 2006. Similar dualization in hospital working conditions due to ownership diversity (central vs. local governments, public vs. privatized hospitals) also emerged in Czechia. However, as 98% of hospitals were privatized earlier, the dualization challenge was less pronounced than in Slovakia (c. f. Veverková 2011). In education, employment relations were not exposed to such challenges as healthcare and remained part of the public service employment system. The regulatory divergence on employment relations in health and educations fueled growing tensions between trade unions in these sectors.

After the 2006 government change in Slovakia, the reform efforts slowed down. This period also brought a return to state dominance and politicization of public service employment relations. The Office for the Civil Service ceased to exist in 2006, giving opportunities for renewal of politicization of employment in the central and local governments and specialized state offices. A lack of transparent monitoring mechanisms and a missing merit-based employment policy encouraged opaque employment relations (Staroňová and Láštic 2011; Jacko and Malíková 2013).

In terms of formalized collective employment relations, the 2000s have shown remarkable stability in Slovakia, with regular social dialogue rounds and separate annually renegotiated collective agreements for the civil service and the public service (Barošová 2008). In Czechia, the Labour Code, a set of government decrees on remuneration rules, tariff determination methods and conditions for the provision of rewards and benefits remained the core regulatory instruments in employment relations in the central government (Hala 2008). In contrast to Slovakia, collective bargaining played a minor role for employment conditions over the 2000s.

In 2009, when the crisis had not yet fully demonstrated its effects on the public sector, the Slovak government amended the legal regulation on civil service remuneration. Legislative changes included a 20% wage increase for selected occupational groups (Staroňová *et al.* 2014). Despite these legislative attempts at improving working conditions, the aftermath of the crisis yielded austerity and increased divergence between occupational groups' working conditions. In Czechia, the most important milestone in the regulation of employment conditions was the adoption of the long-planned Act on the Civil Service in 2014 (Act No. 234/2014 Coll.). This Act was finally adopted after political trade-offs between the government coalition and the newly elected president and a threat of losing EU structural and investment funds in 2015–2010 if the civil service fails to professionalize and depoliticize (Suchardová 2013). An important consequence of the adoption of the Act on Civil Service is a growing role of social dialogue and the opportunity for collective bargaining in central government. Since the Slovak civil service underwent this process in the early 2000s, cross-border learning, exchange of information and cooperation between the Czech and Slovak trade unions and employer associations helps develop the capacities of the Czech social partners in their new roles in public sector social dialogue.

The above legislative developments shaped developments in the public sector remuneration system. In Czechia, government decrees rather than collective bargaining directly regulate pay developments in the central and local governments as well as in education and healthcare in public ownership. The most important decree for pay determination is Decree No. 564/2006. Pay tariffs are defined separately for employees in different subsectors and occupations. Each change to wage levels is determined by the government and may be consulted with trade unions via tripartism, but the role of social dialogue for pay determination remained limited without multi-employer or sectoral collective agreements. The 2014 Act on the Civil Service opens an opportunity for replacing governmental regulation on wages with collective bargaining. A new remuneration system is under development by 2017. This raises expectations on the side of social partners, especially trade unions, on their increasing scope to shape remuneration through higher-level collective agreements for the civil service, which did not exist before. Despite a high degree of decision-making centralization over pay, the system allows some flexibility to account for regional pay differences and establishment-level bonuses and benefits. For example, employees in the capital city of Prague receive additional bonuses and allowances next to their base salaries. Differences in pay also exist between larger and smaller cities and municipalities in direct relation to their budgetary restrictions. Healthcare is partly an exception to the above remuneration rules, because public sector employment regulations apply only to 39% of healthcare workers in hospitals that are directly managed by central government (ÚZIS 2010). Remuneration of healthcare employees in other types of public hospitals is subject to Labour Code rules.

In Slovakia, two relevant resources for remuneration emerged in the past 25 years. The first one is a system of legal regulation on pay determination across particular subsectors of the public sector. The second resource is collective bargaining over wages, which is firmly institutionalized since the adoption of legal regulation for civil (state) service and for public service in 2002. Currently, there are nine legal acts regulating the pay of particular occupational groups in the public sector (e.g., state servants, police department, judiciary, fire and rescue department, tax and customs administration, education and public health). Each legal act supplements the acts described above. Despite the complexity of pay regulation, the current extensive decentralization is driven by the dominance of subsectoral interests and the lack of political will to integrate pay regulations under a single regulatory system (Nebeský 2010; Staroňová *et al.* 2014). SLOVES, the trade union representing employees in the central and local governments, supports an introduction of a single pay regulation covering the whole sector, but finds its implementation in a context of austerity measures and public administration reforms unlikely.

The most important piece of legislation in Slovak remuneration is the Act No. 553/2003 Coll. on the remuneration of some employees upon executing work in the public interest. This act has governed remuneration in healthcare and education and has caused a number of tensions between stakeholders in these subsectors. Until the mid-2000s, both healthcare and education followed the above remuneration rule. Upon NPM reforms in healthcare, all hospital workers, regardless of the hospital's central or local government management, lost their public servant status after 2006. Responsibility for pay determination shifted exclusively onto sector-level social partners and their collective bargaining procedures with reference to the Labour Code (Kahancová and Szabó 2015). Therefore, since 2006, tensions escalated between large and smaller hospitals, with the latter experiencing higher budget constraints. While collective bargaining remained important for shaping healthcare remuneration, social partners found it increasingly difficult to reach agreements. The divergent hospital constraints fueled a growing dualization in working conditions across various hospital types (Kahancová and Szabó 2015). Although formally independent, trade unions maintain that Act 553/2003 Coll. still resembles the most important benchmark for wage setting in healthcare. The fact that healthcare follows different pay regulations than other public sector subsectors in both Czechia and Slovakia suggest some convergence in trends between both countries.

In summary, both Czechia and Slovakia adopted distinct regulations on civil service and public service employment relations and conditions. The timing of adoption, however, differed and was subject to domestic political support. Moreover, both countries possess detailed remuneration rules for various occupational groups in civil and public services and the complex employment structure comprising civil servants, public servants and regular employees under Labour Code provisions. At the same time, the countries differ in the way remuneration rules are implemented, with more scope for collective bargaining in Slovakia and a greater role for direct government regulation of wages in Czechia. Convergence can be observed in the distinct character of remuneration in healthcare and its peculiar relation with remuneration and interest representation in other public services in both countries.

Collective Bargaining Structure

Developments in collective bargaining responded to trends in relevant structural reforms in employment relations. Table 11.3 offers an overview of most important social partners and bargaining structures.

Czechia's bargaining structure shows some rigidity because of the strong role of government decisions on baseline pay developments and bargaining scope limited to individual benefits, bonuses and non-wage working conditions negotiated at the establishment level. While trade unions operate in all studied subsectors, there is a lack of sectoral employers' associations and thus sectoral or multi-employer bargaining. Consequently, the dominant level for collective bargaining is the establishment level, supplemented by tripartite consultations and government decisions. The 2014 Act on the Civil Service opens new opportunities for strengthening the role of multi-employer bargaining in central government. March 2015 saw the

Table 11.3 Bargaining Structure and Actors in Pay Determination in Czechia and Slovakia

	Trade unions		Employers		Collective bargaining	
	Czechia	Slovakia	Czechia	Slovakia	Czechia	Slovakia
Central government	Trade Union Federation of State Organizations (OSSOO)	For civil service: Slovak Trade Union of Public Administration and Culture (SLOVES) and other unions through membership in the Confederation of Trade Unions including the trade union in public service (SLOVES); Independent Christian Trade Unions (NKO) General Free Trade Union Federation (VSOZ)	Ministry of Labour; Ministry of Finance	For civil service: Ministry of Labour, Social Affairs and Family; Ministry of Finance	Collective bargaining launched for the first time in 2015; wage increases through government order	Regularly established sectoral and establishment-level bargaining since 2003 (since regulations on civil service and public service in force); Annually bargained agreements separate for civil service and for public service
Local government	Trade unions of state bodies and organizations	For public service: nine trade unions in public sector through their membership in Confederation of Trade Unions, including the trade union in public service (SLOVES); Independent Christian Trade Unions (NKO) General Free Trade Union Federation (VSOZ)	Ministry of Labour; Ministry of Finance, individual municipalities and local government offices	For public service: five ministries, representatives of the federation of municipalities and higher territorial units	Wage increases through government order but no higher-level bargaining coordination or collective agreement; Decentralized bargaining in municipalities with trade union presence on individual bonuses, benefits, and non-wage working conditions	Regularly established and functioning since 2003 (since regulations on civil service and public service in force) Annually bargained collective agreements separate for civil service and for public service

(*Continued*)

Table 11.3 (Continued)

	Trade unions		Employers		Collective bargaining	
	Czechia	*Slovakia*	*Czechia*	*Slovakia*	*Czechia*	*Slovakia*
Healthcare[1]	Trade Union Federation of Health and Social Services (OSZaSP ČR) Professional Trade Union of Medical Workers of Bohemia, Moravia and Silesia (POUZPČMS)	Slovak Trade Union Federation of Healthcare and Social Services (SOZZaSS) Doctors' Trade Union Federation (LOZ) Trade Union Federation of Nurses and Midwives	Ministry of Healthcare, Association of hospitals (AN ČR), Association of Czech and Moravian Hospitals (AČMN)	Ministry of Healthcare, Association of State Hospitals (AŠN SR) Association of Hospitals of Slovakia (ANS)	Establishment-level bargaining, supplemented by ad hoc tripartite social dialogue without conclusion of higher-level agreements; wage increases through government order; bargaining on individual bonuses and benefits; estimated bargaining coverage 74%[2]	Multi-employer bargaining and establishment-level bargaining; sectoral bipartism and tripartism; separate bargaining and collective agreements for state and for regional hospitals; estimated bargaining coverage 95%
Education	Czech and Moravian Trade Union of Workers in Education	For public service: same actors as in local government above, including trade unions in the education subsector	Ministry of Education + Ministry of Finance	For public service: five ministries including education, representatives of the federation of municipalities and higher territorial units	Decentralized bargaining at school level; wage increases through government order	Bargaining coverage via encompassing collective agreement for public service, with distinct pay scales for education. Establishment-level bargaining also exists.

[1]Hospital subsector only

[2]Estimate of healthcare employees covered by collective agreements (Czíria 2009; Veverková 2011)

Source: authors' compilation based on earlier research and interviews with social partners.

very first attempt by the Trade Union Federation of State Organizations to launch collective bargaining with a view to conclude a higher-level collective agreement. Prior to this, trade unions did not conclude collective agreements beyond the establishment level, but were consulted by the Ministry of Finance and the Ministry of Labour on changes to legislative and regulatory instruments (e.g., the most important government Decree No. 564/2006 on wages of employees in public services and government). Wages stipulated through government decisions covered all relevant employees in the central government, local government and schools. Despite rigidity in basic wage setting, there is a gap between stipulated and actual wages. This gap can be explained by labor market competition, which forces public institutions to adjust wage levels to the private sector (Glassner 2010; Bouchal and Janský 2014).

In Slovakia, multi-employer and sectoral bargaining is firmly established and remains relevant for employment regulation across all subsectors. In contrast to Czechia, the bargaining has been enabled because of a more complex and uncoordinated remuneration system across occupation types and subsectors and an earlier adoption of distinct regulation in the civil and public services. Besides establishment-level agreements, the majority of employees are covered by distinct higher-level collective agreements for the civil service (*Kolektívna zmluva vyššieho stupňa pre štátnu službu*) or the public service (*Kolektívna zmluva vyššieho stupňa pre verejnú službu*). Higher-level collective agreements are concluded annually and include stipulations on wage growth. The only exception to this rule is healthcare, which developed its own bargaining structure after hospital corporatization and a split of employers' associations in the wake of NPM reforms. As a result, organizations of public hospitals managed by the local government and public hospitals managed by the central government each concluded a separate collective agreement with the two dominant trade unions (SOZZaSS and LOZ). The youngest trade union representing nurses and midwives attempted to become the third trade union in multi-employer collective bargaining. Wide-scale healthcare reforms thus served as an opportunity for maintaining coordinated bargaining in Slovak healthcare, which has indeed survived all tensions, austerity and diverging interests of trade unions and hospital managements (Kahancová and Szabó 2015). Because of post-crisis austerity, collective agreements are not renegotiated on an annual basis, but their validity is extended until a new agreement is reached (often through mediation procedures, given the lack of agreement between partners).

In summary, establishment-level bargaining dominates Czechia's public sector while in Slovakia, both the establishment and sector levels (often without vertical coordination between the two) are equally important. Establishment-level bargaining addresses benefits, bonuses and non-wage working conditions, while pay regulation is centralized in government hands in Czechia. In Slovakia, higher-level collective agreements in the public sector regularly stipulate wage increases to tariffs.

Public Employers and Trade Unions

Legislative resources for multi-employer bargaining turned out to be crucial for the formation and sustainability of organized interests. The most important difference between Czechia and Slovakia is the missing interest representation organization at the sector level in Czechia, while sector-level employer organizations and trade unions are important in Slovakia. The enactment of the 2014 Act on the Civil Service in Czechia and the 2012 public administration reform in Slovakia are expected to further impact the structure of employers and the potential to introduce and reinforce their coordinated action in Czechia and Slovakia, respectively. At the same time, post-crisis reforms in public administration will put the structures and interest coordination of public employers to the test. Interviews with trade unions signal that expected reorganization of competences, hierarchy and vertical coordination on the side of employers will significantly influence bargaining conditions and outcomes. This is because some offices and their employees will become subordinated to different central government institutions, which means a shift in establishment-level bargaining provisions and coverage.

Managerial autonomy from political authorities closely relates to the discourse of depoliticization discussed above. While some public employers were granted full autonomy through legal regulation (e.g., school self-governance bodies in both countries and the Healthcare Surveillance Authority in Slovakia), others remain directly subordinated to the central government (and thus political) structures. Yet, recent trends suggest state attempts to decrease the previously granted managerial autonomy in some bodies. The most notable examples include the subordination of the Slovak Healthcare Surveillance Authority to the Ministry of Healthcare upon government changes in 2006 and 2012 and the 2015 attempt to subordinate the autonomous selection process of school principals to local government bodies. In both countries, (de)politicization of public employers remains an enduring challenge both at the collective (organizational and managerial) and individual (merit-based professionalization) levels.

The role of public employers changed because of reforms. This is most notable in healthcare, where both countries introduced hospital corporatization and privatization. Reforms directly contributed to a growing gap in interests of non-corporatized, corporatized and privatized hospitals. Diversity often derives from budgetary constraints. In Slovakia, a gap in budget constraints fueled fragmentation of employers' associations and multi-employer bargaining. In Czechia, this issue is less pronounced due to a more centralized system of wage setting through government decrees.

On the side of trade unions, both countries share a similar union landscape inherited from socialist Czechoslovakia. However, in direct response

Table 11.4 Czechia and Slovakia: Trade Union Membership (Whole Economy), in Thousands (1993–2011)

| | TUM[1] | | NUM[2] | |
	Czechia	Slovakia	Czechia	Slovakia
1993	3500,0	1570,0	2800,0	1413,0
1994	2800,0		2240,0	1269,0
1995	2350,0	1250,0	1880,0	1125,0
1996	2130,0		1704,0	996,0
1997	1975,0		1580,0	867,0
1998	1480,0	820,0	1332,0	738,0
1999	1340,0	750,0	1206,0	671,3
2000	1200,0	700,0	1080,0	623,0
2001	1047,6	668,8	942,8	591,9
2002	985,3	603,7	886,8	531,3
2003	962,1	580,4	865,9	509,0
2004	883,0	512,7	816,8	449,6
2005	849,0	482,6	785,3	439,2
2006	815,0	447,5	753,9	411,7
2007	796,0	411,0	736,3	383,5
2008	787,0	382,6	728,0	359,6
2009	767,0		709,5	340,0
2010				330,0
2011				330,0

[1]TUM = Total trade union membership in thousands
[2]NUM = Net trade union membership, calculated as TUM minus union members outside the active, dependent and employed labor force (retired workers, independent workers, students, unemployed).

Source: ICTWSS Database 4.0 (2013), national data.

to reform trajectories and post-crisis austerity, new trade unions emerged over the past 25 years. Long-term challenges of declining union membership (see Table 11.4) and crisis-driven austerity measures contributed to growing divergence in unions' interests. In turn, this produces fragmentation of trade unions' structures.

Fragmentation of union structures is most explicit in healthcare and education. The relationship between the two Czech trade unions in healthcare (OSZSP ČR and POUZPČMS) is competitive and their cooperation remains ineffective (Veverková 2011). In Slovakia, the past decade saw the fragmentation of healthcare unions by occupational group (doctor, nurse, general healthcare personnel). Repertoires of trade union action adjusted to the long-term trend of declining union membership. Younger trade unions are more active and successful in gaining concessions through protests than through traditional channels of social dialogue. The declining union membership also motivates trade unions to reconsider their attitudes on various institutional mechanisms. The extension of collective agreements onto establishments without a trade union presence is one of the sources of tensions between unions in central and local government and in education in Slovakia. Other tensions have developed between unions in healthcare and education upon their attempts to reach wage increases from the limited state budgets in the mid-2000s. Despite such tensions and fragmentation, the public sector remains well organized. Regulation through collective bargaining is more important than in the private sector.

The dominant position of trade unions is not challenged by alternative forms, e.g. works council representation. Despite 2011 legislative attempts to weaken trade unions through strengthening works councils in Slovakia, works councils cannot engage in collective bargaining. Trade unions seek to maintain their exclusive interest representation role despite membership decline through strengthening their ties with other stakeholders and cementing their position in management structures of public institutions. A 2014 corruption scandal in a Slovak public hospital launched discussions on the greater involvement of stakeholders, including trade unions, in hospital governance boards.

The trade union agenda is strongly driven by efforts to establish higher-level collective agreements for the civil service and for the public service in Czechia and the sustainability of existing agreements in Slovakia. Influencing remuneration remains among the most important union strategies. SLOVES, the Slovak trade union in central and local government, points at a discrepancy between minimum wage stipulations and public sector tariffs in Slovakia because some tariff categories do not meet the respective level of one of the six skill-based minimum wage levels. At the same time, the union accepts the argument that tariff adjustments would be an excessive burden on the state budget in the current post-crisis period.

Consequences of the Crisis for Public Sector Employment Relations

How did the crisis influence trends in public sector reforms, employment relations and the strategies of employers and trade unions? Both countries' GDP growth recovered relatively quickly, with Czechia experiencing only a short period of GDP decline (Myant 2013). In Slovakia, economic growth peaked in 2007 and plummeted to -4.8% in 2009 before recovering to 4.5% in 2010 (Kahancová 2013). The driver of the crisis was declining demand in industry, which caused unemployment growth especially in Slovakia and pushed governments to increase public expenditure on employment policies. Related to this, governments aimed to keep public debt under control and adopted several austerity packages, which affected the public sector (see Table 11.5). Freezing and cutting of wages was a common response of governments across other countries in their effort to restore sound public finances (Glassner 2010; Bach and Bordogna 2013).

Table 11.5 Czechia and Slovakia: Austerity Measures and Consequences

	Czechia		Slovakia	
	Measures	Consequences	Measures	Consequences
Central government	2010–2013: direct wage cuts for selected occupational groups in civil and public service, gradual compensation through wage growth since 2014 2010–2012: internal restructuring across state institutions to cut public spending	Nominal wage cuts for selected occupational groups 10%, (2010), adjusted tariff wages for others; public sector real wages decreased by 7% (2008–2013), compared to a 2% average decrease in the whole economy; wage growth resumed after 2014 by 2.5–3.5% Decrease in employment by 22.5 thousands (2010–2012); out of that, 8,000 job losses in 2011[1]	2009: New Law on Civil Service selectively stipulates wage increases 2010–2013: Budget cuts to contain public debt; wage freeze as government priority; trade off between employment stability and wage freeze 2012–2016: ESO reform, internal restructuring of public administration to optimize public spending	20% wage increase for selected occupational groups of high-level civil servants[2] Collectively agreed wage increases limited: 5–7% annually until 2010, 1% (2010), 0% (2011–2013), 16 EUR flat increase per employee (2014), 2,5% (2015) Estimated decrease in real wages 10–12%[3] compared to 1,4% in the overall economy[4]; Increased tensions between public sector trade unions Planned reduction of state administration offices (from 613 to 79); regional offices of state administration abolished in 2013[5] Due to restructuring some employee groups experience decreasing wages or bargaining coverage General consequence: employment growth, increased use of fixed-term contracts
Local government	2010–2013: direct wage cuts for selected occupational groups in civil and public service, gradual compensation through wage growth since 2014 2013: reform of financing rules for municipalities	Nominal wage cuts 10% for selected occupations (2010) and adjusted tariff wages for others; decrease in employment, concentrated among larger municipalities; Smaller municipalities improved their budgets, employment sheltered from direct exposure to cuts	Same as in central government	Same as in central government
Healthcare	2010–2013: direct wage cuts for selected occupational groups (including healthcare), gradual compensation through wage growth since 2014	Wage cuts and wage freezes, wage growth resumed as part of public sector wage growth by 2.5–3.5% after 2014	Since 2006: austerity in state funding of insurance companies	Increased budgetary constraints for employers (especially regional hospitals), hospital privatization intensifies

(Continued)

Table 11.5 (Continued)

	Czechia		Slovakia	
	Measures	Consequences	Measures	Consequences
	2014: reform to stabilize hospital finance, direct state transfers to hospitals to compensate for income decline after recall of patients' administrative fees; discussions on increased stakeholder participation on healthcare financing (including the state)	Recall of administrative fees affected hospital incomes, effects on employment conditions to be evaluated	2012–2015: wage increases for doctors upon trade union action. Since 2014: attempts to harmonize remuneration across healthcare as a whole through a single legislative act	Growing disputes over wage bargaining, bargaining more often leads to mediation and arbitration. Widening gap of working conditions between different types of public hospitals. Doctors' wage growth subject to wide public discourse; dissatisfaction of nurses and other occupational groups, trade union fragmentation. Increased legitimacy of industrial action instead of bargaining. Dissatisfaction of stakeholders (e.g. Chamber of Nurses and Midwives) with the Ministry's proposal, discussion continues
Education	2010: teachers excluded from adjustments in tariff wages 2013–2015: restored wage growth by 2.5–3.5%; reforming financial rules of regional education (preschool, primary and secondary schools)	Teachers' wages mostly unaffected by austerity measures. Expected increase in quality of public service; employment effects not yet evaluated	2010–2012: Cost-saving measures on investments in schools, wage moderation. Legally stipulated wage increases after trade union strikes	Wage moderation: 4–7% annual wage increase between 2006–2009, 1% (2010), 0% (2011–2012)[6]. 5% annually in 2013, 2014 and 2015 after strike[7]. Trade union fragmentation. Increased legitimacy of industrial action instead of bargaining

[1]Eurofound (2015)
[2]Staroňová et al. (2014: 200)
[3]SLOVES trade union calculation
[4]SME (2011)
[5]Jacko and Malíková (2013)
[6]OZPŠAV trade union internal document
[7]Wage increases for teachers in primary and secondary education, rates for other occupational groups differ.

Sources: European restructuring monitor, Ministry of Education of the Slovak Republic, Ministry of Education, Youth and Sports of the Czech Republic, OZPŠAV Slovakia, SLOVES Slovakia, Collective agreements for civil service and for public service, Týden (2010)

Austerity Measures and Consequences

In both countries, austerity measures to contain public spending converged around two key issues: direct budget expenditures on wages, and internal restructuring and service reorganization. First, wage cuts for many occupations in the civil and public services (including healthcare but excluding teachers) were introduced in Czechia. Slovakia resorted only to wage freezes across all studied subsectors after 2011. Despite wage freezes, sectoral collective bargaining for the civil and public service in Slovakia was not undermined.

Second, austerity packages aimed at public sector reorganization driven by the need for greater efficiency. The Czech government introduced internal reorganizations in central government, decreasing employment by 22,500 persons within two years (2010–2012) but maintaining an overall stability in public sector employment (see earlier discussion). In Slovakia, austerity measures did not have a significant effect on employment levels. In fact, public sector employment grew under austerity. The largest public administration reform, Effective, reliable, and open public service (*Efektívna, spoľahlivá a otvorená verejná správa*, ESO) was introduced only in 2012. Besides increasing transparency and efficiency of public services, cost cutting is an important driver of the ESO reform as part of post-crisis austerity of the social democratic government in Slovakia.

Both types of austerity packages impacted on workforce organization and management by affecting wages, job security, workload and structural factors, including bargaining coverage (in Slovakia only). While wage freezes/cuts can be seen as a short-term measure that terminated after 2013, organizational changes aiming at efficiency through changing managerial practices, workload and forms of employment have a long-term effect on employment.

The consequences of austerity demonstrated themselves through increasing workloads, a challenge to job security for civil and public servants and temporary wage freezes (Slovakia) and wage cuts (Czechia). From a macroeconomic perspective, austerity measures yielded savings on total budgets and helped consolidate public finances in both countries. The reduction in the size and scope of public service provision is still being addressed through various reform packages, including the package to change the financing of regional education in Czechia and the ESO reform in Slovakia. While the Czech experience influences employment and working conditions directly, in Slovakia, the effects are also channeled through the bargaining structure. Trade unions criticize the reorganization because some employees will experience shifts to other state organizations, which affects their collective bargaining coverage and threatens existing benefits. This may contribute to declines in trade union memberships.

Responses of Employers and Trade Unions

The long-term reform trajectory in both countries did not face additional challenges because of the crisis. Employers refrained from using the crisis as an argument vis-à-vis employees to benefit from the power asymmetry and introduce managerial prerogatives. If these trends occurred, they took place in a decentralized, micro-level perspective, but without the undermining of established bargaining structures.

Healthcare is partly an exception to this trend, because employers were pushed to respond to corporatization, managerialization and post-crisis austerity. This was more explicit in Slovakia than in Czechia because of Slovakia's larger share of public hospitals. After corporatization, smaller public hospitals faced increasing budget constraints, and these further intensified with the crisis (through austerity in state financing of health insurance companies and thus hospital services). Prolonged wage freezes and disagreement with hospital corporatization processes fueled action on the side of the strongest occupational group: medical doctors. The 2011 campaign of doctors' trade unions, first in Czechia and later in Slovakia, involved coordinated threats of doctors quitting their hospital jobs and possibly working abroad if wage increases were not granted. Significant wage increases were legally stipulated despite the continuation of austerity measures in the economy as a whole. Upon the doctors' success, nurses in Slovakia launched a similar demand and reached legally stipulated wage increases in 2012 (later revoked by the constitutional court). To meet increased wage demands and save on wage costs, managements in smaller hospitals resorted to changes in working contracts and work content, which further fueled dissatisfaction on the side of nurses. This employer response can be referred to as a managerial offensive, where management unilaterally decided to adjust nurses' contracts under pressure of budget deficits and even hospital bankruptcy.

Other than healthcare, public sector employers did not take large-scale and publicly discussed steps in response to austerity measures. Their decisional autonomy is relatively limited, especially in Czechia, with centralized wage setting and a lack of sector-level bargaining. Therefore, employer responses to post-crisis austerity occurred mainly in a decentralized way, as the above example of hospital management demonstrates.

Trade unions remained the dominant actors representing public sector employee interests after the crisis. The post-crisis years brought both union fragmentation and the emergence of new trade unions, e.g., in healthcare and education. The role of other stakeholders and newly emerging actors remains generally limited, but has played a more important role in healthcare and education than in the central and local governments. For example, Slovakia saw three petitions in healthcare between 2011 and 2014 and three petitions in 2012 in education. Some of these were organized by trade unions, while others emerged from the initiative and support of students, parents, professional organizations, school principals, occupational groups and patient organizations (c. f. Kahancová and Sedláková 2015). These developments suggest a growing importance of interaction of trade unions with other stakeholders for shaping working conditions in some public service domains.

Finally, trade unions' response to austerity is characterized by an interesting shift in union strategies. The post-crisis years saw increased dissatisfaction with working conditions in central administration, healthcare and education, but also other public service subsectors. Wage freezes in education and the central and local governments in Slovakia, next to wage cuts in the central and local governments in Czechia, motivated trade union strikes and protests in both countries in 2011–2015. Public sector strikes are legal but strictly regulated through the Collective Bargaining Act (2/1991 Coll.) and its amendments. Strikes are restricted in some essential public services in both countries. The shift of union agendas from bargaining to strikes and protests forced the government to respond to wage claims. Initial successes in trade union protests motivated a chain reaction, in which unions in other subsectors launched similar actions. Recent examples include the 2011 protests of medical doctors in both countries, the 2012 protests of nurses and teachers in Slovakia and the 2015 protests of judiciary employees in both countries. All of these public actions brought wage increases. This trend puts the role of collective bargaining under pressure where industrial action turned out to bring more success for wage increases. The fact that healthcare workers tend to voice their dissatisfaction directly to the government strengthens the role of central regulation and hollows out more flexible options through the conclusion of higher-level collective agreements.

Conclusions

This chapter reviewed the formation of public sector employment relations in Czechia and Slovakia since the fall of state socialism in 1989. Specific attention was devoted to the role of the crisis in modifying or reinforcing long-standing trends. In this concluding section, we identify common trends across both countries and evaluate the influence of the crisis.

Depoliticization of the civil service, efficient service provision, changed financing of education and municipalities and managerialization/corporatization in healthcare remain the dominant reform efforts over the past 20 years in Czechia and Slovakia. EU accession and the economic crisis served as important external influences on public sector reforms; however, we argue that the domestic political will and stakeholder interests remained equally important in most reform areas. The influence of NPM principles varied across countries and subsectors. Attempts at decentralization, managerialization and merit-based policy making penetrated the central government and local government to some extent in both countries. Decentralization of state powers resorted to modification in local government structures, healthcare and to a lesser degree, in education. Finally, corporatization, or an organizational change fostering market behavior of public corporations without privatization, dominated NPM-style reforms in Slovak healthcare, while the dominant trend in Czech healthcare has been privatization during the 1990s.

The state's role in these reform efforts can be evaluated as varying between a 'directing state' and a 'coping state' (Lodge and Hood 2012). The directive elements remain strongly present in Czechia's public sector remuneration system and in both countries' efforts to optimize service provision and introduce distinctive legislation for public sector employment conditions. Established sectoral bargaining in Slovakia and emerging bargaining structures in Czechia support these long-term strategies. However, in other reform efforts, the governments have shown uncertainty and a responsive (coping) strategy rather than deliberate implementation of long-term strategies. This unstable role of the state can partly be explained by the new institutionalization processes of public sector governance after a regime change and frequent government changes that produced a reversal of earlier reforms or blocked their introduction (e.g., the long-planned civil service regulation in Czechia since 1999, or the recall of hospital corporatization in Slovakia in 2011).

The crisis did not produce significant downsizing, but affected working conditions through wage cuts, wage freezes, changes to work organization and growing job insecurity. Long-term employment trends show stability even in the aftermath of the crisis. To restore employment stability during austerity, both countries resorted to wage freezes or wage cuts, combined with modest growth in temporary contracts.

Finally, our analysis shows a twofold crisis influence on employment relations. First, we argue that levels and processes of social dialogue, employment conditions and their regulation, formed and institutionalized over the past 25 years of the countries' democratic histories, have not been altered under direct influence of the crisis. At the same time, our second argument suggests that social dialogue does face increased challenges. This does not directly result from crisis effects on wages and working conditions, but from an indirect effect of austerity measures (especially wage cuts and wage freezes). This indirect effect is channeled through interests and responses of domestic stakeholders. Social partners, especially trade unions, shifted their strategies to cope with post-crisis austerity in wages from bargaining to public actions including strikes and protests. Although the success of public action leaves collective bargaining and institutionalized employment relations contested, trade unions and employers—especially in Slovakia—still consider bargaining a relevant pillar of public sector employment relations. While collective bargaining did play a comparatively more limited role for public sector employment relations in Czechia, the new regulation on civil service opens new opportunities for public sector bargaining coordination also in this country.

Note

1. Act No. 221/1996 Coll. on the territorial and administrative organization of the Slovak Republic (*Zákon o územnom a správnom usporiadaní Slovenskej republiky*).

References

Bach, S. and Bordogna, L. (2013) 'Reframing Public Service Employment Relations: The Impact of Economic Crisis and the New EU Economic Governance', *European Journal of Industrial Relations*, 19(4): 279–294.

Barošová, M. (2008) 'Industrial Relations in the Public Sector—Slovakia', *EurWORK*, online source. https://eurofound.europa.eu/observatories/eurwork/comparative information/national-contributions/slovakia/industrial-relations-in-the-public-sectorslovakia

Bordogna, L. (2008) 'Moral Hazard, Transaction Costs and the Reform of Public Service Employment Relations', *European Journal of Industrial Relations*, 14(4): 381–400.

Bouchal, P. and Janský, P. (2014) 'Státní úředníci: Kolik jich vlastně je, kde a za jaké platy pracují? [Civil Servants: How Many of Them Are There? What Wages Do They Work For?]', *IDEA—CERGE-EI Study*, 4/2014.

Čerych, L., Kotásek, J., Kovařovic, J. and Švecová, J. (2000) 'The Education Reform Process in the Czech Republic', in *Strategies for Educational Reform: From Concept to Realisation*, Strasbourg: Council of Europe Publishing, 41–66.

Czíria, Ľ. (2009) 'Representativeness of the European Social Partner Organizations Hospitals: Slovakia', *EurWORK*. http://www.eurofound.europa.eu/eiro/studies/tn0802017s/sk0802019q.htm

Darmopilová, Z. and Špalek, J. (2008) 'Brokering Health Policy: The Case of Czech Republic Healthcare Reform', in Staroňová, K. and Vass, L. (eds.) *Public Policy and Administration: Challenges and Synergies*, Bratislava: NISPAcee Press, 1–25.

Dvořáková, Z. and Stroleny, A. (2012) 'Social Dialogue and the Public Services in the Aftermath of the Economic Crisis: Strengthening Partnership in an Era of Austerity—the Case of the Czech Republic', *European Commission Project*: Industrial Relations and Social Dialogue VP/2011/001.

Eurofound (2015) 'Restructuring in the Public Sector', *ERM Annual Report 2014*. Publications Office of the European Union, Luxembourg.

European Commission (2012) 'Industrial Relations in Europe 2012', Publications Office of the European Union, Luxembourg.

Galetto, M., Marginson, P. and Spieser, C. (2014) 'Collective Bargaining and Reforms to Hospital Health Care Provision: A Comparison between the United Kingdom, Italy and France', *European Journal of Industrial Relations*, 20(2): 131–147.

Glassner, V. (2010) *The Public Sector in the Crisis*, ETUI Working Paper 2010.07.

Greger, D. and Walterová, E. (2007) 'In Pursuit of Educational Change: The Transformation of Education in the Czech Republic', *Orbis scholae*, 1(2): 11–44.

Hala, J. (2008) 'Industrial Relations in the Public Sector—The Czech Republic', *European Observatory of Working Life (EurWORK)*. http://eurofound.europa.eu/observatories/eurwork/comparative-information/national-contributions/czech-republic/industrial-relations-in-the-public-sector-the-czech-republic

Hancké, B. (2014) 'Employment Regimes, Wage Setting and Monetary Union in Continental Europe', in Wilkinson, A., Wood, G. and Deeg, R. (eds.) *The Oxford Handbook of Employment Relations: Comparative Employment Systems*, Oxford: Oxford University Press, 317–333.

Hannigan, B. (1998) 'Assessing the New Public Management: The Case of the National Health Service', *Journal of Nursing Management*, 6(5): 307–312.

Hood, C. (1995) 'The "New Public Management" in the 1980s: Variations on a Theme', *Accounting, Organizations and Society*, 20(2–3): 93–109.

ILO (2014) *Collective Bargaining in the Public Service: Bridging Gaps for a Better Future*, Issues Paper for Discussion at the Global Dialogue Forum on Challenges to Collective Bargaining in the Public Service, Geneva: International Labour Office Sectoral Activities Department.

Jacko, T. and Malíková, Ľ. (2013) 'A Chance to Restart Public Administration Reform in Slovakia, Conference Proceedings', 21st NISPAcee Annual Conference *"Regionalisation and Inter-regional Cooperation"*.

Kahancová, M. (2013) 'The Demise of Social Partnership or a Balanced Recovery? The Crisis and Collective Bargaining in Slovakia', *Transfer*, 19(2): 171–183.

Kahancová, M. and Martišková, M. (2015) 'Bargaining for Social Rights at the Sectoral Level: The Case of Slovakia', *BARSORIS—European Commission Project.* Industrial Relations and Social Dialogue VS/2013/0403.

Kahancová, M. and Sedláková, M. (2015) 'New Challenges for Public Services Social Dialogue: Integrating Service User and Workforce Involvement in Slovakia', *European Commission Project.* Industrial Relations and Social Dialogue VS/2013/0362.

Kahancová, M. and Szabó, I. G. (2015) 'Hospital Bargaining in the Wake of Management Reforms: Hungary and Slovakia Compared', *European Journal of Industrial Relations*, 21(4): 335–352.

Lodge, M. and Hood, C. (2012) 'Into an Age of Multiple Austerities? Public Management and Public Service Bargains across OECD Countries', *Governance: An International Journal of Policy, Administration and Institutions*, 25(1): 79–101.

Mandl, I., Curtarelli, M., Riso, S., Vargas, O. and Gerogiannis, E. (2015) 'New Forms of Employment', EMCC Research Report No. EF1461, Publications Office of the European Union, Luxembourg.

Myant, M. (2013) 'The Impact of the Economic Crisis on Collective Bargaining in the Czech Republic', *Transfer*, 19(2): 185–194.

Nebeský, Ľ. (2010) *Desatoro odporúčaní ako zamestnávať vo verejnej správe efektívnejšie* [*Ten Recommendations How to Employ in Public Services More Effectively*], Bratislava: Inštitút hospodárskej politiky.

Nemec, J. (2010) 'New Public Management and its Implementation in CEE: What Do We Know and Where Do We Go?' *NISPAcee Journal of Public Administration and Policy*, 3(1): 31–52.

Pollitt, C. and Bouckaert, G. (2011) *Public Management Reform*, Oxford: Oxford University Press.

SME (2011) 'Reálne mzdy na Slovensku sa prepadli [Real Wages in Slovakia Plummeted]', http://ekonomika.sme.sk/c/6171290/realne-mzdy-na-slovensku-sa-prepadli.html

Staroňová, K. and Gajduschek, G. (2013) 'Civil Service Reform in Slovakia and Hungary: The Road to Professionalisation?' in Neuhold, C., Vanhoonacker, S. and Verhey, L. (eds.) *Civil Servants and Politics : A Delicate Balance*, Basingstoke: Palgrave Macmillan, 123–151.

Staroňová, K. and Láštic, E. (2011) 'Politicko-administratívne vzťahy a ich formálne pravidlá na Slovensku v rokoch 1990–2010 [Political-administrative Relations and their Formal Regulation in Slovakia between 1990 and 2010]', in Beblavý, Beblavá, E., Staroňová, K., Ondrušová, D., Bandúrová, M. and Láštic, E. (eds.) *Koaličná zmluva či zákon?Právna úprava a realita politicko-administratívnych vzťahov na Slovensku*, Prešov: Michal Vaško, 32–81.

Staroňová, K. and Staňová, Ľ. (2013) 'The Role of Central Structures for Coordination, Management and Control of the Civil Service: The Case of Slovakia, in Regionalisation and Inter-regional Cooperation', *21st NISPAcee Annual Conference Proceedings*, Bratislava: NISPAcee PRESS, pp. 1–16.

Staroňová, K., Staňová, Ľ. and Sičáková-Beblavá, E. (2014) *Systémy štátnej služby: koncepty a Trendy [Systems of Civil Service: Concepts and Trends]*, Bratislava: Comenius University Press.

Suchardová, M. (2013) 'EU Loses Patience and 2014–2020 Fund Collection under Serious Threat', *Nadační fond proti korupci [Foundation Fund against Corruption]*. http://www.nfpk.cz/en/glossary/michaela-suchardova/2446

Týden (2010) 'Vláda odklepla snížení platů statních zaměstnanců [Government Agreed to Decrease Wages of State Employees]', *Týden*. http://www.tyden.cz/rubriky/domaci/politika/vlada-odklepla-snizeni-platu-statnich-zamestnancu_188027.html#.VSGbumbcj_5

ÚZIS (2010) ´Czech Health Statistics Yearbook 2010´, ÚZIS. ISBN 978-80-7280-966-0. http://www.uzis.cz/en/publications/czech-health-statistics-yearbook-2010

Veverková, S. (2011) Czech Republic: 'Industrial Relations in the Health Care Sector', *EurWORK*. http://eurofound.europa.eu/observatories/eurwork/comparative-information/national-contributions/czech-republic/czech-republic-industrial-relations-in-the-health-care-sector.

Index